A Quick Index to Twenty Essential Questions

D1716468

BUILDING TYPE BASICS FOR

elementary and secondary schools

SECOND EDITION

BUILDING TYPE BASICS FOR

elementary and secondary schools

SECOND EDITION

BRADFORD PERKINS *with* RAYMOND BORDWELL
Perkins Eastman

WILEY

JOHN WILEY & SONS, INC.

For Lawrence Bradford Perkins Sr., FAIA,
and Dwight Heald Perkins, FAIA,
who led the way for 80 years.

Copyright © 2010 by John Wiley & Sons, Inc. All rights reserved

Published by John Wiley & Sons, Inc., Hoboken, New Jersey
Published simultaneously in Canada

For general information about our other products and services, please contact our Customer Care Department within the United States at (800) 762-2974, outside the United States at (317) 572-3993 or fax (317) 572-4002.

Wiley also publishes its books in a variety of electronic formats. Some content that appears in print may not be available in electronic books. For more information about Wiley products, visit our web site at www.wiley.com.

Library of Congress Cataloging-in-Publication Data:

Building type basics for elementary and secondary schools / Stephen A. Kliment, editor, Bradford Perkins with Raymond Bordwell.—2nd ed.
    p. cm.
  Includes bibliographical references and index.
  ISBN 978-0-470-22548-6 (cloth)
  1. Elementary school buildings—United States—Design and construction. 2. High school buildings—United States—Design and construction. 3. Elementary school buildings—United States—Planning. 4. High school buildings—United States—Planning. I. Kliment, Stephen A. II. Perkins, L. Bradford. III. Bordwell, Raymond.
  LB3218.A1B89 2010
  373.16—dc22

2009033996

Printed in the United States of America
SKY10032559_011422

CONTENTS

CONTENTS

PREFACE

Wiley's Building Type Basics series, conceived more than a decade ago by the late Stephen A. Kliment, FAIA, series founder and editor, who had served as editor in chief of *Architectural Record* magazine from 1990 to 1996, includes one book on each of the major building types that architects design.

Early in the development of the series, Kliment called upon expert architects to each author a volume based on the typology that they had built a career or firm upon.

Who is this series intended for, and what purpose will it serve in your practice? Building Type Basics books are written primarily for architects—from recent graduates working on their first project in a building type, to experienced architects who want the latest information on a building type they already know, to seasoned associates and principals looking to add a new building type to their firm's portfolio. Beyond architects, the series is useful to developers, builders, clients, urban planners urban designers, and related professional consultants working with a given building type. As Kliment had written in the preface to the first editions of the Building Type Basics series: "As architectural practice becomes more generalized and firms pursue and accept commissions for a widening range of building types, the books in this series will comprise a convenient, hands-on resource providing basic information on the initial design phases of a project and answers to the questions design professionals routinely encounter in those crucial early phases."

Each volume of the Building Type Basics series covers what architects need to know about the unique features of a given typology—from site selection and site planning issues related to landscape and parking to predesign programming, project delivery processes, building codes and accessibility, engineering systems, lighting and acoustics, wayfinding, costs, feasibility, financing, and more. The latest editions in this series, including this volume, offer information about sustainable design solutions, the contemporary design trends related to that building type, as well as the most current updates in both information technology and building technology that impact a building type.

Case studies of the best contemporary projects of a given building type help to illustrate the concepts presented in each book. Selected projects are geographically diverse across North America and vary in scale so that one can glean lessons from a given case study that can be applied to the architect's or designer's own work, whether a small-scale project in a remote setting in a southern climate or a large-scale building in a dense, urban setting in a harsh northern climate or somewhere in-between. That is, wherever your project is located and whatever its scale, the case studies in this book offer valuable lessons.

Richly illustrated with diagrams, drawings, and photographs, the Building Type Basics series—through both visual information and narrative—will serve as both a guide and reference with its presentation of relevant concepts, design principles, and techniques to guide your projects.

John E. Czarnecki, Assoc. AIA
Senior Editor, Architecture and Design
John Wiley & Sons

ACKNOWLEDGMENTS

This book includes major contributions from many individuals and firms.

CHAPTER 1 includes material prepared by our Perkins Eastman colleagues Alan Schlossberg and Joanne Violanti, as well as advice from H. Evan Powderly, of the Byram Hills School District, and Blair Perkins Grumman. Food service advice was provided by Adam Millman of Cini-Little International Inc.

CHAPTER 4 includes material from Geoffrey Roesch.

CHAPTER 8 includes extensive advice from Norman Kurtz of Flack & Kurtz Consulting Engineers, LLP, David L. Grumman of Grumman/Butkus Associates, Ltd., and Buro Happold Consulting Engineers, P.C.

CHAPTER 9 includes extensive input from Lenny Zimmerman of Flack & Kurtz.

CHAPTER 10 includes extensive input from William M. Richardson of Educational Systems Planning.

CHAPTER 11 has input from Jennifer Sisak.

CHAPTERS 12 AND 13 are largely the work of Jennifer Beattie, with the advice of Fred Shen of Shen, Milsom, Wilke.

CHAPTERS 14 AND 15 have input from Jennifer Sisak and Pam Loeffelman. Tony Russell of Russell Design helped with Chapter 15.

CHAPTERS 16 AND 18 include extensive input from Charles Williams, Linton Stables, and Fred Petraglia of Perkins Eastman.

Sarah Mechling provided image research and graphic design coordination, with the help of Steven Yates, Katy Gillen, Leslie David, and Janette Sutton. Christine Schlendorf and the staff of our New York School Studio provided graphic support.

Finally, the overall book owes a great deal to our research assistant, Rachael Perkins Arenstein, and two teachers: my nephew Caleb Perkins and my daughter Judith Perkins Schiamberg.

ACKNOWLEDGMENTS

This book includes major contributions from many individuals and firms.

CHAPTER 4 includes material prepared by Paul Chera, Clemson cuisine; Alan Schlossberg and Joanne Wolaniuk, as well as the team at Brandi Lowdermilk of the Brown Hills School District; and Bell Packing restaurant. Food service advice was provided by Adam Kulbaum of Vitit Little Restaurant, Inc.

CHAPTER 6 includes material from Geoffrey Roesch.

CHAPTER 8 includes extensive advice from Norman Kurtz of Flack & Kurtz Consulting Engineers, LLP; David J. Commant of Grumman/Butkus Associates; and Bero/Happold Consulting Engineers, PC.

CHAPTER 9 includes extensive input from Larry Zimmerman of Flack & Kurtz.

CHAPTER 10 includes extensive input from William M. Richardson of Educational Systems Planning.

CHAPTER 11 has input from John F. Stark.

CHAPTERS 12 AND 13 are based on the work of Jennifer Beattie, with the advice of Fred Stitt of Stitt-Wilson, Wilke.

CHAPTERS 14 AND 15 have input from Kenneth Stark and Pam Loeffelman. Davy Russell of Russell Design helped with Chapter 15.

CHAPTERS 16 AND 18 include extensive input from Charles Williams, Linton Sabics, and Fred Perrault of Perkins Eastman.

Sarah Mechling provided image research and graphic design coordination, with the help of Steven Yates, Kay Gillbert, Leslie David, and Janette Sutton. Cindy Dunne Schlendorf and the staff of our New York SEI studio provided graphic support.

Finally, the overall book owes a great deal to our research assistant, Rachael Redman Arenstein; and two teachers, my nephew Caleb P. Penn and my daughter Judith Fedina Solnamburg.

CHAPTER 1

PREDESIGN

INTRODUCTION

The need...

The repair, renovation and construction of new schools is an increasingly complex endeavor in the United States. There are over 97,000 public school buildings comprising an estimated 6.6 billion sq ft of space on over 1 million acres of land.[1]

According to a 1999 study by the National Center for Education Statistics (NCES), the unmet need for school construction and renovation was estimated to be $127 billion. This amount was higher than the previous estimate of $112 billion given by the General Accounting Office (GAO) in 1995.[2] Some other organizations believe the need is actually far larger than $127 billion.[3] In 2000 the National Education Association gave an estimate of $322 billion for fixing and modernizing the nation's schools. The steep increase was due, in part, to the study's more comprehensive state-by-state analysis as well as the inclusion of $54 billion for technology improvements, such as wiring for Internet access.

NCES indicated in 1999 that three-quarters of the nation's schools report needing funds to bring their buildings into a "good overall condition." The Department of Edu-

cation (ED) has documented that the average age of a public school building is 42 years, an age at which schools tend to deteriorate.

The backlog of renovations and repairs is only part of the challenge. After a decline that generally ended in the 1980s, school enrollment steadily increased, reaching in 2005 a record total of 55 million for public and private elementary and secondary schools. A further increase of 10 percent is projected before 2017. This growth has not been and will not be evenly distributed geographically: States in the Midwest, South, and West are projected to experience growth, while enrollment in others is expected to stabilize or in some areas, such as the Northeast, to decline.[4]

Even in communities with stabilizing enrollment, school construction is likely to be an issue. The need arises not only from building age and obsolescence, but also from the evolving nature of K–12 education.

Since the late 1800s schools have been under continuous pressure to accommodate a broader curriculum, reduced class sizes, and more specialized programs, such as preschool, special education, and English as a second language, as well as new administrative, instructional, and communication

1. U.S. Department of Education, National Center for Education Statistics, NCES Common Core of Data (CCD) Survey, *Local Education Agency Universe Survey: 2005–06.*

2. U.S. General Accounting Office report, *School Facilities: Construction Expenditures Have Grown Significantly in Recent Years,* March 2000, http://www.gao.gov/archive/2000/he00041.pdf.

3. Laurie Lewis et al., "Condition of America's Public School Facilities: 1999," NCES website, http://nces.ed.gov/surveys/frss/publications/2000032/index.asp (accessed 6/2009).

4. William J. Hussar and Tabitha M. Bailey, *Projections of Education Statistics to 2017,* NCES website, http://nces.ed.gov/pubsearch/pubsinfo.asp?pubid=2008078 (accessed 6/2009).

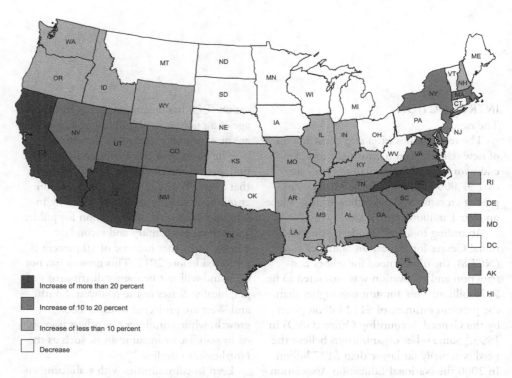

▶ *Projected Education Statistics to 2008. Source: U.S. Department of Education, National Center for Education Statistics.*

Increase of more than 20 percent

Increase of 10 to 20 percent

Increase of less than 10 percent

Decrease

technologies. These developments have generated the need for significant additions to and reconfigurations of existing facilities. Moreover, they have probably contributed to the need for new schools. As graduation requirements have changed and programs such as those listed above have been added, schools built in the 1950s and 1960s that may have originally accommodated 2,000 students now effectively hold 1,800 or fewer.

As education and facilities continue to evolve, demand for additions and reconfigurations is inevitable. Schools constitute one of the building types whose built environment has a direct impact on the quality of the functions they accommodate—in this case teaching, learning, and community activities. So long as educating the next gener-

ation is a primary task for our increasingly connected planet, the planning, design, and construction of schools will be an evolving and essential challenge.

This chapter addresses the educational changes influencing educational architecture and looks at the design process necessary to successfully address new developments. It covers the process of programming and planning, along with the specific types of spaces generally expected for a wide range of school types.

There are quantitative methods for defining and illustrating the spaces required for various school areas. Programming, however, can be as much an art as a science. The types and designs of the spaces we build should be directly related to changes in educational practice. As these changes become more common in the districts for which we design, they influence the size, configuration, and number of program areas in mainstream schools. As improved spaces are developed, they can, in turn, influence educational practices in positive ways. Such a feedback process can help drive innovation in the design of schools that are relevant not only today but also long into the twenty-first century.

THE LEARNING PROCESS

Probably the most important issue school designers (and their clients) must understand is how the physical environment relates to and can support the learning process. As a child grows, he or she typically learns in different ways, and the physical environment of the school should reflect this characteristic and process. A well-designed environment can help stimulate and support teaching, whereas a poorly designed school can inhibit learning. Although some experienced design professionals understand this interrelationship, there have been numerous recent studies to determine the relationship of teaching and learning to the physical environment.

One of the most common references is Benjamin S. Bloom's *Taxonomy of Educational Objectives* (1956). Despite being more

than a half-century old, the taxonomy has needed only a few recent revisions (Anderson & Krathwohl 2001) and outlines the hierarchy of thinking skills that a student uses. Teachers and curriculum providers have used this hierarchy to plan lessons that introduce new material using lower-order thinking skills, such as identification, and then build upon that new knowledge with higher-order skills, such as analysis and evaluation. The design implications of this hierarchy are that teaching is no longer about a teacher standing at the front of a class lecturing to students whose sole job it is to memorize their notes. In order for students to engage in the higher-order thinking skills of Bloom's taxonomy, teachers and students must be free to utilize the classroom space in new ways to create more meaningful lessons.

Although other taxonomies have been introduced, Bloom's provides useful background for programming any school. Information drawn from this important work is included in the table on the following pages. Bloom's work has been fundamental in planning the educational programming for each age group. It has also helped to move school planning away from the rigid standard classrooms that dominated school design in the early decades of the twentieth century. Rooms and furniture scaled to the children,

Those involved in the design of school buildings cannot think only in terms of physical structure. They must think about the individuals who will use the building. Think about the role the building plays in supporting teaching and learning and the full development of all of each student's potentials. If the architect keeps these things in mind, he may be able to contribute...to the achievement of the educator's goals...by creating a building that is a tool for the teacher and an expression of the school's educational approach...by creating an atmosphere, a mood, to aid the student in every learning task set before him...by making the school a place the student looks forward to entering, and one he regrets leaving. (Perkins 1957, p. 62)

DEVELOPMENTAL GUIDEPOSTS FOR CHILDREN AND ADOLESCENTS

	PHYSICAL	EMOTIONAL
Early childhood (ages 3–5)	• Body growth slows, more adult proportions develop. • At 6, neural development 90% complete. • From 4 to 8 years, lymphoid development increases from 40% to 90%. • Most children farsighted. • Muscle development begins at 4 years, but larger muscles dominate.	• Tend to fear imaginary or anticipated dangers. • Begin to understand concept of taking turns and tend to imitate adults. • Crying and tantrums diminish; anger can be expressed in words (often by threatening or yelling). • Anger directed at cause of frustration, retained for longer periods of time, but 4-year-olds begin to seek ways to hide it from others. • Channeling anger and frustration is important.
Middle childhood (ages 6–9)	• Apparent difference between growth rate of girls and boys (girls closer to end growth states, boys taller and heavier). • Nearsightedness may begin to develop at 8 years. • 6-year-olds use whole bodies for activities and large muscles are more developed; 7-year-olds more cautious and show ease with fine motor skills; 8-year-olds develop fine motor skills and increased attention spans. • Nervous habits begin to appear at age 7.	• 6-year-olds begin to assert independence and demonstrate confidence. • 6-year-olds fear the supernatural. • 7-year-olds are more stable, narcissistic, polite, responsive, empathetic, less aggressive, and can draw connections between cause and effect. • 8-year-olds demonstrate greater independence, vacillate between moods, and begin to sense how others feel toward them. • 7- and 8-year-olds discover some of their limitations and may hesitate to try new tasks, but 8-year-olds seek to create an external image of competence and confidence.
Late childhood (ages 9–11)	• More resistance to disease. • Steady increases in body measurements—height and weight (girls more than boys)—and muscle growth. • Have fine motor skills. • May feel uncomfortable with scrutiny. • Many girls begin showing signs of puberty.	• Fear exclusion from peers. • Prone to outbursts but try to control them. • 10-year-olds mild-tempered, seek reassurance from others; anger comes and goes quickly. • 10-year-olds most afraid of heights and dark. • 11-year-olds fear school, friends, for parents' welfare, strange animals, threatening world events; are more easily angered, often resulting in physical violence, but can control outbursts more appropriately.
Early adolescence (ages 12–14)	• Enter pubescence, puberty, and postpubescence. • Activated primary and secondary sex characteristics.	• Emotions vacillate; responses are inconsistent. • 12-year-olds may develop a derogatory sense of humor to control emotions. • 13-year-olds withdraw from others, tending toward secrecy and sullenness. • 14-year-olds use derogatory humor as defense and primary form of communication.
Late adolescence (ages 15–18)	• Height and weight stabilize. • Girls generally physically mature by 18, boys by 19.	• Feel restrained or controlled by adults. • Have insecure self-image; may fear inadequacy. • Focus attention on opposite sex or close peers. • Feel challenged to find comfortable self-image.

SOCIAL

- Begin to understand concept of taking turns and tend to imitate adults.
- 4-year-olds prefer to spend time playing and cooperating with others and can pick up social cues from surroundings.
- 5-year-olds prefer to play with others.
- May create imaginary playmates if deprived of contact with other children, but most will outgrow these playmates by age 5.

- Family influence decreases; peers are more important; teachers become authority figures.
- 6-year-olds have many internal conflicts, resulting in capriciousness.
- 6-year-olds choose playmates on qualities of age and size (not gender or ethnicity), and 7-year-olds are more aware of social status or ethnicity differences among themselves.
- 7-year-olds are self-critical and often disassociate themselves from frustrations.
- 7-year-olds are well mannered unless bored, and 8-year-olds are more developed socially.
- 7-year-olds are more conscious of position among peers; boys and girls play separately.
- 8-year-olds prefer company and approval of peers, and exhibit more self-control and modesty.

- Socialize in exclusive groups with own sex (boys' groups gravitate toward bravado and competition, and girls' groups are well structured and more concerned with maturity).
- Develop important individual friendships, which are often fluid.
- Ties to family less important than ties to peers; adult shortcomings looked at critically, often leading to conflicts.

- Motivated by desire to fit in with peers, which prevents individual expression but emboldens adolescents to assert independence from home.
- Peer groups are exclusive and develop from single-sex to coed.
- Intensely drawn to a best friend, believing that only this other person understands.

- Independence asserted, power struggles with parents, most concerned about social life.
- If uncomfortable with adulthood, may withdraw to former behaviors.

LINGUISTIC

- Age 3: 600 to 1,000 words, simple sentences.
- Age 4: 1,100 to 1,600 words, good syntax, plurals used, fluency improves, 4-, 5-, and 6-word sentences, 3- to 4-syllable phrases.
- Age 5: 1,500 words, nearly perfect syntax, fluency with multisyllabic words, 5- to 6-word complete compound or complex sentences.

EIGHT INTELLIGENCES			
TYPE	**LIKES TO**	**DEVELOPS RELATED SKILLS**	**LEARNS BEST BY**
Linguistic intelligence: "the word player"	Read Write Tell stories	Memorizing names, places, sayings, dates, and trivia	Saying, hearing, and seeing words
Logical/mathematical intelligence: "the questioner"	Do experiments Figure things out Work with numbers Ask questions Explore patterns and relationships	Math Reasoning Logic Problem solving	Categorizing Classifying Working with abstract patterns/relationships
Spatial intelligence: "the visualizer"	Draw, build, design, and create things Daydream Look at pictures/slides Watch movies Play with machines	Imagining things Sensing changes Reading maps, charts	Visualizing Dreaming Using the mind's eye Working with colors/pictures
Musical intelligence: "the music lover"	Sing, hum tunes Listen to music Play an instrument Respond to music	Picking up sounds Remembering melodies Noticing pitches/rhythms Keeping time	Rhythm Melody Music
Bodily/kinesthetic intelligence: "the mover"	Move around Touch and talk Use body language	Physical activities (sports/dance/acting) Crafts	Touching Moving Interacting with space Processing knowledge through bodily sensations
Interpersonal intelligence: "the socializer"	Have lots of friends Talk to people Join groups	Understanding people Leading others Organizing Communicating Manipulating Mediating conflicts	Sharing Comparing Relating Cooperating Interviewing
Intrapersonal intelligence: "the individual"	Work alone Pursue own interests	Understanding self Focusing inward on feelings/dreams Following instincts Pursuing interests/goals Being original	Working alone Individualized projects Self-paced instruction Having own space
Natural intelligence	Acute awareness of patterns in nature	Sensitive to features of the natural world (clouds, rock configurations)	Discriminating between living and man-made things

more flexible classroom configurations, and many other physical modifications have been adopted to reflect the changes that have been incorporated in educational programming.

Howard Gardner's *Frames of Mind* (1983) originally listed seven types of learning "intelligences." In 1996 this listing was expanded to eight, where it remains despite some additional proposed ideas. In theory, all eight forms of intelligence are equally valuable and viable. Historically, school curricula have favored certain styles of learning over others. In the United States a bias toward verbal/linguistic and logical/mathematical intelligences has influenced the facility planning, design, and furnishing of American schools. Yet if a student's strength is artistic, the classroom and teaching can be adapted to make art the door to learning.

This theory does not mean teaching every lesson in eight different ways. Instead, it suggests personalization. Gardner uses the image of a room with a number of doors. The room represents the subject being taught, and the doors symbolize alternative ways for a student to enter the room and access the topic. In outline, this theory suggests structuring the learning process so that the following occur:

- Students enter through the door related to their dominant intelligence. Each access point consists of lessons, learning centers, activities, etc.
- Students also study the topic from the other points of access after having acquired a basic understanding using their dominant intelligence.
- Students work cooperatively with others who may have come to the topic through

a different door. This clarifies ideas and reinforces the subject learned.
- Students synthesize the knowledge they have collected about a topic.
- Students teach what they have learned to others and apply what they have learned to other topics.

▲ *A successful teaching environment still begins with the relationship of a good teacher with his or her students. Photograph by Rachael Perkins Arenstein.*

Many teachers, as well as a growing number of schools, are using this approach. The August 1997 issue of *School Planning & Management* described a renovation program at the Saltonstall School in Salem, Massachusetts. The goal of the renovation was "to create an incubator for innovative programs in elementary education statewide." One of the decisions was to incorporate Gardner's theory, which meant the following:

- A focus on technology, inasmuch as "good multimedia programs present material verbally, spatially, musically, and logically." Instead of having one electrical outlet on a wall, the classrooms were wired to support computers, media presentations, a listening center, an overhead projector, and other such equipment.
- The renovation priorities were ranked by their impact on learning. Money was shifted from a number of typical building renovation priorities to technology and other teaching aids. For example, a decision was made to add sinks in each classroom for art and science projects. This innovation cost $1,000 per sink but eliminated travel to a special room and increased the number of activities that supported students with high spatial and kinesthetic intelligence.
- Multipurpose spaces were created to permit flexible teaching areas. Even the auditorium has no fixed seating.
- Outdoor balconies adjacent to classrooms were used as teaching areas for weather and science topics.
- A "flow room" was created to provide a place where a student can focus on a topic of particular interest. "Flow" is designed to foster a focused state of attention. Flow is connected to the multiple intelligences

theory in that students are more likely to have flow experiences in activities they find interesting, leading them to invest time and effort in difficult tasks——an important learning skill.

Regardless of whether Gardner's multiple intelligences theory or other theories are applied to school design, it is clear that the physical environment should reinforce the educational program. No fixed classroom environment will do the job properly. Training materials for teachers also reinforce the relationship of the classroom's physical environment to the learning process. For example, the materials used by the national program Teach for America make the following recommendations:

- An open, stimulating environment is one that invites students to explore and participate, [and] makes it easy for students and the teacher to carry out learning activities (e.g., students should be able to see the chalkboard, students can easily access learning materials, teachers can circulate easily among the students, etc.).
- Organize students [if you use assigned seating] into heterogeneous groups for cooperative learning, or design seating arrangements to minimize unnecessary talking or maximize collaboration between students.
- Many students need personal space to feel that they belong to the classroom and that they can keep their personal belongings safe.
- Because most people work best in a variety of different settings, you may want to create different opportunities for students to sit up straight, stand, lean, lounge, etc. Some teachers use beanbags or carpets to provide alternative spaces for students.

◀ The classroom has evolved from the rigid seating plan illustrated in Modern School, a 1915 precursor to this book. Courtesy of HMFH Architects.

◀ Contemporary classrooms feature integrated technology with flexible furnishings that allow students a variety of educational settings, including team and project-based learning. Perkins Eastman. Courtesy of Perkins Eastman.

▶ *The changing nature of classrooms is represented here by both traditional and nontraditional studio-style settings. Avenues, The World School, New York, New York. Perkins Eastman. Courtesy of Perkins Eastman.*

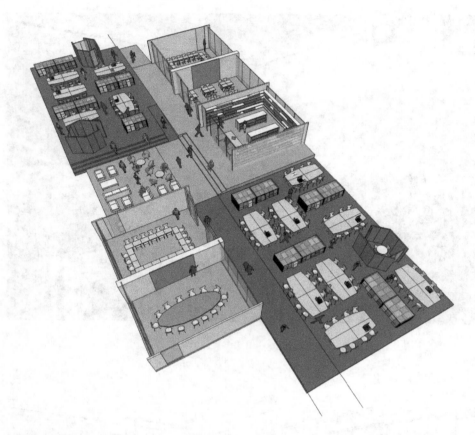

- Learning centers are areas in a classroom where small groups of students can…focus on specific skills or content areas.
- Visual displays are an important aspect of a classroom environment that supports student learning [and offer] a great opportunity to focus your students on their academic goals and reinforce the material that you are teaching.

The Teach for America guidelines reflect a shift in thinking about the learning process. In his book *In School* (1995), Ken Dryden concluded, "This past decade, the focus of education has shifted back to the classroom…. People have come to realize again that a school works in the classroom—or it doesn't work at all; that education may be about teaching and teachers, but really it is about learning and kids; and that education reform may be for *all* kids, but really it is for the majority of kids in every class who are doing just adequately or worse." This shifting focus has been influenced by the impact of self-directed, real-world, project-based learning. Spaces where students can work collaboratively support the evolution of teachers from old-style dispensers of information to present-day "guide-on-the-side" mentors and coaches.

SCHOOL PROGRAMMING AND PLANNING GUIDELINES

General Considerations

In the last 15 years there has been remarkable advancement in the process and guidance available to school districts and private institutions alike. There is a large amount of information on design guidelines and standards available from many sources. The Internet has made it possible to look at a variety of planning and design resources developed by state departments and private organizations, including guidelines from individual states, university think tanks, and online repositories such as www.edfacilities. org, www.designshare.com, and www. eric.ed.gov, which provide access to more than 1.2 million bibliographic records of journal articles and other education-related materials.

Finding information or "standards" to guide the planning, design, and construction of school facilities is not a difficult task. However, these standards vary. They can be influenced by the learning process and curricula of different age groups as well as the issues related to children with special needs. It is not possible to cover every variation in these planning standards; rather, in order to prepare the design team and client to make informed decisions, this chapter introduces representative program guidelines for the four most common types of public schools:

- Kindergarten and preschool
- Elementary school
- Middle school
- High school

These basic school types may be organized in a number of ways:

- Elementary, pre-K–3
- Elementary, pre-K–5
- Elementary/middle, pre-K–8
- Middle, 6–8
- Middle/secondary, 6–12
- Secondary, 9–12
- Elementary/middle/secondary, pre-K–12

This chapter also covers a number of other variations wherein schools may have a specific purpose, focus, or type of leadership, such as the following:

- Special needs schools (for children who are physically or emotionally disabled, blind, deaf, etc.)
- Vocational/technical schools
- Charter schools
- Alternative schools
- Selective academic and magnet schools
- Private (boarding and day schools), parochial, and international schools

Note that this book focuses primarily on public schools. However, much of the guidance given here applies equally to private school design. Although there are subtle distinctions between public and private schools, and the latter are not subject to the same regulations as public schools, most are trying to accomplish the same mission.

Programming and Planning

Determining school building capacity
When beginning the planning process of a new or renovated facility, one of the most common questions asked—and, from a programming point of view, one of the first questions that must be answered—is how many students the facility can accommodate. The answer is generally given as the

programmed *effective capacity*. This number can be calculated in a variety of ways and must be agreed upon by all parties involved before the process of planning the school can begin.

This section outlines the basics of determining the capacity of a school. The method used varies depending on a number of factors. However, there are two basic capacity calculations most frequently used, one for elementary schools and one for middle/high schools.

Before we look at calculations, it is important to understand the terms we will be using. The following definitions are common when discussing the capacity of a school and for the most part are interrelated.

Definition of terms

Teaching stations are defined as areas in which students receive instruction on a regularly scheduled basis. These spaces include not only classrooms but also music rooms, science labs, art rooms, fitness rooms, gymnasiums, media centers, theaters, and so forth. Because each student can occupy only one place at a time, for middle schools and high schools, such "co-curricular" spaces relieve the classrooms of a requirement to accommodate the entire student body at one time.

The *utilization factor,* expressed as a percentage, provides a facility with a certain degree of scheduling and programmatic flexibility in scheduling teaching stations occupied by a section of students. A typical utilization factor is 80–90 percent, and is determined by the specific scheduling and practices of the individual school.

Effective capacity is the number of students that can be comfortably accommodated by a facility at any given moment. To calcu-

late the effective capacity of a school, the number of teaching stations is multiplied by the number of students per teaching station, multiplied by the requested utilization factor. The utilization factor accommodates the desired degree of flexibility. A facility's *maximum capacity* is the total number of teaching stations multiplied by the maximum design value per station. *Efficiency* is a measure of the number of teaching stations occupied during a given period of the day: the more teaching stations occupied during a given period, the higher the efficiency. Likewise, the higher the utilization factor, the higher the facility's planned efficiency will be.

Design value is defined as the number of students intended to occupy a teaching station during any scheduled period. For public schools in the United States, design values may range from 22 to 28 for an elementary school, and from 22 to 30 or higher for a high school. Private schools often focus on reducing class size below public school levels. Design value can also mean the total number of students a school building can effectively accommodate. The definition depends on the context in which the term is used.

Determining elementary school capacity

The method used for determining effective capacity is different for the elementary school than for the middle and high school. For our purposes, an elementary school capacity will be based on a model in which students have a "homeroom" or regular classroom. When attending classes in a specialized classroom, such as art or music, in other parts of the building, no other students occupy their room. Most elementary schools do not operate on a schedule based on specific "periods" of time, and consequently do not change classrooms during the day for different subjects. The number of special classrooms (science labs, art, etc.) will be a reflection of the enrollment and the curricular focus envisioned for the school. Therefore, the capacity of an elementary school is a fairly simple calculation of multiplying the number of regular classrooms by the design value of each one. For example:

26 classrooms × 22 students = capacity of 572

In this case, the utilization rate is assumed to be 100 percent, or maximum capacity, and represents the facility's maximum capacity.

In some cases there may be a difference between lower elementary school design values and those of the upper elementary grades—for example, K–2 may be planned at 18 students per teaching station, and grades 3–5 at 22 per station. It is important to agree on the design values at the start of the planning process, because it gives the facility planners a figure to use in determining the number of classrooms required, and also governs the size requirements for support spaces such as cafeterias, science labs, art rooms, and libraries.

Most newly designed elementary school facilities in the United States include art, music, computer awareness and keyboarding, and sometimes wet lab science and project spaces. Spaces for these programs do not affect the design capacity of the facility because when students are using these facilities, their classrooms will remain empty. This is the main difference in determining building capacity between elementary school facilities and middle/high school facilities.

Determining middle school and high school capacity

The following methodology can apply to both middle and high school planning, as there is no appreciable difference between the two in scheduling utilization. Either can be influenced by the program and scheduling system implemented to operate the school. Most districts have a standard utilization rate, which can vary widely from district to district.

Unlike elementary schools, middle and high schools generally operate on a bell schedule in which students do not "own" a classroom. As they move around the building, students continually settle into teaching stations. It is very difficult to achieve a utilization factor of 95 percent or above in either a middle or a high school, because it is very difficult to schedule every teaching station every period of the day. Efficiency of 100 percent is almost impossible to achieve, and if it is, generally represents an overcrowded or poorly operated school.

Standard utilization rates

95 percent efficiency. Mandated in some states, such as Florida, 95 percent efficiency can be achieved only by "floating" teachers and providing them with offices for use outside of classrooms. Utilization rates this high can impose some restrictions on scheduling flexibility and limit the ability to add programs or operate classes of less than maximum capacity, such as advanced placement (AP) classes, where there might be 10 or fewer students.

90 percent efficiency. More flexible than 95 percent efficiency, a 90 percent rate can provide dedicated classrooms for some teachers and for programs such as foreign language.

85 percent efficiency. The most common percentage used when planning a new school without any specific direction from the district, 85 percent efficiency can be thought of as an 8-period day with each teaching station being used during 7 of the 8 periods (in actuality 87 percent).

80 percent efficiency. Offering great flexibility, 80 percent efficiency opens up the possibility for innovative scheduling (certain types of "block schedules" in which each student has fewer classes per day for a longer period of time). Teachers can have their own rooms, or space can be provided for a greater number of programs with smaller enrollments (less than the design

TEACHING STATION UTILIZATION RATES			
PERIODS PER DAY	**AVERAGE USAGE PER STATION (PERIODS)**	**UTILIZATION RATE (%)**	**NOTE**
8	7.5	94	Most of the teaching stations will be occupied 100% of the time.
8	7	87	Fairly typical utilization rate for planning purposes.
8	6	75	Each teacher might have his or her own room.[1]
6	5	83	Represents some form of modified schedule.
6	4	67	Too low for planning purposes and not recommended.
5	4	80	Some variation of a block schedule,[2] and as low a utilization as is normally permitted.
5	3	60	Too low for planning purposes and not recommended.
4	3.5	88	2 x 4 block schedule; individual teaching stations are shared by more than one teacher.
4	3	75	2 x 4 block schedule; represents utilization with some capacity for growth. Common in international schools and some public schools utilizing a block schedule. This is a typical utilization for this type of schedule.
4	2.5	63	Block schedule; represents utilization when individual rooms are "owned" by a single teacher, teaching 5 of 8 periods. Generally considered too low for planning a new facility.

1. One lunch period and one planning period per teacher
2. A block schedule is a type of academic scheduling in which each student has fewer classes per day for a longer period of time. A 2 × 4 block schedule is an 8-period "day" spread over two days. To keep the table consistent, only one day is shown (4 periods in a single day). Typical block schedule utilizations are built around each teacher teaching either 6 of the 8 periods (3 of 4 per day) or in some cases 5 of 8 periods (2.5 of 4 per day).

value per teaching station), such as AP classes.

75 percent efficiency. Providing tremendous flexibility in scheduling and program opportunities, 75 percent efficiency is used primarily when a district wants to build in capacity for future increases in enrollment.

Schedule can also influence the desired utilization. As outlined in the table at left, the utilization rate is determined by the number of periods per day a teaching station is used as compared to the total number of periods in a day.

Estimating the gross area of a building

Net square feet (NSF) refers to the net usable area of specific program elements as defined in the building's "program." Gross square feet (GSF), or gross building area, is the entire area of the plan of the school building, and usually refers to gross area of a building by measuring from the outside of its exterior walls and including all vertical penetrations, such as elevator shafts, interior and exterior walls, corridors, stairwells, mechanical rooms, and other built space not specifically identified in the program or defined as "net" square footage. For example, if we refer to a 1,000 NSF flexible laboratory space, we mean a space that has 1,000 sq ft of actual usable space within its four walls.

Different regions of the country have different average square footages for their schools. It is typical to find, for example, that schools north of 30° north latitude begin to get larger due to increased mechanical system requirements and the need for virtually all program areas to be indoors. Conversely, schools south of 30° north latitude begin to get smaller due to the lack of major

heating equipment and the ability to accommodate some net and gross area functions outdoors. Especially in Florida, New Mexico, Arizona, and southern California, one might find some gymnasium space replaced with an outdoor court, or corridor space might be on the outside of the building.

Thus, while interesting, national media figures in school size per student are rarely useful in programming. For example, *School Planning and Management*'s "2008 Construction Report" gives median sizes of new schools as follows:

Elementary schools	124 sq ft/student
Middle schools	146.6 sq ft/student
High schools	166 sq ft/student

But their statistics go on to illustrate a wide range:

	Lowest Quartile	Top 10%
Elementary schools	105.5 sq ft/student	178.6 sq ft/student
Middle schools	125.3 sq ft/student	218.8 sq ft/student
High schools	141.1 sq ft/student	460.0 sq ft/student

Therefore, it is usually important to develop a program that reflects the particular needs and aspirations of each school.

Net-to-gross calculations

Once the capacity has been determined and the net programmed areas identified, an estimated GSF can be developed. During the programming phase, this can be calculated using the chart on page 17. "Northern climate" for this purpose is above 30° north latitude. Grossing factors below 30° north latitude can be reduced if certain functions, such as circulation or locker space, are

▶ *In warmer climates, the division between indoor and outdoor portions of a classroom can become blurred. American International School: Riyadh, Riyadh, Saudi Arabia. Perkins Eastman. Courtesy of Perkins Eastman.*

moved to the outdoors. In exceptionally hot climates, these functions tend to remain indoors and thus the grossing factors used above 30° north latitude might be more accurate.

Urban grossing factors are generally higher. When a school building adds floors, a greater percentage of the gross area must be allocated for exiting and mechanical space requirements. Elementary schools generally have fewer rooms and, thus, smaller grossing factors than middle and high schools. Small, single-story buildings are potentially the most efficient from a gross area standpoint (no exit stairs); however, they may be more expensive because of increased exterior enclosure, foundation, and roof area.

The tables on pages 17–18 offer a generalized look at the relationships between size,

location, and grade levels of buildings. The grossing factors given in the tables are based on the experience of the authors, who have found that programmers commonly underestimate the grossing factors required, often at the request or guidelines of the owner/client. The numbers in these tables are given for reference purposes to help establish a starting point. Grossing factors should be carefully reviewed as necessary for each individual project.

For all schools: calculating classroom size
Learning environments include all programmed space within the building where both formal and informal learning takes place. The most common unit is the basic classroom, designed for groups ranging from 16 to 30 students. Groupings smaller than

ELEMENTARY SCHOOL GROSSING FACTORS BY REGION, SIZE, AND POPULATION DENSITY*				
CONDITION	STUDENT POPULATION	URBAN GROSSING FACTOR	SUBURBAN GROSSING FACTOR	RURAL GROSSING FACTOR
Northern climate Large support facilities	500	1.60+	1.52+	1.50+
	750	1.60–1.63	1.52–1.59	1.50–1.55
	1,000	1.58–1.60	1.48–1.52	1.45–1.50
	1,200	1.55–1.58	1.42–1.48	1.40–1.45
Northern climate Compact support facilities	500	1.62+	1.54+	1.52+
	750	1.62–1.65	1.54–1.59	1.52–1.55
	1,000	1.58–1.62	1.52–1.54	1.48–1.52
	1,200	1.50–1.58	1.45–1.52	1.40–1.48
Southern climate Large support facilities	500	1.50+	1.47+	1.45+
	750	1.50–1.55	1.47–1.50	1.45–1.50
	1,000	1.45–1.50	1.45–1.47	1.40–1.45
	1,200	1.40–1.45	1.40–1.45	1.35–1.40
Southern climate Compact support facilities	500	1.52+	1.49+	1.47+
	750	1.52–1.57	1.49–1.54	1.47–1.52
	1,000	1.47–1.52	1.43–1.49	1.40–1.47
	1,200	1.42–1.47	1.38–1.43	1.35–1.40

* To be multiplied by the net programmed area.

this are classified as *small group rooms,* and larger than this are classified as *large group instruction rooms.* Classroom sizes vary depending on the grade level served and the number of students the space is planned to support, as shown in the table on page 19.

Urban school classrooms are often smaller than their suburban counterparts. The cost of land and construction can be considerably more, which often forces these schools to build more spatially economic structures. Conversely, pressure on the classroom square footage can come from class size, which in urban schools can often be larger. The table on page 19 illustrates the potential reduction in area found in urban public schools.

Several factors influence classroom size and groupings. Each of the following factors should be discussed early in the planning process, prior to establishing the classroom size:

• State and district guidelines.
• Maximum anticipated class size.
• Use of any special technologies or projection equipment (change in use to a technology or distance learning lab).

MIDDLE SCHOOL AND HIGH SCHOOL GROSSING FACTORS BY REGION, SIZE, AND POPULATION DENSITY*

CONDITION	STUDENT POPULATION	URBAN GROSSING FACTOR	SUBURBAN GROSSING FACTOR	RURAL GROSSING FACTOR
Northern climate Large support facilities	500	1.65+	1.60+	1.57+
	750	1.60–1.66	1.55–1.60	1.52–1.57
	1,000	1.57–1.64	1.52–1.57	1.49–1.54
	1,200	1.52–1.62	1.50–1.55	1.46–1.51
	1,600	1.45–1.55	1.46–1.52	1.40–1.49
Northern climate Compact support facilities	500	1.65+	1.60+	1.57+
	750	1.60–1.66	1.55–1.62	1.52–1.59
	1,000	1.57–1.64	1.52–1.59	1.49–1.56
	1,200	1.52–1.62	1.50–1.57	1.46–1.54
	1,600	1.45–1.60	1.46–1.55	1.40–1.52
Southern climate Large support facilities	500	1.53+	1.50+	1.50+
	750	1.50–1.53	1.45–1.50	1.43–1.50
	1,000	1.45–1.50	1.43–1.45	1.40–1.43
	1,200	1.40–1.45	1.40–1.43	1.38–1.40
	1,600	1.40–1.43	1.37–1.41	1.35–1.40
Southern climate Compact support facilities	500	1.53+	1.50+	1.50+
	750	1.52–1.53	1.47–1.50	1.45–1.50
	1,000	1.47–1.52	1.45–1.47	1.42–1.45
	1,200	1.45–1.47	1.40–1.45	1.38–1.42
	1,600	1.40–1.45	1.37–1.41	1.38–1.40

* To be multiplied by the net programmed area.

- Potential changes in future programs and room use (e.g., the future use of a classroom as an art room), primarily at the elementary level.
- Number of support and self-directed spaces available for break-out use, especially in middle and high school (fewer small group spaces = larger classrooms).
- Likelihood of increased class size beyond the design value used in planning the classroom (high probability = larger classroom).
- Alignment of classroom size across several grade levels to allow for flexibility in reconfiguration should an enrollment "bubble" in a particular grade require more

TYPICAL SUBURBAN SCHOOL CLASSROOM SIZES[1]			
GRADE LEVEL	16 TO 20 STUDENTS (SQ FT)	21 TO 24 STUDENTS (SQ FT)	25 TO 30 STUDENTS (SQ FT)
Grades pre-K–1	1,000–1,200	1,100–1,200	Not recommended
Grades 1–2	900–1,200	1,100–1,200	Not recommended
Grades 3–5	850–900	900–1,000	950–1,100
Grades 6–8[2]	725–825	750–850	850–950
Grades 9–12[2]	725–825	750–850	850–950

1. Areas given assume typical suburban campus standards. Minimum allowable classroom size may be governed by state regulations and should be verified early in the planning process.
2. In many cases, state and district standards for middle and high school classroom sizes are the same, or the difference between them is negligible. Establishing a common size for both during planning will provide a certain degree of future flexibility in programming space.

TYPICAL URBAN SCHOOL CLASSROOM SIZES[1]			
GRADE LEVEL[2]	16 TO 20 STUDENTS (SQ FT)	21 TO 24 STUDENTS (SQ FT)	25 TO 30[3] STUDENTS (SQ FT)
Grades pre-K–1	800–925	925–1,000	Not recommended
Grades 1–2	750–875	875–950	950–1,100
Grades 3–5	650–800	800–875	875–1,100
Grades 6–8	625–725	725–825	825–1,000
Grades 9–12	600–700	675–850	775–950

1. Areas given assume typical urban campus standards. Minimum allowable classroom size may be governed by state or district regulations and should be verified early in the planning process.
2. In urban districts where building configurations contain two or more of the listed grade-level groupings (e.g., grades pre-K–8 or 6–12), it is advisable to establish a common size for all classrooms to maximize future flexibility.
3. In districts where enrollments are expected to increase, it is advisable to build the largest classrooms feasible to allow for future internal growth.

classrooms in a given year. Establishing a common size also helps in creating a repeatable structural grid and generally produces a building that is simpler and easier to plan.

As mentioned previously, states often provide standards. Depending on how the facility is funded, these standards represent the minimum square footage to be allocated. For special education classrooms, states often require fewer students in the classroom as opposed to mandating larger classroom sizes. The examples in the table on page 21 are typical of state guidelines for special education classrooms.

▶ Tables allow flexibility in student arrangements and can help with class size variations. Harvey Milk School, New York, New York. Perkins Eastman. Photograph by Seth Boyd.

Most districts attempt to keep the number of students per classroom lower than their maximum design value. Typical ranges are 16–20 for pre-K through grade 2, 22–25 for elementary schools, and 23–30 for middle and high schools. The most common design value for middle and high schools is between 23 and 25 students.

Classrooms should be designed to allow an increase in the student population of three to five students above the established design value to allow additional capacity within the classroom to accommodate growth or variations in individual class sizes.

Generally, larger classrooms are preferable to smaller ones, especially in elementary schools. Elementary-age students need to sit either at individual tables and chairs or at group tables. Project areas are needed within the classroom and typically include areas for science, computer clusters, and other equipment-intensive spaces.

Storage needs within the classroom are often underestimated. Larger classrooms provide greater opportunities for built-in or movable equipment to help meet this need. At the elementary school level, cubbies for backpack and coat storage are often provided within the classroom to facilitate the monitoring of students belongings and, particularly in the north, to assist with arrival and departure preparation.

SIZE REQUIREMENTS FOR SPECIAL EDUCATION CLASSROOMS

STATE	REQUIREMENTS
New York	A 770 NSF classroom is sized for a maximum capacity of 12 students, whereas a classroom size of 450 NSF accommodates a maximum capacity of 6 students.
Virginia	Self-contained classrooms for 10 students are sized at 750 NSF.
Florida	Self-contained special education classrooms are sized for 10 students at a range of 90 to 100 NSF per student.

◀ Storage, small project areas, extensive display areas, varied floor surfaces, and other features are important design elements. Whiting Athletic Complex, Whiting, Indiana. Fanning/Howey Associates.

The Planning Process Step by Step

Each school district is unique and will require an equally unique approach to creating a "space" programming process for determining and implementing the needs for a school building improvement program.

Whether involving new construction or renovation and modernization of existing facilities, project requirements must be fully defined. Many larger districts have facility departments that will provide the design team with the project's requirements. Some districts will require the development of educational specifications, or *ed specs*. This is an accepted industry term for the document that sets forth the requirements of a specific building program. The Connecticut State Board of Education regulations concerning School Construction Grants, Section 10-287c-1, Definitions, offers a particularly clear and concise definition of this term:

"Educational Specifications" means a description of the general nature and purpose of the proposed school building project, which may include the applicant's long range educational plan and the relationship of the proposed project to such plan; enrollment data and proposed project capacity; the nature and organization of the educational program; support facilities; space needs; accommodation for educational technology; specialized equipment; and site needs, and any other supporting documents deemed necessary.

The educational specifications are a blueprint, or roadmap, for future improvements or facility design. As such, the contents should be visionary and idealistic. The committee members identified in the following paragraphs should not come with preconceived or limited solution ideas based on past experiences alone, but should instead be prepared to discuss what is needed to meet the educational needs of the district.

Ed specs generally contain information on the type, size, and number of spaces in the project, among other project-related information. Effective ed specs convey more than the numerical parameters of a project; they establish proper guidance for the design team, and will accomplish the following:

- Create a clear and concise document to effectively communicate the scope and needs of the project to the design professional.
- Convey information in such a way as to allow for a creative design solution.
- Set forth the quality expectation of the finished project, including establishing goals for a sustainable solution (e.g., "This project shall be capable of achieving a LEED Silver designation as defined by the requirements set forth by the United States Green Building Corporation [USGBC]…").
- Represent the defined curriculum to be implemented in the facility.
- Account for future changes in use (provide guidance for a *flexible* design solution).
- Limit rigid or fixed descriptions of solutions.
- Ensure development with the complete support of the district's educational professionals and others in the school community.

The term "ed spec" can be misleading if taken literally, as it does not set forth the educational specifications related to curriculum content, nor does it direct teaching methodology. However, a thorough understanding of the district's educational philosophy, objectives, and proposed use of the facility is a basic requirement of a successful ed spec.

In any process involving a broad range of constituents, it is unlikely that all of the participants will agree on every point. Consensus-building is an important part of any planning exercise and should be acknowledged by the entire group at the onset of the process. Consensus for this purpose can be defined as agreement with the proposed direction or outcome of the plan by most of those involved.

Consensus is predicated on the ability of the participants to subjugate their individual "wish list" for the greater cause of developing a workable building solution. If the group can agree to build consensus around ideas and concepts that achieve the prioritized needs of the district, it is possible to reach a solution that will be cost-effective, sustainable, flexible, forward-thinking, and garner the support of the majority of the district's constituents.

Although the specifics may vary, there are seven steps that are common to the majority of successful planning processes. Each planning process should include and address these steps:

1. Assemble the planning committee.
2. Gather data and assess the facility (if an existing building is involved).
3. Workshop 1: Define the opportunity for meeting future educational needs.
4. Generate options.
5. Workshop 2: Validate/evaluate.
6. Workshop 3: Present plans for recommendation and approval.
7. Prioritize and schedule for implementation.

There are a number of variations available within this outline. A general description of each step follows.

Step 1: Assemble the planning committee

Determine who the participants in the process will be. There are a number of constituents who can offer insight and perspective on the use and subsequent solution to a particular facility. The assembled committee can be called a Steering Committee, Facilities Committee, Project Control Committee, or any number of other designations. During this phase, the process is verified, and any subcommittees are assembled that may be required to evaluate specific issues. The size of the overall group varies, but is generally 20–40 people. In general, the committee is made up of any or all of the following:

Board of Education members

Participation by one or more board members can provide valuable insight into district policies and in many districts the board authorizes the services of the architectural/educational planning team and other consultants that may be necessary to fully explore the project. Board members are accountable to the communities they serve and have a vested interest in the recommendations of the committee.

School head, school director, or superintendent

Involvement by the superintendent or other representative of the central administration can provide valuable leadership to the process, help to facilitate communication with other administrators and the board of education, and assist in helping to convey the results of the process to the broader school community.

Working committee of school staff

A representative group of building administrators and classroom teachers can speak on behalf of building users; help to assemble the needs, objectives, and goals of the district; organize the working group; and provide data used in the study. This group is invaluable in supplying the design team with information on building usage.

Architectural/educational planning firm(s)

The consultant team may consist of an architectural firm with programming and planning expertise, an educational facilities planning firm experienced in programming and planning educational facilities, or both. This team of architects and planners is responsible for providing the professional programming and planning services and is tasked with the overall responsibility to produce the final report. This team should provide leadership during the collaborative process highlighted below. The consultant team serves as adviser on major architectural considerations, such as the evaluation of existing buildings; informs the group of current best practices; and helps resolve differences of opinion among group participants.

Community members

Engaging community members in the process will facilitate a number of goals important to the process:

- Inform the group of the community's perceptions of the district or project. This can be viewed as understanding the district's "brand identity" before beginning the process.
- Convey the needs of the community to the committee.
- Identify community concerns about the project.
- Act as subcommittee members if there is an opportunity to form community partnerships with the district.
- Communicate back to the public as the project progresses.

As these committee members are valued for their roles and thereby gain an increasing ownership stake in the solution, they can become positive spokespersons for the process and the ultimate results.

Student representatives

Overlooked and sometimes underserved voices on planning committees are student representatives. Including three to five students on the committee will provide a perspective not available from any other source. Students are the ultimate end user and will usually be some of the more honest and outspoken members of the committee. It is important to have at least three students so that they do not feel overwhelmed in the context of the larger group.

The committee will be assembled for three to six months and will meet on a regular basis, either semimonthly or monthly. The meetings will involve presentations from the consultant team of architects and planners and from any subcommittee reports developed during the process.

Step 2: Gather data and assess the facility

Assembling information on enrollment, demographics, students served, curriculum, and other information specifically related to the needs and scope of the individual project sets the baseline point of departure in determining facility improvements. If the project involves an existing facility, the team should collect information on building capacity, life safety code compliance, use efficiency, maintenance, building envelope conditions, electrical and technology systems condition, mechanical equipment conditions, and Americans with Disabilities Act (ADA) accessibility compliance. This will provide the steering committee with a broad base of knowledge of the facility and identify required improvements. Deficiencies related to structural, life safety, and deferred maintenance issues will ultimately become the highest priorities for improvement. During this phase, the process and schedule are verified, the committees and subcommittees are assembled, and responsibilities are assigned.

Step 3: Workshop 1—define the opportunity for meeting future educational needs

With the information collected in Step 2, the first workshop is scheduled. It can be scheduled for three or four hours, an entire day of six or seven hours, or over two days of approximately five hours a day. The time allocated is dependent on a number of factors, including the ability of the district to provide substitute personnel to cover the regular responsibilities of the committee members and the ability of community members to commit the time on a regular basis. During the first workshop, the scope of the project is verified; or if the scope is unknown, parameters are set in place to be used in determining the scope of the project. It is beneficial at this point for the consultant team to give a presentation on the process to be utilized, the parameters of the committee's responsibilities, and trends or practices that will influence the ultimate solution. The committee can offer feedback on a number of topics to help generate the project's opportunities and design challenges. If a longer workshop can be scheduled, it is advisable to have the participants break up into smaller groups of five or six to discuss a variety of issues. After they have had time to adequately discuss the topics given them, a representative of each group will report back to the entire group on their ideas.

For the first workshop, small group topics might include a forward look at the future of the facility being studied, such as:

• What will students be doing in this school 5, 10, and 20 years from now?
• What will teachers be doing in this school 5, 10, and 20 years from now?
• How will the community be using this school 5, 10, and 20 years from now?
• How will technology affect the use of this school 5, 10, and 20 years from now?
• How will this improved facility benefit teachers, students, and the community?

Or, questions could include topics relevant to known concerns about the project, such as:

• What do you believe the major public concerns over this project will be?
• How important is creating a sustainable or "green" building solution?

The workshop, if time allows, could include a charrette to explore the opportunities and limitations of the site, wherein workshop participants have an opportunity to draw their ideas on large sheets of paper.

The result of this workshop is a "design direction statement" to be used by the architectural and planning team in beginning the first program statement, as well as the possible options to be presented at workshop 2.

Step 4: Generate options

The architectural and planning team assesses the information generated from Workshop 1 and develops a draft program statement of needs. Along with this preliminary program, the team generates two to five options for the proposed facility recommendations, develops a list of criteria on which the options will be evaluated, and prepares a presentation for the committee.

Step 5: Workshop 2—validate/evaluate

The committee is assembled for a second workshop, between three hours and one day long, in which the architectural and planning team presents the options, along with the opportunities and limitations of each. The proposed program document is reviewed to determine if all the needs of the project are being met and if there are issues needing further discussion. The committee works through each one and determines the option (or a new one) that best represents the objectives and goals of the district as established above.

If time allows, small group work by the committee members could include

- Review each option and create a list of comments or recommendations about each.
- Generating a list of pros and cons of each option.
- Comparing the options to the needs identified for students, teachers, and community members.

Step 6: Workshop 3—present for recommendation and approval

The architectural and planning team prepares and presents the draft educational specifications or facilities design guideline to the committee for endorsement. During the workshop, the team will receive any additional comments and assess the ramifications of implementing them. When approved and with any remaining modifications included, the team prepares the final report for presentation to the board of education.

Step 7: Prioritize and schedule for implementation

Depending on the scope of the proposed project work and the agreed-upon services of the architect and planner, the final ed spec is used to potentially establish

- A list of priorities for improvement or implementation.
- A schedule for improvements by phase.
- An order of magnitude cost estimate by phase for consideration by the board of education.
- The sustainability or LEED requirements and their potential impact on schedule, cost, and/or the consultants to be engaged in the project.
- A plan for presentation to the public for finance hearings, bond campaigns, or a referendum, as required in the particular state, to secure financing.

Summary

This is a very general overview of a commonly used process. It is probably not the exact process that will ultimately be used in any individual district. Each project is different, and the process should be designed to meet the particular needs of the school and the community that it serves. At the completion of the planning process, with the financing in place, the project is now ready for the schematic design phase for the entire project or its identified first phase.

EARLY CHILDHOOD AND KINDERGARTEN

Introduction

Kindergarten typically is a child's first introduction to school or a transition from another preschool program—nursery school, Head Start, day care, or any of the many other types of early childhood programs. In most school systems, children enter a program at age 5 or 6, but a growing number of states are mandating early childhood education for younger ages, and it is the stated policy of the administration of Barack Obama to support a significant expansion of these programs.

Kindergarten generally is defined as a form of preschool education in which children are taught through creative play, social contacts, and natural expression. The concept was originated in Germany in 1837 by Fredrich Froebel; kindergarten, "child's garden," was based on the idea that children's play was significant. Froebel employed games, songs, and stories to address the needs of children (at that time, generally ages 3 to 7). The kindergarten served as a transitional stage from home to school, often a child's first formal learning experience. In 1861, American educator Elizabeth Palmer Peabody opened the first kindergartens in the United States, in Boston. By the 1920s, kindergartens were included in public schools in most parts of the United States.

Historically, a child's first day at kindergarten was often his or her first formal learning experience away from home, but today more children have been exposed to other forms of preschool programs or child care. Still, there can be some separation anxiety as the child leaves home and the prima-

ry caretaker to transition to a group social environment made up mostly of faces the child does not know. The facility can play a role as the transition zone between where the student is with the person bringing them to school and where they actually enter the school. This transition should be as seamless and comfortable as possible.

Since the early 1950s and 1960s, neighborhood schools, often within a short walk of home, have been replaced by central

▲ The entire school environment should play a role in the early childhood learning process. Margaret Shadick Cyert Center for Early Education at Carnegie Mellon University, Pittsburgh, Pennsylvania. Perkins Eastman.

▶ *Successful early childhood classrooms require a flexible environment, furniture, and detailing appropriate for small children, as well as extensive storage. Fairfield Early Childhood Development Center, Fairfield, Connecticut. Perkins Eastman. Photograph by Woodruff/Brown.*

school districts and complex busing networks to collect children from many neighborhoods. In recent years many school districts began to reverse districting concepts, particularly at the elementary school level, and focus on the creation of community-based schools. Yet there are many districts that still prefer the Princeton Plan, whereby a central school is built for each age group.

The design of schools for early childhood education has always sought comfortable, supportive, and adaptive settings conducive to a learning process derived from familiar play and hands-on activities. Specific fea-

> The first step of a child's education life must, above all, be an easy one. This means a kindergarten room that welcomes, encourages, and becomes a friend. In design terms, it calls for spaces within the room that are large enough for a wide range of activity, varied and interesting enough to entice the child and hold his attention. The kindergarten should have a generous view of nature…and it should be made easy to enter. (Perkins 1957, pp. 42–44)

tures associated with home, as well as school, are considered in developing an appropriate transitional setting. The type, size, scale, and variety of more public and private spaces underlie appropriate design and planning. Much like a house, containing public spaces (entry hall, living room, dining room, family room) and more private spaces (kitchen, bedrooms, bathrooms), a school should create spaces for comfortable retreat and quiet, reflective play, as well as for small and large group activities. Today, the typical age range of children in kindergarten programs is 4–6 years.

Early childhood programs have attracted many innovators, such as Dr. Maria Montessori, who developed the Montessori method. This is built on the philosophy that children develop and think differently from adults. They are not merely "adults in small bodies." Many schools have been developed over the last century around her ideas that children are capable of self-directed learning. The children are masters of their schoolroom environment, which is designed to be academic, comfortable, and to encourage independence.

Other innovators have also come from Europe. In particular, the early childhood programs developed in Reggio Emilia, Italy, were identified as exemplary in a 1991 *Newsweek* article, "10 Best Schools in the World." This system, which has become one of the most popular international models, is particularly relevant to the subject of this book. In Italy as a whole, preschool programs have been operating for about 35 years, since the enactment of legislation requiring a free education to be accessible to children ages 3–6. This law was followed in 1971 by additional legislation establishing infant/toddler programs.

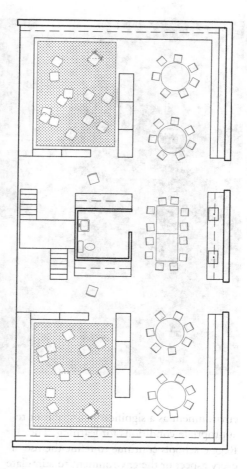

◀ Early childhood program and kindergarten spaces are typically larger, have some soft flooring for naps, and provide adjacent toilet facilities. Perkins Eastman. Courtesy of Perkins Eastman.

In the community of Reggio Emilia, with some 141,000 inhabitants, results have generated international interest in early childhood education programs. The Reggio approach is built on the creation of conditions for learning that encourage a child's construction of "his or her own powers of thinking through the synthesis of all the expressive, communicative, and cognitive languages" (Edwards et al., 1993).

What makes the Reggio philosophy so appealing to architects and designers, as well as educators, is its reliance on the physical

▶ Like a third teacher, the classroom environment should be stimulating, surprising, and comfortable. Margaret Shadick Cyert Center for Early Education at Carnegie Mellon University, Pittsburgh, Pennsylvania. Perkins Eastman.

environment as a significant contributor to appropriate conditions for learning. The Reggio schools continue to refine the use of every aspect of the environment to stimulate curiosity and support creative learning. The following are key principles of the Reggio Emilia approach:

- *Environment as third teacher*—a belief that children learn from their surroundings as well as the people in their lives so the environment should play an equal role to that of the teacher (parents are considered to be a child's first teacher, and classroom teachers their second). The environment must be flexible and adaptable not only to changing teaching styles, but to individual instructors as well. The environment should at once be stimulating, surprising, comfortable, and familiar. It should allow for small and large group projects as well as intimate spaces for one or two children to explore learning. Classrooms should reflect the students' lives and include display space for projects, artwork, and objects of nature. Common space should be available for art classes and dramatic play and for the gathering of children from different classes in group activities.

- *Emergent curriculum/adaptive environment*—builds on the interests of children. Topics for study are captured from the talk of the children, through community or family events, and from

◀ Collaborative small- and large-group work is an important part of the early childhood learning process. Margaret Shadick Cyert Center for Early Education at Carnegie Mellon University, Pittsburgh, Pennsylvania. Perkins Eastman.

known interests (e.g., puddles, shadows, dinosaurs, etc.). Teachers devise specific projects, provide needed materials, and offer possibilities for parent/community support and involvement. The environment should support the spontaneous development of projects and the needs of planned projects, as well as the demands of changing curricula and educational practices.

- *Multiple forms of representation/ exploration*—graphic arts are integrated as tools for cognitive, linguistic, and social development. The presentation of concepts and hypotheses in multiple forms of representation, such as print, art, construction, drama, music, puppetry, and shadow and light play, is essential. The environment

should be able to provide impromptu settings as well as the specific equipment, space, or furnishings needed.

- *Collaborative small and large group work*— considered valuable and necessary to advance cognitive development. Children are encouraged to dialogue, critique, compare, negotiate, hypothesize, and problem solve through group activities. Multiple perspectives promote a sense of both group membership and the uniqueness of self.
- *Curriculum child-centered/teacher-framed*— the teacher's role is complex. Teachers are learners alongside the children. They are resources and guides, lending their expertise to the children. They carefully listen, observe, and document the children's work

▲ Not all learning takes place in the classroom. Tenderloin Community School, San Francisco, California. Photograph by Ethan Kaplan/Esto Photographics.

and the growth of their classroom community. Teachers are committed to reflection about their own teaching and learning, just as they stimulate thinking and promote peer collaboration among the children.

In the United States the primary source of standards—other than state or local regulatory departments—is the National Association for the Education of Young Children (NAEYC) in Washington, D.C. The NAEYC Early Childhood Program issues the most widely used accreditation standards for programs for centers and schools serving children from birth through kindergarten. These standards, which are often higher

than state licensing standards, are, however, voluntary. Among the general goals that all early childhood and kindergarten programs should strive to achieve are the following:

- Create a visually rich, fun, and surprising environment.
- Provide spaces and surfaces for display of children's work.
- Provide a variety of settings for children's works in progress.
- Introduce a variety of social settings for small and large groups.
- Make strong connections between the indoors and the outdoors; above all, use daylighting as much as possible.
- Connect spaces to promote communication, orientation, and flexible programming and staffing.
- Build in flexibility of space to accommodate evolving teaching practices.
- Create a distinctive, pleasing entrance.
- Pay special attention to the scale and height of typical elements such as windows, doors, doorknobs/pulls, sinks, toilets, counters, furnishings, mirrors, steps, shelving/storage, light switches, towel dispensers, and other accessories.

Criteria for High-Quality Early Childhood Programs

Characteristics of the physical environment:

- The indoor and outdoor environments are safe, clean, attractive, and spacious. There is enough usable space indoors so children are not crowded. There is a *minimum* of 35 sq ft of usable playroom floor space indoors per child and a *minimum* of 75 sq ft of play space outdoors per child. Program staff have access to the designated space and sufficient time to prepare the environment before children arrive.

- Activity areas are defined clearly by spatial arrangement. Space is arranged so that children can work individually, together in small groups, or in a large group. Space is arranged to provide clear pathways for children to move from one area to another and to minimize distractions.
- The space for children (three years and older) is arranged to facilitate a variety of small-group or individual activities, including block building, sociodramatic play, art, music, science, math, manipulatives, and quiet reading and writing. Other activities, such as sand play and woodworking, are also available on occasion.
- Carpeted spaces as well as hard surfaces, such as wood floors, and ample crawling/toddling areas are provided for infants and young toddlers. Sturdy furniture is provided so nonwalkers can pull themselves up or balance themselves while walking. School-age children are provided separate space arranged to facilitate a variety of age-appropriate activities and permit sustained work on projects.
- Age-appropriate materials and equipment of sufficient quantity, variety, and durability are readily accessible to children and arranged on low, open shelves to promote independent use by children. Materials are rotated and adapted to maintain children's interest.
- Individual spaces are provided for children to store their personal belongings.
- Private areas are available indoors and outdoors so that children can have occasional solitude.
- The environment includes soft elements such as rugs, cushions, or rocking chairs.

- Sound-absorbing materials are used to minimize noise.
- Outdoor areas include a variety of surfaces, such as soil, sand, grass, hills, flat sections, and hard areas for wheel toys. The outdoor area includes shade, open space, digging space, and a variety of equipment for riding, climbing, balancing, and individual play. The outdoor area is protected by fences or by natural barriers from access to streets or other dangers.
- The work environment for staff, including classrooms and staff rooms, is comfortable, well organized, and in good repair. The environment includes a place for adults to take a break or work away from children, an adult-size bathroom, a secure place for staff to store their personal belongings, and an administrative area that is separated from the children's areas for planning or preparing materials.

For projects involving renovation, state guidelines rarely acknowledge the difficulties inherent in adapting older buildings. It is very important to review local building codes for new and renovated projects. Common amendments/issues that should be given special attention include the following:

- Number of exits and travel distance restrictions
- Special emergency lighting requirements
- Number of floors and/or maximum distance above grade
- Types of special locking permitted
- Separations from other uses, if in a mixed-use building or complex

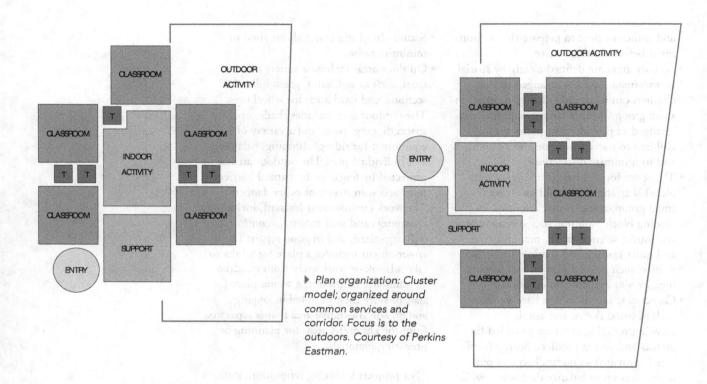

▶ Plan organization: Cluster model; organized around common services and corridor. Focus is to the outdoors. Courtesy of Perkins Eastman.

▲ Plan organization: Cluster model; organized around open play space. Focus is to the interior. Courtesy of Perkins Eastman.

Typical space guidelines are as follows:

• 35–50 usable sq ft/child for indoor activity/ classroom space (This area does not typically include staff workspace, administrative offices, storage areas, toilet areas, etc.)
• 75–100 sq ft/child for outdoor activity space

The required space standards often fall short of those recommended by social and behavioral research, in both quantity and arrangement of space. Research also indicates that facilities with too little space (less than 35 usable sq ft of space per child) may lead to more aggressive/destructive behavior, fewer friendly contacts, and less solitary learning and play. Conversely, too much space (more

than 50 usable sq ft of space per child) can result in reduced attention spans, more supervision required by staff, and an increase in aimless, random behavior. Thus, some current experts recommend plans such as those shown in the figures on page 29 and above.

Sample program
As mentioned previously, state guidelines for the design and planning of early childhood education and kindergarten facilities provide little insight into the space needs of specific facilities and their design. The table on page 36 shows a sample facility program, assumed for 100 children, and a list of typical spaces and design issues for consideration. With facilities of significantly larger size than shown in this example, consideration

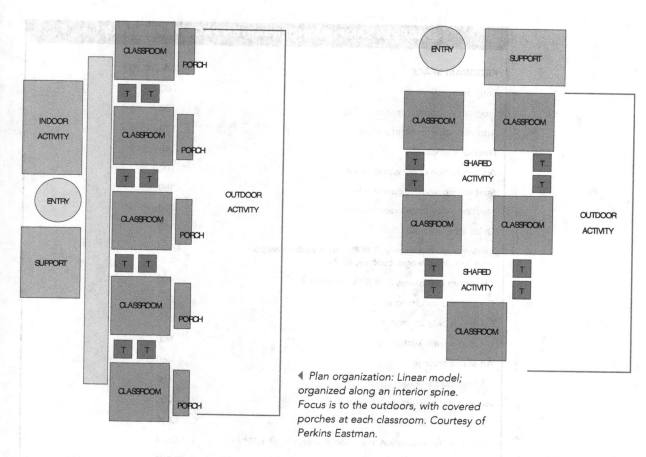

CLASSROOM
PORCH
T T
INDOOR ACTIVITY
CLASSROOM
PORCH
T T
ENTRY
CLASSROOM
PORCH
T T
OUTDOOR ACTIVITY
SUPPORT
CLASSROOM
PORCH
T T
CLASSROOM
PORCH
T T
CLASSROOM
PORCH

ENTRY
SUPPORT
CLASSROOM
CLASSROOM
T
SHARED ACTIVITY
T
T
T
CLASSROOM
CLASSROOM
OUTDOOR ACTIVITY
T
SHARED ACTIVITY
T
T
T
CLASSROOM

◀ *Plan organization: Linear model; organized along an interior spine. Focus is to the outdoors, with covered porches at each classroom. Courtesy of Perkins Eastman.*

▲ *Plan organization: Hybrid linear; organized along a complex spine made up of a series of activity/play spaces. Courtesy of Perkins Eastman.*

should be given to creating smaller clusters of classrooms organized around shared activities that can be arranged to create a sense of multiple neighborhoods or houses.

Other Considerations

Parking and drop-off
- Review applicable local zoning regulations regarding parking, often based on ratio of spaces to children/staff.
- Adequate drop-off/pickup space at the beginning and end of each day for buses and parents who drive their own children is

needed. Consider a long curb pickup lane or short-term loading/unloading spaces at the entrance.
- Adequate lighting at parking and drop-off areas is critical for safety and security.

Entrance
- Welcoming, spacious area with adequate seating and places for informal visiting
- Large enough to accommodate small groups of children and adults
- Often the place where children exhibit the signs of anxiety over separation from parents

SPACES IN SAMPLE KINDERGARTEN FACILITY PROGRAM*

PROGRAM SPACE	AREA (SQ FT)
Entry area	200
Program assistant/reception	120
Administrative assistant's office	120
Director's office	160
Administration copy/supply room	100
Staff workroom/break area/toilet	350
Meeting/parent conference room	200
Quiet room/first aid	100
Kindergarten classrooms (5 @ 800 sq ft each; classroom area includes storage, cubbies, kitchen, etc.)	4,000
Classroom bathrooms (5 @ 80 sq ft each)	400
Central activity/dining area	1,500
Central activity storage	200
Art studio (with kiln)	500
Art studio storage	60
Kitchen/food storage	600
General facility storage	200
Subtotal usable space	8,810
Multiplier for circulation, mechanical area, etc. @ 1.4**	3,524
Total Facility Program (average @ ±123 sq ft/child)	12,334

* Kindergarten program for 100 children
** Assumes ground floor or 1-story space

- Display areas for bulletins/flyers and artwork/children's projects at both adults' and children's eye level
- Close to administrative area to provide security and accommodate parent-teacher/administrator meetings

Corridors/transition spaces
- View as extensions of activity space.
- Avoid long, straight hallways; provide nooks and alcoves for sitting, play, and display and visual connection to classrooms.
- Provide space for wall/ceiling-hung projects, display cases for various art objects.
- Open corridor spaces with interior glass windows looking into adjacent classroom/activity spaces; take advantage of borrowed natural light.

- Avoid designing corridors that have no other use but circulation.
- Use carpeting or other acoustic materials to reduce noise.

Classrooms
- Select materials/finishes to help reduce noise (think in terms of 20 children at active play).
- Create areas for distinct activities (e.g., group meetings, quiet individual concentration, laboratory/semiactive spaces, workshop/studio spaces for art, drama, blocks, games, etc.). These areas are best created through the use of movable furnishings, shelves, bookcases, and so forth, to promote flexibility and the individual character of each classroom. Rectangular spaces are typically easier to configure than square or oddly shaped areas.
- Provide a soft living-room-like area for visiting/relaxing.
- Design space to meet both children's and adults' physical needs. Be sure to provide seating, tables, workspace, and storage suited to both.
- Provide space for cubbies/lockers either between classrooms or within classrooms; allow for adult assistance.
- Provide for display of plants/objects.
- Take advantage of areas below windows for quiet seating nooks or play areas.
- Provide a play area specifically suited to wet or messy activities.
- Include a kitchenette, to serve a group of classrooms or the entire school area, with counters and cabinets at heights for both children and adults; include locking cabinets.
- Provide sinks for both children and adults within the classrooms and near the wet play area.

- If possible, lower sills of windows to 18–24 in. above the floor, to conform to a child's scale.
- Provide ample daylight, with good shade/blind control for nap and quiet activity time.
- Provide flexible lighting levels to accommodate various activity moods.
- Provide bulletin/display boards for children and adults.
- Install an individual temperature control for each classroom.
- Install a child-accessible drinking fountain (can be incorporated with a low sink).
- Provide a toilet room directly adjacent to the classroom; consider special child-accessible fixtures.
- Install hands-free faucets to promote hand washing and general hygiene.
- Provide areas/closets for storage of supplies, games, nap mats/blankets, etc.
- Provide a quiet room/area, possibly shared by adjacent classrooms, for disruptive children or for individual play.
- Balance the need for small, quiet spaces with openness to permit adequate supervision of staff-child interaction.

Administrative space
- Locate near entrance for easy access by families and for view of main entrance.
- Provide administrative offices as required.
- Provide principal's/director's office with adequate space for small meeting table.
- Locate staff mailboxes in or near staff room.
- Provide space for records storage/supplies.

Art studio
- Ample natural light, with good shade/blind control (facing north for indirect light is preferred)

▲ Art studio with ceramics program. Margaret Shadick Cyert Center for Early Education at Carnegie Mellon University, Pittsburgh, Pennsylvania. Perkins Eastman. Photograph by Jim Schafer.

- Bulletin boards/display boards/display shelving for children and adults
- Separate kiln room if ceramics work is part of the program
- Large, flat multiuse tables to support individual and group work
- Ample storage for art supplies
- Sensible finishes for easy cleanup after art activities

- Cleanup area within the art studio for both children and adults, with extra-deep clay-trap sinks
- Locking storage cabinets adjacent to sink and counter areas
- A bathroom for children either in the art studio or nearby

Observation/consultation space
(Optional—used for staff teaching and teacher/parent consultations.)

- Position observation space to observe child-child and child-teacher interaction, often within the classroom. (Such spaces are typically provided in early childhood, daycare, and "demonstration school" facilities, usually not in pre-K or kindergarten.)
- Isolate acoustically to allow for discussion of classroom behavior.
- Consider one-way mirrored glass to conceal identity of observers, particularly when parents are included in observer group.
- Consider designing observation space to be shared by classrooms.
- Design may allow for use as quiet activity room if also accessible from classroom.
- Separate lighting control from classroom to support one-way viewing.
- Design for entry/exit without view from observed area.

Kitchen/pantry
- Position for easy/secure delivery access, adjacent to dining area.
- If possible, allow for view from dining area with interior windows to promote child-staff interaction and learning.
- Arrange space to allow for display cooking; try to maintain free sight lines through the kitchen space.
- Provide adequate ventilation.

Communication systems

- Each classroom/area should have a phone and intercom communication.
- Consider locating data outlets within the classrooms to allow for computers/access to the Internet, as well as internal e-mail communication from classroom to classroom.
- Each classroom should have a computer work area.
- Provide multiple electrical outlets in classroom/activity areas for a range of equipment. Consider specifying childproof outlets.
- Provide data outlets at administrative/staff work areas.

Toilet facilities

- Include some child-size toilets, but plan for transition to full-size/adult toilets.
- A preschool bathroom should be directly accessible from the classroom and should be easily supervised by the teacher.
- Provide a minimum of one toilet and sink per classroom.
- Consider hands-free flush/faucet systems to encourage use and promote general hygiene.
- Provide a separate facility for staff and visitors.
- Adapt at least one toilet fixture for accessibility; *do not* use a typical 17 in. high fixture; provide lowered grab bars at a standard 15 in. high fixture.
- Provide locked storage cabinets for cleaning supplies, etc.

Outdoor space

- Direct outdoor access from each classroom is best, or it may be from a central point in the facility.
- Consider sheltering devices against sun, wind, rain, etc.

- Develop different play zones for active group play, quiet individual play, etc.
- Provide bathrooms close to the outdoor play area.
- Use natural land formations/terrain for exploring; trees, rocks, small hills for running, climbing, sliding, etc.
- Allow for good visibility to all areas of the outdoor play space.
- Provide secure boundaries with fencing; try to buffer/soften the appearance of the fencing with plantings.
- Vary surfaces for play—asphalt, concrete, grass, sand, or synthetic recycled interlocking resilient matting beneath climbing/swinging equipment; *avoid gravel*!
- Provide varied outdoor lighting conditions; use shade structures.
- Provide storage space for all outdoor play equipment, accessible from both outside and inside the facility if possible.

▲ *Outdoor activity space should provide for a number of activities. Coman Hill Elementary School, Byram Hills School District, Armonk, New York. Perkins Eastman. Photograph by Paúl Rivera/ArchPhoto.*

Design of the classroom—scale, variety, and flexibility of space. A well-designed classroom environment is safe for children, supports their emotional well-being, stimulates their senses, and challenges their skills. Subdividing the classroom into well-defined "activity pockets" identifies physical spaces that are each functionally limited to one activity, but not completely closed off from the rest of the classroom or from instructor supervision. Observation of preschool children at play suggests that there is a tendency for them to cluster into small groups of less than five, with a mean of about two children. If activity areas are sized for two to five children and an instructor, they should be 40–60 sq ft each. In addition, space should be provided either within the classroom or in a nearby area to allow for an entire class to meet as a single group. The following are simple suggestions for creating activity pockets:

- Care should be taken to allow as much flexibility and adaptability of small activity areas as possible.
- U-shaped or L-shaped low walls can be used to delineate activity areas. The number of activity areas created with permanent walls should be limited, as they can also restrict flexibility.
- Area rugs or other floor finish changes can be used to delineate areas.
- Bookshelves, low bookcases, or other storage and display cabinets can be used to define edges.
- Other furnishings can also be used to define edges, such as the back of a sofa, the edges of reading chairs or comfortable seating, and display systems.
- Existing columns can be used to define edges or corners.

- Ceiling- and floor-level changes can align with centers' boundaries; it is important to consider accessibility to raised platform areas.
- Bay windows, with built-in benches and the addition of other defining elements such as an area rug or low bookcase, can be used for a small activity area.
- Canopies, curtains, latticework, or fabric can be hung from the ceiling to create an activity area.
- Color, lighting, and other material changes can be used to further enhance the articulation of pockets.

All supplies, work surfaces, materials, storage, audiovisual equipment, and required power sources should be provided. Seating and furnishings should adapt to the needs of the activity as well as the size of the group. Finally, there should be an activity area in each classroom that comfortably supports the play of one child as a place for refuge or solitary activity.

Personalization, display, and storage. Providing inventive and creative ways to display the work and projects of the children is essential to support "habitation" of their space. Every part of the architecture should be thought of as potential display space; walls, ceilings, floors, and furnishings throughout the facility should be used. Care should be taken to provide a variety of display spaces for two-dimensional flat work and three-dimensional pottery, mobiles, sculpture, and small crafts. The display area should be flexible and allow for quick and easy change. A display space should be designed for viewing by both adults and children. Appropriate lighting should emphasize the displays and should be adjustable in both position and intensity.

The following are suggestions for display spaces:

- Picture rails or shelves along walls. Particular attention should be given to corridor areas, where walls may become repetitive.
- Closed display cases arranged for viewing from one side or from all sides.
- Open, adjustable shelving.
- Metal gridwork or other mesh materials attached to walls or ceilings to hang artwork/projects.
- Windowsills or areas in front of windows where natural light and the interplay of light and shadow can enhance the objects viewed.
- Other flexible display systems that can be moved or reconfigured to create different desired effects.

Color, pattern, and light. The use of varied colors and textures can be very desirable. A range of textures friendly to a child's skin and body adds another aspect to a child's experience with the physical environment. A number of textures can be considered: wood, ceramic tile, various plaster surfaces, metal or wire screens, fabric, rubber, various metal surfaces, safety mirror, and glass.

Colors can be vibrant or subdued, but there is no need to limit environments designed for children to the ubiquitous primary colors. Research has suggested that bright red hues create excitement, and deep purples and greens are stabilizing and soothing. Yellow, as well as being restful, is the first color that can be perceived by small infants. There are, however, many facilities designed with little or very simple color to provide the most neutral backdrop possible. James Greenman, a nationally respected expert on the design of early childhood settings, advocates this approach because, he believes, the environment should not compete with the artwork and projects of the children. Moreover, it does not overstimulate the children. A neutral background allows the environment to be personalized and animated by its inhabitants. In essence, the space is regarded as an active representation of the children's work and learning process.

Varied lighting not only adds to the interest of the environment, but also provides options for creating moods, supporting different activities, and learning. Daylighting may be a significant part of the education curriculum. Through observation of the sun, children can begin to understand the passage of time, the changing of the seasons, and the movement of the planet. Daylight should be allowed to enter the building from different orientations and locations. Large windows, skylights, and outdoor sundials all help to connect sunlight with the children's daily lives.

ELEMENTARY SCHOOLS

Elementary school classrooms are typically some of the largest in the district, driven by the need for young students to move fluidly from one activity to the next. Students in this age bracket have limited attention spans and are developing a variety of motor skills. The rooms, therefore, need to provide a wide range of activities that can be set up simultaneously. For this section, elementary schools will be defined as including pre-K (age 3) through grade 5.

As noted in the preceding sections, early childhood classrooms, pre-K through grade 2, can sometimes be larger than those for grades 3 through 5. The exact size of the elementary classroom should be a function of the program to be provided; the number

▶ Many new elementary schools have to be built on tight urban sites. Agassiz Elementary School, Cambridge, Massachusetts. HMFH Architects.

▶ Crow Island School is considered by many to be the first modern elementary school. It became the model for the large postwar school building boom. Crow Island School, Winnetka, Illinois. Perkins, Wheeler & Will with Eliel & Eero Saarinen.

AREA 1: ELEMENTARY SCHOOL CLASSROOM SPACE REQUIREMENTS

PROGRAM ELEMENT	COMMONLY REQUIRED	SPACE REQUIRED
Classroom	Yes[1]	Variable; from 700 sq ft in an urban school to more than 1,200 sq ft when land and funds to build larger buildings are not limiting factors.
Computer/ project commons	Yes[2]	350–600 sq ft (one per 100–200 students); should be designed for flexible use, with access to water and storage areas. *Important*: See footnote 2.
Science instruction	Yes	900–1,200 sq ft (one per 300–600 students); size depends on lab type and whether combined as a "wet lab" with art. Wet labs are typically larger (50 sq ft per student) than dry labs or technology-based labs (35 sq ft per student).
Art instruction	Yes[3]	900–1,200 sq ft (one per 300 students); number required depends on program, student population, and grades served. Elementary schools with more than 850 students may require two rooms.

1. Space within the classroom for student cubbies for backpacks and coats if located in a northern climate. Provide ample space for circulation, seating benches, and cubbies sized for today's backpacks, commonly carried by students of virtually all ages.
2. During programming, Computer commons should be carefully evaluated and discussed before committing to this space allocation. With cost-effective computing solutions and new portability, these areas are rapidly converting to project or team space as computers distribute more evenly throughout the school.
3. Art instruction may require space for two-dimensional art such as drawing and painting, three-dimensional art including clay work and model making, and graphic art involving digital photography and photo editing. These three spaces may be interconnected and share certain storage and support functions.

Source: Perkins Eastman.

of students it serves; in-room support spaces such as sinks, cubbies, and toilet facilities; and conformance to state guidelines.

Program Elements

The program elements of an elementary school can be categorized into six areas:

1. *Classroom spaces*: general-purpose classrooms, clusters of classrooms (the "house"—see the following section), labs, art rooms, special education classrooms

2. *Teacher and administrative support areas*: general offices and waiting area, principal's/assistant principal's suite, psychologist's office, nurse's office, conference rooms, common faculty (team teaching) planning and workrooms, faculty dining room, conference rooms, adult toilets.
3. *Media and technology space*: technology center, library/media center, special use/ club meeting rooms, exhibition space.
4. *Classroom support space*: gymnasium, cafeteria, specialized resource rooms for remediation.

AREA 2: ELEMENTARY SCHOOL ADMINISTRATIVE AND FACULTY SUPPORT SPACE REQUIREMENTS

PROGRAM ELEMENT	COMMONLY REQUIRED	SPACE REQUIRED
Administrative offices	Yes	120–350 sq ft per office; type and size depend on capacity of the building and the program specifics. Common elements include a principal's office, assistant administrator's office (minimum 1), conference room, nurse's office, administrative support, and reception and waiting area.
Nurse's office/sick bay	Yes	Minimum 350 sq ft, including cot area, restroom, nurse's station, and storage. Located near administrative offices and the main entry; should also have access to athletic fields and multipurpose room.
Guidance/counselor's office	Yes	Number and type dependent on a variety of factors and should be programmed individually for each school. Located near administrative offices with easy access to students.
Staff space	Yes	Minimum 650 sq ft for staff workroom, including kitchenette, work tables, copy area, mailboxes, and material storage.
Storage	Yes	Note: The total storage needs of a building are very often underestimated. Storage needs include space for student coats/backpacks, project storage, teachers' resources, building maintenance supplies, book supplies, recycled materials storage (as part of a recycling center), and storage space dedicated to the other major components of the building.

Source: Perkins Eastman.

5. *Performing and visual arts*: art rooms, music rooms, music practice rooms, theaters, auditorium.
6. *Facility management*: central receiving, custodial and maintenance support spaces, recycling room, central storage.

Elementary School Space Guidelines

Elementary schools typically have more basic needs as compared to middle schools and high schools, because a great deal of the instructional program is accommodated in the core classroom. The quantity and type of programs, though, can vary widely, and it is helpful if specialized spaces can accommodate the support of core programs.

The quantity of specialized program areas is determined by the offerings at the school and varies from school to school. The size of each room and quantity of each room type

◀ Elementary classrooms require a space to accommodate special projects such as this one on archeology. Photograph by Judith Perkins.

◀ Art room demonstrating a variety of activities happening simultaneously. American International School: Riyadh, Riyadh, Saudi Arabia. Perkins Eastman. Courtesy of Perkins Eastman.

▶ *Carlin Springs Media Center provides for a more relaxed and informal seating gallery. Carlin Springs Elementary School, Arlington, Virginia. Grimm + Parker Architects. Photograph by Kenneth M. Wyner.*

AREA 3: ELEMENTARY SCHOOL MEDIA AND TECHNOLOGY SPACE REQUIREMENTS		
PROGRAM ELEMENT	**COMMONLY REQUIRED**	**SPACE REQUIRED**
Library/media center	Yes	Provide seating for 10% of school population, minimum 50 seats (approximately two classes), plus additional seating for technology access support.
Media center support space	Yes	Determined on an individual basis; could include small group rooms, computer commons/labs, workroom, office, storage, soft/informal seating area, etc.
Technology lab/studio	Optional	Determined on an individual basis; could include small group rooms, computer commons/labs, work room, office, storage, soft/informal seating area, etc.

Source: Perkins Eastman.

AREA 4: ELEMENTARY SCHOOL CLASSROOM SUPPORT SPACE REQUIREMENTS

PROGRAM ELEMENT	COMMONLY REQUIRED	SPACE REQUIRED
Gymnasium/ multipurpose	Yes	Square footage varies; minimum recommended area is 3,200 sq ft for 600 students. Depends heavily on grade configuration and capacity of school. Very large elementary schools may require two of these spaces. For smaller elementary populations, this room may also function as the cafeteria or auditorium.
Cafeteria	Yes[1]	School population ÷ number of planned lunch periods x 13 sq ft. Additional square footage may be required for faculty dining space and individual lunch period scheduling variation.
Media center support space	Yes	Determined on an individual basis; could include small group rooms, computer commons/labs, work room, office, storage, soft/informal seating area, etc.
Exhibit and display space	Optional	Determined on an individual basis; could include art exhibit hall or commons near entry for display of schoolwork.

1. Warming kitchen and full-service kitchen should be planned at up to 40% of the size of dining area, or a minimum of 3.2 sq ft per meal served per shift, including the back counter of the serving areas (5.2 sq ft would be 40% of 13 sq ft; 4.0 sq ft is a good number for preliminary planning). If not serviced by a district's central kitchen, the kitchen would be about 1.5 times this size, or 6 sq ft per seat. Depending on food styles and offerings, the serving line may be up to one-third of the total kitchen NSF. Again, this depends on whether the kitchen is standalone or serviced from a central kitchen. For preliminary planning, 1.5 sq ft per seat should be provided for the serving line. If more demonstration cooking is desired, this area could approach 60% of the total kitchen. *(Notes on Food Service courtesy of Cini-Little.)*

Source: Perkins Eastman.

are functions of the school's total enrollment. The square footage given below for each space can be assumed as a starting point for a 600-student elementary school, grades K–5, with four sections per grade. Areas are subject to variation by program focus and according to increases or decreases in enrollment. For example, for smaller schools, multiple functions can be accommodated in a single space, such as a cafeteria/auditorium or a science/art room. Larger schools will likely require dedicated space to adequately implement the program. Typical program areas for an elementary school are shown in the tables on pages 43–49.

Sample Program
Refer to Appendix A for a sample program for a 750-student rural elementary school in a northern climate. Each programming area should be arranged together as shown.

AREA 5: ELEMENTARY SCHOOL PERFORMING AND VISUAL ARTS SPACE REQUIREMENTS

PROGRAM ELEMENT	COMMONLY REQUIRED	SPACE REQUIRED
Auditorium	Yes	If provided, calculate area required for the main "house" by determining what percentage of the school's population is to be accommodated at one time. For example, (600-student school) x (percentage of students to be accommodated, 50%) x (9 sq ft per student) = 2,700 sq ft. Additional square footage required for stage and support space.
Theater	Optional	Calculate the area for the main "house" as for an auditorium. Additional square footage required for orchestra space, stagecraft, dressing rooms, projection booth, etc.
Theater stage	Optional (if program provides for theater)	1,200–2,400 sq ft; size for largest performance anticipated.
Music rooms	Optional	1,100–1,450 sq ft each; size for largest group using the room. Number required depends on program, student population, and grades served. Elementary schools with more than 850 students may require two rooms.
Art rooms	Optional	Varies; minimum 1,000 sq ft. May include additional space for kiln, storage, etc. Larger elementary schools may require two art rooms.
Exhibit and display space	Optional	Determined on an individual basis–could include art exhibit hall or commons near entry for display of schoolwork.

Source: Perkins Eastman.

AREA 6: ELEMENTARY SCHOOL FACILITY MANAGEMENT SPACE REQUIREMENTS		
PROGRAM ELEMENT	**COMMONLY REQUIRED**	**SPACE REQUIRED**
Maintenance and receiving space	Yes	Varies; minimum 400 sq ft. Larger if space includes building-wide storage and a recycling center.
Central plant	Optional	Determined on an individual basis; depends on mechanical systems selection, geographic location, etc. Can be programmed as net square footage, or included in gross area if the grossing factors account for it.
Recycling center	Optional	Minimum 400 sq ft; used for separation and collection of recyclables. Located near the shipping and receiving area.
Building-wide storage	Yes	Minimum 400 sq ft; used for maintenance supplies. Can be centrally located or distributed.
Instructional material storage	Yes	Dependent on size of school; provide at least one space of minimum 200 sq ft for book storage, supplemented by other storage areas for teacher resource support. Can be distributed.

Source: Perkins Eastman

◀ *Another good example of providing students with variety in seating options. P.S. 1/ Bergen School, Robinhood Foundation Library Initiative, Brooklyn, New York. Marpillero Pollak Architects. Photograph by Peter Mauss/Esto Photographics.*

▶ *The stage for the multipurpose room at Greenman Elementary School is two-sided, offering an informal stage to the lobby as shown. Amphitheatre seating adjoins the extra-wide stairs leading to the second floor. Greenman Elementary School, Aurora, Illinois. Cordogan Clark & Associates, Inc. Photograph by Ballogg Photography.*

MIDDLE SCHOOLS AND HIGH SCHOOLS

Middle school classrooms are more typically aligned with high school classrooms than with those of an elementary school. They may be dedicated for a specific program (e.g., world language or math), or assigned to a number of different programs in a given day or week. Classroom design for middle schools and high schools is similar and treated similarly in this section. Differences are identified and further defined later in the chapter.

Program Elements

The program elements of a middle school and high school can be categorized into seven major areas:

1. *Academic spaces*: general-purpose classrooms, clusters of classrooms (the "house"—see the following section), special education classrooms

2. *Teacher and administrative support areas*: conference rooms, common faculty (team teaching) planning and work-rooms, faculty dining room, conference rooms, adult toilets

3. *Media and technology spaces*: technology center, flexible lab space, library/media center.

4. *Community and stakeholder space*: cafeteria, student commons, parent centers, special use/club meeting rooms, exhibition space

5. *Physical education and support space*: Gymnasiums, natatoriums, weight and aerobic rooms, health and fitness centers/classrooms, storage rooms, locker rooms, team rooms

6. *Performing and visual arts*: art rooms, music rooms, music practice rooms, theater, auditorium

7. *Facilities management and custodial space*:

Shipping and receiving, maintenance space, mechanical equipment space, building-wide storage/supply rooms, custodial offices

The preceding list comprises the elements of a middle or high school program. The square footage of the building and incremental sizes of basic program elements will vary greatly from locale to locale. Among the factors that will affect the final program of the middle school are enrollment projections, teaching philosophy, special interests (e.g., athletics, technology, and foreign languages), climate, preferred class sizes, and financial resources.

It is often the financial stability of the school district and not the ability and desire of a community to invest its tax resources that shape the final program. However, most states concur that, at a minimum, the school district must provide the "fundamental instruction spaces" necessary to accommodate enrollment projections. Typically, fundamental instruction spaces include general classrooms, library, and gymnasium spaces.

The program component tables on pages 53–72 address the most common spaces found in middle and high schools but are by no means inclusive of all spaces required. Refer to the sample facilities programs below for a more complete listing of potential spaces.

Space Requirements

As with elementary schools, the quantity and type of specialized program areas can vary widely and are heavily determined by the school's programs and curriculum. As middle and high schools are more specialized than elementary schools, their support spaces are more complex. The discussion of common support spaces in this section includes a general outline and does not address needs for schools of specialized focus, which are discussed later in the chapter.

Academic spaces

Calculating classroom size

General-purpose classrooms usually are designed to accommodate 22–30 students, with the most typical range being between 22–25. The permitted maximum number of students per classroom may vary somewhat from state to state or be influenced by district standards. At both the middle school and high school level, the typical average class size noted above allows for an increase in the student population of 3–5 students per classroom without requiring new construction. In most cases, classrooms should be equipped with 2–4 more seats than the planned capacity to allow for scheduling variations and the occasional larger class.

General classrooms in a middle school, which are typically 770–1,000 NSF, have been based on the guideline of 35 NSF per student for classrooms of 22–30 students. With reductions in the size of technology equipment, the development of more ergonomic and flexible seating, and the availability of other space within the building for specialized break-out space, this guideline is now in question. Where the state or local jurisdiction does not specifically dictate a size, 30 NSF per student is sufficient. Minimum area requirements vary from state to state and must be confirmed by the architect. Some private schools use a smaller average size because of smaller class sizes and/or because they do not have to meet state department of education standards.

Science rooms and labs

Science rooms and labs for middle and high schools range in size between 1,000 sq ft minimum and, occasionally, more than 1,400 sq ft. Many science labs are designed to support individual courses such as biology or chemistry, but they can also be designed as interdisciplinary science spaces. Storage can make the difference between a successful science area design and one that will be perceived as too small. Earth science, for example, requires storage for rocks, soil, microscopes, and so forth; while physics may require a wider range of equipment. Storage and prep rooms for chemistry require chemical storage complete with a preparation area, corrosion-proof shelving, and a fire-proof chemical storage cabinet. Storage areas, both in adjacent spaces and in the classroom or lab, should be provided with locks to protect chemicals and expensive equipment.

Science classroom and lab design should take into consideration three main areas or activities as students engage in lecture settings, hands-on experimentation, and technology use for research, simulation, and measurement of experiments. These can be divided into separate spaces or designed to be flexible, multiuse space. It is often desirable to provide an instruction space in which students sit at desks and learn from the teacher's instructions on either a whiteboard or screen, or from a lab station.

Natural gas or propane is typically provided for chemistry, biology, and multiuse labs, but is not as necessary for physics or technology labs. Most labs should be equipped with sinks with hot and cold water, emergency shutoffs, and eye-washing stations.

Fume hoods and special ventilation requirements are often mandated for science rooms and preparation areas or rooms. Durable materials, resistant to chemical and flame damage, should be used for flooring, casework, and countertops.

Designing for flexibility

One of the themes of middle school and high school design is the exploratory nature of its programming. Students at these levels are inquisitive and may take a number of classes to determine if the subject and content interest them. Consequently, flexibility in secondary school classroom design is critical. The size, configuration, and groupings of classrooms are among the planning concepts most important to the success of the increasingly utilized teaming and house methodology.

Demountable partitions may be used between pairs of classrooms but should be carefully placed where they will be used the most. Other keys to flexible design include

- Furniture that can be arranged in a number of different configurations
- Technology access at various points in the room, as well as wireless Internet access
- Digital display technology to allow material to be presented on a number of different subject matters
- Lighting controls to allow multiple levels of illumination
- Visual connections to adjacent space for "pull-out" activities

Flexibility can mean the inclusion of technology centers that are not subject-specific. The same computer lab may accommodate distance learning, interactive foreign

AREA 1: ACADEMIC SPACE REQUIREMENTS FOR MIDDLE SCHOOLS AND HIGH SCHOOLS

PROGRAM ELEMENT	MS REQUIRED	HS REQUIRED	SPACE REQUIRED
Classrooms	Yes	Yes	Size and quantity of classrooms required are described in the text section "Calculating Classroom Size."
Computer labs	No[1]	No[1]	850–1,200 sq ft; if provided, plan as a flexible space that can be reconfigured in the future, or as a technology project lab with more specialized graphics or media capabilities.
Project/ study commons	Probably	Probably	500–1,200 sq ft (for programs that rely on project-based, self-directed activities, provide one for every 150 middle school students, or one for every 100 high school students). Commonly found in schools with an international baccalaureate (I.B.) program.
Small group rooms	Yes	Yes	250–450 sq ft each (minimum 2 rooms); approximate quantities for establishing a baseline: 1 for every 4–6 general middle school or high school classrooms; number required depends on program, student population, and grades served.
Science spaces	Yes	Yes	1,050–1,450 sq ft (per 125–200 students); size depends on lab type. Wet labs are typically larger (50 sq ft per student) than dry labs or technology-based labs (35 sq ft per student). A combination of both is generally required. Number required is dependent on science course-taking patterns and requirements, types of science classes offered, and utilization goals of the facility. If teachers have their own classrooms, the number required will generally be higher.
Technology/ vocational/ project labs	Optional	Optional	1,050–2,400 sq ft; size depends on lab type. Project labs that are equipment-intensive require a minimum of 50 sq ft per student, less equipment-intensive labs require minimum 35 sq ft per student.

1. Computer labs or commons should be carefully evaluated and discussed before committing to this space allocation. With cost-effective computing solutions, the decentralizing of computer technology, and improved portability and wireless networks to distribute computer access more evenly throughout the school, these areas are rapidly converting to project or team space. Although there may be "computer labs," they are commonly dedicated to a specific function, such as graphic arts, and therefore not labeled as computer labs.

▶ *Informal breakout space provides support to the adjacent classrooms. Sunset Ridge Middle School, West Jordan, Utah. VCBO Architecture. Photograph by Dana Sohm, Sohm Photografx.*

language studies, language arts, graphic design, and other programs.

Faculty and administrative support areas

The quality of support areas is a significant factor in motivating teachers, fostering a collaborative environment, and facilitating interaction between faculty and students. In addition, a growing body of research has shown that space where teachers can collaborate has tangible benefits for the teaching environment in a school. Administrative areas attract both internal and public visitors. See the table on page 56 for space requirements.

Administration areas should be located adjacent to the main public entrance to enable direct visual supervision of visitors. It is important to provide a reception area for visitors to deter them from wandering through the school unattended. Security has become an ever-increasing concern in school facilities. The inclusion of metal detectors and security cameras is becoming more common. The reception area can act as a control point for the administration area and the school in general.

Private offices should be provided at 100 sq ft minimum for the principal and vice principal(s). The principal's office is often larger to accommodate meetings with students or parents. A second means of ingress/egress for the administrative suite is recommended for security and privacy. A conference room can be a shared facility; if only one is provided, it should be designed to accommodate a minimum of 10 to 15 people at 15 sq ft per person.

In some districts, the superintendent and associated staff (business official, administrative assistants, etc.) may be located in the same area. The same space requirements apply.

Work areas for copiers, fax machines, printers, public announcement systems, faculty mailboxes, and storage should be provided. A vault to secure examinations and petty cash is often included.

The size of the guidance suite will depend on the level of service and requirements as established by the school district and determines the number of guidance counselors, offices, conference rooms, and support spaces required. It is recommended that an area be provided for students to access materials such as information on colleges and other topics of interest. Separate offices for counselors, at a minimum of 120 sq ft per office, should be provided to allow for individual meetings with a student or a student and parents. A conference room is also desirable for somewhat larger gatherings, but may be shared with another area of the school, such as the administration suite.

The nurse/health suite is generally located near, or within, the main offices of the school and close to the physical education area and outdoor play fields. It should also be convenient to a main entry for easy access by EMS personnel. These seemingly contradictory requirements often lead to the design of "satellite" areas, such as a trainer's room, that can be used as a health suite for injuries related to physical education or athletic events. The size of this area will vary greatly depending on the total population of the building. There should be a waiting area for students and staff. A private office directly adjacent to the waiting area should allow direct visual contact for supervision. This office should also have direct visual contact with a "resting room." The resting room

should have cots or beds; the number included will depend on the level of service provided by the nurse, but as a general rule there should be one bed or cot for every 200 students. The suite should be equipped with a refrigerator and restroom and should have access to ice.

Dining and food service spaces

The size of the cafeteria/kitchen space varies greatly, depending on the student enrollment, number of scheduled lunch periods, and type of kitchen facilities required. Some school districts require full-service kitchens, whereas others may contract with a food service provider that prepares meals off-site. Whatever the specific situation, it is safe to say that 15 sq ft per person is an adequate size for the purposes of planning the seating area in the initial design; and some schools design to a standard of only 12 sq ft per person.

Kitchen and food service spaces will most likely be more expensive per square foot because of the special equipment required. Particular attention must be given to the mechanical systems, electrical systems, and fire protection of these spaces.

These facilities are often used for activities beyond the cafeteria function. Therefore, the placement of the kitchen, serving areas, and possibly vending machines is critical. It is often desirable to be able to close off the kitchen after lunchtime to allow for other activities. Storage of food products, both dry goods and food requiring freezers and coolers, must be taken into consideration.

Sanitary concerns also affect the design of these facilities. Ease of maintenance and general cleaning of equipment is extremely important. Quarry tile floors and wall bases are often used in the kitchen/cooking area

PROGRAM ELEMENT	MS REQUIRED	HS REQUIRED	SPACE REQUIRED

AREA 2: ADMINISTRATIVE SPACE REQUIREMENTS FOR
MIDDLE SCHOOLS AND HIGH SCHOOLS

PROGRAM ELEMENT	MS REQUIRED	HS REQUIRED	SPACE REQUIRED
Principal's office suite	Yes	Yes	Usually part of an administrative office area located near the building entry; contains at a minimum: 200–400 sq ft waiting area 75–150 sq ft secretary's area 250 sq ft principal's office 200 sq ft assistant principal's office 200–400 sq ft work areas (requirement bsed on school population of 600–800 students, for mail, copying, processing, etc.) 120 sq ft coat and storage 120 sq ft restroom 120 sq ft waiting area
Counselor's office	Yes	Yes	Historically located as part of an administrative office area located near the building entry, guidance and counselor spaces are becoming more centrally located, such as near the library or cafeteria, and contain at a minimum a small waiting area, one or more offices, filing space, access to conference rooms, and restroom facilities.
Faculty offices	Depends	Depends	Depends on the staffing model employed at the school. If staff are to share teaching space, it is common to provide a staff office/workroom. Offices can be either departmental or collaborative (mixed subjects in one office). Offices should be located where students are for passive supervision and ease of access for staff. Minimum size of each should accommodate the largest department's staff, or one-fourth to one-third of the teaching staff at any one time.
Teacher/student/parent meeting rooms	Probably	Probably	125–450 sq ft each; approximate baseline is 1 per every group of 125 students
Small group rooms	Yes	Yes	250–450 sq ft each; number required depends on program, student population, and grades served. Approximate baseline is 1 per every 4–6 classrooms.
Faculty dining room	Depends	Depends	If not provided, allow enough room in the student cafeteria for teachers to eat with students. If provided, faculty dining space should have a window or serving line directly to the kitchen or servery. Area can be computed by (total population of students) ÷ (number of lunch periods) ÷ (average students per class) x 20 to 25 sq ft per person (allows for a counter with magazines and papers, etc., as well as lounge area if needed; if seating only, 16–18 sq ft is enough). Capacity example for determining the size of a faculty dining room at a 600-student school: 600 students ÷ 3 lunch periods = 200 per seating. 200 ÷ average class size (assume 24) = 8.3 (use 9); teachers minimum x 1.5 for variations in schedule and guests = 13.5 adults; provide adult dining seats for a minimum of 14.
Faculty toilet	Yes	Yes	Provide one male and one female toilet per 125 students (or use larger toilets of two stalls each, male and female, per 250 students); accessible to classroom areas and teacher workroom (or locate inside workroom).
Private phone area (optional)	Yes	Yes	Provide a "phone booth" for staff to make private phone calls, or utilize staff conference rooms by equipping with telephones with outside lines. 32 sq ft minimum if not used as a conference room.
Nurse's suite personnel	Yes	Yes	Accessible to the athletic area and located for easy access in case of emergency

◀ *Cafeterias can double as entry commons to increase the size of public space for functions beyond dining. Syracuse High School, Syracuse, Utah. VCBO Architecture. Photograph by Paul Richer, Richer Images.*

because these materials are easily cleaned.

The placement of the kitchen within the school building and its relationship to the site require the consideration of at least two factors. Access for the delivery of products and storage facilities for garbage must be conveniently located near the service areas of the kitchen.

Library and media center spaces

The school library/media center is usually a major focal element and often very important to the image of the school. The space requirements for libraries vary greatly, depending on the existing number of volumes and the anticipated growth. The number of stored periodicals and paperback books must also be considered. Books will be important for the foreseeable future, but with the advent of technology-based search engines, the need to browse rows of books will

be challenged. High-density shelving may find its way into school library planning as the cost to build and operate space continues to rise and schools seek ways to build more efficient facilities.

The library should include an office for the librarian and a circulation desk, and it often incorporates seminar rooms and small group study rooms. Adequate space should be wired with Internet connections and other technology for research via computers. Some schools incorporate computer labs, teaching/gathering areas for small group instruction, and separate workspaces and private offices.

Visual access to every area of the space by the librarian and staff is important to maintain ongoing supervision. To achieve this, careful placement of the reception area, book stacks, reading areas, and computer areas is critical.

▶▲ Food courts offering a variety of meal choices reduce the institutional atmosphere of traditional cafeterias. West Brazos Junior High School, Brazoria, Texas. SHW Group, LLP. Photograph by Richard Payne, FAIA.

AREA 3: STUDENT DINING AND FOOD SERVICE AREA REQUIREMENTS FOR MIDDLE SCHOOLS AND HIGH SCHOOLS

PROGRAM ELEMENT	MS REQUIRED	HS REQUIRED	SPACE REQUIRED
Cafeteria	Yes[1]	Yes[1]	(School population) ÷ (number of planned lunch periods) x (15 sq ft). Additional square footage may be required for faculty dining space and individual lunch period scheduling variations.
Kitchen	Yes[2]	Yes[2]	Warming kitchen and full-service kitchen: up to 40% of dining area NSF; or 3.7 sq ft per meal served, including serving areas.
Food service	Yes[3]	Yes[3]	Depending on food styles and offerings, up to one-third of total kitchen NSF. If more demonstration cooking is desired, this area could approach 60% of total kitchen NSF.

1. As noted, 15 sq ft is a solid planning number for determining the area required per seat. How the actual number of seats is determined may vary based on district policies. Typically, for equal populations of middle school and high school students, there will be fewer high school students participating than middle school students, as there will be a percentage of students who will skip lunch in favor of other activities.

2. It is generally safer to use 4.5 sq ft for high schools, as they generally have slighter bigger portions and more beverages and variety, especially for more diet-related reasons (allergies, etc)

3. Use 2 sq ft per seat basic, and 1.5 times that (or 3 sq ft per seat) if school is not served by a separate central kitchen.

Courtesy of Cini-Little International, Inc.

◀ Media commons like that of the new American International School in Riyadh, shown here, combine state-of-the-art technology with food service in an informal atmosphere. American International School: Riyadh, Riyadh, Saudi Arabia. Perkins Eastman. Courtesy of Perkins Eastman.

▶ Libraries can be wonderful, light-filled spaces, such as the one at Cass Technical High School, Detroit, Michigan. TMP Associates, Inc. Photograph by Balthazar Korab.

AREA 4: LIBRARY AND MEDIA CENTER SPACE REQUIREMENTS FOR MIDDLE SCHOOLS AND HIGH SCHOOLS			
PROGRAM ELEMENT	MS REQUIRED	HS REQUIRED	SPACE REQUIRED
Library/media center	Yes	Yes	Provide seating for 10% of school population, minimum 50 seats (approximately two classes) plus additional seating for technology access support. See Media Center section, p.57.
Media center support space	Yes	Yes	Determined on an individual basis; may include small group rooms, computer commons/labs, work room, office, storage, soft/informal seating area, etc.
Media, exhibit and display space	Yes	Yes	Determined on an individual basis; may include art exhibit hall or commons near entry for display of schoolwork.

◀ *A variety of seating types helps attract students looking for a more informal reading environment. Saline High School, Saline, Michigan. TMP Associates, Inc. Photograph by Christopher Lark Photography.*

Seating should accommodate approximately 10 percent of the school population. This may vary according to the types of seating, number and locations of computer stations, and alternative-use spaces planned. For this 10 percent figure, 25 sq ft per person should be provided. The placement of reading areas of various sizes throughout the library is recommended. This arrangement will make the task of allowing adequate visual supervision from the reception area more difficult, but not impossible. Seating areas may be divided into either class-size groupings, group-size tables, or more informal soft seating for general reading.

Boarding school libraries tend to be much larger than those of public schools because the collections are often much more extensive; however, there is continuing discussion of the role books will play in the future design of school facilities. The library

▶ *The library/media center at Roger Ludlowe Middle School, Fairfield, Connecticut. Perkins Eastman. Photograph by Woodruff/Brown.*

typically has a distinctive appearance and is prominently located on the campus.

Fitness and wellness spaces

Physical fitness, wellness, and competitive sports are all included in this section. These areas of the schools are often accessible not only during the school day, but also after hours for practice or community use, and as spectator venues for athletic competition.

An official high school basketball court measures 50 ft × 84 ft. A gymnasium used by a middle school can be smaller, but the architect should thoroughly discuss size with the district. If a school participates in competitive athletics, the designer of the gymnasium should verify the size noted above for official court size. These dimensions do not take into consideration the recommended 10–15 ft safety zones behind each main backboard. Bleacher seating is commonly included in middle and high school gymnasiums. The capacity of bleacher seating can be calculated by dividing the length of a bleacher row by 18 linear in. per person and multiplying this figure by the number of rows to be provided.

Careful attention must be given to acoustic and mechanical systems. Because the intended use of the space is for vigorous physical activity and for potentially large spectator groups, its mechanical requirements usually surpass those of a general-use space. Lighting is critical in such a space, often requiring an increase in footcandles to provide sufficient illumination for sports as well as for potential video filming. Sound systems and sports equipment, such as scoreboards, time clocks, volleyball nets, and the like, will also affect the design of the space.

Larger gymnasiums are often designed to be dividable into two or more sections by means of either a folding wall or a retractable curtain. In these cases special attention must be given to egress requirements, acoustics, and prevention of interference with baskets, exit doors, bleachers, and other fixed elements.

Special provisions must be incorporated for the protection of such equipment as fire alarms and strobes, scoreboards, time clocks, lighting, and speakers. Wire mesh covers can be placed over these items to protect them from basketballs, volleyballs, and the like. Protection of the lighting is particularly important to prevent shattered pieces of glass from showering the floor. Shatterproof protective safety lenses should be provided for all lighting fixtures.

One gymnasium should be provided for every 500 students. Secondary gymnasiums for every additional 500 students or fraction thereof may be smaller, depending on the student population, school policy, and available funding. Smaller gymnasiums allow more flexibility in scheduling classes and constrain classes to smaller groups that are more readily supervised.

Other physical education
and support spaces
Swimming pools, sometimes referred to as natatoriums, are not as common in high

schools as gymnasiums and auditoriums, and are even rarer in middle schools. Attention to mechanical and electrical requirements is critical because of the amount of moisture produced by this type of space. Separate mechanical rooms and pool equipment rooms are often required to accommodate the specialized equipment. It is important to choose materials that resist moisture (see also chapter 11 on materials and chapter 8 on mechanical systems).

At minimum, a pool should be 25 yards or meters (depending on the school's standards) × 6–8 ft lanes. The number of lanes

▲ Athletic netting allows larger gymnasiums to be divided into smaller physical education teaching stations without compromising the mechanical systems operation. Chickering Elementary School, Dover Massachusetts. Earl R. Flansburgh + Associates. Photograph by Peter Vanderwarker.

▶ *Climbing walls are a popular addition to physical education programs. Lincoln-Sudbury Regional High School, Sudbury, Massachusetts. OMR—The Office of Michael Rosenfeld, Inc., Architects. Photograph by Robert Benson Photography.*

is determined by the school district, designer, and project budget. Pressure to provide pools with a 25 m length is increasing. It is now common to see pools built as 25 m in one direction and 25 yd in the other, or with a movable bulkhead to vary the length of the swimming lane.

Locker rooms and shower spaces should

be located in close proximity to the gymnasium and pool. Many jurisdictions require the pool deck to be entered through the locker room shower area and may require locker rooms for the pool separate from those used for the gymnasium. Often called "wet" and "dry" locker rooms, this refers to their proximity to the spaces they support.

Design Note:
One of the first areas reduced to save on construction costs is the amount of deck space around the pool. This can create problems, however, as water safety and physical education classes and swim teams find it difficult to use the pool building when not in the water. Try not to reduce the amount of deck space beyond the amount required to accommodate a minimum of two typical classes or swim teams.

◀ The pool at Lyons Township District 204 illustrates the integration of lighting, mechanical, and acoustic components into the overall design. Lyons Township High School–South Campus, Western Springs, Illinois. DLA Architects, Ltd. Photograph by Alexander Romanovsky/DLA Architects, Ltd.

Locker rooms for boys and girls should be located next to or very near each other. This is important for supervision during school-day use and allows supervision for use by a visiting team during athletic competition. If the school district has an extensive sports program, separate facilities for visiting teams or community use may be appropriate.

Adequate space must be provided to avoid tight quarters in these areas. The activity level of students before and after gym classes and sporting events is often increased. A combination of full-length and smaller box-type lockers is recommended to accommodate clothing, shoes and boots, and gym gear. Lockers should be constructed of durable materials such as heavy-gauge metals or plastics. Lockers should have vents, as well as flush-mounted or recessed lock spaces to avoid sharp edges. Locker benches should be permanently mounted to the floor or wall to avoid hazards and ensure adequate aisle space in front of the lockers.

A gymnasium office should be provided that allows for visual supervision of these spaces. Separate offices are often desirable for male and female gym instructors. These offices should also have visual access to the gymnasium areas. Avoid sight-line views from public areas into the locker room through the offices.

Showers can be provided as a large, single shower room, individual stalls, or a combination thereof. Handicapped-accessible facilities must be provided in adequate numbers to meet local codes. Schools are often used as disaster relief centers during local crises; therefore, this use should be considered in regard to its potential impact on any design.

Flooring materials should be durable and comfortable when walked on barefoot. Ceramic tile is often used; however, it is important to consider the slip resistance of

▶ This flexible health sciences lab integrates space for the athletic trainer and school nurse and space for the health sciences programs. American International School: Riyadh, Riyadh, Saudi Arabia. Perkins Eastman. Courtesy of Perkins Eastman.

AREA 5: FITNESS AND WELLNESS SPACES FOR MIDDLE SCHOOLS AND HIGH SCHOOLS			
PROGRAM ELEMENT	**MS REQUIRED**	**HS REQUIRED**	**SPACE REQUIRED**
Gymnasium	Yes[1]	Yes[1]	5,800–12,000 sq ft (one teaching station minimum, two preferred). Full-size basketball court, minimum seating, and clearances. Number of health and fitness teaching stations dependent on district program requirements, total population, and other facilities provided, such as swimming pool and fitness rooms. Provide a minimum of one health and fitness teaching station per 200 students.
Locker rooms	Yes	Yes	For both physical education use and team use, the number of lockers provided should be sized for the anticipated use (factors including, how many students use the locker room at one time, do students store gym clothes in the locker room, do teams store uniforms in the locker room, how big is the largest team using the locker room, how many teams use it at once) and by the districts' physical education requirements.
Health classrooms	Yes	Yes	750–1100 sq ft

1. Number of gymnasium courts provided is a function of the physical education classes required per day, and the number of team sports and their schedules for practice.

selected materials. These factors should be taken into consideration for wall materials. The designer should be aware of the ease of maintenance for products selected. Surfaces and finishes that are not easily maintained are often not maintained, which can lead to hazardous conditions.

Performing and visual arts spaces

As a general design rule, an auditorium and theater can be categorized as follows: A theater has a large stage and smaller house, while an auditorium has a smaller stage and larger house. This is something of a generalization, but in most cases it holds true. For an auditorium with fixed seating, a guideline of 7–9 sq ft per person may apply, depending on the age group it is designed for and the quality and size of the planned seating. Larger, more padded seats require more space than molded plastic or wood seats. If fixed seating is provided, the space will be dedicated to specific use as an auditorium, lecture hall, and general assembly space for large groups. This type of space will most likely have a stage. The design of a stage varies greatly, depending on the district's needs. A true stage, by definition, has fly space to allow for movable scenery, lighting, and other required equipment; such a stage is generally found in theaters, whereas auditoriums usually have smaller, more open stages or platforms and may or may not have a curtain system.

Sloped floors with fixed seats in auditoriums and theaters will enhance the viewing sight lines. Acoustics, sound equipment, and lighting equipment are critical to the design. General house lighting and special theater lighting are often provided, including a dimmer system for control. For these components, specialists are usually consulted by the design professional.

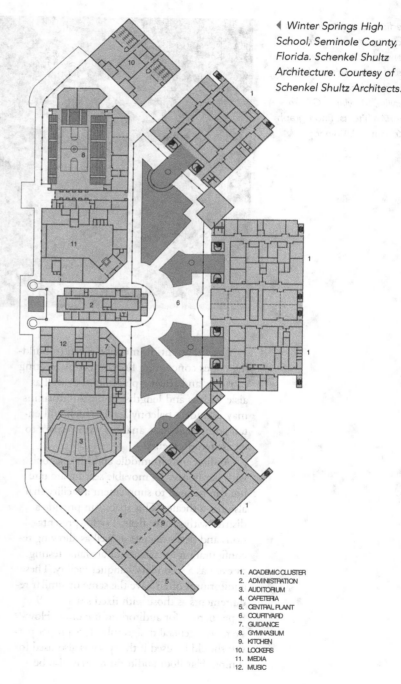

◀ *Winter Springs High School, Seminole County, Florida. Schenkel Shultz Architecture. Courtesy of Schenkel Shultz Architects.*

1. ACADEMIC CLUSTER
2. ADMINISTRATION
3. AUDITORIUM
4. CAFETERIA
5. CENTRAL PLANT
6. COURTYARD
7. GUIDANCE
8. GYMNASIUM
9. KITCHEN
10. LOCKERS
11. MEDIA
12. MUSIC

Careful attention must be given to building codes concerning fire protection, seating capacity, and seating placement, as well as aisle widths and lengths. Some auditoriums may include a balcony level, which will entail additional code analysis with respect to egress requirements.

Auditoriums in middle and high schools with flat floors and movable seating are rare but can be used to supplement a facility that also has a theater. This space can provide a district with greater flexibility for presentations and performances as well as allowing reconfiguration for science or art fairs, testing, or even as a secondary banquet facility. These auditoriums often have the same or similar requirements as those with fixed seats—7–9 sq ft per person for auditorium use only. However, as a general design rule, 15 sq ft per person should be used if the space is also used for dining. Flat-floor auditoriums may also be

equipped with folding partitions to increase flexibility. Acoustical design is again critical if the space is used for multiple purposes.

A music room can range from the size of a general classroom up to a large multiuse music and orchestra room. One classroom should be provided for every 500 students; size and design are governed by the music program's requirements. Special attention must be given to the acoustics. The use of acoustic wall padding and/or acoustic concrete masonry units is suggested.

Instrumental/band room

As a general rule, the space requirements for this area are 1,400 sq ft minimum; 15 sq ft per person. One such area should be provided for every 500 students. Substantial storage is required for this space, considering the sizes and types of instruments. Daylight is not necessary but recommended. Sometimes

◀ *The multiuse cafeteria and auditorium at Carlin Springs Elementary School, Arlington, Virginia. Grimm + Parker Architects. Photograph by Kenneth M. Wyner.*

◀ *This instrumental music room maximizes natural light and uses curtains to vary the acoustic qualities of the space. Concordia International School, Shanghai, China. Perkins Eastman. Photograph by Tim Griffith.*

a tiered floor is desirable. Incorporating this feature will result in a space that is less flexible and will require a greater square footage per student. The placement of this space and the function of adjacent spaces are critical because of the acoustic considerations. Often a separate wing or dedicated area is designated to create a music suite including music classrooms, band rooms, auditorium, choir rooms, and music practice rooms.

Vocal/chorus room

As a general rule, the space requirements for this area are 1,200 sq ft minimum; 7 sq ft per student. One classroom should be provided for every 500 students. The design of this space should follow the same guidelines as for a band room, but less storage is needed for this space. A piano, depending on its size, may increase the required square footage. As in a band room, a tiered floor may be included, again resulting in less flexibility and requiring a greater square footage per student.

Music practice rooms

Music practice rooms vary in size, depending on whether they are used for instrument or vocal practice. As a general rule, the space

---

AREA 6: PERFORMING AND VISUAL ARTS SPACES FOR MIDDLE SCHOOLS AND HIGH SCHOOLS

PROGRAM ELEMENT	MS REQUIRED	HS REQUIRED	SPACE REQUIRED
Art instruction studio	Yes[1]	Yes[1]	1,050–1,450 sq ft; 1 per 250 students; generally, 2 rooms minimum (number required depends on program, student population, and grades served).
Auditorium	Yes[2]	Yes[2] (if not provided with a theater)	(School population) ÷ (number of planned seatings to accommodate the entire population) x (9 sq ft). Additional square footage required for stage and support space.
Theater[2]	Optional	Optional (if program specifies)	Size of the "house" can be determined by the desired capacity x 9 sq ft. Additional square footage required for orchestra space, stagecraft, dressing rooms, projection booth, etc.
Theater stage	Optional	Yes (if program provides for theater)	2,400 sq ft (minimum stage size for largest performance anticipated)
Music instruction	Yes	Yes	1,100–1,650 sq ft each; for a typical middle or high school of more than 850 students, provide minimum 2 music instructional rooms (number required depends on student population, music and orchestra program, and grades served).
Music practice	Optional	Optional	36–250 sq ft each; number required depends on student population, music and orchestra program, and grades served.

1. Art instruction may require space for two-dimensional art such as drawing and painting, three-dimensional art including clay work and model making, and graphic art involving digital photography and photo editing. These three spaces may be interconnected and share certain storage and support functions.

2. During programming, the needs for an auditorium versus a theater should be determined. As a rule of thumb, an auditorium has a "large house and small stage." Primarily used for presentations, movies; with the correct floor-space flexibility, may be reconfigured for model UN simulation or mock-courtroom experiences. A theater has a "small house and big stage"; usually provided with some form of fly space for scenery, its use is geared more toward performance art of plays, musicals, and recitals, both small and large group.

An example in determining the size of the "house": a 1,200-student high school wants to seat the entire school population in two seatings. 1,200 students total ÷ 2 seatings = 600 seats + 10% for staff and scheduling flexibility = 660 seats.

◀ *Outdoor art terrace at Concordia International School, Shanghai, China. Perkins Eastman. Photograph by Tim Griffith.*

requirement for a practice room is 25 sq ft minimum. Daylight is not necessary, but increased ventilation for these spaces may be appropriate.

Facility management and support spaces
Adequate storage facilities must be provided to accommodate the mass quantities of reading materials, paper goods, furniture, and other materials and equipment required by a school but not used on a daily basis. The amount of space needed varies from one school to another. Storage areas should be placed throughout the building to allow proper access from areas that will use these facilities; storage room sizes vary according to what will be stored.

All schools require spaces for varying degrees of laundry services, staff lockers, vari-

Design Note:
In designing the mechanical systems for music rooms, be sure to avoid large duct connections between music rooms or between music rooms and other adjacent spaces. Such connections can potentially create a situation where sound will be transferred down the duct, causing considerable distraction in the adjacent room.

ous workshops, and storage for furniture and equipment. Garages may be required to store and maintain the school's maintenance vehicles and the vans or buses used to transport students to athletic and social events, if these are not provided from a separate central location.

Adequate parking should be provided for faculty, visitors, and staff. Parking for major events like graduation or theater productions may often be handled with overflow lots on lawns and fields to minimize the need for paved areas.

Sample Middle School Facility Space Program

A sample program is shown in Appendix B for a typical 1,200-student suburban middle school in a northern climate. It represents a wide range of potential spaces that might be found in a middle school. Several of the program components are to support an exploratory program and are considered optional depending on the specifics of the program's requirements; these are included in the total student capacity of the building.

AREA 7: FACILITY MANAGEMENT AND SUPPORT SPACES FOR MIDDLE SCHOOLS AND HIGH SCHOOLS

PROGRAM ELEMENT	MS REQUIRED	HS REQUIRED	SPACE REQUIRED
Shipping and receiving	Yes	Yes	300 sq ft minimum; staging requirements of deliveries should be considered. (What other storage areas are provided may determine how long deliveries of paper and other building maintenance supplies will remain in this area.)
Custodial and maintenance offices	Yes	Yes	150 sq ft minimum for one person. Verify program with client if locker or changing areas are required.
Storage areas	Probably	Probably	300 sq ft minimum; storage areas required could include book storage, furniture storage, instructional materials, and maintenance supplies. Verify program with client.
Security office	Verify	Verify	150 sq ft minimum for one person. May include video display terminals for monitoring the schools video security system. May require office space for more than one person, and waiting area or interview room. Verify security personnel requirements with client.
Recycling room	Verify	Verify	250–450 sq ft; many schools provide janitorial and support space for recycling materials from the school's operation. Verify recycling program requirements.
Janitorial and maintenance closets	Yes	Yes	Size, location, and quantity are dependent on the final building design. Maintenance closets to provide for cleaning supply and paper storage, mop storage, and sink.
Telecommunications closets	Yes	Yes	Size, location, and quantity are dependent on the final building design. Provide ample clearance in front of all electrical and communications panels.
Exterior requirements	Yes	Yes	Space should be provided for large trash containers and delivery and service vehicles. Equipment storage may be required for maintenance of buildings and grounds (lawn mowers, field striping machines, rakes, shovels, etc.).

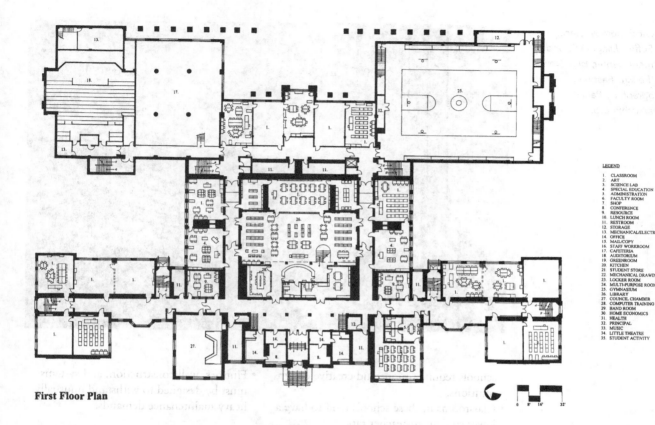

First Floor Plan

LEGEND

1. CLASSROOM
2. ART
3. SCIENCE LAB
4. SPECIAL EDUCATION
5. ADMINISTRATION
6. FACULTY ROOM
7. SHOP
8. CONFERENCE
9. RESOURCE
10. LUNCH ROOM
11. RESTROOM
12. STORAGE
13. MECHANICAL/ELECTRICAL
14. OFFICE
15. MAIL/COPY
16. STAFF WORKROOM
17. CAFETERIA
18. AUDITORIUM
19. GREENROOM
20. KITCHEN
21. STUDENT STORE
22. MECHANICAL DRAWING
23. LOCKER ROOM
24. MULTI-PURPOSE ROOM
25. GYMNASIUM
26. LIBRARY
27. COUNCIL CHAMBER
28. COMPUTER TRAINING
29. BAND ROOM
30. HOME ECONOMICS
31. HEALTH
32. PRINCIPAL
33. MUSIC
34. LITTLE THEATRE
35. STUDENT ACTIVITY

Sample High School Facility Space Program

Appendix C shows a sample program for a typical 1,600-student high school. It represents a suburban school in a northern climate.

SPECIAL SCHOOLS

Today many children with disabilities are "mainstreamed" into general-population schools. These schools, which typically provide rooms for special education in addition to general classrooms, should be handicapped accessible as required by the Americans with Disabilities Act (ADA). However,

there is still a need for special schools, and many have been built for both emotionally and physically disabled students. To design these schools, the design team must study and understand these children's special characteristics. There are excellent examples of schools built for children who are blind, deaf, nonambulatory, emotionally disturbed, or with other disabilities. The following are basic points to consider when designing these schools:

• The design team must become extremely knowledgeable of the characteristics of the children's specific disability. Most special

▲ A compact middle school floor plan. Collins Middle School, Salem, Massachusetts. Earl R. Flansburgh + Associates. Courtesy Earl R. Flansburgh + Associates.

▶ *Physical therapy space.*
UCP Suffolk Diagnostic and
Treatment Center, Islip, New
York. Perkins Eastman.
Photograph by Paúl
Rivera/ArchPhoto.

schools require unique and creative design solutions.

- Classrooms in these schools tend to have a lower student-to-teacher ratio.
- Nonambulatory children touch and view their environment and perceive space from a different height than other children. The design should not follow typical standards for mounting heights, windows, and other building elements.
- Toilet rooms should be part of or adjacent to classroom spaces to reduce distance and time without supervision.
- Travel distances to core functions should be minimized.
- Tactile surfaces are important to children who are missing other senses.
- Rooms or spaces, apart from the general classroom, should be provided for working with students one on one.

- Finishes, wall construction, and systems must be designed to withstand unusually heavy maintenance demands.

In addition, there are particular issues that should be considered in each of the more common types of special schools, as described in the following sections.

Schools for Children with Severe Physical Disabilities

United Cerebral Palsy, hospitals for severely disabled children, and other sponsors have created special schools for children with severe or multiple physical disabilities. Most such schools are designed to provide a combination of physical therapy and education that make it possible for the children to return to their families or to be adopted. The basic design considerations include the following:

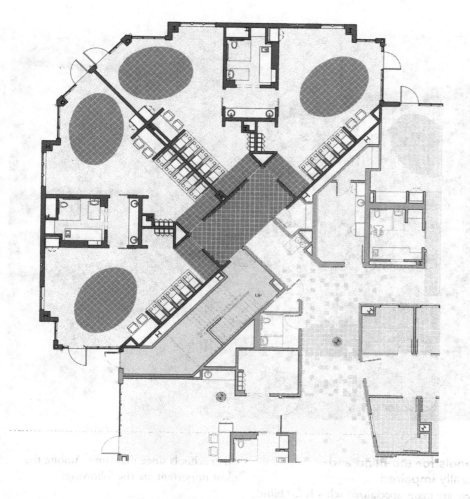

◀ *Classrooms designed for children with multiple disabilities have many special features, including adjacent toilet facilities, soft floor surfaces, and wheelchair storage. Elizabeth Seton Pediatric Center, Yonkers, New York. Perkins Eastman. Courtesy of Perkins Eastman.*

1. Full wheelchair accessibility is essential.
2. Materials and systems should be selected that minimize hazards (sharp corners, exposed heating elements, hard surfaces that can hurt a child in a fall, etc.), floor surfaces should facilitate wheelchair movement, and lighting levels should be sensitive to potential visual impairment.
3. Design flexible classroom spaces, keeping in mind that the children may be seated on the floor. A warm floor, low win-dowsills, and other special features are appropriate responses to this issue.
4. Class sizes are small, but the rooms must accommodate wheelchairs and a variety of special equipment.
5. Bathrooms should be convenient to all program areas.
6. Outdoor play areas should be designed to facilitate appropriate exercise and play in a very safe setting.
7. All educational environments are typically combined with therapy areas.

▶ *The typical classroom at the Coleman School in the New York Foundling Hospital is designed to let severely disabled students sit on the floor. It includes a mirror at eye level, low windowsills, radiant heating, and a flexible layout. Coleman School at New York Foundling Hospital, New York, New York. Perkins Eastman. Photograph by Fred George Photography.*

Schools for the Blind and Visually Impaired

There are many specialized schools for blind and visually impaired students, as well as programs in public and private schools for children with this disability. The oldest—and most famous—is the Perkins School for the Blind in Watertown, Massachusetts. Helen Keller (who was both blind and deaf) and her teacher, Annie Sullivan (who was visually impaired), studied there before Helen entered Radcliffe, where she was graduated with honors. Many of the educational concepts for visually impaired children were developed at Perkins and have been adopted in other schools since that time. Among the most important are the following:

1. The term "visually impaired" is used because many so-called blind people have some sight. Therefore, the environment should be planned to maximize students' independence and use of their limited sight.
2. Class sizes tend to be small and are usually set up for flexible teaching using a variety of special teaching aids, toys, and other items requiring storage.
3. Appropriate lighting is very important. Illumination should be planned to pro-

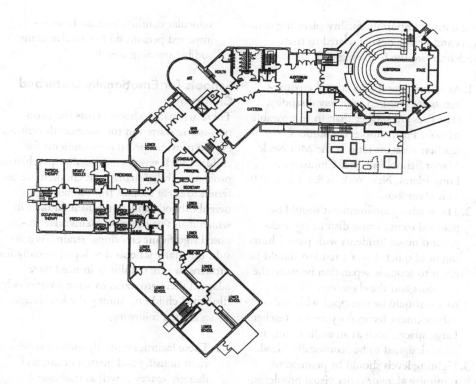

vide a high level of even light without glare or similar problems.

4. Contrasting colors and surface texture changes are typical navigational aids. Braille (for elevators and signs) is also used, but a minority of visually impaired students read braille.

5. Low furniture and sharp edges should be avoided.

6. Single-story buildings and carefully graded sites have the obvious advantage of presenting minimal challenges to this student population. Where multistory buildings are used, elevators that call out the floor, stair handrails that are continuous along the landings, and other such details are important.

7. Most schools for visually impaired stu-

dents include a number of special therapy and training areas to give students the skills to function as independently as possible when they leave the special educational setting. Many children with visual impairment must deal with other disabilities as well.

8. Life safety devices should have clear annunciator features because auditory cues are important to the visually impaired student.

Schools for the Deaf

The most famous educational institution for the deaf is Gallaudet College in Washington, D.C. Like Perkins School for the Blind, it has helped develop educational guidelines for students with certain disabilities. Some of the more important facility-planning concepts and design details related to these guidelines are the following:

1. As with all good educational environments for children with any disability, class sizes are smaller than in comparable schools. For example, the student: teacher: assistant ratio at the Mill Neck Manor School for Deaf Children on Long Island, New York, is 8:1:1 in a 550 sq ft classroom.
2. The teaching environment should be planned to minimize distracting background noise. Students with partial hearing need quiet. Extra attention should be given to acoustic separation between the corridors and the classrooms. These rooms should be equipped with audio enhancement technology for the teacher. Large spaces, such as an auditorium, are often designed to be acoustically "dead."
3. Lighting levels should be planned to minimize glare or other visual problems, because many students will rely on lip reading, computers, TV monitors, or other techniques and devices to help with their learning.
4. Technology is playing an increasing role.
5. Schools for the deaf also typically include extensive facilities for special therapy, physical therapy, and occupational therapy. This last area focuses on giving students the skills to live independently with their disability.
6. Life safety devices must take hearing disability into account. Flashing lights, for example, are an important part of any alarm system. A closed-caption TV system often serves as the public address system. In addition, the site should be planned to minimize potential student-vehicular conflict, because hearing-impaired persons do not receive many audible warning signals.

Schools for Emotionally Disturbed Children

There are many schools across the country—some started in the nineteenth century—to provide special environments for children with severe emotional or psychiatric problems. Today many such children are referred to these schools from inner-city neighborhoods and come from families in which drugs or other problems have imposed significant emotional strain. As a result, the many schools developed initially for orphans or other children in need have adapted their programs to serve emotionally disturbed children. Among the key design issues are the following:

1. These facilities typically include supervised housing and mental health and therapy spaces as well as traditional school spaces.
2. The class sizes are typically small and the rooms flexible. Quiet rooms and other features may be part of the program.
3. The facilities must be robust and able to withstand heavy use.
4. Some schools have a special character, such as a farm setting, which is integrated into the program.
5. Some areas may have to have special security features built in, but a non-institutional character is usually a priority.
6. Outdoor activity areas may be a particularly important part of the program.

Vocational Schools

Vocational high schools were a common building type in earlier decades. Their

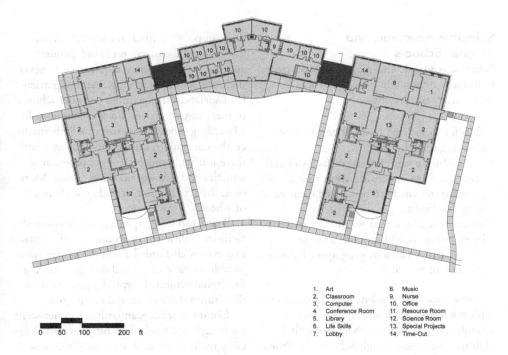

1. Art
2. Classroom
3. Computer
4. Conference Room
5. Library
6. Life Skills
7. Lobby
8. Music
9. Nurse
10. Office
11. Resource Room
12. Science Room
13. Special Projects
14. Time-Out

0 50 100   200 ft

◀ *The design of the new building at the Green Chimneys School for emotionally disturbed children reflects the school's farm theme. Animals are an important part of the children's education and therapy. Green Chimneys School, Brewster, New York. Perkins Eastman. Courtesy Perkins Eastman.*

numbers have diminished, but they remain an important educational resource for children who are best served by less academic and more career-specific educational programs.

Vocational schools are most often found today in larger school districts. In most secondary schools, vocational education is a department within the school. The old home economics and shop areas have been replaced with more contemporary trades and occupations, many of them computer aided. While, several trends have made dedicated vocational schools a less popular school type, there is still a need to train a workforce of welders, engine repair specialists, auto body repair specialists, and other trades. At a November 2009 presentation by the Department of Education there was, in fact, an emphasis on "vo-techs" for workforce devel-

opment in fields such as allied health and computer production.

- The division between industrial and academic skills has eroded. Today's workplace requires more academic skill to deal with technology, and schools include more technology in academic curricula.
- Many vocational courses are now offered at community colleges and by a wide variety of for-profit providers.
- Some vocational programs—such as those providing the technical skills required in science and medicine—require interdisciplinary training.

In general, these trends mean that vocational programs should not be isolated. Instead, they should be integrated into a broader secondary school curriculum.

Selective Academic and Magnet Schools

Selective academic and magnet schools have been created by public school districts for a wide variety of reasons:

- To offer specialized facilities and instruction to gifted children.
- To combine a critical mass of facilities and resources so as to provide a specialized program too costly to be offered in more than one facility.
- To create a school that will attract students from various neighborhoods so as to achieve better racial or geographic balance in a school system.

New York City was one of the first to establish selective academic and magnet schools, including high schools for gifted children: Stuyvesant High School, the Bronx High School of Science, and La Guardia High School of Music and Art and Performing Arts.

Boarding Schools

Not counting specialized therapeutic schools, there are more than 290 boarding schools in North America today. These may be coed or single-sex schools and may have a specific focus, such as military, international, or specialized academic schools. Most boarding schools serve children in their high school years, but there are also junior boarding schools for children in elementary and middle school grades. Many are more than 100 years old, located on large campuses with hundreds of acres, elaborate facilities, and distinctive atmospheres.

The planning standards and guidelines for these schools are very different from those of public schools for several reasons. Generally, the curriculum is independent and not subject to state requirements; nevertheless, a school may subscribe to a particular association that requires member schools to meet certain criteria for accreditation. In a boarding school, class size usually is smaller, the curriculum can be more diverse, and there is often a much stronger program of athletics and extracurricular activities. Moreover, the school must provide the elements of a home.

There can be a large disparity between the facilities at different boarding schools. Some may have well-funded facilities that are comparable to those of a small college. Funding for capital projects is typically generated by the alumni through capital campaigns.

Common space standards are nonexistent for boarding schools. Planning for such a facility requires detailed analysis of the mission, history, strengths, and focus of the school. Boarding schools compete with each other for students and teachers. Most fill a particular niche, which makes them attractive to their target markets. The image of the school is very important to both parents and alumni. A strong determinant in assessing programmatic need can be an evaluation of how a school's facilities compare with those of its peer institutions.

As a 24-hour community, the school must also serve as home and extended family to its students. Faculty are often encouraged to live on campus and to eat meals together with the students. The faculty may be instructors during the day, coaches in the afternoon, and monitors on weekends and evenings. There are often extensive community service programs, as well as many weekend and evening activities.

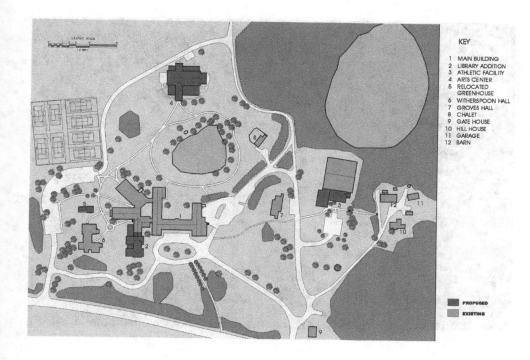

KEY

1 MAIN BUILDING
2 LIBRARY ADDITION
3 ATHLETIC FACILITY
4 ARTS CENTER
5 RELOCATED
   GREENHOUSE
6 WITHERSPOON HALL
7 GROVES HALL
8 CHALET
9 GATE HOUSE
10 HILL HOUSE
11 GARAGE
12 BARN

PROPOSED
EXISTING

◀ *Some boarding schools, such as Miss Hall's, are small campuses with a few buildings, whereas others, such as Philips Academy, resemble small college campuses. Miss Hall's School, Pittsfield, Massachusetts. Perkins Eastman. Courtesy Perkins Eastman.*

Housing

Dormitories are often arranged by grade. Most schools prefer a mix of predominantly double rooms with some single rooms.

Common lounge facilities should be located centrally within a building or on each floor. Toilet facilities are typically centralized. Faculty apartments are often included in a dormitory for convenience in providing supervision and counseling.

Some schools wire dorm rooms for technology; others prefer to have students use the school's common computers. The use of laptop computers, the decreasing costs of hardware, and the availability of wireless technologies are causing a shift to access throughout student housing rooms and common areas.

Related facilities include a laundry for linens (sometimes contracted out) as well as coin-operated laundry facilities for students to wash their clothing.

Boarding schools typically include an infirmary, either within one dorm or as a freestanding building. The number of beds and toilet facilities are a function of the school's population, and there is often a residence for the attending nurse.

Incorporating faculty housing on campus is an important goal of many schools. This arrangement aids in retention of faculty and creates a feeling of community and security that is important to students and their families. Typically there is a large home for the head of school that is also used for receptions and special activities, as well as freestanding

▶ *Philips Academy, Andover, Massachusetts.*

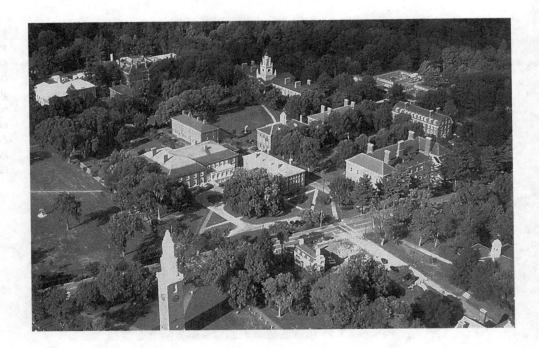

homes for faculty with families, and staff apartments in the dorms or other buildings.

Other boarding school facilities

Theater
Drama production can be a major after-school activity at many schools. Depending on the preference of the school, performances may be given in a theater with fixed seating and a formal stage, or in a black box theater. Provisions should be made for an adequate lobby and support areas such as scenery workshop, prop and costume storage, dressing rooms, and toilets.

Depending on the type of theater, it is often supplemented by a large flat-floor assembly space to gather the student body in one location for morning meetings and dances (often with students from other schools).

Art gallery
Most schools have a gallery or dedicated exhibition space for displaying students' work. Some schools may also have a more formal gallery for traveling exhibitions. Depending on the nature of the gallery, issues of security, climate control, and flexible lighting should be considered. The school gallery should be centrally located and convenient for visitors.

Student center
The student center is a lounge that serves as a place for students to spend time and so-

cialize between classes and on weekends. This space is often furnished with comfortable seating, stereo equipment, a large TV, and games such as pool or board games. It should be centrally located and convenient to classrooms and dormitories.

Dining facilities

Most schools have a centrally located dining room serving three meals a day to students, faculty, and staff. Buffet-style serving lines, rather than table service, are typical for most meals. Many schools want the room to be able to accommodate the entire student body at one sitting. The dining room is often part of the main building and convenient to both dormitories and classrooms. Adequate space should be provided for the servery, kitchen, and support areas.

Administrative and support areas

A boarding school usually has several administration spaces in addition to those found in a typical public school:

- *Development offices.* A school's development office often plays a large part in maintaining alumni relations and raising funds for endowment and capital projects. This department is often located in a separate building on campus.
- *Admissions suite.* The admissions suite is often the first impression for prospective students and their families. It is important to have a space that is prominently located and that creates a good impression of the school.
- *Administration.* The office of the headmaster or headmistress and his or her support staff, the monitors' office, the switchboard,

and other administrative functions that deal directly with the students on a daily basis should be centrally located and are often found in the main academic building. The business office component can be more remotely located.

- *Document storage.* Boarding schools often maintain fairly extensive documentation for historical purposes, including transcripts, students' files, old business records, and memorabilia. Dry, heated, secure space should be provided for these collections.

FUTURE SCHOOL FACILITY SPACES

Schools in the future will most certainly continue to reflect the society that they serve. Keeping school facilities relevant and future-proofed will mean creating facilities that

- Are flexible and can be configured to meet changing programmatic or curricular needs.
- Support a variety of learning styles.
- Create opportunities for project-based interdisciplinary work.
- Incorporate ever-changing and complex technology platforms and tools.

This could mean any number of variations and probably means the creation of new space types for schools that will improve their utilization, reduce operational and maintenance costs, and be reconfigurable without major construction renovation. As we move toward designing facilities that reflect a more global approach and curriculum influence, the following pages illustrate some examples of what might be found in the twenty-first century schoolhouse.

The Whole Brain Lab

We hear a lot about people's bent toward left- or right-brain thinking, but few of us often remember which is which. The website www.funderstanding.com explores this topic, making some interesting points well worth exploring further. As it points out, an easy way to remember them is

<u>L</u>eft = <u>L</u>ogical and <u>R</u>ight = <u>R</u>andom.

This is why we think of left-brained people as those who are sequential, rational, and analytical and tend to look at the parts of a problem as opposed to the whole. Right-brained people are intuitive, more holistic, and subjective, and look at the big picture over the parts. According to the Funderstanding website, "Most individuals have a distinct preference for one of these styles of thinking. Some, however, are more whole-brained and equally adept at both modes." And here is the important part for planners: "In general, schools tend to favor left-brain modes of thinking, while downplaying the right-brain ones."

The following list represents a studio or suite space concept, intended to provide students and teachers with wide-ranging opportunities to study subject matter through a variety of activities that would support both left- and right-brain approaches to learning. The suite would be capable of being used by one to three classes simultaneously to explore topics in a multidimensional way and using different strategies of comprehension. The suite would be comprised of three main areas:

5. http://www.funderstanding.com/right_left_brain.cfm.

Exploration Lab: on-line and connected
- Research
- Reading
- Writing
- Collaboration
- Printing
- Production

Investigation Lab: hands-on and real
- Experimentation
- Project based
- Scientific
- Mathematical

Creation Lab: artistic expression
- Drawing
- Two-dimensional
- Three-dimensional
- Model making
- Pottery

The individual areas are visually connected but have the ability to be separated physically. Supported by storage, offices, and prep spaces, this suite of rooms is virtually self-contained, offering the ability to run extended-period programs. These types of spaces are a logical implementation of Howard Gardner's theory of multiple intelligences.

Physical Education and Health Lab

The Centers for Disease Control estimates that the prevalence of overweight children aged 6 to 11 has more than doubled in the past 20 years, and has almost tripled for children aged 12 to 19. For these children, an estimated 61 percent will have at least one additional risk factor for heart disease, such as high cholesterol or high blood pressure.[6] Obviously there is a need for schools to explore new ideas about curriculum, programs, and physical space to deal with these staggering statistics. The lack of an appropriate amount of physical activity can contribute to these statistics and create a number of health risks that include obesity, diabetes, and cardiovascular and other diseases.

Physical education and health-related programs, which focus on teaching the life-long importance of leading a healthy lifestyle, are gaining in popularity. Each generation continues to live longer than the previous one—partially due, of course, to advancement in medical sciences, but also to our knowledge of maintaining physical health.

Health and wellness suite

The health and wellness suite would be capable of being used by one or more classes simultaneously to explore topics in a hands-on and interdisciplinary environment. Located near the training room, locker rooms, and coaches'/instructors' offices, it would be comprised of three main lab components.

Nutrition and fitness research lab

Workstations provide students with the latest research on health-related nutrition and exercise programs, allowing them to create individualized exercise, diet, and wellness programs. Student can monitor, track, and make adjustments to their individual programs on a weekly basis. Activities conducted in this lab include

- Research
- Writing

6. D. S. Freedman et al., "The Relation of Overweight to Cardiovascular Risk Factors among Children and Adolescents: The Bogalusa Heart Study," *Journal of Pediatrics* 103, no. 6, (1990): 1175–1182.

- Fitness program design
- Analysis of fitness test results
- Computer simulation
- Nutritional planning
- Results documentation

Physiology lab

Equipped with various aerobic- and anaerobic-type exercise equipment, a weight scale, body mass index (BMI) measurement device, and the like, this portion of the lab is intended for students and faculty to learn about exercise and engage in it; to understand their fitness level and monitor their metabolic changes during exercise. Equipment here can be used in fitness instruction as part of a total program or as a rehabilitation center for students recovering from injuries or surgery. Equipment used to measure breathing and lung capacity might serve as aids in athletic training, or the music department might use it in assisting wind instrument students to improve their conditioning. Activities in this lab include

- Fitness testing
- General exercise instruction
- BMI testing
- Student experiments in conditioning
- Heart rate and stress test monitoring

Testing lab

Lab stations equipped with sinks for simulation and experimentation of health-related science programs. This lab might be used as a forensics lab or for other specialized programs not able to be accommodated in other science classes. Activities in this lab include

- Biology and health-related science experiments, testing, and simulation

- Student presentation of work
- Forensic sciences
- Nutritional experimentation
- Foods analysis
- Individual projects and team work projects

The testing lab as outlined above used with other areas of the health and wellness suite, which together try to address the challenges of creating a healthier future for our students. With the majority of the equipment being movable for future changes, the testing lab is built to accommodate a variety of programs.

The ARC—A New Kind of Library

One area of the twenty-first-century schoolhouse that has been pressured to change is the library. Debate is ongoing over books versus digital media, allowing food and drink near books, hours of operation, and the functional value of the library space. There are a number of variations being designed that include several interesting ways to combine space. Some characteristics include

- The inclusion of snack bars (similar to the modern bookstore)
- Larger areas of informal seating
- The use of high-density shelving for the storage of nonfiction books
- Flat-screen displays for collaborative work with presentation and research materials.
- Small group team space
- Self-checkout for print materials
- Printing and copy capabilities

All of these attributes could be supported by supporting the three main functions of the twenty-first-century library: Archives,

Research, and Collaboration—or, for short, the ARC.

Archives

This area combines digital and print media resources for access by students and faculty in preparation of lessons, reports, term papers, and homework assignments. It includes periodicals and is supported with both formal and informal seating areas. Books, for the foreseeable future, will still occupy a significant amount of space in the twenty-first-century library; however, they will not all be stored in a "browsing area." Instead, books may be stored and retrieved as needed from lower-cost space, such as temperature- and humidity-controlled basements or storage rooms.

Research

The research area of the ARC provides the furniture and resources necessary for a variety of research modalities, including workstations, conference space/tables, and informal seating, where students might work individually or in groups. There is direct-wired and wireless access to on-line resources, printers, and copy machines, and drop-in terminals are available for student use.

Collaboration

Collaboration can occur in any area of the ARC and is more operational than physical, supported by creating large, flexible spaces and by the use of appropriate furnishings, strong environmental planning, and interior design. The ARC could include a snack bar area and table seating for all-day food service opportunities and could be located near the school's dining facilities. In this way, cafeteria seating may be used for expanded ARC use when not being used for lunch periods.

Conversely, the more formal seating of the ARC located near the snack bar may be used during lunch periods and beyond.

Variable Teaching and Learning "Theaters"

When planning a facility to support a variety of instructional programs, broad user input by faculty, staff, community, and students can offer valuable insight. Typically, "theater" spaces designed for varied programs include an unobstructed performance area with a wood or synthetic floor similar to a theater's stage. It may include a sprung floor, such as those used in dance studios, and state-of-the art sound and lighting systems, and could be supported by back-of-house facilities such as a kitchenette, reception area, dressing rooms, and restrooms. These flexible and multifunction theater classrooms should be located for easy access from inside the building as well as for audience access from outside and they can be configured in a number of different ways.

"Black box" theater

Designed for teaching performing arts of all kinds, a black box theater has a flat floor with movable seating; it accommodates theater in the round, ensemble performances, and films or other video presentations. With black walls and variable acoustics (usually provided by movable curtains), a fixed lighting and sound grid over the entire ceiling, and a sound/projection booth, it is equipped technically for the presentations and performances anticipated. If sized appropriately and with proper protection of its sound and lighting systems, it can even support certain types of athletic activities, such as volleyball, various forms of martial arts, or wrestling. In some instances, the proportions of the theater can be configured to resemble the "stage" of an actual theater.

A typical black box will be between 2,300 and 3,200 sq ft and a minimum of 18 ft in height. At the smaller size, the box should accommodate approximately 150 people, including performers, audience, and staff. A typical performance might have up to 15 performers and accommodate an audience of 130.

"Gray box" theater

An ideal venue for meetings and conferences of all kinds, a gray box is equipped similarly to a black box. With a flat floor and lighter walls (gray perhaps), the space allows a more comfortable venue for tabletop activities with multiple configurations. A gray box may have windows for natural light. It is equipped with sound and lighting systems applicable for the type and scale of the use intended. Somewhat less technical than a black box, this venue is appropriate as a banquet hall, meeting room, or testing center, or for art or science fairs.

"Green box" theater

Similar in design and equipment to the black box described above, this space has a flat floor with movable (portable) seating and accommodates a variety of teaching and performing configurations. The key distinguishing characteristic is the ability to open one wall of the "box" onto an adjacent large room, either a gymnasium or cafeteria, for the purposes of converting it to a "stage" and the adjacent space to a "house" to create a larger theater configuration.

"Blue box" theater

A blue box theater is a performing arts facility that combines the flexibility of a black

▶ *The blue box theater at Concordia International School, Shanghai, China. Perkins Eastman. Photograph by Tim Griffith.*

box reconfigurable stage area with the acoustics of a recital hall. Somewhat less flexible than black or gray boxes, the room has a sloped floor, fixed seating, and possibly a balcony level. A good example can be seen in the photograph above, showing the blue box theater designed by Perkins Eastman for the Concordia International School in Shanghai. The stage can be reconfigured to support a wide range of spectator participation for performances, team debates of various configurations, mock UN, spelling bees, or chess tournaments, and it is appropriate for any music, drama, or limited athletic event where spectator participation is desired. Seating can range from 130 to 175 or more.

A Case for One Science Lab

The precedent for having a single science lab serve an entire department was established by Mitchell-Giurgola Architects of New York for East High School in Columbus, Indiana. The school, which won an AIA Honor Award in 1975, was designed for an open-classroom curriculum and team teaching. One of the most interesting design features still in use today is the science lab. East High School's science department is unique in that its program is housed in a single large laboratory facility capable of accommodating several science classes in different subject areas at one time. Designed as one large room where physics, chemistry, and bi-

◀ This successful school has a single multistation lab to support its science program. Columbus East High School, Columbus, Indiana. MGA Partners Architects. Photograph by Columbus East High School.

ology students all work on experiments at the same time, this lab is open all day so that students can return to finish a lab or do an extension activity when they choose.

- A large percentage of science instruction is conducted in nonlab space.
- To date, technology space usage has been underplanned in most science labs.
- A single multistation lab would provide higher utilization in less square footage, allowing for higher-quality lab space at the same cost. Following the formula *size x quality = cost,* smaller space and higher quality equals the same cost as larger space and less quality.

There are many other possibilities, and these will become more accepted as school officials, planners, and architects design space to reflect the needs of the program and the students it serves.

CONCLUSION

The type and use of educational technology, availability of increasingly vast amounts of information, and a greater focus on individualized and self-directed instructional models will continue to influence planners and architects in seeking new way of improving the spaces schools build. The ideas represented here are only a sampling of possibilities for new and flexible learning space expected to beome more accepted as school officials, planners and architects, design space to reflect the influences of the twenty-first century.

CHAPTER 2
CIRCULATION

DESIGN CONCEPTS

The organizational strategies that designers utilize for schools take numerous factors into consideration. The size, number, and configuration of individual program components as defined in the *facility space guideline* or *educational specification (ed spec)* significantly influences the building's final configuration or shape. Other factors include the size and shape of the proposed site, the adjacencies between school program elements, and planned use of the facility during nontraditional hours of operation by any number of groups. Factors to consider when assessing these influences include the following:

Entry sequence. How do students enter school each day, and where do they go? Do they immediately report to a homeroom, or do they first gather in a larger area such as the gym or the cafeteria? How do staff and faculty enter the building? How does the public enter the building during the school day? Is central administration the security checkpoint? How does the public enter the building for community events?

Internal circulation. During the school day, where do students have to go, and how often? Do they travel the corridors as a class, such as in elementary school, while other classes are in session? Do they travel individually at each class period, such as in the upper grades? How much time is allotted between periods, and how far are the distances? How are student lockers used and distributed in the school?

School size. How large is the school's enrollment? Is there a need to create subgroup-

ings within the building to mitigate the anonymity created in facilities with large enrollments? If subgrouping is a goal, what is the differentiating factor for grouping: by grade level, by full-grade groupings such as "houses," by different magnet programs, or by other elements?

Number of stories. How many floors is the facility, and how are big-box spaces such as gymnasiums and cafeterias stacked within the overall volume of the building? Are grades separated by floor, or do they share floors?

Community use. What areas of the buildings are accessible after school hours?

Teaching methodologies. What are the teaching methodologies employed? Are there magnet or multiple magnet programs? Is there a team teaching approach?

Efficiency/cost. How much corridor space is needed to serve each room in the building? This is a major component in the determination of building efficiency and resultant costs. Different organizational strategies yield varying efficiencies.

Natural light. Almost all spaces in a school building can benefit from some amount of natural light. The light requirements for many rooms are established by local codes and regulations.

Site access. Many spaces, including classrooms for lower age groups, benefit from direct site access.

BUILDING CONFIGURATIONS

There are a number of possible building configurations for schools; most are based on the

> The corridor is the school's thoroughfare. But shouldn't it be a pleasant avenue, not a forbidding tunnel? Physically, the corridor is a space for people moving from room to room. Psychologically, it can be a place for refreshment of the mind, for unwinding and relaxation and for pleasant socializing. (Perkins 1957, p. 15)

▶ *Student workspace at A. E. Stevenson High School, Lincolnshire, Illinois. OWP/P. Photograph by James Steinkmap.*

▼ *Dumbbell double-loaded classroom wings (the "H" plan). Perkins Eastman. Courtesy of Perkins Eastman.*

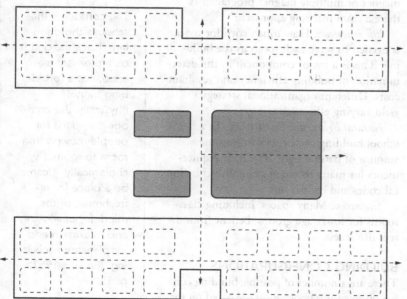

internal organization of the school's individual components as well as its site opportunities and limitations. Historically, the double-loaded corridor school has been the primary influence in school planning. Commonly referred to by a number of nicknames—"factory model," "egg crate," "assembly line school"—this form dominated school planning from the post–Civil War urban models of the Northeast until recently.

In the twenty-first century, program requirements include more variety in student groupings. This variety of groupings requires a wide range of spatial size, flexibility, and arrangement. Contemporary programs have pushed school planning away from the double-loaded corridor and generated a new series of partis (organizational models). Seen originally in elementary schools, the pod or

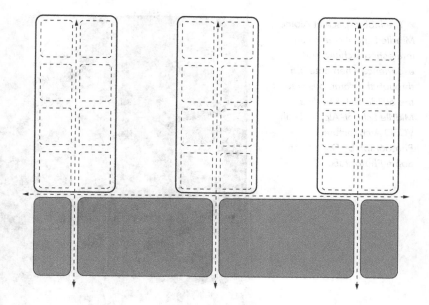

house plan school has graduated to the middle school and beyond. This model tends to generate a squarer plan with an internal focus toward breakouts and common areas that at times also includes student work space, faculty offices, building services, and other support spaces.

Even as variety increases, configurations can still be synthesized into several basic spatial organizations. Site-specific issues such as site size, geometry (square, rectangular, L-shaped), topography, orientation, natural features, and/or the designer's intent to create specific forms can mold these basic parti models into more idiosyncratic solutions. In the three building partis discussed below, the first typically represents the double-loaded corridor while the second and third tend to be more organic, less axial or square in plan.

1. *Double-loaded corridor schools.* These facilities are a variation on the traditional factory model plan. The plan often resembles a single letter, such as an L, E, or H. This parti can be improved by adding another letter, such as two opposing Ls providing nonstandard connectors to provide "off-grid" spaces, such as theater space, cafeterias, libraries, music and art facilities, and gymnasiums and other supporting physical education facilities.
2. *Studio-based, self-directed, and project-based schools.* These are more organic and random in plan and can be more responsive to the site and climate. Warmer, drier climates tend to generate smaller, separated parts as opposed to larger mega-buildings found in colder climates and limited-site urban locations. The plan is flexible in the variable

size of learning spaces, integrating breakouts and other forms of interaction space with the circulation system.
3. *Urban, multistory schools.* Characterized by tighter sites and stacked programs, these buildings tend to be more geometrically consistent.

Double-Loaded Corridor Schools

Centralized resources with double-loaded classroom wings ("E," "L," "I," or "H" plan)

Historically, this has been the most fundamental building form. The essence of this concept is the centralization of all shared resources, from auditorium and gymnasium to school administration. In contemporary design, this type is found mostly in elementary schools or to accommodate programmatically or spatially simple or smaller urban schools on tight sites.

▲ *Spine with double-loaded classroom wings (the "E" plan). Perkins Eastman. Courtesy of Perkins Eastman.*

CIRCULATION

▶ *The lobby space at Alpine Middle School creates an interesting architectural experience when entering through the commons area of the building. Timberline Middle School, Alpine, Utah. VCBO Architecture. Photograph by Dana Sohm, Sohm Photografx.*

Positive attributes
- Centralization of shared-resource functions minimizes travel distances from classrooms.
- This concept is readily used for elementary schools, where shared facilities are typically fewer in quantity and less sophisticated than they are for the upper grades.
- By dividing the classrooms into wings, it is possible to create subgroupings within schools, thereby generating a number of smaller "school-within-a-school" components.
- It is still possible to create visually interesting buildings by using the more architecturally interesting common spaces as a visual centerpiece, with the more neutral classroom wings as a backdrop.

Limitations
- It can be difficult to isolate separate functions for after-hours or nontraditional uses.

- The uniform grid is often based on a regular structural plan using bearing walls and mechanical system that limits future flexibility.
- It is often difficult to integrate variable-size spaces for different-size learning groups immediately adjacent to the more structured and regular plan elements.

There are at least three common variations of this parti, as discussed in the following section.

Centralized resources with single-loaded or double-loaded classroom bars/wings
This double-loaded configuration allows for visual differentiation of corridors and increased opportunity for subgrouping classroom areas (the "H" plan). In lieu of centralizing resources, this basic concept places shared resources at either end of a

94

double-loaded classroom corridor. The single-loaded corridor variation is more compact (see diagram at right).

Positive attributes
- This model is internally efficient, and isolates each wing for potential variation by grade or curricular focus.
- It is possible to isolate different parts of the building for nontraditional hours of operation.
- Centralized resources provide ease of access to shared facilities.

Limitations
- This model results in long travel distances from classrooms to central resources.
- There are fewer spatial opportunities for creating "school-within-a-school" subgroupings.
- This model often works best when symmetrical in plan; however, contemporary schools (except for schools with limited grade levels, such as an elementary school for grades 4–5) are seldom best accommodated by symmetrical program space.

Spine with single-loaded classroom wing
In this model, a "main street" separates classroom areas from shared resources. This configuration allows for visual and programmatic differentiation of the sides of the corridor. In this model, double-loaded classroom wings are organized perpendicular to (or off) a "main street" corridor spine (the "E" plan). The shared resources of the school are also located along this spine.

Positive attributes
- This model begins to organize subgroups of classrooms within the overall school.
- The placement of shared, centralized

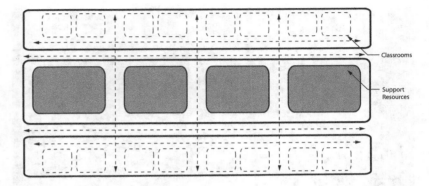

building blocks along the main spine allows the designer to organize the nonstandard grid components of the building in one area (gyms, cafeterias, auditoriums/theaters, and other big box or collected small group practice or office spaces).
- This model provides natural opportunities for future expansion to the spine or wings.

▲ *Centralized resources flanked with single-loaded classroom wings. Perkins Eastman. Courtesy of Perkins Eastman.*

▼ *Courtyard with double-loaded classroom wings (the "donut" or "O" plan). Perkins Eastman. Courtesy of Perkins Eastman.*

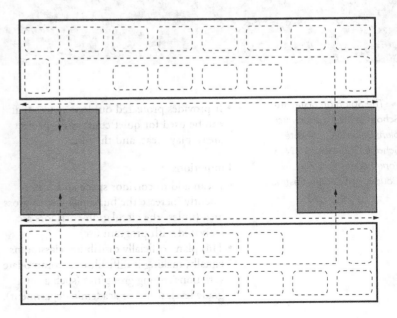

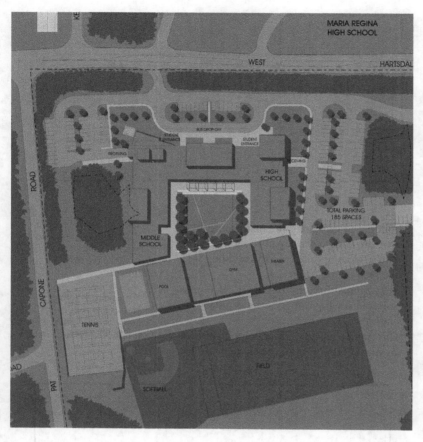

▲ The Solomon Schechter School utilizes a courtyard plan. Solomon Schechter School, Greensburgh, New York. Perkins Eastman. Courtesy of Perkins Eastman.

- It provides protected outdoor spaces that can be used for quiet courtyards, project areas, play areas, and the like.

Limitations

- It can add to corridor space and consequently increase the building's net to gross area (unless the circulation corridors are activated with program use).
- This plan artificially distributes classrooms equally, making it difficult to accommodate variations among groupings (such as by grade level, team, or academic department).

- Creates a large amount of exterior wall, which can add to construction and energy costs.

Centralized resources with classroom clustering

In this concept, classroom wings are replaced with a small number of classrooms formed around central nodes (the "donut" or "O" plan). The courtyard model is widely used in school design. It typically consists of up to four classroom blocks or support wings arranged around a central courtyard. This model can work for small or large schools and can provide natural groupings for multigrade clusters. It can also create one or more protected courtyards.

A variation on the donut model can be created by forming a courtyard with classroom clusters and shared resource areas. Once again, major circulation is differentiated from secondary circulation feeding the classrooms. This helps to enable subgrouping and mitigates heavy traffic in front of classroom doors. The shared resource nodes are typically programmed for functions that are utilized by the surrounding classrooms. The nodes can include such program elements as faculty offices, tutorial rooms, project areas, and other essential functions, such as restrooms and egress stairs. The classroom cluster establishes clear subgrouping within the overall school building, which enhances some teaching methodologies, such as team teaching. This concept centralizes school-based shared resources, with classroom clusters located around the central resource zone.

Positive attributes

- This model can provide a natural light-well at the center of the donut that enhances sustainability and educational goals for natural light in the majority of the learning environments.

- It can create an efficient perimeter (exterior wall to enclosed area).
- It can be appropriate for tighter, urban environments.
- It can provide one or more outdoor environmental areas for use in water collection or heat island effect reduction, as science project areas, or for other academic support functions.

Limitations

- It can be difficult to isolate individual functions for after-hours or nontraditional uses.
- It can limit the planning module in multistory schemes because of the floor plan regularity.

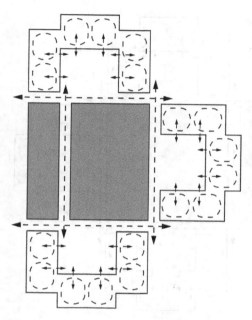

◀ Centralized resources with classroom clustering. Perkins Eastman. Courtesy of Perkins Eastman.

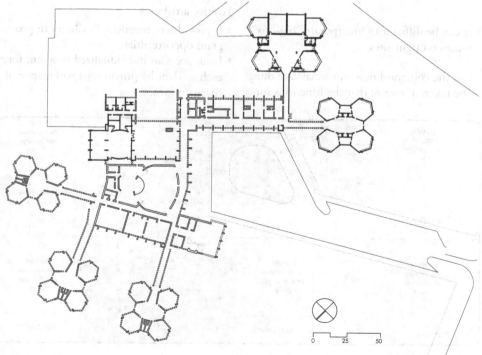

◀ One of the most famous early cluster plans. Heathcote Elementary School, Scarsdale, New York. Perkins+Will original building. Peter Gisolfi Associates addition. Courtesy of Peter Gisolfi Associates.

0   25   50

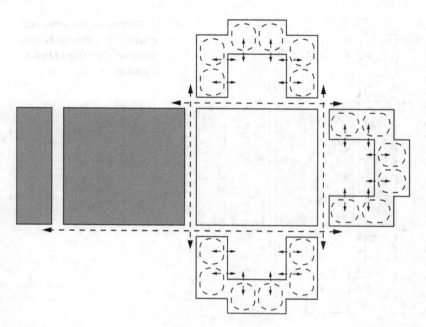

rounding the courtyard and the uses for the courtyard are compatible and do not disturb each other. In addition, local regulations should be checked for requirements concerning egress from courtyards. Sun-study analysis should also be undertaken to ensure that these open spaces remain sunny and usable. In regions of severe climate, snow removal should also be considered.

Studio-Based, Self-Directed, and Project-Based Schools

The main attribute of this planning model is that it supports a large variety of the student grouping options and houses a percentage of its population in studios or self-directed space. It has fewer overall classrooms than a traditional factory-model school.

▲ A variation on the "O" plan, consolidating the shared resource area. Perkins Eastman. Courtesy of Perkins Eastman.

▶ Studio-based model showing the combination of enclosed and open instructional and project areas. Perkins Eastman. Courtesy of Perkins Eastman.

• It can be difficult to incorporate "big-box" spaces on tight sites.

In the courtyard design, special care must to be taken to ensure that the functions sur-

Positive attributes
• It provides tremendous flexibility in program opportunities.
• It supports an individualized program for each student by providing a wide range of space options.

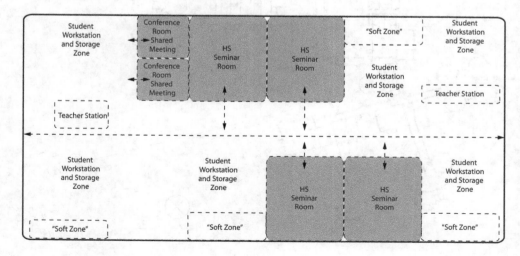

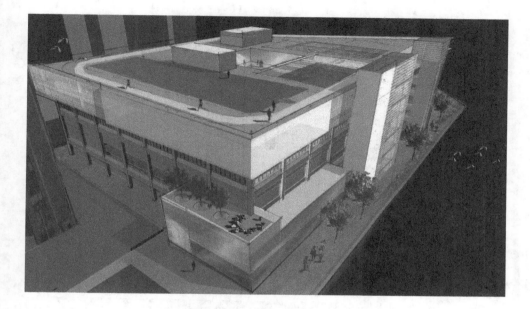

◀ *Tight urban sites, such as this platform created in the East River for a multistory K–12 international school, often require unique vertical stacking of spaces. United Nations International School. New York, New York. Perkins Eastman. Courtesy of Perkins Eastman.*

- It supports freer movement of students in self-directed teams that can allow them to progress according to their ability rather than age level.
- The building plan can be more compact than an axial double-loaded corridor.
- It utilizes more circulation space as programmed area and can improve the square-foot-per-student planning efficiency.

Limitations

- It can be difficult to implement without a committed and innovative district or school.
- It has less application for elementary schools that use typical self-contained instructional units.
- Such a model can drive up the overall size of the building if it also simultaneously tries to provide a traditional number of standard classrooms (thus resulting in a doubling of student workstations).

- It is difficult to implement without an adequate furniture budget to support the style of learning.

Urban, Multistory Schools

Of necessity, many urban schools are built on small sites and organized vertically. This can present a number of difficulties for the planner and architect. Nevertheless, some of the most famous urban private and public schools have functioned within this site-imposed parti.

Positive attributes

- It can produce very efficient square-foot-per-student numbers.
- If used in northern climates, it is more appropriate for high school campuses.

Limitations

- Although smaller and more compact space can reduce the square footage requirements

CIRCULATION

▸ Multigrade model with grade-based classroom wings and shared facilities. Perkins Eastman. Courtesy of Perkins Eastman.

▸ Multischool model at the NYSCA Mott Haven Campus, New York, New York. Perkins Eastman. Courtesy of Perkins Eastman.

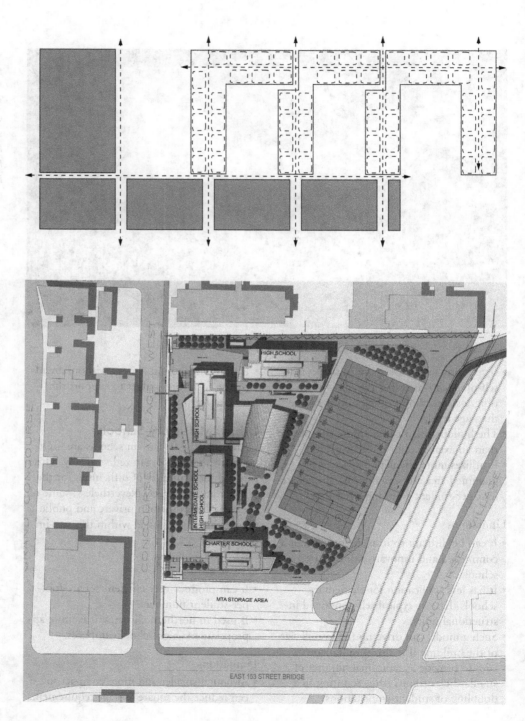

per student, increased need for elevators
and stairwells (especially if exiting big box
spaces from upper floors) and mechanical
shafts can increase the overall square
footage of the building.

- It is difficult to integrate large, big-box
spaces efficiently.
- If deep floor plates are created, it can be
difficult to provide daylighting and natural
ventilation.
- Separation of multigrade-level groupings
can be difficult.
- It can be difficult to accommodate programs or grades on single floors.

Multigrade Campuses

In some districts—and most international
schools—elementary, middle, and high school
grades may share the same campus. Although
cost savings can be realized, there are a number of planning challenges to address.

Positive attributes

- All grade levels can share back-of-house
functions such as central administrative
functions, a main kitchen, shipping and
receiving, centralized recycling, central mechanical plant, centralized security, technology "head-end" or equipment room
space, and outdoor athletic support/stor-
age.
- Space is flexible when enrollments between
grades vary (e.g., space used for grade 9
one year could be used for grade 8 the following year).
- It provides immediate vertical integration
of students with greater abilities to move
up in the program; conversely, students
who need additional help may likewise be
closer to the needed resources.
- It can reduce the need for paving and site-
related improvements because a staggered

schedule can use a single bus drop-
off/pick-up for all grades.

Limitations

- On smaller sites, it can be difficult to provide
an identifiable entry point for each school.
- It can be difficult to control unwanted or
random interaction among age groups.
- On tight sites with compact plans, it can
be difficult to schedule multiple-school,
after-hours activities simultaneously.

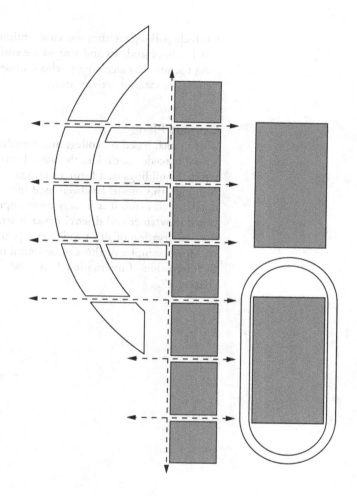

▲ Campus plan. Perkins
Eastman. Courtesy of Perkins
Eastman.

- Vehicle parking requires special attention if high school students and visitors are entering the site near elementary school student entries or exterior activity areas.

Campus Plan

This model, based on college and boarding school precedents, divides the school into separate buildings that form a campus. Although this model has been used in northern climates, it is usually more appropriate in warmer and drier climates where the conservation of site area is not a priority. More examples of this can be found in the discussion of international schools chapter 17.

Positive attributes
- This plan can be appropriate in areas where the weather facilitates outdoor circulation.
- There is more opportunity for natural lighting and ventilation, supporting a more sustainable facility.
- If used in northern climates, it is most appropriate for high school campuses.
- It facilitates opening of certain functions for after-hours use.

Limitations
- This model is not recommended for elementary schools in northern climates.
- It can create security issues by limiting naturally observable space.
- It can create a higher ratio of building exterior envelope (and cost).

CHAPTER 3

DESIGN CONCERNS AND PROCESS

This chapter focuses on four major issues in school planning, design, and construction:

- The major steps and tasks involved in planning, designing, and implementing a school building program
- The most common management problems that occur in school building programs
- Major trends
- Unique design concerns relevant to school building programs

THE PLANNING, DESIGN, AND IMPLEMENTATION PROCESS

Most design professionals consider educational facility design to be one of the more challenging project types. At times, school-building design has settled into a routine, but at its best the design of an educational facility has a dynamic relationship with the lives and activities of the children, teachers, and communities that use the school. School design is challenging and typically involves many client representatives, outside agency and public reviews, complex functional issues, rapidly changing technology, restrictive codes, and other significant design influences. Even relatively small school projects can take two to three years, and larger projects take from four to six years from initial conception to completion. The design professionals who are successful in dealing with the combination of issues involved are those who understand not only the issues but also the implementation process during which these issues are resolved.

The implementation process for most school designs can be divided into 11 steps:

1. Strategic planning
2. Identification and scoping of need
3. Selection and organization of the project team
4. Programming and predesign work—defining scope
5. Schematic design
6. Obtainment of public approval and/or financing
7. Design development
8. Construction documentation
9. Selection of the construction and installation teams, and purchasing
10. Construction and installation
11. Occupancy

The first part of this section discusses the design team's tasks for each of these steps. Understanding all the steps, as well as the design team's potential role in each, is an essential responsibility of any design professional.

Strategic Planning and Preliminary Definition of Need

Many educational facility projects are done within existing facilities or on existing campuses. Therefore, any project must be planned within the framework of a long-range plan. Even in new facilities, the initial building design must assume growth and change in the future.

An effective strategic plan incorporates more than site and facility issues. It must

▶ *Graphic outline of the major steps in a five-year facility master plan for a public school district. Courtesy of Perkins Eastman*

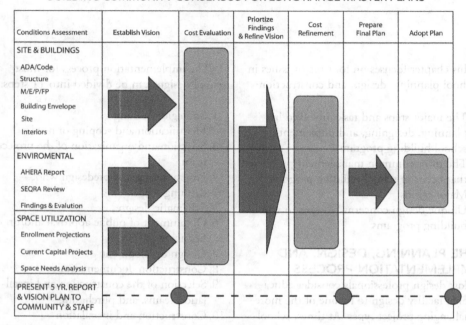

BUILDING COMMUNITY CONSENSUS FOR LONG RANGE MASTER PLANS

Conditions Assessment	Establish Vision	Cost Evaluation	Priortize Findings & Refine Vision	Cost Refinement	Prepare Final Plan	Adopt Plan
SITE & BUILDINGS						
ADA/Code						
Structure						
M/E/P/FP						
Building Envelope						
Site						
Interiors						
ENVIROMENTAL						
AHERA Report						
SEQRA Review						
Findings & Evalution						
SPACE UTILIZATION						
Enrollment Projections						
Current Capital Projects						
Space Needs Analysis						
PRESENT 5 YR. REPORT & VISION PLAN TO COMMUNITY & STAFF						

reflect the potential impact of changing approaches in education, technology, demography, funding, and other factors that will determine the future need for and use of the facility. The role of the design professional in this initial phase can be very important.

Typically, the design professionals evaluate existing conditions—from mechanical systems to interior finishes, operational issues, code compliance, and the ability of the facility to support the academic mission. Once these issues or problems are defined the design team can develop available options and determine the potential cost and schedule for each major facility action implied by a potential development strategy. In

most strategic plans, the facility's addition/expansion/modernization options are then evaluated against how well they help achieve the institution's key goals. The facility options can then be realized.

Once the strategic planning framework is set, the next step is to define the scope of the specific project or projects. This preliminary definition is sometimes determined by the facility owner, but it is more efficient and productive to include the educational planners and design professionals in the process.

The primary tasks within this step include establishing an outline program and statement of project objectives, setting a realistic schedule, outlining a preliminary project budget, and defining the professional services that have to be retained. In certain cases this step also includes some preliminary test of feasibility. Most school projects must be judged by their impact on property tax, tuition, or the ability to raise the necessary funds. As a result, clients must have early confirmation that the project is financially feasible.

Selection and Organization of the Project Team

The design of any educational facility is a team sport. It is not uncommon for fifteen or more professional disciplines to be involved:

Architects
Educational planners
Equipment specialists
Interior designers
Civil engineers
Geotechnical engineers
Mechanical engineers
Acoustical engineers
Electrical engineers
Plumbing and fire-protection engineers
Cost consultants and/or construction managers
Telecommunications and technology consultants
Lighting designers
Theater consultants
Food service consultants
Pool consultants
Landscape architects

In some large urban schools, elevator and exterior wall consultants are also needed.

Typically, most of the various disciplines are retained by the architect as a single cohesive team, thereby providing the school with

a single source of responsibility. In addition, the following professionals may be involved:

Accountants
Financial consultants
Investment bankers
Attorneys
Bond counsel
Fund-raising consultants
Environmental consultants
Traffic consultants
Parking consultants

Other specialists may be involved in the financing and public approval process.

The client typically focuses on the lead professionals—usually the architects. Selection of the other members of the design team is often left to the lead firm or firms. The key issue, however, is to have a team that incorporates all the critical professional skills. Financial limits sometimes curtail the scope of the specialists' involvement, but the complexity of many educational facility projects demands that the team find a way to cover most of the specialist disciplines listed earlier.

The selection process for the lead professionals varies considerably, but a thorough process would include the following:

1. Research is done on firms with relevant experience.
2. A written request is sent to a "long list" of firms, asking them to submit letters of interest, lists of references, and information on relevant projects. This request, sometimes known as a Request for Qualifications (RFQ), includes a statement of the project objectives, an outline of the program, a schedule, and an assumed budget.

▶ *Typical project organization for a large new public school. Courtesy of Perkins Eastman*

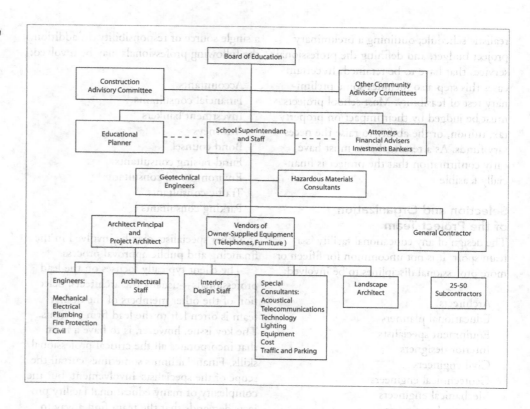

3. After a review of the submittals, four to six firms are selected for a short list and asked to make a formal presentation.
4. In some cases the short-listed firms are asked, via a request sometimes known as a Request for Proposal (RFP), to submit a written proposal summarizing the following:

   • The firm's understanding of the project
   • Proposed work program
   • Proposed schedule
   • Key personnel and subconsultant firms that will work on the project
   • Proposed fees and expenses

Following the formal presentation and interviews, a contract is negotiated with the selected firm. In some cases the fee is discussed only after a team is retained, based on qualifications, and there has been a comprehensive discussion of scope, schedule, proposed specialist consultants, and other variables. In the past—and even today in some districts—the fee is set after reference to a standard fee schedule. Most experienced design teams and their clients, however, know that no two projects are the same and that the appropriate fees should be carefully calculated in each particular case. For a small, phased renovation of an occupied building, a fee equal to 10–14 percent of the project construction cost may be too little.

Conversely, for a large, new high school on a flat site, a lump-sum fee equal to 6 percent may be adequate. The form of contract is typically based on one of the standard contract forms of the American Institute of Architects (AIA), but many public school districts and private schools have their own forms.

Once the lead firm is selected, the entire team must be organized. This organization must begin with the client, because only the client can

- Select the professional team.
- Set the overall project goals (including the budget and schedule) and monitor to determine whether they are being met.
- Select—from among the options prepared by the design team—the program and design solutions that best meet the objectives.
- Resolve differences and problems between team members (e.g., design team and builder).
- Administer the contracts with the team members.
- Lead the relationship between the project team and the public.

Most successful projects have clients who create a clear decision-making structure and a strong team relationship with all the firms involved in the process. Some clients have even used partnering sessions at the beginning of a project to build team relationships. This widely employed technique has the key members attend a one- to three-day workshop to establish a positive framework for their future working relationship. Recognizing the importance of the client's role in this relationship, the renowned Finnish-born architect Eero Saarinen liked to start a project by saying to the design team, "Let's see if we can make this guy into a great client."

Educational Specifications, Programming, and Predesign

The programming phase usually begins with the preparation of the "educational specifications" ("ed specs"), or facility design guidelines. These are typically prepared by an educator who knows the school system, relevant codes, and educational trends nationwide.

For the design team, one of the most challenging steps is the translation of the educational specifications or design guidelines into an architectural program and initial concept. In the past the client would prepare a detailed statement of its requirements or program for a project during the scoping phase. Today the increased complexity of the average project has meant that the full, detailed scope must be analyzed and defined with the assistance of the design team.

Program analysis has become a basic service provided by the architects, facility planners, and interior designers on educational facility projects. Among the additional particulars that the design team, with the help of specialists, must define are the number of each type of space; the detailed functional requirements (amount of pinup and chalkboard/whiteboard space, desired lighting levels, etc.) and dimensions of each space; equipment requirements; mechanical, electrical, plumbing, and other services needed; and the required relationships between

▶ Room data sheet for an
elementary school classroom.
Courtesy of Perkins Eastman.

Room Data Sheets

| Room | ELEMENTARY SCHOOL CLASSROOM | | |

Net Area (sm)	Primary Adjacency	Secondary Adjacency	Normal Occupancy
56	Commons	Little GEMS Café, Elementary Library	25 students

Finishes

Floor	Base	Wall	Ceiling	Window Treatment			
Vinyl/ Carpet	Vinyl	Paint	ACT	Shade Pockets			

Lighting

Natural Daylight	Fluorescent	Emergency	Task	Zoned Switching	Dual Level Switching
X	X	X			X

Power/Communication

Convenience Outlets	Other	Network Data	Floor Outlet	Intercom	Clock	Telephone	Video Projector	Security
X	X*	X	X	X	X	X	X	

Plumbing | **HVAC**

Sink	Hot Water	Cold Water	Floor Drain	Room Control	Unconditioned Space	Special Exhaust	Natural Ventilation	Humidity Control
X		X		X			X	

Millwork/Built-ins*

	Countertop	Under Counter Shelves	Over Counter Shelves	Full Height Shelves	Base Cabinet	Wall Cabinet	Teacher Closet	Cubbies
Depth	600 mm	300 mm	300 mm		600 mm	600 mm	600 mm	
Height	850 mm	850 mm	2150 mm		850 mm	2150 mm	2150 mm	

*Special Requirements: The architect shall seek opportunities to utilize movable furniture and fixtures in lieu of built in casework.

Fixtures

Smartboard	Markerboard	Tack Surface	Hanging/ Map Rails	Retractable Proj. Screen			
X	X	X		X			

spaces. This important initial step is discussed in more detail in chapter 1.

The project team also has several other tasks before design can begin:

• A detailed assessment of existing conditions in the project area

• Preparation of base plans showing existing conditions in structures, a site survey, utility analyses, and geotechnical analyses (if new construction is involved)

• An analysis of the zoning, building code, and public-approval issues that will influence the design

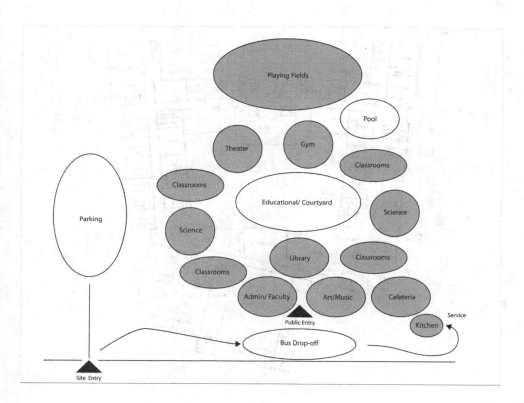

◀ *Conceptual diagram for a new, private 7–12 upper school, the Solomon Schechter School, Greenburgh, New York. Perkins Eastman. Courtesy of Perkins Eastman.*

• Special analyses of any other issues (asbestos, audiovisual needs, structural capacity, etc.) that may affect the design, cost, schedule, or feasibility of the project

The results of the programming and related analyses are then combined into one or more preliminary concepts, an expanded statement of the project goals, and an updated project schedule and budget.

Once these project documents are available, in many cases two important parallel series of tasks begin—obtaining land-use approvals and securing financing. Public schools typically do not require zoning or other formal land-use approvals, but they usually must achieve community acceptance. Private institutions, however, typically must obtain formal land-use approvals for their proposed projects.

When required, the local land-use approval process typically starts with informal meetings with the municipal officials or planning department staff. They will help outline the steps in the process, identify any special approvals (such as zoning variances) that are required, and specify the information required at each step in the process. Most local approval processes for projects that involve more than renovation within an existing structure require a detailed site design and a schematic building design for

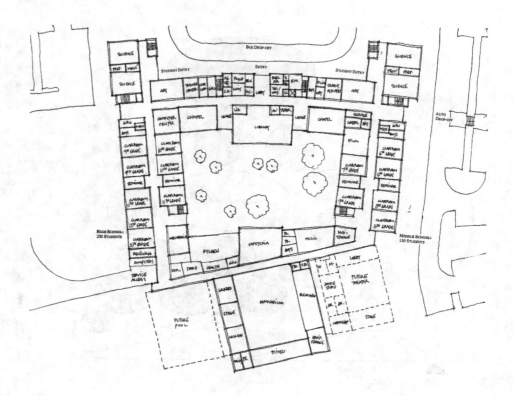

▶ *An early schematic design plan for the Solomon Schechter School, Greenburgh, New York. Perkins Eastman. Courtesy of Perkins Eastman.*

land-use approval. On larger projects the process may also require detailed analyses of the environmental impact of increased traffic, noise, storm drainage, and other issues before local officials give their approval. It is not unusual for the land-use approval process to take one year to complete. In many cases, the design team must take the lead in this effort.

The second series of tasks that typically begins during predesign involves securing the financing for the project. Few major projects are paid for from the school system's current income. Many involve borrowing, and most larger public projects require an issue of tax-exempt bonds after a public referendum.

It is usually preferable to hold the referendum after the more refined design materials are specified and cost estimates are developed during the schematic design stage, but many schools do not want to risk the fees involved without a favorable vote or fund-raising effort.

Fund-raising is also important for private institutions. This process can take more than a year to complete. During the financing process, the design team is often asked to assist in the required documentation, public presentations, and other steps.

Once these predesign tasks are nearly completed, it is time to start the traditional design process.

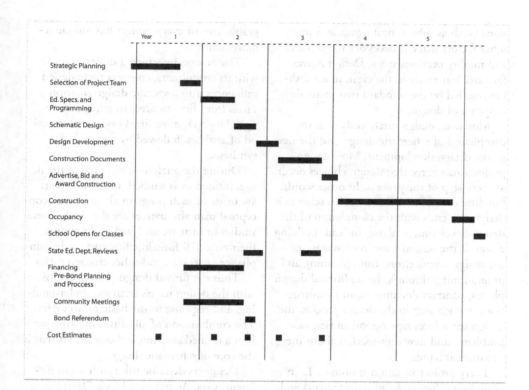

Typical schedule for the planning, design, and implementation of a large, new school building. Courtesy of Perkins Eastman.

Schematic Design

Schematic design is the first phase of the traditional design process. For most public school projects, this phase may not begin until after the school bond issue passes or funding is secured. During this first phase, conceptual options are studied and a preferred design concept is developed for all major components of the project. The standard forms of agreement for design services provide brief definitions for the schematic design phase, as well as the subsequent phase.

The standard contractual definitions of design services are based on a theoretical process that, if it were followed, would per-

mit the design team to move in an orderly way through the most common steps in the design, documentation, and construction of a building. This theoretical process assumes that a clear definition of the client's program exists. It also assumes that the process can progress in a linear fashion from the definition of client requirements through a series of steps—each of which results in a more complete definition of the design—until the project is sufficiently detailed to go into documentation for bidding (or negotiation) and construction.

The reality is not so orderly. Evolving program requirements, budget considerations, increased knowledge of site considera-

111

tions (such as subsoil problems), and many other factors make it necessary to go back and modify previous steps. Design moves forward, but rarely in the clear, linear fashion implied by the standard two-phase description of design.

Moreover, design rarely ends with the completion of schematic design and the next phase, design development. Most design professionals agree that design choices occur at every step of the process. In other words, building design neither starts with schematic design nor ends with the completion of the design-development phase. Instead, building design is the central issue in each stage of the design team's effort, from planning and programming through the traditional design phases, contract documents, and construction. At each step in the design process, the design team faces new opportunities, new problems, and new information about the situation at hand.

Every project situation is unique. Each presents a different set of requirements and limitations; a particular set of programming, cultural, environmental, technological, and aesthetic contexts to be considered; and its own set of challenges and opportunities. Design brings to the surface the major considerations inherent in the situation. It is both a problem-seeking and a problem-solving process.

Although every project has a unique combination of design influences, some of the most important are the program, the codes, the site, the constraints imposed by existing structures, the technological requirements of the systems to be incorporated (structural, mechanical, electrical, etc.), sustainability goals, the cost, the schedule, and the client's particular goals. Thus, although many schools are built to house similar pro-

grams, almost every project has unique requirements.

The process by which a design team, with its consultants, converts these design influences into a specific design solution varies from firm to firm. In schematic design, however, most firms begin with a period of analysis, followed by a period of synthesis.

During the analysis stage, each of the design influences is studied. Often diagrams are made of each program element, and conceptual plan alternatives are sketched. These studies in turn are analyzed to determine their potential functionality, cost, code compliance, aesthetic, and other characteristics.

Thus the formal design process begins with the design team's analyses, understanding, and response to the basic project data. The combination of all of this information into a unified solution is the synthesis that is the core of schematic design.

Designers describe this synthesis in different ways. As architect Lewis Davis has noted, "Very few designers—no matter how consistent their work—can trace all influences. Some are external: technology, available materials, codes, etc. Some are internal: the designer's own education or the experience of the building just seen in Europe."

Some firms like to generate and test several alternatives before settling on a single approach. Others prefer to seek out a single strong idea around which they can organize the rest of the design.

But there is more than logic at work. Any experienced designer will note the importance of the nonrational, the nondescribable, and the poetic in the creation of a successful building design. At key points judgment, taste, intuition, and creative talent take over.

Underlying this diversity of approaches, there are some common themes and design tasks. The first is an expansion of the client's original goals statement to include clear design goals. These will help in making the inevitable decisions on trade-offs between budget and quality, appearance and energy efficiency, as well as the thousands of other major decisions in which competing priorities must be reconciled.

The next basic task is the development of a parti, or basic organization, for the project concept. As architect Edward Larrabee Barnes put it, "It is not just a case of form following function. Sometimes function follows form."

Designers also choose a design vocabulary, which includes the essential formal or aesthetic ideas that will govern the development of the design concept. Some designers develop a personal vocabulary of ideas, details, preferred materials, and so on, and refine it on each project. Others approach each project as a unique problem, selecting an appropriate vocabulary to fit the situation.

It is common for design teams to consider several conceptual solutions to a design problem. For this reason, most have developed a process for narrowing the choices to a single concept. In some cases, selection is based on a formal grading of a concept against the original project objectives. In others, it is an intuitive judgment based on experience. In most instances, designers use a combination of both.

Beyond the first conceptual steps, however, the process becomes more complex. In all but the smallest and simplest projects, the steps that follow concept development involve a team of people. Although it is true that significant projects are usually developed under the guidance of a single strong design leader, it is important to realize that not many projects have fewer than ten people involved in the decision making—architects, engineers, interior designers, specialist consultants, construction managers, public agencies, and, of course, clients. Thus, design excellence results in part from the effective management of a complex team, all of whose members contribute to the quality of the final product.

The result of all these steps is a completed schematic design. Although different projects, clients, and design teams have different definitions of the completion of this phase, there are certain commonly agreed-upon objectives and products.

1. *Objectives.* The primary objective is to arrive at a clearly designed, feasible concept and to present it in a form that achieves client understanding and acceptance. The secondary objectives are to clarify the project program, explore the most promising alternative design solutions, and provide a reliable basis for analyzing the cost of the project.
2. *Products.* Communicating design ideas and decisions usually involves a variety of media. Typical documentation at the end of this phase can include the following:

- A site plan
- Plans for each level, including conceptual reflected ceiling plans
- All elevations—exterior and conceptual interior elevations
- Two or more sections
- An outline specification
- A statistical summary of the design area and other characteristics in comparison to the program

Design Options

Design Options	1	2	3	4	5
Program Fit	Good	Good	Acceptable	Good	Good
Site Utilization	Good	Acceptable	Acceptable	Acceptable	Good
Appropriate adjacencies	Good	Acceptable	Poor	Acceptable	Good
Clear circulation	Acceptable	Acceptable	Poor	Good	Good
Disruption	Acceptable	Acceptable	Acceptable	Poor	Poor
Phasing	Acceptable	Acceptable	Acceptable	Poor	Poor
Cost & budget	Acceptable	Acceptable	Acceptable	Prohibitive	Poor
Acceptability to neighborhood	Good	Poor	Acceptable	Prohibitive	Acceptable

Key
- ● Good
- ⊖ Acceptable
- ○ Poor
- ⊗ Prohibitive

▲ Some architects and clients use graphic tools to analyze and present design options. Perkins Eastman. Courtesy of Perkins Eastman.

- A preliminary construction cost estimate
- Other illustrative materials—renderings, models, or drawings—as needed to present the concept adequately:

  a. *Drawings.* These are typically presented at the smallest scale that can clearly illustrate the concept (perhaps 1/16 in. = 1 ft for larger buildings, and 1/8 in. = 1 ft for smaller buildings and interiors).

  b. *Outline specifications.* This is a general description of the work indicating major systems and materials choices for the project, but usually providing little detailed product information.

  c. *Preliminary estimate of construction cost.* The schematic design estimate usually includes a preliminary area

analysis and preliminary construction cost estimate. It is common for preliminary cost estimates made at this stage to include contingencies for further design development, market unpredictability, and changes during construction. These estimates are often developed by professional estimators or a builder selected by the client, but some design teams do their own cost estimates.

3. *Other services.* As part of the schematic design work, the design team may agree to provide energy studies; special program and design studies; life-cycle cost analyses; or other economic studies, renderings, models, brochures, or promotional materials for the client.

4. *Approvals.* The final step in schematic design is to obtain formal client approval. The importance of this step cannot be overemphasized. The schematic design presentation must be clear enough to gain both the understanding and the approval of the client. Most design teams recommend that once this has been accomplished, each item in the presentation be signed and dated by the client prior to initiation of the design development phase.

Obtaining public approval and/or financing

At this stage, and again at the end of construction documentation, the design may also be subject to review by the state's department of education or the technical arm of a city's board of education. This review usually focuses on conformance with established standards and the relevant codes. Financing is typically subject to voter approval of a bond issue.

Design Development

The objectives of the design development phase are different from those of schematic design. The primary purpose is to define and describe all important aspects of the project so that all that remains is the preparation of the formal construction contract documents.

As the pressures of tight schedules and the amount of fast-track construction have increased, some design firms have attempted to shorten or even eliminate this phase. However, there are strong design, technical, and economic arguments against doing so. Design development is the period in which all the issues left unresolved at the end of schematic design can be worked out, and this can be done at a large enough scale to prevent the risk of major modifications during the construction contract document phase. Working drawings and specifications are complex and intricately interrelated; changes in these documents are costly and likely to lead to coordination problems during construction.

In addition, design development is the period in which the design itself achieves the refinement and coordination necessary for a really polished work. Without this step, too many important areas of design exploration are compressed into the schematic phase or left to be addressed in the working drawings.

Effective design development results in the design team's working out a clear, coordinated description of all aspects of the design. This description typically includes fully developed floor plans, interior and exterior elevations, reflected ceiling plans, wall and building sections, and key details—usually at the same scale used in the construction contract documents. It also includes the evaluation of alternative interior finishes and furnishings. In addition, the basic mechanical, electrical, plumbing, and fire-protection systems are accurately sized and defined, if not fully drawn. No major issues should be left unresolved that could require significant restudy during the development of construction contract documents phase.

The products of the design development phase are similar to those of schematic design—drawings and specifications that fix and describe the size and character of the project, as well as any recommended adjustments to the preliminary estimate of construction cost. It is important to bring the design development phase to a close with formal presentation to, and approval by, the client.

Construction Documentation

The design process does not really end with the completion of the design development phase; rather, the emphasis shifts to the effort necessary to have a complete, coordinated set of documents to guide the purchasing, construction, installation, and initial operations steps that follow.

The construction documents typically include drawings, specifications, contract forms, and bidding requirements. Each of these four documents plays an important role.

1. The drawings provide a graphic description of the work that is to be done.
2. The specifications outline the levels of quality and standards to be met.
3. The contract forms include the actual contract, the bond and insurance requirements, and general conditions outlining the roles, rights, and responsibilities of all parties.
4. The bidding requirements—if the project is being bid—set the procedures for this process.

▶ *The Solomon Schechter floor plan at the end of schematic design. Solomon Schechter School, Greenburgh, New York. Perkins Eastman. Courtesy of Perkins Eastman.*

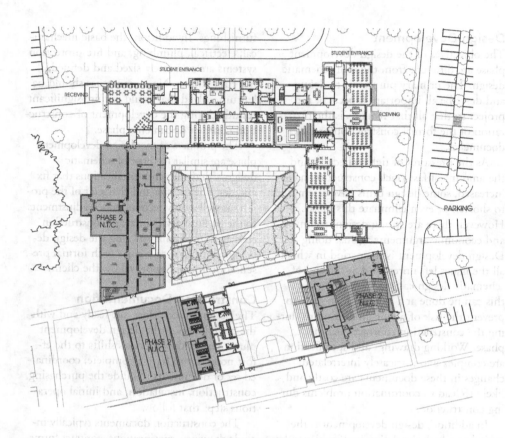

The professional design organizations (such as the AIA and others) have model documents for specifications, contract forms, and bidding requirements. These are good starting points, but all standard forms must be adapted to incorporate each project's unique requirements. The largest part of this step in the process, however, is the production of a comprehensive set of drawings and technical specifications. This task often takes four to six months for the large teams on many educational facility projects. A new building or a substantial renovation of a middle school or high school can involve more than 100 sheets of drawings and

several hundred pages of technical specifications. Each sheet of the drawings may involve 100 to 200 hours of work to complete, as the drawings must provide a clear, accurately dimensioned graphic description of the work to be done, and these drawings must be coordinated with the drawings of the other design professionals working on the same part of the project.

Experienced design professionals plan this step carefully and seek productivity savings. Computers and advanced software, such as building information modeling (BIM), in particular, are beginning to bring some noticeable improvements in both

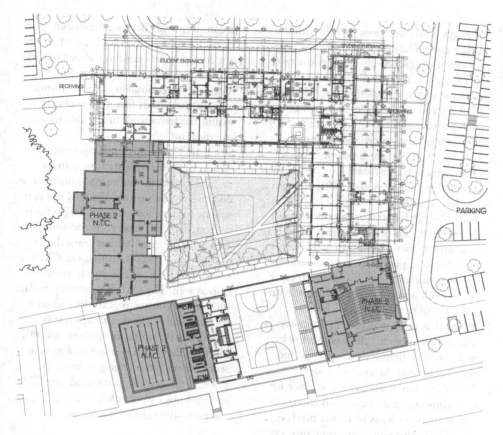

◀ Construction
documentation, including
detailed dimensions for the
Solomon Schechter School,
Greenburgh, New York.
Perkins Eastman. Courtesy of
Perkins Eastman.

speed and quality, but the human element is still key.

Selection of the Construction and Installation Teams and Purchasing

Once part or all of the construction documents are available, the next critical step is the selection of the builders, furniture and equipment manufacturers, and others who will provide the construction and other installed elements of the facility. Typically, the design team either manages the selection process or is an active participant with the client.

Experienced design professionals believe that if the right companies are selected, the

remaining implementation phases are straightforward. Even one bad selection, however, can make completion of the project very difficult.

There are a number of choices available. In the selection of a builder, there are six major alternatives:

1. The most common procedure is for the construction documents to be completed and put out for a bid to companies attracted by public advertisement or selected from a list of prequalified general contractors.
2. For major educational facilities projects, a frequent choice is to have a construction

manager (CM) work side by side with the design team. During design, the CM gives advice on cost, schedule, and constructability issues. When the construction documentation nears completion, the CM bids all of the various subtrades and then provides a guaranteed maximum price (GMP) and becomes the general contractor.

3. For projects in which the scope is unclear or construction must start long before the completion of design, some clients retain a builder to work on a cost-plus basis. Most clients do not like the open-endedness of this method, but there are times when it is necessary. Because most public school work must be purchased by competitive bidding, this approach is limited to emergency work and projects in which the various parts of the work can be bid.

4. A variation in approach sometimes occurs wherein components such as sheetrock walls, outlets, light fixtures, playground equipment, and doors can be identified. The client may negotiate a unit price for each component and can then choose to buy as many units as he or she needs or can afford. This works for some projects, such as window replacement programs, repaving of parking lots, and replacement of light fixtures.

5. An increasingly common option is *design/build*, whereby the client typically retains a team that includes either a builder and a design team or a design team that includes a "builder" component. Some clients like the simplicity and the assumed higher degree of cost control. The success of the design/build approach, however, depends on the selection of a design/build team committed to the client's interests, inasmuch as the normal quality control provided by an independent design team

is compromised. Because the design team works for or with the builder, it often cannot communicate concerns about quality and value directly to the client. For furnishings, the equivalent is the furniture manager, who bids furniture packages within the framework of a performance specification.

6. Since the 1970s an increasingly popular option has been construction management. During the design and construction documentation process, the CM is a consultant to the client and the design team on cost, schedule, and constructability issues. This approach differs from the second option, however, in that the CM is a consultant to the client during construction as well. The CM may actually replace the general contractor, but does so on a fee basis. All of the construction subcontracts may be bid (as in the first option), but the CM—in his or her professional service form—does not guarantee the price. If the price is guaranteed, the CM can no longer work solely in the client's interest—the risks are too great.

The selection of an approach, as well as the selection of appropriate companies, is important and should be carried out in a systematic fashion. Advertising for bidders and hoping the right people show up to bid is rarely enough. Most experienced design teams and school districts research the options, identify the most qualified firms, solicit their interest, confirm their qualifications, and then—where public bid laws permit—limit the final proposals to the four to six best candidate firms. Again, AIA and other professional organizations have standard forms to facilitate the process: prequalification questionnaires, bid forms, contract forms, and other commonly required documents. Sometimes these forms are adapted by the client's attorney to fit specific project requirements, but they provide a helpful starting point.

In the case of many public school programs, the process, forms, and administrative procedures must be carefully planned to conform to the applicable bidding and purchasing procedures established by local or state law. These are often set out in documents available from a state's department of education. For a summary of the laws and procedures that underlie most public bidding laws, the National Organization on Legal Problems of Education's *Planning and Financing School Improvement and Construction Projects* is good source (Bittle 1996).

A number of the same options are available in purchasing interior finishes, furnishings, and equipment. Dealers, who represent several manufacturers, or individual manufacturers will provide fixed-price bids for furniture and/or finishes. There are also many firms prepared to provide cost-plus services with or without a guaranteed maximum price, and there are a growing number of services offering the equivalent of a design/build approach.

Construction and Installation

With the start of construction and the production and delivery of furnishings and equipment, many additional companies and individuals take on major roles. In most educational facility projects, the design team is expected to provide both management and quality control throughout this process.

The management role typically includes administration of the various construction and supplier contracts; review of payment requests, change orders, claims, and related contract issues; and assistance in resolving problems in the field. On educational facility projects, both roles can require a major commitment of the design team's time. It is not uncommon for 20–30 percent of the design team's total project effort to be expended during this phase.

Occupancy

Schools require their buildings to be complete one to two months prior to occupancy by students. This time is necessary for teachers and staff to prepare. New schools are typically opened for the fall semester and sometimes in January, but are rarely opened midsemester.

The design team's work is not complete when the facility is ready for occupancy by the students. Virtually all clients moving into new facilities require assistance during the first few months.

The design team's tasks during the occupancy, or "commissioning," phase often fall into two categories: following up on incomplete construction, furnishing, and equipment issues, and organizing and transferring the information necessary to occupy and maintain the facility.

Most clients will not or cannot wait until everything is complete. They often choose to move in when the building achieves substantial completion—the point at which it can be safely occupied and used. Schools typically must be occupied before a term begins to permit teachers and staff to prepare for the start of classes. This circumstance often complicates the resolution of the open punch list (the list of still-to-be completed or corrected building items) elements.

Occupancy also often reveals construction, furnishing, and/or equipment that does not perform as intended. Sometimes these issues (such as an underperforming air-conditioning system) can be resolved with a limited amount of adjustment. Others require ongoing monitoring and additional work. Experienced design teams prepare their clients for the probability of some lingering issues and assure the clients that they will be there to help resolve them.

It is important, however, to wean clients from dependence on the design team for routine operation and maintenance. The first step in the weaning process is to collect and transfer to the client all operation and maintenance manuals, training information, and related materials. This information should include a set of record drawings describing what was actually built. These

drawings are usually prepared from marked-up working drawings provided by the contractors. In recent years it has become common for this information to be delivered in both electronic disk and hard-copy form. The electronic form can be a useful tool in future management of the facility by the client. Some design teams also prepare a reference manual containing samples, supplier data, and other information on all furnishings and finishes.

COMMON PROBLEMS AND CAUTIONS

The 11 steps outlined earlier constitute the process within which the design professionals must work. To properly serve most school facility clients, the design team must bring expertise to each step. The design team (in conjunction with the facility's owner/sponsor) is the thread that ties all 11 steps into a unified planning, design, and construction process. Thus, it is essential that design professionals be able to provide more than their particular technical service; they must also understand and be able to manage a very complex, multistep project delivery process. To be effective, design professionals should know not only how this process should proceed; they must also understand how it can go wrong. There are thousands of school construction programs each year. Some finish on time and within budget, and meet or exceed their objectives. Others encounter serious problems—some so serious that administrative staff lose their jobs, voters and school boards lose confidence, and the school suffers long-term repercussions. Many of these problems are repeated in projects across the country. Ten of the most common and serious problems are discussed in the following paragraphs.

10 COMMON PROBLEMS IN SCHOOL DESIGN AND CONSTRUCTION

- Failure to plan
- Unclear and/or unrealistic goals
- Inadequate or inconsistent client leadership
- Selecting the wrong professional team for the wrong reasons
- Ineffective management
- Placing too low a priority on quality or too high a priority on first-cost reduction
- Poor cost management
- Failure to plan for maintenance
- A drawn-out or interrupted schedule
- Failure to match the project with the best available construction resources

Failure to Plan

In some cases, careful planning may reduce the need for construction. For example, the need to build a brick-and-mortar solution may be avoided by revising class schedules or implementing other lower-cost solutions identified in the planning process. For example, one institution avoided most of a proposed building program by rescheduling the school day and improving the departmental sharing of resources. Another avoided new construction by identifying and converting underutilized spaces within the district's schools. School building programs should be driven by curriculum, teaching, and learning needs. Not every demographic shift requires a construction response.

Often, however, brick-and-mortar solutions are necessary. Many districts under budgetary pressure have deferred maintenance projects for years. Others are responding to evolving education requirements. Even districts with significant declines in student population face space shortages. The incorporation of new programs such as English as a second language (ESL) and other program changes require more rooms to serve the same number of children. Careful planning can minimize the need for building, but eventually all districts have construction needs. When the need for construction is identified by and justified through the planning process, planners should rank options in terms of their ability to effectively meet demands, and provide a clear, staged master plan for implementation.

Unclear and/or Unrealistic Goals

A building program is a complex but manageable task. The first step in effective management requires a clear statement of the program objectives. Many school systems ignore this step. Others fail to apply realism to their goal setting. Serious problems for a building program begin with goals that cannot be met because of a budget that is too low, a schedule that is too short, or an educational outcome that cannot be realized.

An unrealistic initial budget can haunt an entire building program. An initial budget estimate, publicly discussed, has a life of its own. It creates a target that everyone remembers and a standard for evaluating how well the program is managed. No school should ever publicly announce a budget target that is not based on a clear outline of all goals to be accomplished within the building program. A budget prepared at the beginning of a building program can be accurate for a project, but this happens only when it is preceded by careful planning and meticulous budget preparation processes.

The same care is needed in setting the other basic program goals. A frequent error is to expect too much from a renovation program. "Parity" between older and newer facilities is often not attainable even after amounts are spent that approach replacement cost. In some instances older facilities cannot be renovated to support modern teaching methodologies, new technology, or even current life safety requirements. The resultant compromises may point to replacement rather than renovation as the better, although harder to sell, course of action.

Goal setting, of course, should cover every other aspect of the program—from a program's ability to respond to future growth and change to a realistic target date for completion. These goals cannot be set arbitrarily but must evolve logically from a careful master-planning effort.

Inadequate or Inconsistent Client Leadership

Selection of a strong, professional team does not relieve a school district of its role as the team leader. As any experienced design professional will quote, "You cannot create a good building without a good client."

Some tasks cannot be delegated. One of these, public presentation of the proposed building program, is typically an essential part of the client's leadership obligation as well as the design team's service. The core of an effective justification of need for a building program is an effective planning process. The school leadership must make sure that the results of this planning process are clear, defensible, and effectively presented.

All school spending plans face potential opposition. The easiest ways to attack a proposed building program include pointing out lower-cost alternatives that were overlooked, highlighting shortcomings in the current management of the district's facilities, and asking questions about the accuracy of the budgeting and planning. If opponents can make a credible case concerning potential waste, lax management, or future cost overruns, a bond issue may be in trouble. If a bond issue fails initially, passage on a second round may be even more difficult. The result is often a reduced and compromised program in the future. The antidote is a thorough planning phase, with the plan properly reviewed and presented.

Once the project is funded and proceeding, it is not uncommon for the school superintendent or the board of education to change. Often these changes lead to late and costly changes in project direction.

Selecting the Wrong Professional Team for the Wrong Reasons

Few school clients can analyze their needs and present a realistic plan without some technical assistance. They require professional advice from architects and engineers as well as legal and financial advisers. There are many architectural and engineering firms with the expertise to provide the planning, design, and project management services required for a successful program. Legal and financial counsel provide guidance to ensure compliance with the expanding regulatory environment of public funding.

To identify qualified consultants able to work as a team with district personnel is a key step, which begins with a good selection process, such as that described earlier in this chapter. A professional team can be selected for the wrong reason, however.

The lowest fee proposal, or renderings, cost estimates of theoretical solutions, or other free services, are foolish bases for selection. Fees can be negotiated, in most cases, to acceptable levels. Free up-front work, completed on speculation, is rarely of any real value. A school design that is not produced in a close working relationship with the client is rarely appropriate. Most such studies rarely resemble the final, appropriate design solution. A successful school design comes from a careful process carried out by a design team that can bring design and management skills to bear over the several years it takes to implement a building program.

Ineffective Management

Although most school systems recognize their management responsibilities, a number of common errors in management compound the problems encountered in construction programs. In some cases, a district may fail to organize clear decision-making procedures. In others, micromanagement or poor interpersonal relationships between client and team members interfere with the coherent work process and team effort necessary for a successful building program.

There are several ways to organize management responsibilities for a building program:

- In some cases, the school or district administrative staff provides the day-to-day leadership and the board reviews, and approves the major policy issues (budget, team selection, major design choices, etc.).
- In other instances, the administration and board assume leadership and are supplemented by a building committee and/or additional staff with the skills to help manage the program.
- In the latter case, a building committee typically includes among its members a design professional, an attorney with construction experience, and a builder.
- Many schools also retain a professional project representative to provide day-to-day liaison with the design team and builder. This "clerk of the works" function can be ineffective if the person has limited experience or authority.

Whether the administrative staff or a committee has management responsibility, one individual should have authority for day-to-day decision making within the framework of the project plan. This individual should have the ability to build consensus among members of the committee and, when necessary, to make the decisions needed to advance the project even if a consensus does not exist. Clear allocation of responsibilities will go a long way toward enhancing program management.

Placing Too Low a Priority on Quality and Too High a Priority on First-Cost Reduction

The quality of a school building has a direct impact on the people who use it. A school building is a long-term—often 50 years or more—community asset. It provides the environment for learning. A well-planned and maintained school can facilitate its education program. A badly planned or maintained building can create barriers.

No school system wants to build a low-quality school, but poor quality may result. The most common culprits include an overemphasis on cost, an initial budget that is too low, planning only for the short term, substituting systems with a low first cost for more energy-efficient options with a lower life-cycle cost, failure to build in the capacity to grow or change in the future, and overreliance on outdated and unimaginative models.

One of the primary benefits a design team can provide the district is a clear understanding of the trade-off between cost and quality. The team must ensure that all participants in the planning process understand the differences between first cost and life-cycle cost, and between short-term and long-term needs. In addition, the design team should challenge traditional school building models and present the client with alternatives that reflect the client's specific needs and academic objectives.

Poor Cost Management

Most building programs are dominated by a focus on first cost, an overemphasis that stems from a fear of cost overruns. Construction costs—and even life-cycle costs—can be managed. There is no reason that a school program should not finish within budget, but this can be accomplished only with the help of an effective cost-management process.

An experienced design team can help a district set a realistic budget that properly reflects the district's goals, program, and master plan. Once the budget is set, the design team should present the options and their cost implications at each stage of the process. Thousands of planning and design choices are made during each phase of a building program, ranging from major program and floor plan choices in the early phases to the selection of specific building components (light fixtures, hardware, floor tile, etc.) in the later phases. For example, during schematic design a choice may be whether or not to air-condition, during design development the location and type of equipment must be selected, and in creating working drawings there are many details to resolve. In a well-structured design process, the most important of the choices—as well as their costs and benefits—should be presented to the building program's decision makers.

It is particularly important, once decisions have been made, that the client and the project team stick to them. One of the most common sources of serious budget overruns in any building program is a team that changes decisions and adds scope during construction. Although some builders count on this eventuality to increase their job profit, most find it disruptive—and even the high markups they assign to the changes barely cover the costs and aggravation. Once the scope is set and the construction contract has been bid and awarded, the natural tendency to make changes—a common weakness of most design teams and their clients—should be strongly discouraged.

Failure to Plan for Maintenance

No matter how well-built the facilities, they will not last unless they are maintained. An overemphasis on low initial construction cost (versus life-cycle cost) or poor choices in the initial planning can accelerate the need for a maintenance program. All building systems—from roofs to boilers—must be maintained. When properly maintained, their life span can often be extended. When school systems fail to plan for maintenance or balance their budgets by deferring essential repairs and preventive measures, they are increasing a long-term liability and cost. Schools across the country continue to pay a high price for this short-term thinking.

The design team can help a school system plan for and structure a maintenance program that will minimize life-cycle costs. No one, however, can eliminate the need for ongoing annual capital and maintenance expenditures. Owners should be careful in the selection of unduly complex controls and technologically advanced facility management systems that are costly and require sophisticated personnel to operate and maintain them. Sophisticated computer-based management of the mechanical systems, for example, may be too complex to be maintained and operated by a janitorial staff. Sometimes simpler is better.

A Drawn-Out or Interrupted Schedule

A school building program's leadership should not ignore the importance of momentum and continuity. A project that proceeds in a steady, orderly fashion from planning through implementation is far easier to manage. Not only is a longer process often more expensive, it can also lead to other problems. When a project stops and starts, or is stretched too far, decision making loses continuity. Key leadership or design team members will change, and the rationale for decisions will be obscured. Moreover, because even a well-run program can extend over four or five years, key team members can simply become exhausted by the process. Once a building program is initiated, there should be a commitment to seeing it through as quickly as possible, while understanding of the need is clear and the team is fresh.

Failure to Match the Project with the Best Available Construction Resources

A strong client and an experienced design team are only two-thirds of the core leadership of a building program. The third part is the construction manager. Although selection of this team member is often constrained by public bidding laws, it is essential that a school seek out the best construction resources available, both at the management level and at the subcontractor level.

In some school systems the client itself brings in the management resources via a professional construction management service, additions to its own staff, or supplemental services from the design team. In other systems, there is an intense, proactive effort to attract bidder interest from construction companies with proven track records on comparable projects. What does not work is a passive reliance on advertising and word of mouth to attract the key construction resources.

The design team can help attract the right builders by investigating the local construction industry, contacting the preferred bidders, and designing the project to fit what local construction resources do best. A poorly planned building program can be packaged in a way that discourages local

subcontractors, because it is too big, has too short a schedule, requires too much sophistication, or has too onerous contract requirements. These errors can lead to higher prices or the wrong bidders.

With a good construction team, even a difficult project can run smoothly. Yet one bad major subcontractor can make the whole process difficult.

All 10 of the above problems can be avoided. In fact, many school systems initiate high-quality building programs that finish on time and within budget and enjoy broad public support. All building programs, however—even the most successful—face problems. A well-run program will surmount these challenges. The difference between a successful program and a program that encounters severe problems typically does not depend on the wealth of the school system. The difference is sound planning and effective management.

TRENDS IN SCHOOL PLANNING AND DESIGN

School building is influenced by many of the same general changes and trends that influence almost all building types, such as the general economy, construction costs, and development of new building systems and materials, but schools are also affected by issues that are specific to educational facilities. Among the most important issues and trends relevant to school design are the following:

- Enrollment trends
- Universal preschool
- Program requirements
- Condition of the existing facilities
- Schools as community centers
- Changes in school utilization
- Research

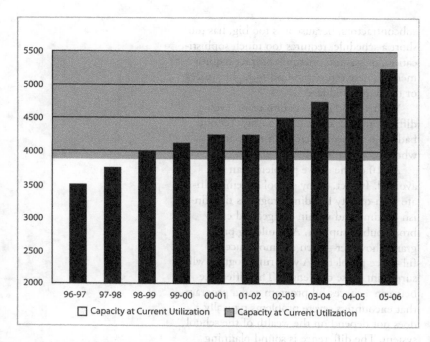

5500
5000
4500
4000
3500
3000
2500
2000

96-97 97-98 98-99 99-00 00-01 01-02 02-03 03-04 04-05 05-06

☐ Capacity at Current Utilization   ☐ Capacity at Current Utilization

▲ This graph shows high school enrollment trends in a small city school district, illustrating the growth commonly experienced in many districts in the 1990s and early 2000s.

Enrollment

One of the most important factors is the number and age of the students that must be accommodated by the school or school system. This has been the issue most vexing for many schools, because of the difficulty in predicting long-term trends. Many school districts saw steady declines until the mid-1980s. Schools were closed and converted to other uses just as the trend reversed. By the 1990s the same systems suffered overcrowding. As this book was being written, this growth in student population appeared to be leveling off except in communities still experiencing general population growth. As a result, many school systems now have professional staff or consultants addressing this issue. Private schools have had to focus on research and marketing to manage their enrollments.

Universal Preschool

It is likely that the Obama administration will support the growing consensus that investment in expanded preschool has strong long-term benefits. If this is the case, the expansion of facilities for these programs will be a major component of future school building programs.

Program Requirements

Growth in the school-age population is only one of the reasons for the severe shortage of school space that began to appear in the 1990s in so many areas of the United States. A typical school today has to accommodate a very different program. In many school systems, spaces must be created for special and remedial education, preschool programs, and classes for English as a second language (ESL), as well as for use by the broader community. In most schools average class sizes have been reduced (from 38 to 40 in public schools in the 1960s, to fewer than 22 today in many elementary schools), and new curricula have been added. Even more change can be expected to result from evolving teaching concepts.

Over the past decades the teaching of children has been based on a discipline-by-discipline model—in other words, a period for science, math, language, sociology, history, and so on. Typically, the sources of these subject matters were textbooks, supported by lectured instruction. More and more learning is now centered on projects, whereby teams of students attack a problem with a multidisciplinary approach, using any number of resources. This change in education methodology should influence the physical design of schools.

Classrooms can no longer be thought of in the traditional sense—having an instruc-

tor at the front of the room at the blackboard, with students at desks and chairs or
tablet armchairs in regimented rows. Ideally
classroom needs total flexibility; however,
total flexibility is difficult to achieve while
there is still a need to bring utilities (power,
data, or gas and water to lab benches, etc.)
to student locations. In addition, project-
based instruction may require that a physical
model or construct stay in place during a
period of study, which may last several
weeks or months. Perhaps the future classroom has to be much larger, allowing for a
traditional instructional area surrounded by
clusters of project work areas. If multidisci-
plinary/multisource instruction is advanta-
geous, then we may begin to see fewer
single-purpose rooms, such as the biology
lab or the computer lab, and instead the
common model may become a general classroom outfitted for student teams to have all
of these resources at their immediate disposal. The computer laboratory is already beginning to disappear, as students need
increasingly less pure computer and keyboarding instruction, and teachers are more
comfortable having computers integrated directly into classrooms.

   Multidisciplinary/multisource instruction
also supports the notion that teachers, more
than students, will move from class to class.
In other words, students studying a multifaceted project in a particular classroom
(with all resources at their disposal) will
have a specialist instructor visit the classroom. Middle schools are close to this approach. In kindergarten, this model has
been used for years, with the creation of activity centers within the classroom and art
and music teachers visiting the class. It is interesting to note that most state standards
require larger classroom sizes for kinder-

garten than for upper grades. This is clearly
inversely proportionate to the size of the
student, but has been deemed necessary for
the multidisciplinary/multiresource instruction traditionally used at lower grade levels.
A few decades ago, open-plan schools, or
classrooms without walls, were the rage.
This trend, for the most part, failed, and
many open-plan schools were renovated
with hard walls built to divide class areas.
Perhaps this physical model was flawed, but
it may also have failed because teaching
methodologies had not yet advanced to the

▲ Some schools built early in
the twentieth century, such as
New Trier High School, have
been maintained and
modernized to remain
examples of educational
excellence in the twenty-first
century. New Trier Hish
School, Kenilworth, Illinois.
Perkins, Fellows and Hamilton.

▶ *At the Community Education Village in Perry, Ohio, the community shares fitness, swimming, auditorium, and music spaces with a K–12 school. Perkins+Will. Photographs by Hedrick/Blessing.*

same state as the physical model. The American Architectural Foundation, in its 2006 publication *School Design and Student Learning in the 21ˢᵗ Century,* summarized this issue as follows: "The design community must respond more quickly to the ongoing changes in teaching and learning…. Flexibility must become a defining principle in school design" (p. 5).

Condition of Existing Facilities

If properly maintained, the shell of most school buildings can last more than 100 years. Many of their other systems, however, become obsolete much sooner. Because of budget pressures or poor planning, or for other reasons, obsolescence and severely deferred maintenance are common across much of the existing stock of school facilities. Nevertheless, there are more than 80,000 existing schools in the United States, and each such structure constitutes the core resource to be considered in the planning of any school building program.

Schools as Community Centers

School facilities need not be just for children. Lifelong learning (adult education) programs, the increasing incorporation of early childhood programs in school campuses, the desire by other age groups to use school athletic and cultural (theater, art, etc.) facilities, and the limitations on land and funds for duplicate community facilities are all encouraging a trend to treat schools as community centers rather than isolated precincts for teaching children and adolescents. The implications of this broader community use tend to promote a closer integration with other community facilities such as the park system and library. Community use also can lead to greater space requirements to provide for both students and adults. Art studios may need storage, athletic facilities may need separate locker rooms, and some facilities—such as a theater or auditorium—may have to be larger or better equipped to accommodate broader community use. Balancing the increased costs, however, is the increased community support that this wider usage should generate. The American Architectural Foundation's 2006 report noted, "In the coming decade, we will reach a point where 75 percent of all Americans will have no direct links to schools. Designing schools for this new age wave will increase the likelihood that this important voting bloc will continue to support public education" (p. 6).

Changes in School Utilization

In recent years more school systems have been experimenting with changes in the traditional school hours and year. Such utilization has gone far beyond traditional summer school and after-school programming. Some schools are experimenting with longer school days and year-round programming. This innovation is, in part, a response to the need to accommodate more class hours without building new facilities, but it is also a response to the need for greater flexibility and access. Adults and others need programs that are available in the evening and on weekends. Even some children can benefit from a school year that is not confined to the traditional September-to-June span. And, as noted earlier, many schools are being opened to use by the broader community.

Even during the school year, schools are experimenting with nontraditional scheduling. Instead of the usual 50-minute periods, some are using block scheduling, whereby classes are taught in longer periods, but not every day.

Such change puts more pressure on facilities by reducing or eliminating the periods when modernization, maintenance, and repairs are traditionally performed. Thus, schools are having to give greater attention to robust materials and systems that require less maintenance and have longer useful lives. Many schools are also experiencing pressure to add air-conditioning so that they can be used during the summer.

Research

One of the saddest comments on the state of K–12 education in the United States is the lack of spending on research. Chris Whittle, the founder of Edison Schools, is just one of the educational innovators who has argued for an investment in education comparable in scope to the NIH in healthcare (2005, p. 204).

The American Architectural Foundation's 2006 report noted, "Although there is a growing body of evidence regarding the link between student achievement and teacher retention, and such factors as daylight and indoor air quality, little has been done in the way of research. The link between school design and other conditions for successful learning needs to be investigated, including student mobility, truancy, graduation rates, personalization, and ways special education accommodations affect the achievement of other students" (p. 8). It is to be hoped that this consensus view will be heeded and that future schools will be strongly influenced by evidence-based design concepts.

UNIQUE DESIGN CONCERNS
Beyond the general trends are a number of design imperatives that influence most schools. Among the most important are the following:

- Making the school an inviting place for children and adolescents
- Size
- Teacher support and professional learning communities
- Technology
- Flexibility
- Regional influences
- Energy conservation
- Sustainability
- Security
- Storage

Making the School an Inviting Place for Children and Adolescents
One of the major problems the school designer must consider is

the "first impression" [the] building gives. Those of us who began our education in one of those big, ugly, fortresslike school buildings remember that First Day as a frightening experience. The grim face of the building was awesome; it was bullying. Here

was a witches' castle, a place of fierce teachers and cruel older children....But just how can a school building be made to say "welcome"? First, both the school building and approach should be designed with just that in mind. Open-armed and friendly, they greet the student without overwhelming. (Perkins 1957)

Size
The ideal size for schools has been widely debated for decades. In former Harvard president James B. Conant's influential 1959 study, *The American High School Today*, he noted, "The enrollment of many American public high schools is too small to allow for a diversified curriculum except at exorbitant expense" (p. 77). Because of the inherent problems and inefficiency of small schools, this milestone study recommended consolidation of many smaller districts.

Today, however, the debate is often more about schools being too large to be manageable and sensitive to the needs of the individual child. Recent research supports the 1997 study by Valerie Lee at the University of Michigan and Julia Smith at the University of Rochester, which argues that 600–900 students is the optimal size for secondary schools (pp. 205–207). There is, of course, no magic number for any school or even any class, but there are guidelines, as discussed in chapter 1.

Across the board, smaller elementary and middle schools are good for everyone. Small high schools have a demonstrated a generally beneficial effect in disadvantaged communities, although the variables in what makes these schools successful are more complicated. The beneficial effect of smaller size is less noticeable in high schools in more affluent neighborhoods.

Teacher Support and Professional Learning Communities

One of the major concerns about the small school movement is the potential impact on teacher collaboration. As a 2008 article in *Education Week*, "Working Smarter By Working Together," noted: "Teacher collaboration is hailed as one of the most effective ways to improve student learning."

Teacher collaboration, which some call "professional learning communities," is viewed as important to improve teaching in many schools. As the *Education Week* article illustrated in its discussion of a successful school in Illinois, the concept was described as "teachers working smarter by working together...the idea was not to create something new or different, but simply to foster an atmosphere in which teachers could learn from one another and share their colleagues' expertise so that, in the end, students would benefit."

The wide view that this is important can run counter to school sizes that only support one math teacher or one science teacher. In addition, teacher collaboration requires spaces for teachers to meet and work together. Too often, teacher support space is shortchanged.

Technology

As discussed in chapter 10, technology is finally having a profound impact on school design. The growing use of computers, Internet access, and other technologies has created major design issues.

Flexibility

Change is inevitable and accelerating. School design today must assume both growth and contraction in future enrollment; changes in average class size; new

Although computer labs are declining in importance, there is still a need for a place to teach computer skills. Park City High School, Park City, Utah. VCBO Architecture. Photograph by Dana Sohm, Sohm Photografx.

technology, teaching concepts, and curricula; and other issues that will require significant adaptation. In the 1960s one response was the open-plan school—a concept that involves the inclusion of large open spaces within the school. These large spaces were supposed to encourage flexible teaching, larger group teaching situations, and other less traditional teaching approaches. Many teachers never committed to the concept, and the spaces themselves were often anonymous, unattractive, and hard to use. Now many of these earlier experiments with flexible design have been subdivided into traditional classrooms.

Even though these earlier efforts may have been misdirected, the issue remained. Today more typical responses include the following:

• Plans that facilitate the combination of spaces

- Circulation patterns and site planning that allow for future additions
- Technology distribution that facilitates replacement and expansion
- Increased use of demountable partitions to permit reconfiguration of space
- Mechanical/electrical distribution designs that can easily accommodate changes in partition layout

These are just some of the techniques that are used to build in flexibility.

Unfortunately, such built-in flexibility is still the exception in school design. Most existing schools and too many new buildings have been designed to a more rigid model. George H. Wood wrote in *Schools That Work* (1992):

It should come as little surprise that in rooms with all desks facing the front (some bolted to the floor) the predominant mode of instruction will be lecture, drill, and recitation. Hands-on experiences require classroom arrangements that facilitate movement, group work, and varied activities. Why then are classrooms so oppressively alike in arrangement and decor?... Part of the answer is in the way schools equip classrooms. Individual desks are the norm, as opposed to tables, lounge chairs, or workstations. The rooms themselves, especially in schools built during the 1950s, are a testament to the lack of imagination of most school architects. Carbon copies of one another, designed to meet square footage requirements, each room is adaptable to any program—as long as the program works well in an open square or rectangle with windows on one side,

chalkboard on another, and little or no storage or private space for teachers or students (pp. 122–123).

Regional Influences

Schools in different parts of the country should reflect their particular regions. At times school design relied too heavily on national models, but more recently styles reflecting regional building traditions, different climates, and other variables have reemerged. Buildings that use a lot of wood are common in the Northwest, and stucco and concrete are the common materials in Florida and the Southwest. Campus-plan schools, where the components are in separate buildings, are more appropriate in milder climates—even though there are many examples of this concept in northern states. Schools in regions where the circulation can be in open corridors—as in Southern California and Florida—often have a much lower overall size (or net to gross square foot ratio) because of the reduced requirement for enclosed circulation.

In 1957 Lawrence Perkins made the following observation:

Traditional classroom design, with its rigidly arranged seating, high-silled windows on the left, and authoritarian location of the teacher, was based on several assumptions: That all students were right-handed. That daylight beamed on just a few rows was enough for the whole room. That neither teacher nor students should ever move into groups, or change location. That teacher-to-student lectures, recitations, and at-desk study were the sole activities in the classroom.

That the world around the classroom had nothing to teach the student....Today's classroom design [should be] based on other principles, most basic of which is flexibility—flexibility to keep pace with changing concepts of education's role in society, and of the teacher's role in the learning process. Also, the classroom must reflect the teaching methods of the school; it must be an efficient tool and a suitable atmosphere for education, regardless of the educational approaches used (Perkins 1957, p. 23).

This basic principle is still valid today.

Energy Conservation

The oil embargo of 1973 made energy conservation an important consideration in building design. In the first years of the energy conservation movement, this issue led to some very unfortunate concepts: very compact floor plans to reduce the amount of perimeter exposed to heat loss or gain; overinsulated, tight buildings that often created indoor air-quality problems; and even the concept (briefly implemented in Florida and a few other locations) of windowless schools. Although greater public awareness, together with the desire to minimize operating costs, have kept energy conservation an important issue, there has been a trend toward more natural design responses. There has even been a return to earlier design traditions that facilitated cross-ventilation, the use of overhangs and other shading devices to reduce solar gain, and building orientation to maximize the use of natural light to illuminate spaces. This subject is discussed further in chapter 6.

Sustainability

Closely related to energy conservation is the issue of sustainability, covered in more detail in chapter 6. The basic principles of "green" architecture (use of renewable resources, energy conservation, daylighting, avoidance of materials that cause indoor air pollution, etc.) are being incorporated in school design.

Security

Security has, unfortunately, become a major issue in many school districts. In some cases security concerns have led to designs that limit access, provide for video surveillance, or permit screening for weapons. In many others it involves the incorporation of the basic principles of "defensible space" design, such as the elimination of spaces that are not subject to random or constant visual supervision, and functional locks and other devices to discourage opportunistic crime and vandalism. In some particularly difficult areas, schools have had to be designed to provide a safe island in an otherwise dangerous neighborhood.

Storage

Storage may seem at first to be a programmatic detail, but it is typically an important issue in supporting a teaching program. As Lawrence Perkins noted, "Ask any teacher about basic requirements for classroom and school design. Storage space ranks high on the list" (Perkins 1957, p. 34). Teaching requires a wide variety of materials, and both the classroom and school must meet this need.

CHAPTER 4

SITE PLANNING

As with most other aspects of school planning and design, there is great variation in site plans. These variations stem from program, size, site cost and availability, climate, and a large number of other considerations. Therefore, this chapter focuses on the issues that are most frequently addressed in school site plans.

URBAN SITE SELECTION

Urban sites are typically constrained. Finding affordable and appropriate sites proximate to the neighborhoods being served is often a challenge. The basic criteria for site selection typically include:

- Available building area (Is it big enough to provide for a building design that, depending on the program and number of grades, allows for separate entries for several age groups or staggered schedules, vehicle drop-off and pick-up, student waiting areas, exterior play space or athletic facilities, and so on?)
- Shape (Rectangular sites are usually easier to plan.)
- Noise and other potential pollutants that could affect the site
- Soil conditions (rock, wetlands, poor structural bearing capacity, high water table, etc.)
- Environmental condition (Is a "clean-up" or environmental remediation needed because of past use?)
- Legal and regulatory constraints (easements, height and setback controls, etc.)

- Access to public transportation
- Costs of purchase and improvements
- Safe access
- Appropriate buffering from incompatible land uses, such as industry or highways
- Adjacency to other compatible land uses, such as parks, libraries, and other facilities

SUBURBAN SITE SELECTION

As with urban sites, proximity to the population being served is a central issue. There are, however, a number of unique issues that set suburban sites apart from urban sites. Student transportation needs often become an important consideration and can have a significant impact on the district's operating budget. In addition to the considerations listed for selecting urban sites, additional attention should be given to:

- Size and available buildable area— taking into account a number of factors, including:
  - Wetland reserves
  - Setbacks
  - Mandated tree preserves
  - Access to utilities such as sewer and water (If the site is remote from other major developments, the availability may be limited.)
  - Availability of roadway infrastructure (for potential major increases in car and bus traffic)
- The number of potential access points (The potential to access the site from a number of different streets may provide a

▶ *Careful planning of safe vehicular circulation and student drop-off is a key site planning consideration. Solomon Schechter School, Greenburgh, New York. Perkins Eastman. Courtesy of Perkins Eastman.*

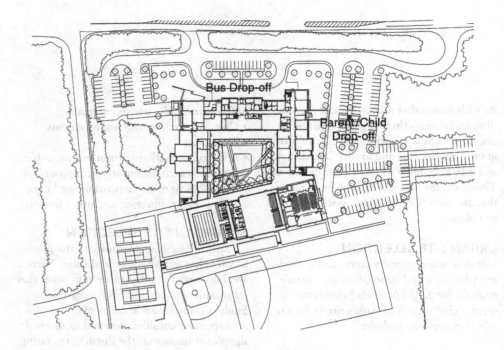

natural opportunity to separate cars from buses or to isolate service drives.)
- Optimization of the building's location and footprint to
  - Minimize the tendency to expand the footprint of the building and thereby increase the exterior wall, operational costs, and internal travel distances.
  - Make sure the building is placed "high and dry" on the site.
  - Provide more of the site for athletic and play fields with the appropriate orientation.
  - Provide more contiguous and easily observable outdoor space.
- Ability to locate the building as close as possible to roadway and utility access to reduce onsite utility runs and roadways
- Limitation of site development costs due to

- Clearing large areas of trees
- Topographic variation requiring extensive cut and fill, especially for play fields
- Variations in subsurface considerations requiring special foundations or waterproofing

SITE SIZE

Most state or district standards for site size are based on the needs of suburban schools. Although it's good to have these standards, it's not always possible to comply with them. A school in Maryland may have 35 acres, while a school with the same program and student count in New York City might have a site of 60,000 sq ft, or less than an acre and a half.

It is difficult to suggest a minimum site size for an urban school other than to look practically at the program. For example, the area required for the footprint of the largest program component, such as a gymnasium (and an appropriate amount of circulation, support, and access), might suggest the minimum site required. Urban sites are often properties with irregular footprints that reduce their commercial value for other uses. Urban sites need to be studied for their opportunity to support a school with the sustainable opportunities that include the provision for natural light in all learning spaces. This can become difficult if the site is too square or has multifloor buildings built to the lot-line on more than two sides of the site. Site size requirements such as the examples shown in the accompanying table are intended primarily for suburban sites and should be considered minimums in that context.

In addition to building size, there are several other exterior elements to be considered in determining site size:

- Administration/faculty parking
- Visitor parking
- Student parking
- Bus drop-off areas
- Service/loading areas
- Playing fields
- Playgrounds for younger children

Requirements for overall school site size are relatively consistent from state to state.

State guidelines shown in the table do not apply in a number of instances, such as many urban schools, schools that share sites with other community facilities, or in the current trend toward development of small schools.

SITE CIRCULATION
Site circulation planning begins with an understanding of the issues discussed in chapter 2:

TYPICAL STATE SITE REQUIREMENTS

STATE	BASIC ACREAGE	ADDITIONAL ACREAGE PER 100 STUDENTS UP TO MAXIMUM ENROLLMENT
New York		
Grades K–6	3	1
Grades 7–12	10	1
Florida		
Primary	3	1
Elementary	4	1
Junior high, junior-senior, or senior high	10	1
Combined schools	10	1
Virginia		
Primary or elementary	4	1
Middle school, intermediate, or junior high	10	1
Senior high or combined school	10	1

▶ Two high schools, an intermediate school/high school, and a charter middle school all share a playing field as well as other facilities built on a 6.6-acre platform over a rail yard. NYSCA Mott Haven Campus, New York, New York. Perkins Eastman. Courtesy of Perkins Eastman.

▶ This small inner city Catholic school was built on a 5,500 sq ft site with access to an adjacent park. St. Ignatius School, New York, New York. Perkins Eastman. Courtesy of Perkins Eastman.

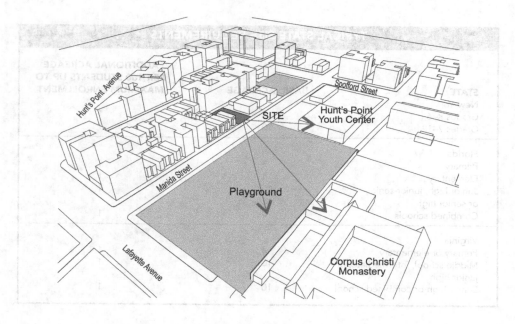

◄ *St. Ignatius School, New York, New York. Perkins Eastman. Photograph by Sarah Mechling/Perkins Eastman.*

- Entry sequence
- Internal circulation
- School size
- Plan efficiency
- Natural light and views
- Site access
- Service access
- Solar orientation and related issues
- Barrier-free access

Designing to mitigate conflicts between the several types of vehicular circulation (buses, parents, staff members, and service vehicles) and pedestrian circulation is one of the most difficult site development tasks. In addition to determining the amount of parking required, it is also important to determine the amount of busing and volume

of anticipated parent/caregiver drop-off, which varies with grade level, location, and demographics. The vehicular circulation types (bus drop-off, parent/caregiver drop-off, and parking) should be kept as separate as possible, and the walking routes of children must be kept clear of these areas. Bus drop-off areas must be designed so buses do not have to back up and children do not have to leave the safety of sidewalk areas to board. Bus stack areas must also be considered. In designing entrance drives, it should be noted that most traffic enters and leaves the site at the same peak times. These roadway systems must be designed to be long enough and wide enough to allow for this traffic. In addition, emergency vehicles must have access even during peak traffic events.

SITE PROGRAMMING

Starting with a clear understanding of the school's curriculum allows the designer to determine the appropriate types of outdoor learning opportunities and plan them as an integral part of the site. As described in chapter 1, building components of a school can be divided into generalized space categories. For initial site planning purposes, the following list is a summary of the most common building components to be accommodated on the site:

- Student assembly (classrooms, small group rooms, etc.)
- Administrative and staff
- Community and stakeholder (cafeterias, public lobbies, etc.)
- Library/media center
- Fitness and wellness (gymnasiums, pools, locker rooms, etc.)
- Performing and visual arts (theaters, music rooms, art rooms, etc.)
- Facility management and support (central plant, maintenance, shipping/receiving, etc.)

Look for these designations on the site illustrations at right. The benefit of applying this approach to site planning is twofold:

- First, it allows for design options to be explored that organize each part as it best relates to the other six parts along with analyses of options that maximize the opportunities presented by the site.
- Second, it provides the facility planner an organized kit of "parts" with which to organize the building on the site. The priority of relationship between components will vary by project. The final site plan will be influenced by curricular or district need, as well as by site-related issues such as available area, access to site, solar orientation, and zoning conformance.

Proper organization of the components will maximize the use and efficiency of the building. The table at left represents the desired relationship of these components to various exterior requirements.

The site plans and examples illustrated on page 141 indicate by number these components and show their relationship to each other in the final solution. In addition, many schools will program parts of the site for educational and recreational purposes, including:

- Pathways/walkays
- Play structures
- Free-play areas (free from equipment for creative play)
- Hard-surface open space (rectangular or square, with a variety of game markings)

▼ Building relationships to exterior areas. Source: Perkins + Will.

Legend:
- ● Primary Importance
- ◐ Secondary Importance
- ○ Optional but Not Necessary

Planning Areas		Public Access and Entrance	Located Near Parking	Located Near Transit Access	Located for Easy Recognition by Visitors	Located Near Service Entrance	Exit Directly to Outdoors	Direct Access to Playground	Has Solar and Site Orientation as a Priority	Located in a Private Zone	Located in a Moderately Quiet Zone	Can be Located in a Noisy Zone
①	Student Assembly Space		○	○			◐	◐	●	●		
②	Administrative and Staff Space	●	●	●	●	●	◐		◐	○	◐	
③	Community and Stakeholder Space	●	●	●	●	◐	◐		◐	◐	◐	●
④	Media Center Space	○	○		○				●	●	●	
⑤	Fitness and Wellness Space	◐	◐	○	●	○	◐	●		○	◐	●
⑥	Performing and Visual Art Space	◐	◐	○	●	○	○		◐	◐	◐	●
⑦	Facility Management and Support Space					●	●				◐	●

Site Planning Criteria

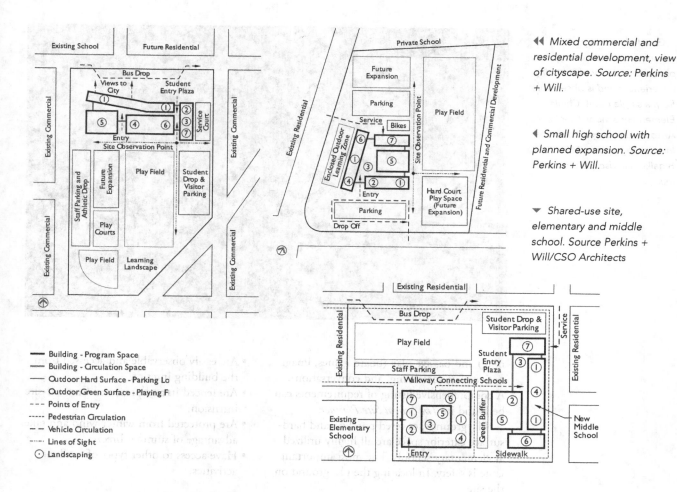

Legend:
— Building - Program Space
— Building - Circulation Space
— Outdoor Hard Surface - Parking Lo
— Outdoor Green Surface - Playing Fi
--- Points of Entry
····· Pedestrian Circulation
— — Vehicle Circulation
-·-·- Lines of Sight
⊙ Landscaping

◀◀ Mixed commercial and residential development, view of cityscape. Source: Perkins + Will.

◀ Small high school with planned expansion. Source: Perkins + Will.

▼ Shared-use site, elementary and middle school. Source Perkins + Will/CSO Architects

- Soft-surface areas, such as sand boxes or aquatic features
- Fixed seating areas for conversation, teaching, reading, or other forms of individual and group interaction
- Dramatic, musical, or other large-muscle play areas, such as amphitheaters, covered pavilions, or open-air porches

Larger, less urban or suburban sites may include the following additional outdoor areas:

- Sport and play fields
- Expanded on-site parking and bus access
- Wooded or naturally preserved areas

ELEMENTARY SCHOOL PLAY AREAS

School grounds are an important part of the school's educational experience and should be considered as carefully as the building plan. For elementary schools, the exterior program is a critical part of a school's appearance. It should include a combination of space for active play (ball games, play equipment, run-

▶ *Good elementary schoolyard equipment provides a variety of safe play experiences and is observable from a single point. Chinle Elementary School, Chinle, Arizona. Landscape Structures Inc. Photograph by Mike Bigalke/ Landscape Structures Inc.*

ning) and passive play (board games, imaginative play, socializing, and conversation). A comprehensive listing of requirements can be found in *The School Site Planner*.[1]

Playgrounds, covered porches, and hard-surface exterior space are all highly utilized at elementary schools. The most important issue is safety. In locating the playground on the site,

- Understand the curriculum and how the exterior facilities will support learning.
- Consider the locations that
  - Have good views.
  - Have a combination of sunny and shaded space.
  - Are protected from noisy roads.

- Are easily observable and accessed from the building interior.
- Are fenced in and protected from off-site intrusion.
- Are protected from winter wind and take advantage of summer breezes.
- Have access to other types of outdoor activities.

Site planning practices can vary widely between urban, suburban, and rural school districts. In urban school planning on tight sites, the building can be part of defining the site boundary or edge. Basic considerations include the following:

- Clear signage to indicate public entries should be provided, with easily controllable entry lobbies.
- The student drop-off area (bus and car) may be in the street or public right-of-way,

1. *The School Site Planner*, Public Schools of North Carolina, State Board of Education, Department of Public Instruction.

◀ This horizontal climbing wall is low to the ground for younger climbers. Normal Heights Elementary School, San Diego, California. Zagrodnik + Thomas Architects, LLP. Photograph by Dan Manlongat.

and should be connected to the building entries by wide, well-illuminated open walkways.

• Exterior play areas and open space should be rectilinear, with a minimum of blind spots.

• The building envelope should sensitively respond to its proximity to pedestrian walkways. (Consider window size and location, climbing access to the roof, etc.)

Playing Fields

The tables on page 144 show approximate sizes for playing fields. Check the local league or state association governing the play of the sport in question before determining the final court or field layout. It is also important to locate these fields with appropriate solar orientations. It is typical for courts and fields to be oriented north–south when feasible. Baseball fields should be ori-

ented on an imaginary line running east-northeast from home plate through the pitcher's mound and second base, so that the pitcher is throwing across the sun and the batter is not facing the sun when looking at the pitcher.

In many instances where field space or costs are limited, playing fields are used for multiple sports. For example, lacrosse and soccer fields can become interchangeable and restriped from one semester to the next. In most cases a football field is placed within a quarter-mile track. The track should be constructed of a synthetic all-weather surface and have a minimum of six lanes. It should include an eight-lane sprint track with appropriate overrun extension on each end and when possible. If the school participates in interscholastic track and field competitions, provision needs to be made for the following field events:

TYPICAL PLAYING FIELD DIMENSIONS

ACTIVITY	SPACE REQUIREMENTS (FT)	REQUIRED AREA (SQ FT)
High school basketball court	50 × 84—playing area only, without bleachers or out-of-bounds area; minimum 5 ft clear on sidelines, 8 ft on end lines	6,000, including minimum clearance at perimeter
American football (without bleachers)	360 × 160—playing area only, without bleachers	57,699, without additional clearances at perimeter (varies)
Soccer	Varies. Standard for high school: 195 × 330—playing area only, without bleachers	64,350, without additional clearances at perimeter (varies)
Tennis courts	60 × 120 (fence line to fence line)—should provide 4 minimum; 6 are preferable for match play	7,200, including clearances
Lacrosse	159 × 330—playing area only, without bleachers	52,470

TYPICAL PLAYING FIELD DIMENSIONS

ACTIVITY	SPACE REQUIREMENTS	DISTANCE BETWEEN BASES (FT)	PITCHING RUBBER TO HOME PLATE	APPROXIMATE AREA REQUIRED ON SITE (ACRES)
Baseball	Varies; approximately 325 ft long measured along foul lines to end of outfield. Center field distance varies, approximately 380 ft from home plate to the end of center field.	90	60 ft 6 in.	3–3.85 minimum, 4.5 preferred
Softball	Varies; 200 ft to center field fence is typical.	60	40 ft for high school in most states / 35 ft for age 10 and under	1.4 minimum
Little League baseball	175 ft long measured along foul lines to end of outfield, and approximately 180 ft from home plate to the end of center field	60	46 ft 0 in.	1.0

* More detailed field layout information is available from a variety of sources, including the National Federation of State High School Associations at www.nfhs.org.

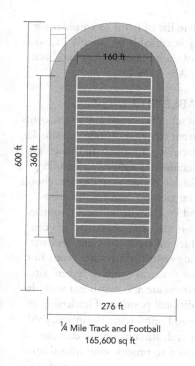

160 ft

600 ft

360 ft

276 ft

¼ Mile Track and Football
165,600 sq ft

120 ft

60 ft
Tennis
7,200 sq ft

330 ft

195 ft

Soccer
64,350 sq ft

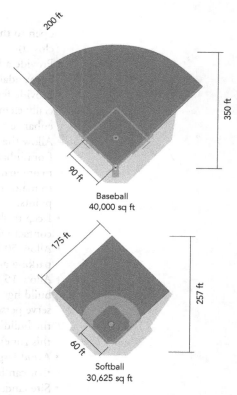

200 ft

350 ft

90 ft

Baseball
40,000 sq ft

175 ft

257 ft

60 ft

Softball
30,625 sq ft

▲ *Typical sports field regulation dimensions. Perkins Eastman. Courtesy of Perkins Eastman.*

- Jumping events
  - High jump
  - Pole vault
  - Long jump
  - Triple jump
- Throwing events
  - Shot put
  - Discus
  - Hammer
  - Javelin

SECURITY AND SAFETY CONCEPTS IN SITE AND BUILDING DESIGN

Increased security attention could be required by expanded hours of use, community use, nontraditional schedules, and increased neighborhood crime or external threats. This issue requires a clear set of guidelines be established for each project. The National Crime Prevention Council (NCPC) recommends the following for schools with significant security concerns:

- Minimize vehicle access points to those required for operation and life safety.
- Provide means for vehicle speed reduction, minimizing perpendicular vehicular approaches directly into buildings occupied during normal operation.
- Plan the site to eliminate the need for students to cross roadways to access playgrounds or other campus facilities.
- Locate playgrounds and exterior learning environments with good visibility from the building interior and by security personnel during off hours (if the facilities are to be

open to the public when the facility is closed).

- Provide adequate site lighting to discourage vandalism.
- Provide fencing around play areas, especially elementary school playgrounds, to enhance a sense of security.
- Allow the maximum practical distance from inhabited buildings (excludes maintenance, storage facilities, etc.) to major roadways and vehicular access points.
- Keep trash containers away from direct contact with inhabited buildings.
- Allow 50 ft from inhabited buildings to parking areas (excluding drop-offs).
- Allow 15 ft of unobstructed space around buildings to allow the opportunity to observe persons or unusual objects next to the building (avoid low landscaping within this zone).
- Avoid large recesses in the perimeter wall that can be used for hiding.
- Site landscaping and lighting can also help with security-related site concerns.
- Use high trees and low bushes (less than three feet high) to deter hiding and provide shading of paved areas (to reduce heat-island effect).
- Use fencing around the site perimeter.
- Place building along the site perimeter to protect site open space.
- Provide general, nonintrusive site lighting in all parking, pedestrian, and entry areas.
- Install security lighting with photocell timer and on/off capacity at selected building and parking lots.
- Separate athletic fields from informal gathering areas.
- Install fences between athletic facilities and school buildings.

A complete list of items to consider for school safety is available on the NCPC website as part of their School Safety and Security Toolkit, Appendix D.[2]

SUSTAINABLE SITE DESIGN

Because of a school's central role in the community, current trends in sustainable site design are especially appropriate in the design of school facilities. As with other building types, sustainable design practices for schools can reduce impacts on community infrastructure and local environmental resources. These lower-impact site improvements can likewise reduce up-front construction costs as well as long-term maintenance costs. But beyond these practical benefits, "green" site design initiatives are also consistent with the school's traditional position of leadership in establishing and reinforcing community values. To that end, sustainable site elements can be designed to provide educational opportunities, promoting an awareness of environmental stewardship and conservation in the school population as well as the community at large.

Through efficient site design, site disturbance can be minimized to reduce erosion and soil loss and to limit the destruction of natural habitat. Efficient building design along with the thoughtful layout of roads and parking areas can also minimize the amount of site coverage by impervious surfaces, thereby reducing potential storm water runoff. For those areas that must be paved, practices such as specifying perme-

2. National Crime Prevention School Safety and Security Toolkit, Appendix D: Basic School Safety and Security Assessment, available at http://www.ncpc.org/cms/cms-upload/ncpc/files/BSSToolkit_D_Assessment.pdf (accessed 6/2009).

◀ *Sustainable features of an addition include a green roof, solar chimneys, outdoor classrooms, and photovoltaic panels. Sidwell Friends Middle School, Washington, D.C. KieranTimberlake.*

able pavement, using vegetated buffers and swales to control runoff, and including bioretention areas to convey and infiltrate storm water can all contribute to dramatic reductions in impacts on local sewer systems as well as lowering infrastructure costs. In suburban and rural settings, school sites are often relatively large, offering opportunities for natural drainage and infiltration systems that may not be feasible for smaller or more compact sites. Other practices include the use of "green roofs" to reduce solar heat gain, rainwater harvesting for reuse, landscape design that features native plants and the restoration of natural habitat, and the use of site lighting that complies with "dark sky" guidelines to minimize light pollution (see chapter 6).

Opportunities for environmental learning can be enhanced by site amenities that could include

• Water gardens
• Outdoor laboratories
• Preservation of soil that can support native vegetation
• Formal and informal opportunities to interact with the site

▲ *Perry Community Education Village; Perry, Ohio.* The "village" comprises a K–4 school, a grades 5–8 school, a high school, and a phys ed/community fitness center—all located on 162-acre site rich in mature trees, creeks, and ravines. One ravine separates the earlier and later grades. Buildings are arranged around formal courtyards and include a 850-seat theater. Perkins + Will associated with Burgess & Niple Ltd., architects. Photo: Hedrich/Blessing.

◀ *Concordia International School Shanghai; Shanghai, China.* This K–12 campus was built on a rural site that is now surrounded by the rapidly growing city. The final two phases include the elementary school, a new high school, and this fine arts center that incorporates both presentation and learning environments, including a 400-seat theater, art studios, and music practice areas. Phase 1, Perkins + Will; Phases 2, 3, Perkins Eastman. Photo: Tim Griffith.

▶ *Dena Primary Center; Los Angeles, California.* This colorful 25,000 sq ft center provides a variety of services for young children and their families in an urban neighborhood in East Los Angeles. Rachlin Architects Incorporated. Photo: Tom Bonner.

▼ *Family Development Center and Charter School; University Park, Illinois.* This center incorporates a charter school for the early grades, an early childhood training facility for the university, and a child therapy program. Ross Barney Architects. Photo: Steve Hall/Hedrich Blessing Photographers.

▲ **St. Matthews Parish School; Pacific Palisades, California.** This elementary school for grades 1–4 is built into the side of a hill. Outdoor connections between program areas, made possible by the local climate, result in a significant reduction in the gross square footage of the building. Lake | Flato Architects in collaboration with Gensler. Photo: Fotoworks/Benny Chan.

◀ **Dr. Theodore Alexander Science Center School; Los Angeles, California.** This widely published K–5 charter school is tucked into a park, of which its green roof is a visual extension. Morphosis Architects. Photo: Gary Leonard.

▶ **PS 189; Bronx, New York.**
This facility combines an
elementary and a middle
school, which share a library,
cafeteria, art and music
rooms, gymnasium, and a
300-seat auditorium.

The school also houses
nine classrooms and related
administrative space for
special education students.
Perkins Eastman.
Photo: Paúl Rivera/ArchPhoto.

◀ **Camino Nuevo Charter
Academy; Los Angeles,
California.** This 12-classroom
school adaptively reuses a
minimall as the core of the
first phase of a new charter-
school campus. An addition
to the original structure
provides a new secure entry
and a protected courtyard for
recess, lunch hours, and safe
pickup and drop-off.
Daly Genik Architects.
Photo: Tom Bonner.

◀ **St. Ignatius School; New York, New York.** *This small new Jesuit school was built on an infill site in an inner-city neighborhood. The school serves a Latino and African-American neighborhood and uses an adjacent park and playground for physical education and recreation. Perkins Eastman. Photo: Sarah Mechling/Perkins Eastman.*

▼ **Roger Ludlowe Middle School; Fairfield, Connecticut.** *The design team for this new 200,000 sq ft, 875-student middle school was selected following an invited competition. It was built next to one of the community's two high schools, which was renovated at the same time. The project took advantage of the sloping site to put the gymnasium and auditorium at the level of the playing fields, with the classrooms on the upper floors and the other common areas surrounding a midlevel patio. Perkins Eastman. Photo: Woodruff/Brown.*

◀ *Concordia International School Shanghai, High School; Shanghai, China.* This new high school is the final phase of a large international school's Shanghai campus. In addition to providing a full complement of academic and physical education facilities, the building features a state-of-the-art information commons/library. The building also incorporates a number of sustainable design features, including geothermal heating and cooling, a green roof over the gym and library, skylights that bring daylight into large spaces, and sustainable materials throughout. Perkins Eastman. Photo: ShuHe.

▶ *Fairhaven High School; Fairhaven, Massachusetts.* The original 1906 school building is an historic landmark. This structure was carefully restored while converting the existing gymnasium into a library. A carefully sited addition provides a new gymnasium, auditorium, art classrooms and science labs. Flansburgh Architects. Photo: Steve Rosenthal.

◀ **Greenwich Academy Upper School; Greenwich, Connecticut.** *The design team for this new upper school and library addition to this well known private academy used the building to link the campus's upper and lower levels across a topographically complex site. Skidmore, Owings & Merrill LLP. Photo: Robert Polidori.*

▼ **Mariner High School; Everett, Washington.** *Additions at both ends of this school transformed its image and gave it a new, much stronger identity in the community. DLR Group. Photo: Chris J. Roberts Photography.*

▲ *Green Chimneys School; Brewster, New York.* A farm-based boarding school for children and teenagers who have been unsuccessful in a traditional educational setting and require a small, structured, and therapeutically supportive setting. Perkins Eastman. Photo: Chuck Choi.

▶ *The Reece School; New York, New York.* A private, nonprofit elementary school in Manhattan serving psychologically fragile, special-needs children. Platt Byard Dovell White Architects LLP. Photo: Jonathan Wallen.

CHAPTER 5

CODES

Almost all construction is governed by a variety of codes and related regulations. Because of the importance of the health and safety of children, school buildings are among the most carefully regulated. Many states, for example, have at least eight to ten codes that govern the construction of a school's major building systems.

Most states have detailed regulations written specifically to govern school building design and construction. Some of these are more than 100 pages long and cover everything from space standards (also discussed in chapter 1) to bidding procedures to specific provisions for emergency evacuation. Many of these regulations are also available on the Internet.

In general, all of this regulation is directed at seven primary issues: life safety; adequate space and facilities for teaching, appropriate building systems and construction practices, public policy (historical preservation, energy conservation, accessibility for disabled persons), enforcement, fiscal and anticorruption controls, and land-use policy.

The National Conference of States on Building Codes and Standards (NCSBCS) published the *Directory of Building Codes and Regulations*,[1] an extremely useful directory of the relevant codes that apply in each state as well as in the cities that have their own supple-

mental codes. Since the first edition of this book, one particularly important change in the code framework governing schools has been the widespread acceptance of the International Building Code (IBC) as the national model building code. The IBC and its implications for school design are covered in detail in *Building Codes Illustrated for Elementary and Secondary Schools* (Winkel et al. 2007). This reference provides an even more recent source on the subject than the NCSBCS directory.

The codes are applied unevenly to public and private schools. Public schools are often subject to state rather than local regulation. Therefore, they are often exempt from local land-use controls. Private schools, on the other hand, may be subject to local land-use controls but are often exempt from meeting state department of education standards for classroom size and other factors.

LIFE SAFETY

The most important issue in the development of any code is life safety. For obvious reasons, all state and local codes—as well as enforcement—start with this issue.

This subject is covered in exceptional detail by *Building Codes Illustrated for Elementary and Secondary Schools* (2007). The key life safety considerations built into the codes include fire safety, environmental safety, and elimination of hazards.

1. *Fire safety.* The following are key issues in fire safety:
    * Reduction of the likelihood of fire through use of noncombustible

---

1. The *Directory of Building Codes and Regulations* can be obtained from the National Conference of States on Building Codes and Standards, 505 Huntmar Park Drive, Suite 210, Herndon, VA 22070 (703-437-0100). The information is also available online to NCSBCS members at http://www.ncsbcs.org/.

materials in construction. For example, wood-frame construction is discouraged or prohibited in many states, and there are often restrictions on the use of flammable interior finishes.

- Reduction of the potential of fire-related structural collapse. Many codes require

structural assemblies that will withstand some period of exposure to fire.

- Early detection through the use of smoke and/or heat detectors—particularly in highly hazardous areas such as kitchens and mechanical spaces—is now commonly required.

NCSBCS CODE SUMMARY, MINNESOTA

TYPE OF CODE	STATE CODE	TECHNICAL BASIS	APPLICABILITY	PREEMPTIVE APPLICATION
Building	State Building Code	1994 UBC with state amendments	All buildings	Mandatory. Local jurisdictions may not amend.
Mechanical	Minnesota Mechanical Code	1991 UMC with state amendments	All buildings	Mandatory. Local jurisdictions may not amend.
Plumbing	Minnesota Plumbing Code	State-written	All public buildings or buildings connected to public use water or sewer system.	Mandatory. Local jurisdictions may not amend.
Electrical	State Building Code	1996 NEC	All buildings	Mandatory. Local jurisdictions may not amend.
Energy	Minnesota Energy Code	State-written	All buildings	Mandatory Local jurisdictions may not amend.
Gas	Minnesota Mechanical Code	1991 UMC with state amendments	All building	Mandatory. Local jurisdictions may not amend.
Fire prevention	Fire Safety, Chapter 7510	1991 UFC with state amendments	All buildings	Mandatory. Local jurisdictions may amend to make more stringent.
Life safety	Fire Safety, Chapter 7510	NFPA 101, 1991 edition, as Supplement to fire code	All buildings	Mandatory. Local jurisdictions may amend to make more stringent.
Accessibility	State Building Code	1994 UBC, Chapter 11 and Appendix Chapter 11, with state amendments	All buildings	Mandatory. Local jurisdictions may not amend.

Source: Directory of Building Codes and Regulations, April 1998. National Conference of States on Building Codes and Standards Inc., p. 96.

- Fire and smoke containment through use of compartmentalization and rated assemblies between floors is also commonly required. Highly hazardous areas, including mechanical rooms, storage areas, and the like, must typically be enclosed with fire-rated walls, floors, and ceilings.
- Fire suppression through mandatory installation of extinguishers, fire-suppression systems in highly hazardous spaces such as kitchens, and, increasingly, the use of sprinklers. The National Fire Protection Association points out that there has never been a multiple-death fire in a building with a functioning sprinkler system.
- Evacuation in case of fire or other emergency is the most universal concept built into the codes. Almost all codes require that there be two means of egress from most spaces. For classrooms, this is typically accomplished by having one exit go into a fire-rated corridor leading to a fire stair or directly outside, combined with an "escape window" or door to the outside. Providing a choice of evacuation routes—in case one is blocked—is fundamental. Most codes also define exit widths and the spacing of fixed seating in larger spaces such as gyms and auditoriums.

Typical of the standards applied are those in the New York State Education Department's *Manual of Planning Standards*:

Main corridor width without lockers 8 ft
Main corridor width with lockers one side 9 ft
Main corridor width with lockers two sides 10 ft
Secondary corridor without lockers 6 ft
Secondary corridor with lockers one side 7 ft
Secondary corridor with lockers two sides 8 ft
Auditorium and cafeteria required exit units net sq ft 600
Back to back spacing of seating not less than 33 in.
Minimum clear distance between seating in the up position 12 in.
continental seating 16 in.
Maximum number of seats if aisles at each end 15

- *Fire fighting.* Some codes require emergency and fire access to all sides of a school building. They usually establish requirements for the standpipe, hydrant, or other devices required for fire fighting. Typical requirements call for hydrants to be located so that any fire can be reached with 500 ft of hose and that they be able to provide 500 gallons per minute.

2. *Environmental safety.* The codes dealing with environmental safety issues vary from state to state; the following are among the most common:
- Required ventilation (see "Ventilation" in chapter 8) and indoor air-quality standards (see "Indoor Environmental Quality" in chapter 6)
- Required removal or containment of asbestos
- Required removal or containment of lead-based paint
- Requirements for food-service equipment (stainless steel, easily cleaned, etc.) and food-preparation and service spaces

- Requirements for safe drinking water and water fountains
- Minimum lighting standards (see chapter 13)

3. *Elimination of hazards.* Most state codes and departments of education also try to minimize potential hazards. Typical requirements and prohibitions in the codes include the following:
   - Use of flooring materials that minimize slipping
   - Marking of glazed doors and sidelights
   - Use of safety glass or glazing within 18 in. of the floor, corridor glazing within 48 in. of the floor in corridors, and glazing in areas such as gymnasiums
   - Site designs that minimize pedestrian-vehicular conflicts, with particular emphasis on drop-off and pickup areas (see chapter 4)
   - Physical restrictions on access to highly hazardous spaces such as boiler rooms, electrical closets, etc.
   - Elimination of overhead power lines that cross school property
   - Restrictions on the location and use of high-pressure boilers
   - Availability of emergency showers in chemistry classrooms
   - A variety of guidelines for natural gas use and distribution
   - Prevention of child access to electrical heating devices

SPACE STANDARDS
Most states establish standards for classroom size as well as the sizes of many other school facilities. This subject is discussed in chapter 1. It should be noted, however, that meeting these standards may not be required in private and parochial schools.

APPROPRIATE BUILDING SYSTEMS AND CONSTRUCTION PRACTICES
The largest quantity of code material regulates the selection of appropriate building systems and methods of construction. The Building Officials and Code Administrators (BOCA) International Code is one of the most widely used compendiums of building codes. Many of its codes also refer to other codes or standards, such as those of the National Electrical Code (NEC); the American Society of Heating, Refrigerating, and Air-Conditioning Engineers (ASHRAE); and the American National Standards Institute (ANSI). State codes typically include separate codes or code sections for mechanical, electrical, and plumbing systems.

PUBLIC POLICY
Schools are often subject to laws and codes passed to further a certain public policy, such as historic preservation, energy conservation, and/or accessibility for disabled persons.

Historic Preservation
Preservation regulations vary widely across the United States. In some states, schools are exempt. In others, a school designated as a landmark or as historically significant may involve additional public reviews, restrictions on renovations and additions, and/or a prohibition against demolition.

Energy Conservation
Most states have an energy code, which usually focuses on the energy performance of the building envelope (see chapter 6). Other sustainable design objectives, such as recycling, are becoming code requirements as well.

Accessibility

One of the most discussed—and often mis-understood—code issues is the Americans with Disabilities Act (ADA). Many people think it is a building code when it is, in fact, a civil rights law whose intent has now been built into many existing codes. The general intent of this important legislation is stated in Title II of the law: "Subject to the provisions of this subchapter, no qualified individual with a disability shall, by reason of such disability, be excluded from participation in or be denied the benefits of services, programs, or activities of a public entity, or be subjected to discrimination by any such entity."

Although the law applies only to a "public entity," ADA's supplemental technical guidelines and most building codes have been developed or revised so that they apply to virtually all schools, including private schools. They apply to faculty and staff, students, and—in the case of some school facilities that have community functions—the general public.

This section of this chapter summarizes some of the guidelines that generally govern the application of this law and the related codes, but these have been subject to myriad local and state variations and interpretations. This discussion should not be considered either legal advice or an interpretation of every accessibility code, but is intended as a framework to help in understanding and interpreting this evolving area of building regulation. For a more complete discussion of the legal issues, the National Organization on Legal Problems of Education's (NOLPE) *Planning and Financing School Improvement and Construction Projects* (1996) has an informative chapter, and technical guidelines are typically provided in state or local acces-

sibility codes as well as in the ADA and ANSI guidelines. Probably the best source on this topic is *Compliance with the Americans with Disabilities Act: A Self-Evaluation Guide for Public Elementary and Secondary Schools*, published in 1996 by the U.S. Department of Education, Office of Civil Rights. The text, listed as ED401688, is available online through the Educational Resources Information Center, an online digital library of education research and information, at www.eric.ed.gov.

Although most people are aware of the need to create an accessible route for mobility-impaired individuals to all functions, ADA also covers other disabilities, including sight, hearing, and other impairments. Thus, properly sloped curb ramps, elevators, accessible toilet stalls, accessible telephones and drinking fountains, and other such accommodations are not necessarily enough. Alarms suitable for hearing-impaired persons, hardware appropriate for people with hand impairments such as arthritis, and other changes may be needed as well. The codes in most states establish the minimum standards, but the definitions of disability are still evolving.

An area that is the subject of particular debate is the degree to which design guidelines should be adjusted for children. Some code officials believe that children should learn to use the same aids as the general public, whereas others argue for aids that reflect children's size, strength, and experience.

The main issue facing school systems, of course, is what to do with the barriers in existing facilities. There are choices. For example, a school can use ramps, lifts, or elevators to permit a disabled student to get to the library, or it can have an aide take a book cart to each classroom. The spirit of law, however, requires the barrier-free route because it offers library services to disabled students in the same setting as others.

The regulations suggest several possible methods of compliance:

- Redesign of equipment
- Reassignment of services to accessible buildings
- Assignment of aides to beneficiaries
- Home visits
- Delivery of services at alternative accessible sites
- Alteration of existing facilities
- Construction of new facilities
- Use of accessible rolling stock or other conveyances

New buildings built or significantly altered after January 26, 1992, however, are to be designed and built so that they are "readily accessible to and usable by individuals with disabilities." The state codes are now reasonably clear, but the federal government references the *Americans with Disabilities Act Accessibility Guidelines for Buildings and Facilities* (ADAAG), published as 28 CFR Part 36 (1994) and available through the Department of Justice website at www.ada.gov under ADA Design Standards. Some state codes may reference the International Code Council (ICC) and American National Standards Institute (ANSI) standard ICC/ANSI A117.1–2003.

Most codes also outline the enforcement procedures that will be used.

FISCAL AND ANTICORRUPTION CONTROLS

State laws and other regulations typically govern the purchasing of design services, construction, equipment, and furnishings.

Although most states permit qualification-based selection of professional services, construction, equipment, and furnishings are typically purchased via a competitive bidding process. The NOLPE monograph *Planning and Financing School Improvements and Construction Projects* mentioned earlier also has a good chapter on this subject, "Fundamentals of Competitive Bidding."

Many districts also impose a number of disclosure and procedural requirements to avoid conflicts of interest and other problems. After this screening, most jurisdictions require the school to award the contract to the "lowest responsible and responsive bidder." A responsible bidder is one "who has the capability to perform the contract requirements and the integrity and reliability which will assure good faith performance." A responsive bidder is one "who has submitted a bid which conforms in all material respects to the Invitation for Bids."

LAND-USE POLICY

Many states exempt public schools from most local land-use controls. Private and parochial schools, as well as a minority of public schools, may be subject to some or all of the following:

- Planning and/or Zoning Board review, which typically focuses on issues such as vehicular access, storm water management, landscaping, and other site planning considerations, as well as compliance with the height, setback, lot coverage, parking, and other requirements of local zoning.
- Coastal Zone, State Historic Preservation Office, and other reviews, which typically deal with one of the public policy issues noted earlier in this chapter.
- Board of Architectural Review scrutiny,

which typically focuses on the materials and aesthetics of the proposed design.

- State or local department of transportation regulations, which often govern the road improvements, curb cuts, and other actions necessary for vehicular access.
- Environmental-impact review, which is often mandated in the expenditure of significant public monies.

CONCLUSION

Navigating the increasingly complex code and public-approval environment has become a major task for most schools and their planning and design teams. It is not unusual for the various reviews to add 6–18 months to the time normally required to plan, design, and start construction of a school.

CHAPTER 6

SUSTAINABLE DESIGN ISSUES

The U.S. Green Building Council (USGBC) released its landmark LEED (Leadership in Energy and Environmental Design) Green Building Rating System Version 2.0 as the first edition of this book was in production. This now widely used rating system, combined with the growing concerns about global warming, the deteriorating environment, and high energy costs, has catapulted sustainable design into a central design issue for most building types.

One of the largest groups to embrace a sustainable design agenda has been the leadership of both public and private schools. This is understandable. As long-term owner/operators, schools are constantly seeking ways to contain and/or reduce operating costs. Moreover, because their mission is to educate children in a safe, healthy, and supportive environment; it is incumbent on them to ask their facility teams to incorporate best practices, as validated by research and evidence-based design.

The interest by school clients has also led to a number of specialized efforts to bring sustainable design to educational facilities.

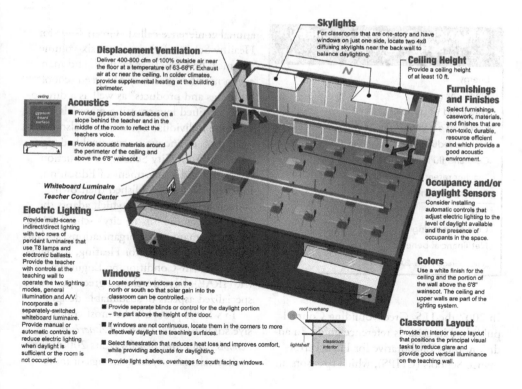

Skylights
For classrooms that are one-story and have windows on just one side, locate two 4x8 diffusing skylights near the back wall to balance daylighting.

Displacement Ventilation
Deliver 400-800 cfm of 100% outside air near the floor at a temperature of 63-68°F. Exhaust air at or near the ceiling. In colder climates, provide supplemental heating at the building perimeter.

Ceiling Height
Provide a ceiling height of at least 10 ft.

Furnishings and Finishes
Select furnishings, casework, materials, and finishes that are non-toxic, durable, resource efficient and which provide a good acoustic environment.

Acoustics
■ Provide gypsum board surfaces on a slope behind the teacher and in the middle of the room to reflect the teachers voice.
■ Provide acoustic materials around the perimeter of the ceiling and above the 6'8" wainscot.

Occupancy and/or Daylight Sensors
Consider installing automatic controls that adjust electric lighting to the level of daylight available and the presence of occupants in the space.

Whiteboard Luminaire
Teacher Control Center

Electric Lighting
Provide multi-scene indirect/direct lighting with two rows of pendant luminaires that use T8 lamps and electronic ballasts. Provide the teacher with controls at the teaching wall to operate the two lighting modes, general illumination and A/V. Incorporate a separately-switched whiteboard luminaire. Provide manual or automatic controls to reduce electric lighting when daylight is sufficient or the room is not occupied.

Colors
Use a white finish for the ceiling and the portion of the wall above the 6'8" wainscot. The ceiling and upper walls are part of the lighting system.

Windows
■ Locate primary windows on the north or south so that solar gain into the classroom can be controlled.
■ Provide separate blinds or control for the daylight portion – the part above the height of the door.
■ If windows are not continuous, locate them in the corners to more effectively daylight the teaching surfaces.
■ Select fenestration that reduces heat loss and improves comfort, while providing adequate for daylighting.
■ Provide light shelves, overhangs for south facing windows.

Classroom Layout
Provide an interior space layout that positions the principal visual tasks to reduce glare and provide good vertical illuminance on the teaching wall.

roof overhang
lightshelf
classroom interior

◀ Sustainable concepts can have a profound impact on classroom design. Courtesy of Collaborative for High Performance Schools.

SUSTAINABLE DESIGN ISSUES

▶ *USGBC LEED for Schools.*
U.S. Green Building Council.
Graphic by Post Typography.

FINANCIAL BENEFITS OF GREEN SCHOOLS ($/SQ FT)	
Energy	9
Emissions	1
Water and wastewater	1
Increased earnings	49
Asthma reduction	3
Cold and flu reduction	5
Teacher retention	4
Employment impact	2
Total	74
Cost of greening	(3)
Net financial benefits	71

Source: Gregory Kats, 2006. Table A.

annual conference called "Green Tools for Healthy Schools," maintains a six-volume technical best-practices manual, and manages a member directory of "green school buildings and products" as well as a directory of "certified low-emitting materials."

Some individual districts have also developed tools to encourage sustainable design. The New York City School Construction Authority and Department of Education, for example, have published their own "Green Schools Guide," which adapts the USGBC material for the city's schools. And, of course, many other organizations, such as the American Society for Heating, Refrigerating, and Air-Conditioning Engineers (ASHRAE), have developed green guides on specialized aspects of sustainable design.

In what is probably the most comprehensive study to date, *Greening America's Schools: Costs and Benefits* (Kats 2006), the author calculates typical savings of more

In 2007 the U.S. Green Building Council published its schools reference guide. In addition, the Collaborative for High Performance Schools (CHPS), which sponsors an

◀ Photovoltaic panels doubling as a shading device. Fossil Ridge High School, Fort Collins, Colorado. RB+B Architects, Inc. Photograph by David Patterson Photography.

than $70 per sq ft versus an average premium for sustainable design of $3 per sq ft. Even if one challenges some of the details, the report makes a compelling case that sustainable design pays for itself.

Sustainable design research, bibliography, and experience have grown rapidly. In addition, a large number of school clients are now mandating green design. For many, "green design" means more than energy conservation. Today, many accept the USGBC's

broader definition, which calls for sustainable sites, water efficiency, energy and atmosphere conservation, materials and resources management, and indoor air quality. This chapter follows this widely used outline.

SUSTAINABLE SITES
The objectives of sustainable site design include improving the interaction of the built environment with its surroundings. This

▶ *Part of this school's LEED Gold rating came from renewable energy sources, but more came from creative reuse of a convent. Felician Sisters Our Lady of the Sacred Heart High School, Coraopolis, Pennsylvania. Perkins Eastman. Photograph by Alexander Denmarsh.*

subject was touched on in chapter 4, but the USGBC and many others have created checklists of site selection and development strategies that contribute to an overall sustainable design goal. The major recommendations include:

1. *Prevent pollution from construction activity.* Erosion and sedimentation control, as well as mitigation measures for storm water contamination, air pollution, and construction noise, are now becoming standard requirements for any major construction project in many communities.
2. *Select appropriate sites.* Sustainable design guidelines discourage siting schools on previously undeveloped land that is the habitat of an endangered species, or is within 100 ft of designated wetlands or within 50 ft of a significant water body. For obvious reasons, these same guide-

lines discourage the use of parkland unless this land is replaced with land of equal or greater value. A corollary of this is a preference for sites that can use existing utilities and other infrastructure and that have appropriate adjacencies with other compatible community uses.
3. *Use sustainable design factors in site and building layout.* Sustainable design factors include orienting buildings to take advantage of daylighting and avoid unwanted shadows from adjacent structures; minimizing shadow impacts from the proposed school buildings on adjacent properties; using adjacent buildings, natural land formations, and landscape to shelter the school from extreme weather and excessive solar gain; and creating appropriate locations for renewable energy generation.
4. *Rehabilitate damaged sites.* Adaptive reuse of existing structures and/or reclamation of damaged sites, such as remediated brownfields, is a common sustainable design objective. The lack of affordable, appropriately located sites in many urban areas has made use of these options an increasingly common practice. Moreover, on reclaimed sites, restoring part of the site with native or adapted vegetation is encouraged.
5. *Reduce pollution and land development from automobile use.* Siting schools near public transit and providing on-site, safe bicycle storage can reduce the demand for on-site parking and automobile use. Some schools are also providing preferred parking spaces for low-emitting and fuel-efficient vehicles.
6. *Minimize water pollution.* Sustainable design guidelines call for implementation of a storm water management plan that

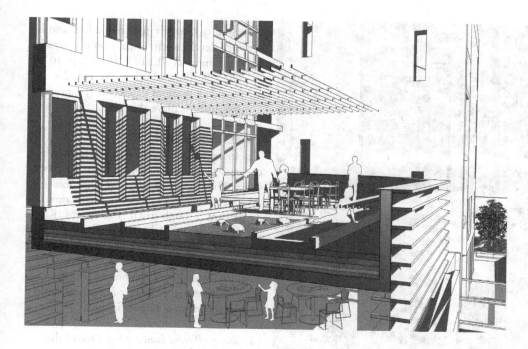

◄ *Careful sun control is part of a comprehensive lighting program. Cairo American College, Cairo, Egypt. Perkins Eastman. Courtesy of Perkins Eastman.*

▼ *Bicycle storage is a basic site requirement. Courtesy of Dero Bike Rack Company.*

reduces impervious surfaces, promotes natural infiltration, eliminates contaminants, and removes suspended solids in storm water runoff.

7. *Reduce heat island effect.* Heat islands (thermal gradient differences between developed and undeveloped land) are believed to have a negative impact on microclimates and habitats. This guideline calls for limiting the amount of impervious hardscape, use of open-grid pavement systems that are at least 50 percent pervious, use of light-colored paving systems, and use of landscaping to shade paved areas. Related guidelines cover the roof surfaces of the school. The guidelines call for the use of roofing materials with a high solar reflectance index (SRI) to reduce heat buildup, and/or use of a vegetated "green" roof.

8. *Reduce light pollution.* According to the USGBC, the intent of this guideline is to "minimize light trespass from the building and site, reduce sky-glow to increase night sky access, improve nighttime

visibility through glare reduction, and reduce development impact on nocturnal environments" (LEED-NC 2.2, p. 101). The USGBC and other green guides provide a number of specific recommendations to achieve this goal.

WATER EFFICIENCY

The importance of conserving water—in particular potable water—is increasingly obvious. The study *Greening America's Schools* calculated an average water-use reduction of 32 percent through sustainable design (Kats 2006, p. 7). Sustainable design focuses on reducing or eliminating the use of potable water for landscape irrigation, employing advanced wastewater technologies, and reducing water usage. Some of the most widely employed design solutions include

1. *Water-efficient landscaping.* One of the major uses of water in schools is irrigation of fields and other landscaped areas. Sustainable design strategies include the use of landscape material that requires little or no irrigation, installation of water-efficient irrigation systems, use of captured rainwater, use of recycled wastewater, and use of other sources of nonpotable water.
2. *Innovative wastewater technologies.* A second approach to a reduction in potable water demand is to reduce generation of wastewater and introduce technologies that use alternative sources of water for normal plumbing functions. These include specification of high-efficiency and/or dry plumbing fixtures such as toilets and urinals, use of storm water or gray water (recycled wastewater) for sewage conveyance, and use of on-site wastewater treatment systems.

◀ This new high school incorporates geothermal heating and cooling; green roofs grown in a bed of crushed recycled bricks; light monitors; an environmental instructional garden adjacent to the science suite; bamboo veneer and flooring; and other features as part of a comprehensive sustainable design strategy. Concordia International School, Shanghai, China. Perkins Eastman. Photograph by Shutte.

3. *Water-use reduction.* A related set of water-use reduction strategies includes water-saving fixtures such as aerated metered faucets, dual-flush toilets, low-flow showers, and high-efficiency urinals. In many cases, repairing leaky faucets alone can lead to significant reductions in water usage.

ENERGY CONSERVATION

The 1973 oil embargo is generally regarded as the beginning of a broad-based concern about energy conservation. Low energy prices and poor public policy cooled this concern in the 1990s, but the high energy prices and the growing dependence on foreign oil at the time this second edition was being written have refocused public concern on energy conservation. The study *Greening America's Schools* calculated an average ener-gy reduction of about one-third in the schools it analyzed (Kats 2006, p. 4). At the same time, there is a growing recognition that the environmental impact of mechanical systems should be managed. This subject is covered in the energy codes and industry standards (ASHRAE and others) as well as in a number of detailed texts, including the *ASHRAE GreenGuide: The Design, Construction, and Operation of Sustainable Buildings,* 2nd ed.

Energy conservation in schools has focused on the six major sources of energy consumption in this building type:

- Lighting
- Heating
- Air-conditioning
- Ventilation
- Domestic hot water

◀◀ In a central courtyard, an integrated water system includes a biology pond, rain garden, and terraced wetlands that recycle wastewater with a treatment tank, sand filter, and gray-water storage. Sidwell Friends Middle School, Washington, D.C. Courtesy of KieranTimberlake. Photograph by Michael Moran.

- Miscellaneous other pieces of mechanical and electrical equipment (pumps, elevators, computers, kitchen equipment, audiovisual equipment, etc.) found in school buildings

New technologies and systems are continuing to be developed in each area, but some of the most effective conservation techniques remain the commonsense design solutions developed long before energy was cheap and plentiful.

Lighting

Some of the most dramatic conservation gains have been made in lighting. In the 1960s the typical design standard for lighting called for 2–3 watts per sq ft for classroom lighting. Today the same or better lighting levels can be achieved with 0.7 to 0.9 watts per sq ft. The source of these dramatic reductions can be traced to the development of high-efficiency ballasts, high-efficiency lamps, and fixtures that are more efficient in directing low-glare, adequate light levels to the work surface. (These more efficient fixtures and their incorporation in school design are also discussed in chapter 13.) In terms of energy conservation, many school systems have found complete replacement of their older lighting to be cost-effective.

Some further reductions in lighting usage have also been achieved by a combination of simple technology and commonsense operating procedures. Among the more common are the following:

- The obvious step of turning out lights when a room is not in use.
- Similarly obvious is the reduction of light-

ing to the levels actually needed for a task. In the past, lighting standards were often unduly influenced by manufacturers and energy suppliers. As a result, many schools have excessive lighting levels.
- The use of double circuiting so that only the number of light fixtures required are turned on. In many classrooms, half the fixtures will provide the desired lighting levels during a normal sunny day.
- The use of photocells in some areas—such as the major public areas and circulation spaces—where more automatic adjustment of light levels using this technology may be justified. Photocell-actuated lighting may also be appropriate in some exterior applications.
- The use of time clocks and motion detectors to automatically turn off lights in spaces that are not in use. Motion detectors (if not a code requirement) have not been cost-effective in many classrooms but can work well in smaller spaces that get sporadic use. There are many central-lighting, programmable control systems available to manage lights automatically with digital controls.
- Design of the school to maximize the use of daylight. As discussed in chapter 13, however, it is important that natural light be used properly. High-intensity direct sunlight on a school desk is not a good alternative to the proper balance between artificial and natural light.
- Use of low-energy fixtures, such as light-emitting diode (LED) fixtures and exit lights or high-pressure sodium lamps for parking lots, is important where permitted by code. LED fixtures have a long expected life, and sodium vapor lighting produces twice as much light per watt as

▶ *A retrofitted daylighting solution includes vertical sunshades to keep heat out and allow for filtered light, while motorized blinds and low-e glazing on the east and west minimize heat gain and maximize sunlight. Sidwell Friends Middle School, Washington, D.C. Courtesy of KieranTimberlake.*

mercury vapor lighting and five times per watt as incandescent fixtures. Sodium vapor, however, may cause disturbance to neighboring homes and may not provide a pleasing color rendition.

Heating

Until the increased use of air-conditioning in schools changed the equation in many school systems, the next major consumer of energy was heating. This was a major focus of the initial efforts toward energy conservation. Tighter building envelopes, more compact floor plans, greater insulation, more efficient heating systems, lower heating levels, more sensitive controls, and more exotic measures were all tried by hundreds of schools and school systems. As energy prices declined and the negative consequences of some measures became apparent (poor indoor air quality, oppressive designs with little natural light in many spaces, discomfort, disappointing savings, etc.), a more balanced view of energy conservation in the heating system has evolved.

By the late 1990s the most common areas of emphasis in heating conservation were the following:

• Tightening the performance of the building envelope by adding wall and roof insulation, building vestibules for the main

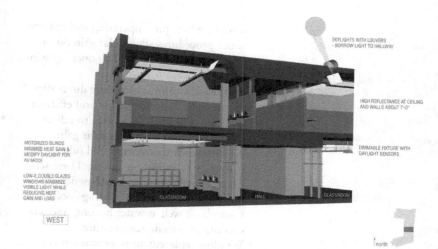

SKYLIGHTS WITH LOUVERS - BORROW LIGHT TO HALLWAY

HIGH REFLECTANCE AT CEILING AND WALLS ABOUT 7'-0"

DIMMABLE FIXTURE WITH DAYLIGHT SENSORS

MOTORIZED BLINDS MINIMIZE HEAT GAIN & MODIFY DAYLIGHT FOR AV MODE

LOW-E, DOUBLE GLAZED WINDOWS MAXIMIZE VISIBLE LIGHT WHILE REDUCING HEAT GAIN AND LOSS

CLASSROOM   HALL   CLASSROOM

WEST

north

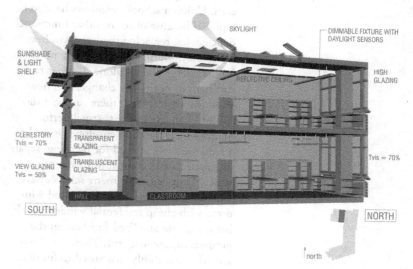

SKYLIGHT   DIMMABLE FIXTURE WITH DAYLIGHT SENSORS

SUNSHADE & LIGHT SHELF

REFLECTIVE CEILING   HIGH GLAZING

CLERESTORY Tvis = 70%   TRANSPARENT GLAZING

VIEW GLAZING Tvis = 50%   TRANSLUSCENT GLAZING   Tvis = 70%

HALL   CLASSROOM

SOUTH   NORTH

north

entrances, and weather-stripping doors and windows.

• Improving the balance and increasing the number of room-by-room controls of the heating system to eliminate the need to open windows in some areas of a school on cold days to compensate for excessive heat. This is a common problem in older

▲ *North-facing windows admit diffuse light while sunshades and light shelves on the south bounce light onto classroom ceilings. Sidwell Friends Middle School, Washington, D.C. Courtesy of KieranTimberlake.*

schools, where poor operating and maintenance procedures allow solar gain on one facade to be counteracted by opening windows.

- Improving controls, including direct digital controls, to more quickly and efficiently adjust heat levels in a space to reflect changes in occupancy and solar gain. Night setback thermostats and other controls are now common as well. These setback controls are often combined with morning warm-up and evening cool-down controls, as well as water heating reset according to outside temperature.
- Window replacement is a common concern. Unless a school's windows have to be replaced because of rot or other functional deficiencies, replacing the large windows common in most schools is rarely justified by the energy savings alone. If other factors help to justify the change, and new windows are installed, there can be a significant increase in the thermal performance of the building envelope, as well as a reduction in the need for painting, repair of balances, and other routine maintenance. Unfortunately, many schools have replaced their large, attractive wood windows with cheap residential windows with inappropriate anodized finishes, on the grounds of low first cost. These windows are often too thinly structured to fill the entire opening, and a fixed metal panel is added to fill in the top of the opening. These windows not only disfigure schools, but often fail early because they were meant primarily for the smaller openings typically found in apartment buildings. There is no reason for this mistake, inasmuch as many competitively priced high-performance window systems are available.

- The addition of low-emissivity (low-e) coatings to windows is now common. This technological innovation significantly improves the performance of the windows and often approximates the benefits of insulated (double-glazed) window units.
- More efficient boilers and related systems save energy costs through flue gas heat recovery, flue dampers, dual-fuel combustion, high-efficiency combustion, and other features. In addition, it is often recommended that boilers be selected to more efficiently match the heating demand (e.g., modules of 50–60 percent of demand to operate at low loads).
- More efficient distribution systems, such as variable-speed pumping and independent zoning for temperature control, help to reduce the heating and cooling energy lost in distribution.

Air-Conditioning

In recent decades more schools have air-conditioned more of their facilities to improve teaching conditions and to make the schools suitable for year-round use. In many school districts air-conditioning has become the standard, rather than a luxury feature for a few priority spaces (such as the principal's office). This shift has added a significant new source of energy consumption.

Among the major steps that schools are taking to control the increase in energy consumption caused by this new demand are the following:

- Use of separate systems to serve areas with unique usage profiles (e.g., auditoriums, computer-intensive areas, offices, community centers, etc.).
- Steps to reduce the power required by a system's fans, often the major energy user

in an air-conditioning system. This has been accomplished in part with variable-speed fans, use of radiant cooling (common in Europe but still rare in the United States), and lower-temperature air supply.

- Utilization of high-efficiency heating, ventilation, and air-conditioning (HVAC) equipment, variable-speed drives on the fans, high-efficiency motors, and refrigeration equipment with good energy efficiency ratio (EER) ratings.
- Use of roof insulation, low-e window coatings, and lighter-colored roofing materials to reduce the cooling load.
- Strategies employed to minimize solar gain through glazing while maximizing the penetration of daylight, include massing, orientation, use of deciduous trees, light shelves, glazing analysis, reflectivity, etc.

Ventilation

Ventilation is a mandatory part of most codes, and it contributes to energy consumption in two primary ways: via the energy used when ventilation air is heated, cooled, and/or dehumidified; and via the energy required to operate the fans in the system. The primary energy-saving opportunities in ventilation include the following:

- Heat-recovery systems that transfer the exhaust heat to the incoming cold air or, reciprocally, the exhaust "cooling" to the incoming hot, humid air.
- Installation of a warm-up cycle during fan start-up on cold mornings. Energy savings will result from heating indoor air, instead of colder outdoor air, to bring the building up to the desired temperature.
- The installation of relief vents and exhaust systems if necessary to relieve pressurization for rooftop units with inadequate relief vents.

Reduction in Other Energy Demands

There are further energy demands that can be reduced. Microprocessor-based energy management and control systems (EMCS) can be very cost-effective in controlling HVAC systems (e.g., start/stop, temperature reset, system optimization, maintenance logs, etc.).

Schools are incorporating an increasing number of mechanical and electrical devices,

▲ This new middle school is bounded on two sides by open space and has unobstructed views, providing daylight through continuous clerestories and light shelves. Wayne Carle Middle School, Westminster, Colorado. RB+B Architects, Inc. Photograph by Paul Brokering.

such as televisions, VCRs, DVD players, computers, audiovisual equipment, kitchen equipment, specialized vocational teaching equipment, and elevators, all of which demand energy. Some of these systems can be controlled by an EMCS to minimize waste. Energy input ratings, available for much of this equipment, should be evaluated as part of the performance specifications.

Domestic Hot Water and Other Plumbing-Related Energy Demands

Although it is not a major source of energy consumption, water usage is an important energy and environmental consideration. Among the conservation measures most frequently employed are the following:

- In some warm-weather states, solar power has been employed to provide domestic hot water and for other uses.
- Use of energy-efficient separate domestic hot-water heaters to allow the large heating boilers to be shut off during mild weather.
- Operating with lower hot-water temperatures (120°F vs. 140°F).

Calculating the Costs and Benefits of Energy-Conservation Measures

There are many methods of calculating the costs and benefits of energy-conservation measures, but probably the most common (and most widely accepted) is the simple payback calculation. With this method, the projected cost of the measure (for example, the cost of a program of light-fixture replacement or more efficient boilers) is estimated. Then the projected annual savings in

gallons of fuel oil or kilowatt-hours are converted to dollar savings. The cost of the measure is then divided by the savings to yield an estimated payback period—in other words, an approximation of the time it will take to recover the capital cost of the measure with the money saved from lower operating costs. When the payback period is less than seven or eight years, many school systems consider it a worthwhile investment. Some will even consider payback periods of ten to twelve years adequate to justify the change.

The payback method is a useful, if somewhat crude, tool. Its reliability depends on the accuracy of the estimates of both costs and savings. Estimates of savings and costs for replacement of light fixtures are relatively easy to calculate, but many other measures are far less exact. Most require the input of an engineering or energy-conservation professional, who often uses more sophisticated methods of calculation, such as the life-cycle cost analysis. This technique is summarized in chapter 19.

As a final note, designation as a LEED-certified school does not always translate into high energy efficiency. As the Environmental Protection Agency's studies have shown, many LEED-certified buildings do not perform (on energy use per sq ft) well enough to earn an Energy Star rating. It is necessary to use more than one set of metrics to guide the design of a really energy-efficient building.[1]

1. For more on the EPA's Energy Star program, visit their website at http ://www.energystar.gov/ index.cfm?c=k12_schools.bus_schoolsk12.

Alternative and Renewable Energy: Solar Energy and Geothermic Systems, Passive Heating and Cooling, and Photovoltaics

There is a strong emphasis in sustainable design on the use of alternative, renewable, and net-zero-pollution energy sources. Schools are logical users of solar energy because the building use is typically concentrated during the day when energy from the sun can be used to maximum benefit. Projections of higher energy costs in the future, steady technological advances, increased public awareness and support for sustainable design, greater design team sophistication, and expanded government support have stimulated experimentation and implementation of these renewable energy systems.

The following are among the systems being used in schools:

- *Active solar thermal*. Solar panels are used for hot-water production and part of the heating load. These systems are often tied into a school's conventional hot-water production system. Many school districts throughout the United States have experimented with this technology and participated in demonstration projects.
- *Passive solar*. Building envelopes can be designed to reduce solar gain for cooling and increase solar gain for heating.
- *Photocell-controlled lighting*. Photocells can control the amount of lighting needed both within classrooms and in outside installations such as parking lots. This technique, combined with proven daylighting design, can significantly reduce lighting energy demand.

- *Photovoltaics (PV)*. PV technology is steadily advancing, and a growing number of school districts have installed such systems. In most cases these systems are designed in combination with normal grid-supplied electricity. For example, it is possible for a school to use such a system to run the electric pumps and blowers of a solar thermal desiccant air-conditioning system at high speed on a sunny afternoon, and then switch over to grid-supplied power for low-speed nighttime demand.

Demonstration projects in Maryland, Michigan, Wisconsin, and many other states have been targeted for schools, and the results have been encouraging. For example, Wisconsin Public Service Corporation's SolarWise for Schools installed solar systems in three Wisconsin schools. The annual output and environmental impacts of the three systems are shown in the table on page 170. Based on the success of this program (both in energy savings and student education) the program was expanded to an additional 44 schools with more in progress.

Other energy technologies are also being tested in schools:

- *Geothermal*. Low-level geothermal systems use geothermal heat pumps and water in wells, where the water stays at a constant temperature. Proponents of these systems point to their use of a nonpolluting renewable resource, lower operating costs, reduction in rooftop equipment, and other advantages. There are also geothermal systems that use naturally heated water, but there are no prominent examples of their use by schools.

▶ *An existing 10,000 sq ft industrial building was completely gutted, renovated, and transformed into a comfortable, light-filled environment. Mother's Club Learning Center, Pasadena, California. Harley Ellis Devereaux. Photograph by RMA Photography, Inc.*

IMPACT OF SOLAR-GENERATED SYSTEMS

	ANNUAL ENERGY OUTPUT (KWH/YR)	ANNUAL COAL CONSERVED (IB/YR)	ANNUAL AVOIDED EMISSIONS (IB/YR)			
			CO_2	SO_2	NO_2	Particulate
Current impacts (3 schools; 12 kW each)	50,000	68,100	120,000	560	640	20
Extended project impact (63 schools, 177 kW total)	249,000	319,000	562,000	2,600	3,000	99

Source: SolarWise for Schools, Chip Bircher, Wisconsin Public Service Corporation, personal communication, November 2009.

• *Wind generation.* A school in Spirit Lake, Iowa, has housed a demonstration project for wind-generated electrical power. Its wind turbine generates more power than is consumed by the school. The payback calculation was enhanced by a Department of Energy grant, but according to the school's figures, even without the grant the annual savings are almost enough to justify a normal capital investment by the school.

BUILDING ENVELOPE

The energy performance of many new buildings is now governed by code. Typical of the energy code requirements are those based on the American Society of Heating,

Refrigerating, and Air-Conditioning Engineers (ASHRAE) Standard 90.1-1999. In existing buildings, retrofits are frequently used to upgrade the energy conservation performance of the building envelope. Among the more common envelope upgrades are the following:

- New thermal pane or low-e glazed windows
- Additional roof insulation added during roof replacement
- Additional wall insulation
- The addition of vestibules
- Weather-stripping and other actions to reduce air infiltration and heat loss

As noted in a following section, however, care must be taken to balance the energy savings of a tighter building envelope with the steps necessary to preserve indoor air quality.

Refrigerant Management

The objective of this part of the program is to reduce ozone depletion. It calls for zero use of chlorofluorocarbon (CFC)-based refrigerants and the phase-out of these refrigerants from use in any existing equipment.

Commissioning and Management

Most comprehensive sustainable design programs call for a more formal definition, monitoring, and handover of the building's systems at the time of occupancy. The purpose of this "commissioning" effort is to "verify that the building's energy related systems are installed, calibrated, and perform according to the owner's project requirements, basis of design, and construction documents" (LEED-NC Reference Guide Version 2.2, p.151).

Commissioning may be carried out by the design team, but it is supposed to be a separate group with specialized skills doing the work. This work is over and above the design team's normal responsibilities and typically calls for a separate commissioning fee—particularly when the school is going for LEED certification.

In addition, as noted above the performance of the systems must be monitored and managed over time. In a growing number of cases this is aided by energy management and control systems (EMCS). Most sustainable design programs emphasize measurement and verification.

MATERIALS AND RESOURCES

This part of sustainable design focuses on building reuse, recycling, construction waste management, use of recycled materials, renewable and/or local materials, and other techniques. As the USGBC notes, both the development and the removal of building materials are major users of nonrenewable resources as well as huge generators of solid waste. It is estimated that "construction and demolition wastes constitute about 40 percent of the total solid waste stream in the United States" (LEED-NC 2.2, p. 233). Thus, the recommended materials and resource sustainability strategies include:

1. *Storage and collection of recyclables.* This includes the provision of an easily accessible area that serves the entire school and facilitates the collection and storage of recyclable materials such as paper, cardboard, glass, plastics, and metals.
2. *Building reuse.* The adaptive reuse of existing structures can be an important part of a sustainable design strategy. The

In new kindergarten classrooms, large north-facing clerestories admit diffuse daylight, while fixtures adjacent to the ceiling maximize reflected light. Santa Rita Elementary School, Los Altos, California. Gelfand Partners Architects. Photograph by Mark Luthringer.

reasons for this are obvious, but there are many existing buildings that are obsolete or inappropriate for reuse. Moreover, in such cases the cost of reusing the existing building can at times approach or exceed the cost of new construction.

3. *Materials reuse.* The LEED program provides a credit if at least 5 percent of the building materials used are salvaged, refurbished, or reused. For example, the Felician Sisters Convent and Sacred Heart High School in Coraopolis, Pennsylvania, achieved a LEED gold rating in part through an extensive program of reuse of existing materials in the design. Over 300 hardwood doors and transoms were refinished and rehung, over an acre

of hardwood floor was lifted, cleaned, and relaid, over a mile of trim was removed and reinstalled, and over 275,000 pounds of roof ballast was removed and reused as underlayment for paving.

4. *Recycled content.* LEED also provides a credit in its rating system if at least 10 percent (based on cost) of the total value of the materials employed incorporate recycled content.

5. *Regional materials.* Another one-point credit is awarded if at least 10 percent of the materials and products are extracted and manufactured within the region. This supports the use of indigenous resources and reduces the environmental impact of transportation.

6. *Rapidly renewable materials.* Another point is awarded if at least 2.5 percent of the total value of the building materials and products use rapidly renewable materials (made from plants that are typically harvested with a ten-year cycle or shorter).

7. *Certified wood.* One LEED point is awarded if at least 50 percent of the wood-based materials and products are certified as being in conformance with the Forest Stewardship Council's (FSC) Principles and Criteria. These standards are designed to encourage environmentally responsible forest management.

Indoor Environmental Quality

The oil embargo and energy crisis of the 1970s caused the owners of most buildings—including schools—to tighten the building envelope and reduce the infiltration of outside air. These measures are often cited as the primary cause of the well-documented health problems that have resulted from poor indoor air quality.

In fact, the causes of many specific indoor air problems are complex, and it is clear that inadequate flow of outside air into a building is only one cause. As more schools are air-conditioned, aging systems, dirty ducts, and deferred maintenance are also issues of concern.

ASHRAE has addressed this issue with the recommendations in its published Standard ANSI/ASHRAE 62.1-2007 along with the accompanying addenda. In many outdoor weather conditions, increased ventilation not only improves indoor air quality but also reduces cooling energy consumption. Well-designed and controlled air-economizer systems can readily achieve this objective. The Occupational Safety and Health Administration's (OSHA) indoor air-

quality (IAQ) rules and the Environmental Protection Agency's (EPA) "Tools for Schools" kit both refer to this standard.

Other issues are addressed by common sense, better maintenance, and growing knowledge about the emission of volatile organic compounds (VOCs). More attention is now paid to the location of air intakes away from the sources of building or vehicular exhaust, to regular cleaning of HVAC ductwork, to better ventilation in special-use classrooms (chemistry, biology, fine arts, etc.), to the selection of better air-filtration systems, and to regular vacuuming of carpets and other dust- or mold-trapping materials.

At the same time, more design teams are being careful to specify materials such as paints and adhesives that are certified as "low emitting" in regard to VOCs.

The EPA and their Tools For Schools program have brought the issue of indoor air quality in our schools to the forefront of importance when considering new or renovation projects. Gregory Kats's study *Greening America's Schools: Costs and Benefits* cites a large number of studies that quantified significant positive health impacts from improved indoor air quality (2006, p. 9). More information is available at www.epa.gov/iaq/schools.

The USGBC and others have expanded on this to include the following guidelines:

1. *Establish a minimum IAQ performance standard.* This should at least meet the requirements of Sections 4 through 7 of ASHRAE 62.1-2007.

2. *Tobacco smoke control.* For obvious reasons, smoking should be prohibited in the building as well as near air intakes, operable windows, and entries.

3. *Outdoor air delivery monitoring.* The LEED rating system encourages incorpo-

rating a monitoring system to monitor outdoor air ventilation. This system should generate an alarm if the system varies by more than 10 percent from the design minimum.

4. *Increased ventilation.* Ventilation rates at least 30 percent above the ASHRAE minimums in number 1, above, are encouraged, as is the use of natural ventilation where feasible. The study *Greening America's Schools* cites the many studies that found improved ventilation and air quality reduces a range of respiratory illnesses, including common colds and influenza. This reduction translates into significant real savings.

5. *Construction IAQ management plan.* A careful management plan should be developed and implemented to reduce problems resulting from new construction and/or renovation.

6. *Low-emitting materials.* Adhesives, sealants, paints, carpets, and composite wood and agrifiber products can emit indoor air contaminants that are odorous, irritating, and/or harmful. Careful selection of these materials is an essential step in an IAQ program.

7. *Indoor chemical and pollutant source control.* The building design should build in features that minimize and control pollutant entry into buildings and later cross-contamination of occupied areas. This ranges from removing dirt and particulates at the main entries to filtering or blocking emissions such as garage exhausts.

8. *Control of lighting and heating systems.* Sustainable design encourages the design to provide for individual or group control of lighting and thermal comfort systems so that they can be adjusted to suit individual task needs and preferences, as well as conformance of the HVAC systems and building envelope with the requirements of ASHRAE 55-2004 to "provide a comfortable thermal environment that supports the productivity and well-being of building occupants" (LEED-NC 2.2, p. 363). A review of 14 studies by Carnegie Mellon on the impact of improved temperature control supports the position that this improves productivity, teaching quality, and student performance (Kats 2006, p.10).

9. *Daylight and views.* Daylight and visual connection to the outdoors are both considered to be very important in schools. LEED encourages both in at least 75 to 90 percent of occupied areas.

CAVEATS

Sustainable design is now generally accepted and a central part of the design process. Moreover, we are learning more each year about successful design strategies. Sustainable design has even become an important addition to the curriculum in many schools.

Nevertheless, some of the early work in sustainable design has been oversold. The achievements have been overstated and the costs understated. This is not an argument against sustainable design, but rather for the careful and thoughtful application of sustainable design concepts. Each project is different, and not all concepts apply. There is little doubt, however, that virtually all projects will benefit from the application of the most relevant sustainable design ideas.

CHAPTER 7
STRUCTURAL SYSTEMS

Because of differences in age; geographical diversity; design team preferences; various federal, state, and local codes; construction costs; and many other factors, virtually every common structural system—and some unusual alternatives—have been used in school construction. Masonry bearing wall, wood frame, poured-in-place concrete, precast concrete, steel frame, and Teflon-coated fiberglass fabrics are just a few of the systems employed. Therefore, it is not possible to provide general guidelines for the selection of the appropriate structural system.

It is possible, however, to summarize ten of the typical factors that school systems and their design teams consider in evaluating structural systems, as discussed in the following sections.

BUILDING LIFE
Most schools are built to last a long time. Although virtually all structural systems can last indefinitely if properly maintained, most new schools prefer structural systems with indefinite life spans and minimal maintenance requirements, such as concrete, steel, bearing wall, and the like. Cost, however, can distort this preference. To reduce first cost, many school buildings use exterior wall systems such as structural stud back up to masonry veneer and exterior insulated facade systems (EIFS). The reduction in first cost is usually accompanied by higher maintenance costs and a shorter system life span.

FIRE SAFETY
Although most fire experts will note that the structural system has little to do with fire safety in a typical low-rise school structure, a growing number of codes now direct or encourage the selection of fire-resistant structural systems, such as fireproofed steel, concrete, glue-laminated beams, and the like.

SEISMIC CONSIDERATIONS
A building's ability to withstand seismic events is probably of greater concern than the combustibility of the structural system. An increasing number of states are recognizing the potential dangers and are addressing seismic design in their codes. Seismic design, however, can significantly affect the choice of systems as well as their cost and flexibility.

FLEXIBILITY
Bearing-wall construction was common in older schools and is frequently used even today. A bearing-wall structure, particularly when the partitions between classrooms or the corridor walls are load bearing, is one of the least flexible systems. Poured-in-place concrete walls and a number of other systems create similar constraints. In an era of accelerating change in educational environments, flexibility is important. Thus, the selection of a structural system should not preclude or inhibit future reconfiguration of space or additions to a school. At one time, during the 1950s and 1960s, flexibility was such a major consideration that it led to prototypes—such as in the School Construction Systems Development (SCSD)—that were developed around the concepts of speed and flexibility.

▶ *Illustration of the systems integration built into the SCSD prototype.*

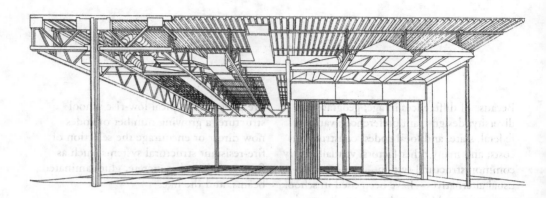

MINIMUM LIVE LOADS, NEW YORK STATE		
OCCUPANCY	**UNIFORM LIVE LOAD (PSF)[1]**	**CONCENTRATED LOAD (POUNDS)**
Assembly areas:		
Fixed seats	60	
Lobbies	100	
Movable seats	100	
Platforms (assembly)	125	
Projection and control rooms	50	
Stage catwalks	40	
Stage floors	125	
Gymnasiums, main floors, and balconies	100[2]	
Libraries		
Reading rooms	60	1,000
Stack rooms	150[3]	1,000
Corridors above first floor	80	1,000
Schools		
Classrooms	40	1,000
Corridors above first floor	80	1,000
First-floor corridors	100	1,000

Source: BOCA National Building Code, 1996 (pp. 16–8, 16–9).

1. psf = 47.9 Pa; 1 pound = 4.4 N.
2. In addition to the vertical live loads, loads of 120 pounds per lineal foot on footboards and seat boards shall be utilized. Lateral sway-bracing loads of 24 lb per lineal foot parallel to and 10 lb per lineal foot perpendicular to seat boards and footboards shall be utilized.
3. The weight of books and shelving shall be computed utilizing an assumed density of 65 lb/cu ft and converted to a uniformly distributed load, which shall be utilized if this load exceeds 150 lb/sq ft.

COST

The structural system typically makes up 10–15 percent of the construction costs of a new school. Most school systems and their design teams try to minimize this part of the budget (subject to code, flexibility, life expectancy, and other considerations). The cost-effectiveness of any system will vary according to changes in market conditions, regional preferences, code requirements, relative labor and material costs, and other factors. Nevertheless, the choice of lowest cost is typically the system that combines the local construction industry preference with simple fabrication and readily available materials.

Although the structural systems of schools are rarely complex as compared with other building types, one of the challenges to cost control is the lack of repetition. The specific needs of the different areas in a school call for a variety of heights, bay sizes, cladding requirements, and even utility systems. Repetition—a typical goal in simplifying a structure and managing cost—is very hard to achieve in the design of a school's structural system.

Among the issues that any school structure must address are code requirements. Typical of the basic code requirements are the loads that the structure must support. The specifications of New York's code, for example, are shown in the table on page 176.

◀ A school's structure can be an important design feature. Frenchtown Elementary School, Trumbull, Connecticut. Fletcher-Thompson, Inc. Photograph by Robert Benson Photography.

Example of exposed wood and steel structure used for aesthetic effect. Lincoln Elementary School, Lincoln, Massachusetts. HMFH Architects. Photograph by Wayne Soverns Jr.

LONG-SPAN SPACES

Typically, the most structurally complex spaces are the large ones—cafeterias, gymnasiums, auditoriums, swimming pools, and the like. Where availability of land is not a constraint, these spaces are typically designed as one-story structures and rarely have other structures above them. These spaces use most of the typical long-span material options, such as steel, trusses, precast concrete, and glue-laminated beams.

PREFABRICATED AND PREENGINEERED STRUCTURES

Many school systems investigate the cost-effectiveness of prefabricated and preengineered structures. Prefabricated structures are widely used to provide temporary classroom space, but their attraction typically is speed of acquisition rather than cost or quality. Thus, the primary reason prefabricated structures are used is to solve short-term shortages of space. They are also commonly used for long-span spaces such as gyms and field houses. Such structures can often be planned, acquired, and made operational in less than a few months. More permanent factory-built structures are also used in some school programs.

Preengineered structures—used particularly for long-span spaces—are quite common. The major advantage of such structures is the reduction in design, fabrication, and delivery time. The costs are not necessarily significantly different from those of other structural alternatives.

Preengineered structures also have disadvantages. Many require pitched roofs with greater volume to heat and cool, and more complex interior partitioning. Another disadvantage of many of these structures is the metal siding and roofing often used as an

AESTHETICS

The structural system can be a major aesthetic consideration in the design of schools. Some architects have chosen to express structure with dramatic effect, as shown in the illustrations on pages 177–179.

◀ Example of exposed wood and steel structure used for aesthetic effect. Andover High School, Andover, Massachusetts. Earl R. Flansburgh + Associates, Inc. Photograph by Wheeler Photographics.

exterior cladding material. Many of these metal cladding systems have limited lives and are viewed as unattractive.

FOUNDATIONS

In more developed areas, available sites often pose problems, one of which is poor soil conditions. As a result, early geotechnical analysis is important. In most cases an analysis should be performed prior to site acquisition. More detailed analysis is also often necessary at the start of construction, inasmuch as the initial tests are only spot checks.

SPECIAL ISSUES

There are a number of other structural issues that arise in some school planning programs:

Special consideration must be given to the selection of the structural system for swimming pools. The high humidity and chemicals used corrode many structural systems and are a frequent source of problems.

The desire for flexibility has led many schools to use operable partitions between spaces. In most spaces—and especially in large ones such as gymnasiums—these partitions create a significant structural load (and associated cost) that many school systems, and some design teams, fail to recognize in the initial budgeting.

There are continuing experiments with structural systems—such as Teflon-coated fiberglass—for roofing large spaces such as tennis and pool areas.

Overall, structure is a less challenging issue in school design than in the design of other building types. Nevertheless, the proper planning and design of the structural system are important to a school's long-term life.

CHAPTER 8
MECHANICAL SYSTEMS

The American Society of Heating, Refrigerating, and Air-Conditioning Engineers (ASHRAE) is one of the best sources of mechanical systems information. The *2007 ASHRAE Handbook—HVAC Applications,* chapter 6, provides an introduction to the major issues for educational facilities. Other sources of reference are as follows:

- NYSERDA High Performance School Design online training course
- USGBC *Green Building Design and Construction*, version 3, which includes what was known as the *LEED for Schools Reference Guide*
- ASHRAE *Advanced Energy Design Guide for K–12 School Buildings*
- ASHRAE *GreenGuide*

This chapter summarizes some of the major issues stated by these references, and several experienced engineering consultants, to be most relevant.

GENERAL

Interior Environment
Interior environmental conditions have a direct impact on a school's occupants. Inadequate heating, cooling, humidity control, air cleaning, ventilation, and noise control can all impede learning.

Simplicity
Most schools cannot support sophisticated engineering and maintenance staff. Therefore, systems should be easily understandable

and maintainable. Ideally, boilers, chillers, pumps, and air-handling equipment should be in easily accessed enclosed rooms, with space around the equipment adequate for service and replacement of major components when needed.

Life-Cycle Analysis
As long-term owners know, schools are ideal candidates for life-cycle cost analysis. In selecting systems, schools should be aware that energy savings and lower maintenance costs often justify the higher first costs of more efficient systems.

Ability to Accommodate Growth and Change
Because schools often have to grow and change, mechanical systems should be designed to accommodate change easily. Piping should not be buried in concrete, mechanical rooms should be expandable, and so forth. Boiler equipment should be designed in modules so as to be easily expandable and to provide redundancy, with no unit providing more than two-thirds of peak heating demand.

Ventilation
Mechanical ventilation is required by code for virtually every school space. The *ASHRAE Handbook* recommends ventilation rates. ASHRAE Standard 62.1 (latest version) is more current, with addenda, and is often the basis for the ratios in codes. It is important to establish ventilation rates required by the relevant state codes and other

local authorities to ensure that adequate ventilation is provided. Other voluntary standards, such as the USGBC LEED rating system, give credit for introducing additional ventilation into spaces, but if desired this should be planned so there is no increase in overall system energy consumption. The following is a summary of the requirements of the New York State Mechanical Code and New York City Mechanical Code for "Required Outdoor Ventilation Air" in educational facilities.

Auditoriums 15 cfm* per person
Classrooms 15 cfm per person
Corridors 0.10 cfm per sq ft
Laboratories 20 cfm per person
Libraries 15 cfm per person
Locker rooms 0.50 cfm per sq ft
Music rooms 15 cfm per person
Training shops 20 cfm per person
Locker and shower rooms 1 cfm per sq ft of floor area
Toilets 2 cfm per sq ft of floor area

Air-Conditioning
An increasing number of schools have incorporated air-conditioning to improve the teaching environment and allow year-round use. In hot, humid climates, air-conditioning and dehumidification are also used to prevent mold and mildew.

Impact of Program
Year-round school, adult education, night classes, community use of auditorium or athletic facilities, and other program variables can have a significant impact on selection and provision of appropriate mechanical systems.

*cfm = cubic feet per minute

One example is the use of schools in South Florida for hurricane shelters. When used for this function, a school's dining hall and associated ancillary spaces may be used for shelter, and ventilation is provided by backup generator-powered ventilation fans. Backup tanks provide for emergency domestic water needs.

Regional Variability
There is still great variability between school districts, and even within school systems. Age, budget, and program, as well as climate, make it hard to generalize. Nevertheless, the accompanying table, a modified version of an ASHRAE table, summarizes "recommended winter and summer design dry-bulb temperatures for various spaces common in schools."

Regional variability also has a significant impact on the selection of appropriate mechanical systems. Listed below are elements of the design that will be significantly affected by regional climatic conditions, and must be selected appropriately by the engineers:

1. Use of natural ventilation
2. Type of cooling system selected
3. Energy recovery potential and type of energy recovery
4. Evaporative cooling potential and type
5. Use of air-side and water-side economizers
6. Type of heating system selected
7. Potential for use of earth-coupled cooling and heating technologies

Indoor Air Quality
A school's indoor air quality (IAQ) should be a major consideration (see also chapter 6). The USGBC LEED for Schools rating system and handbook highlights the major concerns for reduction of volatile organic

RECOMMENDED DESIGN TEMPERATURES			
SPACE[A]	WINTER DESIGN, °F	SUMMER DESIGN, °F DB	SUMMER DESIGN, RH = (%)
Laboratories	72	76–78[d]	50–55
Auditoriums, libraries, administrative areas, etc.	72	76–78	50–55
Classrooms			
Pre-kindergarten through grade 3	75	76–78	50–55
Grades 4 through 12	72	76–78	50–55
Shops	72	76–78[b]	50–55
Locker, shower rooms	75[d]	c,d	
Toilets	72	c,d	
Storage	65	c,d	
Mechanical rooms	60	c	
Corridors	68	78–80[b]	60[c]

DB = dry-bulb temperature. RH = relative humidity. a. For spaces of high population density and where sensible heat factors are 0.75 or less, lower dry-bulb temperatures will result in generation of less latent heat, which may reduce the need for reheating and thus save energy. Therefore, optimum dry-bulb temperatures should be the subject of detailed design analysis. b. Frequently not air-conditioned. c. Usually not air-conditioned. d. Provide ventilation for odor control.
Source: ASHRAE

compounds (VOCs) within construction materials. It also recommends ventilation air quantities and highlights requirements for post-construction flushing with ventilation air before occupancy.

Noise and Vibration

Mechanical systems produce noise and vibration that must be controlled. The location of mechanical rooms and the selection of partition materials are important in school design. Major equipment should have vibration isolation mountings, particularly with a suspended floor. Piping in mechanical rooms should have vibration-isolation joints and hangers. See also chapter 12.

Program Area

The space required for mechanical systems varies widely inasmuch as some schools pro-
vide limited mechanical services with rooftop equipment and others have central mechanical areas for sophisticated heating and air-conditioning equipment. Most school programmers allocate 4–6 percent of total area for mechanical and electrical spaces in a new building prior to design. Engineers argue, however, that if air handlers are within the building, they can take up 6 percent by themselves. This percentage is lower if the heating, ventilation, and air-conditioning (HVAC) equipment is housed in rooftop package units. However, it is important to understand the implications of rooftop equipment, such as reduced life of equipment, maintenance inconvenience, vandalism potential, and other local variables such as equipment noise concerns and protection of equipment during natural disasters.

Construction Budget

Mechanical systems costs (not including electrical or plumbing) also vary widely, ranging from less than 10–15 percent of the construction budget for schools that require only heating and ventilation, to more than 15–25 percent of the budget in air-conditioned high schools that include a pool, auditorium, and sophisticated science rooms.

PRESCHOOLS AND KINDERGARTENS

Some of the specific issues regarding mechanical systems in preschool and kindergarten are discussed in the following paragraphs.

Use of Existing Facilities

Many early childhood programs must adapt spaces originally designed for other uses. Thus, their mechanical systems are often retrofits or replacements. Many old heating systems can be retrofitted, with temperature-control valves added at each space-heating element to provide improved temperature control.

Warm Floors and No Drafts

Because young children often play or sit on the floor, a warm floor with minimal drafts is important. To this end, radiant heating, including in-slab systems, can be effective. Air supply intakes should be located to minimize drafts. Floor-mounted heating equipment with exposed hot surfaces or sharp edges should be avoided. In addition, care should be exercised in zoning to avoid overheating and slow "pickup."

Hours of Operation

Many school programs operate from early in the morning to early in the evening to match parents' working hours. The design of systems should assume 12–14 hours of operation for these programs, with minimal night and weekend use.

Ventilation

Well-designed provisions for ventilation and humidity control, to minimize formation of microbial growth and the spread of communicable diseases and odors, are particularly important. The location of air intakes and the selection of filter media are critical; use of duct lining, which when damp can be a source of mold, is discouraged.

Teacher Work Spaces

Teacher work spaces may call for a separate temperature-control zone.

ELEMENTARY SCHOOLS

The HVAC requirements of elementary schools incorporate some of the preschool requirements but also have their own special issues.

Program Areas

Elementary schools typically are more complex programmatically than preschool facilities. Gymnasiums, auditoriums, and cafeterias are often part of the program, as are specialized teaching spaces (media center, music, art, etc).

Hours of Operation

An elementary school's primary hours of operation are from 7:00 A.M. to 3:00 P.M. Usually, the peak cooling load occurs in the afternoon, and peak heating demand is in the morning at start-up.

Basic Classroom HVAC Needs

The basic ASHRAE recommendations for classroom HVAC systems include the following:

- Heating and ventilation in all classrooms
- Air-conditioning for classes used year-round in warm, humid climates
- Summer dehumidification in humid climates
- Economizer cycles for use during winter months
- Separate temperature-control zone for each classroom

Gymnasiums

Gymnasiums often have independent systems to accommodate a variety of uses, both during and after normal school hours. Locker rooms, if provided, are typically positioned so they can be vented directly to the outside; toilets and/or showers are also provided. These spaces require a great deal of ventilation. Air may be transferred from adjacent spaces to make up for that displaced by exhaust requirements.

Administrative Areas

Administrative areas typically are occupied beyond normal class hours and when school is not in session. They are often served by separate systems and are air-conditioned. At the very least, they should be designed to permit future air-conditioning.

Science, Art, and Computer Rooms

An increasing number of elementary schools have dedicated teaching spaces for science, art, computers, and other classes. Odors, such as caused by animals in science rooms and some art media, require adequate ventilation. These spaces should have sufficient exhaust (that is, exceeding air supplied) to yield a negative pressure relative to adjacent space. Computers almost always require air-conditioning, and a separate system is usually desirable for computer labs and server rooms.

Libraries and Media Centers

In most climates libraries and media centers should be air-conditioned to better preserve their books and other materials. Humidification may also be considered to alleviate excessive winter dryness. Large temperature and humidity variations throughout the year should be minimized.

MIDDLE AND SECONDARY SCHOOLS

Middle and secondary schools share the mechanical systems requirements of elementary schools, but they have more varied facilities as well as different hours of use. Some of the issues involved in providing systems for the additional spaces in such facilities are discussed in the following paragraphs.

Auditoriums

Auditoriums require an especially quiet and draft-free system. Air-conditioning is increasingly common because of year-round and community use. Independent systems should certainly be considered. In addition, auditorium design should take into consideration a number of other factors:

- The ability to precool the building mass can reduce the volume of air-conditioning required during peak occupancy for programs lasting just a few hours.
- Careful air distribution is important to minimize drafts. Some air should be exhausted near or in the ceiling to remove pockets of hot air.
- Returns near seating where face velocities exceed 275 ft per minute (fpm) may cause objectionable noise and drafts.
- Mechanical equipment rooms should be buffered from seating and stage areas to avoid acoustical problems.

- Lobbies and ancillary spaces such as toilet rooms have different heating and cooling requirements and should probably be served by separate systems or temperature-control zones.
- Stages require special consideration because of the unusual loads created by lighting and the activities on stage. Exhaust mechanisms are often included high in the space near the lights. However, care must be taken to minimize stack effect by creating low air velocities, wide distribution, and properly designed exhaust equipment.
- New technologies such as Displacement Ventilation should be considered for auditoriums. With this system very low velocity air is supplied below the seats to ventilate and cool the occupants. This air then rises up, taking away heat, carbon dioxide and occupants' odors. This system, if designed correctly, can also be very quiet in operation.

Kitchens and Dining Spaces

Kitchens require large amounts of ventilation air to serve as makeup for exhaust hoods over cooking appliances. In some schools with dining spaces adjacent to the kitchen, the ventilation air serving the dining space can be transferred and used for makeup to the exhaust hoods. In some kitchens air-conditioning is provided to maintain acceptable working conditions.

Computer Classrooms

Additional cooling is almost always required in computer classrooms, and it is important to designate which rooms will serve these needs, so that the additional cooling and air-handling equipment can be adequately accommodated.

Science Classrooms

Science classrooms may require fume hoods with special exhaust systems, as well as a makeup air system. At minimum the ventilation system should be carefully designed to maintain negative pressure relative to adjacent spaces, even when some fume hoods are not in operation. Independent temperature controls should be provided for each science classroom.

Natatoriums and Ice Rinks

Natatoriums and ice rinks require special heating, air-conditioning, and dehumidification systems. There are also a number of further requirements:

- A natatorium design must address humidity control, ventilation requirements for air quality (outdoor and exhaust air), air distribution, duct design, pool-water chemistry, and evaporation rates. A humidity-control system will not work if any of these items are overlooked.
- A natatorium requires year-round relative humidity levels of 40–60 percent for comfort, energy conservation, and protection of the building.
- Strategic use of glazing should be studied carefully to avoid condensation and "fogging."
- All glazing and cold perimeter structural elements should be washed with hot air in the winter to prevent condensation.
- Ductwork should be appropriately selected to resist the corrosive environment.
- Ice rinks present equally complex design challenges. The mechanical system must be designed to reduce refrigeration loads, avoid fogging (owing to introduction of moisture-laden outside air), deal with the

heat load of lighting, skaters, and spectators, and address a number of other special technical issues.

- Ventilation must be adequate to avoid high content ratios of exhaust fumes from an engine-powered ice resurfacing machine (Zamboni).

Vocational Education Spaces

There are a wide variety of vocational education spaces. Many require special mechanical systems:

- Auto mechanic instruction typically requires outdoor air supply, an exhaust system that can deal with odors and fumes (such as carbon monoxide), and controls that maintain the negative pressure of the space.
- Other industrial arts shops often have special requirements to accommodate the exhaust, dust, and heat associated with painting, welding, soldering, and similar activities.
- Home economics spaces often produce high heat loads resulting from cooking, washing, drying, and sewing equipment, and the plumbing and HVAC systems should be designed to handle such demands.

CHAPTER 9

ELECTRICAL/COMMUNICATIONS SYSTEMS

REFERENCE STANDARDS

The most important reference standards for a school's electrical systems are the following:

NFPA 70—National Electrical Code
NFPA 101—Life Safety Code
EIA/TIA 568-B—Commercial Wiring Standard
EIA/TIA 569—Commercial Building Standard for Telecommunication Pathways and Spaces
ANSI/J-STD—607-A-2002 (formerly EIA/TIA 607) —Grounding and Bonding
ADA—Americans with Disabilities Act

IMPACT OF TECHNOLOGY

As in all other areas, personal computers are proliferating throughout the country's educational system. The U.S. Department of Defense Education Association's Technology Program Standards call for one personal computer per two students throughout its worldwide program. This concentration of technology affects the design of electrical systems in many ways.

Although the design unit power density for lighting systems is decreasing to approximately 1.0–1.5 watts per sq ft in classroom occupancies, the density for receptacle power is now up to 3.0–4.0 watts per sq ft.

In providing branch circuits for devices that utilize power supplies to convert AC power to DC for use within solid-state equipment such as computers, printers, and even fluorescent lighting fixtures with electronic ballasts, the effects of harmonics on the power system must be considered. In the common practice of using three-phase homeruns for receptacle circuits, with a shared neutral conductor, the neutral will likely be carrying more current than any of the three-phase conductors because of third harmonic currents. Thus, from a practical perspective, neutral conductors must be enlarged or, alternatively, each circuit must carry its own neutral.

The increase in power density also implies larger electrical distribution equipment and transformers. These devices are likely sources of electromagnetic interference (EMI). Because the effects of long-term exposure to high levels of EMI on people are not known, it is appropriate to practice "prudent avoidance." That is, because EMI levels are inversely proportional to the distance from their sources, it is prudent to avoid locating electrical panel boards, transformers, and so forth within 8 ft of classrooms, offices, and other areas occupied by people for more than a few minutes at a time.

Many jurisdictions allow the use of flexible, metal-clad cable for the concealed installation of branch circuits, rather than the traditional method of wiring in conduit. Although there are potentially considerable first-cost savings in using the metal-clad cable method for both lighting and branch circuits, there is a downside that must be considered. As discussed earlier, technology in the classroom is rapidly changing, and thus the electrical infrastructure must be flexible enough to accommodate the change. The wiring in metal-clad cables cannot be adjusted or augmented as the need arises; it must be removed and replaced. The wiring in conduits, however, can usually be upgraded or augmented at any time.

POWER SOURCE

Many schools, other than those in dense urban environments, are usually low-rise (1–3 story) buildings or campuses, spread out so that the distance from the incoming source of utility power to the most remote area is greater than 200 ft. This circumstance, coupled with the fact that virtually all schools that have air-conditioning use electricity as the energy source, leads us to consider three-phase 480/277 volts as the voltage for distribution of bulk electricity throughout a school. This means that large-load mechanisms such as air-conditioning, elevators, pumps, and fans are powered at three-phase 480 volts. Fluorescent lighting systems can also take advantage of this plan, powered at single-phase 277 volts. Moreover, electrical closets local to the areas remote from the power source can contain transformers to step down the voltage to three-phase 208/120 volts for use mostly by 120-volt convenience outlets. Some schools still use 208/120 volts for the primary services if the higher voltage is not available at installation or the school started as a small structure.

EMERGENCY POWER

Unless a school building is a code-mandated "high-rise" (more than 75 ft above fire truck main access), the typical items re-

quired to be backed up by an on-site power source are exit signs and those light fixtures that lead people to exit the building in case of a power failure.

Because these lights typically consume only 0.5 watts per sq ft of power, it is usually more cost-effective to provide them with local battery packs than to install an on-site diesel emergency generator.

LIGHTING SYSTEMS

Energy efficiency and visual comfort are the key words in lighting systems designs for schools. As discussed in chapter 13, a balance of direct and indirect illumination provides a classroom with sufficient light for children to perform paper-oriented tasks and computer operations. Care should be taken in the design stages of a school project so that maintenance personnel need only to stock a limited number of replacement lamp types. This measure helps to ensure timely replacement to maintain proper levels and quality of illumination.

FIRE SAFETY

Today's multiplexed, addressable fire detection and alarm systems simplify fire safety design tremendously. Classroom detectors, sprinkler-system tamper and flow switches, manual pull stations, air-handling duct detectors, and so forth, can all be looped together and then identified separately at the fire alarm control panel or remote annunciator location. This allows instant identification of the device that "called in" the alarm so that a response by staff and fire personnel can be appropriate. Alarm notification devices are now typically combination speaker/strobes. Not only alarm tones but also voice announcements can be transmitted to better manage the actions of people in the event of a fire. The strobe function allows visual notification of hearing-impaired people. The entire system must follow the guidelines of the Americans with Disabilities Act (ADA).

COMMUNICATIONS

Communications systems in schools include various types of voice, data, and video information. For example, voice systems include telephone, intercom, and public-address functions. Data systems include local-area networks (LAN), access to wide-area networks (WAN), time-of-day clocks, and class-change tones. Video systems include access to distance-learning video programs, cable TV, and in-room playback of recorded DVDs.

Fortunately, today's technology allows for the integration of many of these systems. For example, a telephone PABX can allow the placing and receiving of outside telephone calls (with access restrictions to avoid unwarranted toll charges), room-to-room intercommunications, public address (PA) to various PA zones throughout the school complex (again, with access restrictions), as well as transmission of class-change tones. With appropriate interfaces to outside program source providers such as local cable television companies, satellite antennae, and local broadcast antennae, specific areas of the school can receive selective video and television programming. Media centers can connect to the WAN resources of the Internet, its World Wide Web, and other subscribed outside data services, and the information available can be shared in-house via LANs.

While a growing number of communication systems are using wireless technology, as this book wsa being written, most systems still require wiring. A structured backbone cabling system consisting of the proper infrastructure of fiber-optic and unshielded twisted-pair copper cabling, with appropriate electronic interface devices, can also integrate and simplify the installation of all these systems. For example, a typical classroom can have an intercom/telephone located at the teacher's desk and several data outlets strategically located in the room. This room can be reconfigured with the telephone at one of the data locations and conversion of the telephone outlet to data use by means of a simple "patch cord" change within the local telecommunications closet. Proper electronic equipment located in the telecom closets can allow any of the data outlets to be configured to one of the school's LANs or directly connected to a specific printer. Again, with proper electronics, the television located in the classroom can receive selected programming via its channel selector, or possibly even be configured as a remote monitor for the teacher's personal computer (PC).

SPACE REQUIREMENTS: RULES OF THUMB

The Electronics Industry Association/ Telecommunications Industry Association (EIA/TIA) publishes standards that address the space requirements and configurations for equipment rooms, closets, and similar space. These standards also include environmental requirements (air-conditioning), as well as electrical power and grounding. The space standards should be applied judiciously, as they address "all-inclusive" equipment rooms and closets, and a particular school may not house all the components anticipated by the standards.

The electrical power systems discussed in this chapter can be housed in a series of electrical closets, placed strategically throughout the facility, and a centralized main distribution room. The closets can be located on every floor at every 15,000 sq ft or at a maximum horizontal spacing of 250 ft, whichever is less. They should each be a minimum of 8 ft × 10 ft to allow for wall-mounted panel boards and equipment, space for transformers, and adequate working clearances for installation and mainte-nance. The closets should be ventilated, taking into account the heat produced by the equipment located therein. The size of the main distribution equipment can vary greatly depending on a number of conditions— the incoming service voltage, capacity, branch circuit panel boards in the room, emergency system configuration, and so forth. It is always important, however, to consider the requirement for ventilation to dissipate the heat produced by the equipment.

CHAPTER 10

TECHNOLOGY AND SPECIAL EQUIPMENT

Thirty years ago a television set, a tape recorder, a film projector, and an overhead projector made up the typical electronic technology found in the average classroom. In every decade of the twentieth century a new technology was hailed as the harbinger of a revolution in teaching. As summarized in *Technology and the Future of Schooling* (Kerr 1996, pp. 2, 133), enormous expectations were rarely matched by results. In the 1920s film was expected to have a major impact; in the 1930s radio was expected "to bring the world into every classroom"; in the 1950s and 1960s the "new media" (television, super-8 film loops, language labs) and programmed instruction seemed to have potential; and in the 1970s there were "the novelties of distance learning and dial-access audio and video." All of these have had some impact, but it has been only in the last 25–30 years that "technology" has truly become a central issue in curriculum planning, facility design, and capital budgeting.

The number of computers and other new educational technologies grew dramatically from the early 1980s to the mid-1990s. In 1983 the ratio of students to computers was 125:1, by 1990 it was 20:1, and by 1995 it was 9:1; since then the ratio has continued to decline (Kerr 1996, p. 52). The same trends exist for CD-ROMs (up from 7 percent access by students in 1991–92 to 37 percent by 1994–95), Internet connections (up from 35 percent in 1994 to virtually 100 percent in 2005), school-wide networks, closed-circuit TV, new media in the libraries, and other technology. According to the *New York Times*, in 1999 the annual expenditure on school computers was $5 billion, and technology expenses continue to increase rapidly.[1]

Any discussion of the role of technology in education is certain to be out of date by the time it is published. The potential for new technology is being explored in thousands of schools, and a flood of new tools, curricula, and concepts have been developed. One report listed technology utilizations as number four of the top ten trends in education.[2] Yet surrounding this excitement is a raging debate on the role and limits of technology in education.

The debate is unlikely to end soon, but there appear to be several preliminary conclusions:

- The new technologies have created a wide variety of new educational tools, some of which are described later in this chapter.
- The new technologies are tools to help in teaching, but they are only tools.
- The cost of these tools competes with other educational budgets. If technological investment is made at the expense of smaller class size, music and art, physical education and

1. Statistics from U.S. Department of Education Institute of Education Sciences Fast Facts website, http://nces.ed.gov/fastfacts/display.asp?id=46 (accessed 6/2009), and "School Districts Merge Studies and Technology," *New York Times*, May 9, 1999.
2. Kenneth R. Stevenson, 2007, "Educational Trends Shaping School Planning and Design," National Clearinghouse For Educational Facilities, Washington D.C., http://www.edfacilities.org/pubs/index.cfm.

sports, expanded hours, higher teacher salaries, or better facilities, it can have a negative impact on the quality of education.
- The cost of technology has also increased the inequalities in facilities. As noted at one conference on the subject, "In one district, you can have multiple machines, an integrated curriculum, and well-trained teachers. Step across a district line, and you have schools with one or two computers in an entire school."[3]

Nevertheless, computers and other new technologies have become an essential part of life in America. More than half of all jobs in the United States require some use of computer skills. Although some of the required skills can be learned quickly later in life, many can and should be learned in school. As Chris Whittle, the founder of Edison Schools, noted in his 2005 book *Crash Course*, "in schools of the future, computer ubiquity and computer reliability will equal what we see in most modern business enterprises" (p. 140). Thus, computers and other technologies will continue to have an increasingly important role in elementary and secondary education. Among the most important of these technologies—and their school design implications—are the following:

- *Computer labs*. Most schools initially put the majority of their computers in a dedicated space or lab where computer skills could be taught and special computer-based projects could be carried out with the help of specially trained staff. The photo on page 131 illustrates a typical dedicated lab.
- *Computers in the classroom*. As more computers, computer expertise, and computer-based curricula have become available, computers have moved into the classroom. In wealthier districts and private schools, new classrooms are being planned on the assumption that every student will eventually have a laptop, plus access to classroom computers linked to school-wide networks and the Internet. This trend can have profound implications for seating design and the wiring of the classroom. Today, wireless connections reduce some of the impact, but hardwired connections are likely to remain an important planning consideration.
- *Internet, local-area network (LAN), and wide-area network (WAN) connections*. School renovations, as well as new construction, now routinely include the provision of wiring and connections.
- *New educational software*. There is a rapidly growing library of software that replaces traditional teaching methods. These programs can simulate science experiments and create entirely new ways to teach geography and other subjects. This has the potential to change the future design of teaching labs and other special classrooms.
- *Library as media center*. As noted in chapter 1, libraries are rapidly evolving. The school library still has books and story time, but now it must also accommodate and manage a growing number of new media (Internet connections, tapes, CDs, DVDs, etc.). A major problem is that there is too much information. Part of the librarian's role is to teach information management and research skills and to integrate content and skills in collaboration with the classroom teacher. Thus there is a need for more dedicated space for libraries, as well as rooms where these new media can be used.

3. "School Districts Merge Studies and Technology," *New York Times*, May 9, 1999.

"I believe that the motion picture is destined to revolutionize our education system." (Thomas Edison, 1922)

"The time may come when a portable radio receiver will be as common in a classroom as...the blackboard." (William Alexander, 1945)

"I was soon saying that, with the help of teaching machines and programmed instruction, students could learn twice as much in the same time and with the same effort as in a standard classroom." (B. F. Skinner, 1986)

• *Distance learning.* The concept of distance, or remote, learning and technology is still evolving. A 2008 report in *Technology and Learning* by Pamela Livingston noted that in 2007, 42 states reported some virtual learning, and that there are 147 virtual charter schools currently operating in the United States.[4] The U.S. Department of Education reports that during the 2004–05 school year, 37 percent of public school districts and 10 percent of all public schools nationwide had students enrolled in technology-based distance education courses.[5]

• *Audiovisual equipment.* Overhead projectors, and even slide projectors, remain common audiovisual (AV) equipment in some schools; but the computer—including PowerPoint and other programs and equipment—is typically replacing these traditional teaching tools.

• *Radio and television studios.* Radio and television production have become part of both school activities and curricula in many districts. TV studios often require large rooms with high ceilings.

The impact of technology in schools is evolving rapidly. The American Architectural Foundation's *Design for Learning Forum* in 2006 noted: "Standards have fully embraced new information and multimedia technologies and that educators will have to adapt

4. Pamela Livingston, "E-Learning Gets Real," *Technology & Learning*, May 22, 2008, http://www.tech-learning.com/article/8856 (accessed 6/2009).
5. U.S. Department of Education, National Center for Education Statistics, 2008, "Technology-Based Distance Education Courses for Public Elementary and Secondary School Students: 2002–03 and 2004–05," http://nces.ed.gov/pubsearch/pubsinfo.asp?pubid=2008008 (accessed 6/2009).

◀ *SMART board interactive white board. Courtesy of SMART Technologies.*

more quickly. Students commonly have personal computers and multimedia communication tools, and this shift is leading to a major redefinition of work spaces in school facilities" (p. 6). In 2009, some of the most important factors for consideration were the following:

• The use of individual classrooms will continue, with the teacher being supported by enhanced technological, administrative, and instructional systems. Technology will allow learning environments to adapt the following desirable features:
• Small-group instruction
• Individualized instruction
• Nonpaper instructional materials
• Collaborative, multisensory instruction
• On-demand access to information and resources

• The general-purpose computer lab will become increasingly unnecessary and will make prime classroom space available for future enrollment growth. All classrooms will be able to function as computer labs,

Steven Jobs, one of the founders of Apple Computer, once stated, "What's wrong with education cannot be fixed with technology.... No amount of technology will make a dent.... You're not going to solve the problems by putting all knowledge on CD-ROMs. We can put a Web site in every school—none of this is bad. It's bad only if it lulls us into thinking we are doing something to solve the problem with education." (*Wired*, February 1996)

as each student has a small laptop or other type of individual computer device connected to the school-wide data network.
- Wireless technology significantly expands access to data and video networks within and around the school building.
- Technology-intense (high bandwidth) special-use learning areas, such as technology education or media/information technology pathway labs, will continue to exist and contain high-end desktop computers hardwired to the school-wide data communications network.
- The library/media center will continue to function as the technology distribution center of the school, housing the main head-end room for voice, video, and data, large-group presentation area(s), open-access computer labs (electronic cafés), video broadcasting, long-distance learning and digital-media production facilities, and student research workstations.
- One-to-one e-learning environments will be supported by a hybrid hardwired and wireless communications infrastructure, utilizing a combination of traditional telecommunications room and fiber optic–based "collapsed backbone" topology to provide each school with seamless data connectivity.

The technologies expected to play an important part in creating this new learning environment include the following:

- Large-screen wall presentation of video-display systems
- Individual laptops, tablets, or other personal computer devices for all students
- Wireless network communications within the classroom
- School-wide one-to-one e-learning

- Distance learning capabilities in multiple learning areas

Additional resources are available at the North Central Regional Educational Laboratory Technology in Education website.[6]

TECHNOLOGY'S IMPACT ON LEARNING SPACE DESIGN

One leading technology consultant (and a contributor to this book), William M. Richardson of Educational Systems Planning, projects a number of changes in classroom design. In his view, basic learning-lab/classroom technology components consist of the teaching station, student learning and technology centers, small-group presentation areas, and student data connectivity locations. His recommendations for the design of these components are discussed in the following text.

Teaching Station

Connectivity for the instructor's station should be located off-center in the front of the classroom space, adjacent to a white dustless marker board (or electronic whiteboard) and pull-down screen, and may include space for peripheral devices. A high/low audiovisual presentation capability may be provided by a ceiling-mounted LCD projector and/or video monitor located at the teaching station. The teacher's desk is to be located adjacent to a combination of voice, data, and video outlets. A possible high-mounted video monitor allows display of a video source from the classroom VCR/DVD or the video distribu-

6. Jan Gahala, "Critical Issue: Promoting Technology Use in Schools," North Central Regional Educational Laboratory website through Learning Point Associates, available at http://www.ncrel.org/sdrs/areas/issues/methods/technlgy/te200.htm (accessed 6/2009).

tion system. The front row of ceiling lights should be capable of being dimmed and controlled separately from the remainder of the lights in the learning space to allow for maximum contrast of images on the pull-down screen.

Student Learning Center and Technology Center

Learning environments should promote extensive use of project based learning opportunities. One or more areas should be located in each space to accommodate groups of two to six students for collaboration and team-building activities. The student learning center in the classroom should include tables with space for students to work with different materials, data network connectivity provided via wireless network access point, and electrical power available to support learning stations consisting of different types of media devices such as recorders, scientific instruments, PDAs, and other hands-on equipment.

Additional elements within this space should include a technology center allowing two to four students to work as a team or independently using computing devices. This space should include specialized networked equipment such as printers, scanners, and desktop PCs connected through hardwired connections to the data network.

Small-Group Presentation Area

An integral part of the lab/classroom should be a presentation space so that students can effectively present their projects to their classmates and instructor. An ideal situation is to have areas that can accommodate both small and large groups.

The front presentation wall serves to allow for presentation to the entire learning

lab/classroom while a smaller area located in the rear of the classroom will allow for smaller presentations and practice space. This latter area should include general space to allow for different activities within a small group, electrical connectivity to power presentation devices and, at a minimum, be adjacent to network connectivity to allow access to stored information.

Student Data Connectivity

Student data connectivity locations should be provided via a combination of hardwired and wireless topology. Learning labs/classrooms should have at least six hardwired student data outlets. In addition, a single data drop dedicated for a wireless access point should be included in

▼ *A middle-school classroom layout incorporating technology. Courtesy of Educational Systems Planning.*

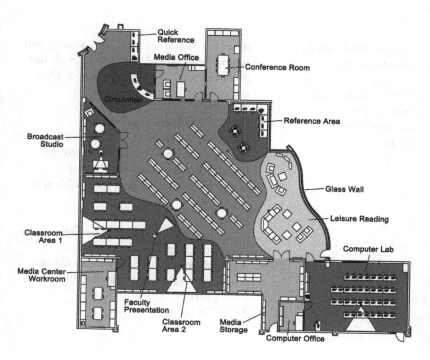

197

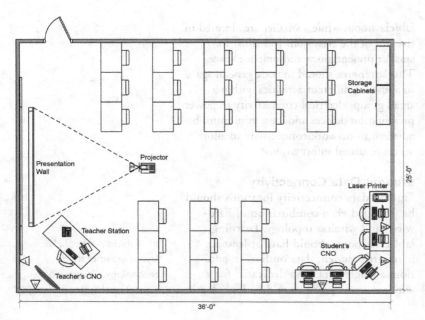

Storage Cabinets

Presentation Wall

Projector

Teacher Station

Laser Printer

Student's CNO

Teacher's CNO

25'-0"

36'-0"

▲ *A conceptual plan for a student learning and technology center as an extension of the school library. Courtesy of Educational Systems Planning.*

the infrastructure design. The access point should be mounted high on the wall, out of harm's way, or above the drop ceiling out of sight.

Typical Elementary School Classroom Layout

The integration of technology into the learning lab/classroom requires basic components that support several "design drivers":

• Arrangement of student furniture in learning clusters rather than rows
• Flexible, technology-friendly furniture with an emphasis on student tables rather than desks.
• Flexible layout

• Direct and controllable lighting where appropriate to allow effective use of presentation components

Typical Secondary School Classroom Layout

The integration of technology into the secondary classroom requires basic components that support several "design drivers" that differ from elementary school classrooms:

• Individual student tables to allow for flexibility in use, varying from traditional rows to perimeter peninsula arrangements of four to six students for team projects and collaboration
• Flexible, technology-friendly furniture with an emphasis on student tables rather than desks so that technology equipment can be allocated per student if necessary
• Standardized communications infrastructure layout allowing for customization based on the learning activities that will take place in that space over time
• Indirect and controllable lighting where appropriate to allow effective use of presentation components

The use of flexible, technology-friendly furniture will allow the same structured cabling system to be used for both of the interchangeable classroom layouts shown in the accompanying figures. This furniture consists of individual student tables with both electrical and data connections that allow it to be configured and reconfigured in either traditional classroom or team/cluster layouts, as shown, utilizing the same communications network outlets.

Science Lab Layout

The ideal technology implementation in science labs should include an AV projection system integrated with sound enhancement, data, and video connectivity at each lab station for four students, as well as a small data-analysis and printer station.

Media Center

A typical media center layout might include an open-access computer lab or electronic café, a mini television broadcast studio, student research workstations, quick-access student research workstations, a leisure reading area, small-group instructional areas, large-group presentation area(s), and possibly the main telecommunications equipment room. The mini television broadcast studio should double as a distance learning facility, with portable cart equipment that can be relocated to any learning area.

CHAPTER 11

MATERIALS

INTRODUCTION

School buildings are among the public structures that are called upon to endure. Many schools in use today across the country are housed in buildings more than 50 years old. The need for these buildings to withstand decades of accommodating schoolchildren and various educational programs should be a major factor in the selection of materials. The materials used to construct a school building should be durable and maintainable. They should withstand years of use and abuse while continuing to provide an atmosphere conducive to learning.

COMMON MATERIAL SELECTIONS FOR PRIMARY SPACES

The decisions made regarding material selections, as well as the accessories to protect them, may have a most profound effect on the physical environment and its appeal to children. We often associate the most institutional and, unfortunately, intimidating settings with endless vinyl tile floors, painted concrete-block walls, cold fluorescent lighting, and numerous wall and corner protection accessories. Although these materials will last a long time, they convey a stronger sense of factory than of home. There are, however, many new products on the market that can provide the durability and maintainability needed without significant compromise of the environment. The following are the general material selection criteria used by experienced school designers for the major spaces in a school:

- *Walls*. The use of gypsum board for walls is more than likely, given today's budget considerations, but this material does not provide very suitable impact resistance. Highly susceptible to gouging, dents, and corner damage, standard gypsum products must be enhanced or protected. The use of new high-impact gypsum products now on the market, more commonly specified in public housing projects, or the addition of a "skim coat" of diamond-hard plaster to at least a height of 4 ft, can help to improve the durability of the walls. Painted or ground-race block is a common alternative.

- *Floors*. Consideration should be given to new carpet materials for classrooms and large play areas to both enhance acoustic quality and reduce injuries associated with slippery, harder surfaces. In many schools area rugs are used so that they can be moved, replaced, or quickly cleaned. Solution-dyed products with integral moisture backing should be specified to ensure color retention and easy cleanup of soils and spills. In areas used for artwork, toilet rooms, and wet or messy activities, the use of VCT or sheet-vinyl products, which provide long-term durability and maintainability as well as many aesthetic options, should be considered. Some products offer an attractive wood-flooring appearance with 6 ft wide sheets capable of welded seaming and flash cove base details for watertightness.

- *Ceilings*. Acoustics should be addressed for each area designed. The use of acoustic ceiling tile in most areas is important, and carpeting should be considered wherever possible. In areas with harder surfaces, such as large expanses of glass wall or hard tile flooring, acoustic-tile ceilings will not be enough. Consideration should be given to the use of acoustic wall treatments such as fabric-wrapped panels. Care should be taken not to locate these panels in high-impact areas, which generally extend up to 4 ft above the floor.

- *Wall protection.* The protection of openings and corners, always a consideration, will ultimately help the facility maintain its appearance. The use of corner guards at key impact areas is recommended, and consideration should be given to recessed guards with carefully coordinated coloring, which helps them to blend with the interior design.
- *Trim and casework.* The use of natural wood to enhance the quality of a space is often desirable and can provide a very durable low-maintenance alternative to

painted trim and cabinets. Among the common woods used for their durability and affordability are maple and oak. Many manufacturers producing children's furnishings work in maple or other light woods, such as birch or beech. These woods are worth considering in determining the color and aesthetic for trim and casework. If painted cabinets are desired, factory polyester or vinyl paint coatings offer good durability as well as easy cleanup. Unfortunately, colors are often limited to white or almond. Countertops of plastic laminate are quite functional, but cabinet fronts, doors, and drawer fronts on lower cabinetry may peel and delaminate over time. Melamine materials should be used on concealed surfaces only.

The materials selected for a school building should support the educational programs and objectives of the client. The environment should be comfortable for the activities within the space, and the materials chosen should add to the comfort in the

STANDARD MATERIAL OPTIONS

INTERIOR WALLS	FLOORS	CEILINGS	ROOF	STRUCTURE	EXTERIOR WALLS
Concrete block	Resilient tile	Acoustical tile	Membranes	Concrete block	Clay masonry
Gypsum board	Hard tile	Gypsum board	Built-up system	Concrete	Cast/precast
Plaster	Carpet	Exposed structure	Shingles	Poured	Concrete block
Wood	Wood	Metal	Slate	Precast	Prefaced block
Metal	Sheet flooring	Wood	Metal	Steel	Stucco
Glass	Poured floors			Stone	Panel systems
Tile	Concrete			Wood	Stone
Partition	Terrazzo				Glass
Glass block	Stone				
	Cork				

students' environment. For example, kindergarten children spend much of their day on the floor, working as groups or in centers, and require a soft play surface such as carpeting. In a high school science classroom, students work at a lab station with chemicals that could be damaging to certain materials. The lab space should have hard, smooth work surfaces and floor finishes that are easily cleaned and chemically resistant. See the table at left for a summary of standard material options.

DURABILITY AND MAINTENANCE

In a school building project, the architect is continually challenged to provide a durable building on a very tight budget, especially for public schools. It is critical that the budgeted or bonded taxpayer funds buy the most space or largest number of classrooms possible. To meet the demand of providing more square footage and program areas, a decision may be made to forgo the more expensive quality materials in favor of more building area. The architect should educate the client to the trade-offs associated with up-front versus life-cycle costs of the materials. The life-cycle cost includes the initial cost, maintenance cost, operating cost, and other costs over the useful life of the material. For example, a poured-in-place terrazzo floor may be less expensive than a vinyl tile floor when the total cost of each is compared over the life of the material. The vinyl tile floor, although less expensive initially, requires frequent waxing and polishing and is subject to damages that may require replacement of sections. The terrazzo floor requires much less maintenance and is not subject to as much damage.

The client should understand the impact of material selections from the perspective of maintenance and replacement. The client will be responsible for maintaining the facility once constructed and thus should be directly involved in the selection of finish materials. This is also true for the structural and exterior construction materials. When asked to provide a brick aesthetic, the architect may investigate a brick veneer cavity wall with masonry unit backup, and a brick tile system backed up by metal studs. Both systems can provide the look the client has requested, but the full brick-on-masonry-unit backup will outperform the brick tile system and require much less maintenance.

As mentioned earlier, it is important to balance material selection with available construction and maintenance funds. In a school building, durability is a major concern and should be a major focus in selection. Often, the more durable material is also more costly. The client may wish to pursue the more expensive material because it promises lower life-cycle cost or because a manufacturer provides a longer warranty period or additional warranty coverage.

The client should incorporate scheduled maintenance for the selected materials into the school staff's work plan. Maintenance has a direct effect on the longevity of a product. Because it is likely that difficult procedures will lead to a lack of maintenance for the product, the ease or difficulty of maintaining a material should be part of the decision to use it in the building. A sheet-flooring system that can be dry-mopped may be easier to maintain than vinyl composition tile that requires waxing and buffing several times throughout the year. Before a product is specified, the client should be made aware of the proper maintenance techniques, the expected life of the product, and any concerns about the performance of existing installations.

CODES

The codes governing the region where construction is to take place will play a role in the selection of materials. Most codes dictate a minimum construction type based on building occupancy. Typically, schools are more demanding construction types than many other buildings and must meet more stringent regulations. A school must adhere to many fire code regulations, such as those involving limits on building area or area increases, fire separations, fire-rated construction, and so on. The fire rating requirements for walls, floors, roof, and vertical circulation paths may limit the materials available for construction. For example, the New York State Education Department requires that exit stairs be one-hour fire-rated construction, which can be provided with masonry construction or fire-rated gypsum board on metal studs. The fire code addresses finish materials by specifying a classification that is based primarily on the flame-spread rating of the material. Design loads mandated for different areas of the country will affect the materials considered for use as structural elements. Structural systems installed along the East Coast, for example, are required to meet high wind ratings because of the possibility of hurricanes. Possible requirements for long spans within a building also inform the structural framing system. Site conditions, soil type, and weather conditions all play a role in the selection of a structural system.

In addition to the building and fire codes, sanitation and health agency regulations affect material selection. There are some very specific requirements for food-preparation areas. These code requirements are intended to eliminate design elements that allow the growth of bacteria and other microscopic organisms by providing environments that can be disinfected. An example is the use of nonseamed stainless in commercial kitchens. Medical areas, such as the nurse's office in a school, also require materials that will minimize the spread of infection and disease from patient to patient. In these areas, finishes and furnishings must be disinfected. Thus, all applicable codes should be carefully reviewed during material selection to ensure compliance.

REGIONAL ISSUES

The availability of building materials in a region will affect construction in that region. For example, trees are rare in Southwest desert climates, and thus wood is not traditionally used in such areas as a major component in construction. Wood is, however, abundant and highly utilized for building in the Northwest. The level of local craftsmanship and skill with certain readily available materials should also be considered. When introducing a relatively new building system or material to an area, the architect should investigate the local resources for achieving a proper installation. Regional preferences in construction, as well as limits on available skills and materials, are common. Occupant heritage, immigrant cultures, economic circumstances, and many other factors, in addition to availability, influence the selection of materials. The traditional ways of building in a region may relate to or reflect the community's values and should be considered in design.

ENVIRONMENTAL CONSIDERATIONS

Materials should be selected to create a healthy, sustainable environment for all occupants. In new construction, selections should not contribute to the creation of the indoor air quality (IAQ) problems that currently plague many existing school buildings. Poor IAQ is a major contributing factor to "sick building syndrome" (SBS). The symptoms of SBS are flu-like, including headache; nausea; irritation of the eyes, nose, or throat; persistent coughing, wheezing, or upper respiratory complaints; hypersensitivity; and lethargy. These symptoms usually appear in a person one to two hours after occupying the building and disappear one to two hours after vacating the building. (See also chapter 6.)

The following are major causes of SBS:

- Outdoor chemical contaminants: motor vehicle exhausts, fumes from plumbing vents, and building exhausts brought inside via mechanical air-supply intakes or improperly located openings in the building
- Indoor chemical contaminants: adhesives, upholstery, carpeting, copy machines, manufactured wood products, cleaning agents, pesticides, tobacco smoke, and combustion products
- Biological contaminants: pollen, bacteria, viruses, molds
- Inadequate ventilation

Corrective measures for existing buildings that have poor IAQ and whose occupants show symptoms of SBS include the following:

- Increase ventilation of outside air.
- Increase air changes to seven or more per hour.
- Remove the source of the pollutant.
- Thoroughly clean mechanical systems and ducts.
- Provide air filtration.
- Reduce excessive moisture.

All building-design professionals should ensure that ventilation systems are properly designed to eliminate any possibility of biological growth, to change air frequently, and to provide uncontaminated fresh-air intake. In addition, materials that do not add contaminants to the environment should be specified. Volatile organic compound (VOC)-containing materials are major contaminant sources that off-gas once installed in a construction project. VOCs are found in adhesives, finishes such as paint and varnish, carpet and carpet padding, treated wood, some pressed composite wood products, some roofing materials, various insulation materials, and pesticides, among other products. Low- or non-VOC-containing materials should be specified. Water-based or natural finishes that do not contain formaldehyde, halogenated solvents, mercury, lead, or chromium are preferred. Earthen materials such as brick, stone, and natural wood should be used over chemical-containing materials. Several wood species have natural decay-resistance properties (e.g., cedar, redwood, black locust). Should any dangerous materials have to be used, care must be taken to contain them in the installation and keep them away from food-preparation areas and water supplies.

Most people now believe that designers should try to help maintain the ecological balance of the environment (see also chapter 6). The Earth's resources should be preserved, and the production of toxic products should be limited. The use of products containing recycled materials and the reuse of products such as doors and windows will aid in this effort. There are many alternatives to the chemically laden off-gassing materials in current use. However, these alternative materials are often more expensive and difficult to obtain. They are slowly becoming more available as they are specified for building projects. As demand increases, research and development is under way on a wide range of environmentally safe building materials.

CONSIDERATIONS IN MATERIAL SELECTION FOR SCHOOLS

The following lists contain considerations for the selection of interior materials, by area, within a school building project:

Administration
- Soft flooring for comfort and acoustics
- Acoustical barrier walls
- Appropriate lighting
- Cleanable surfaces in workrooms
- Ventilation for copying area

Offices
- Private, quiet environment
- Acoustical barrier walls for privacy
- Proper air change and ventilation
- Durability (but not as critical as in student environments)

Nurse's area
- Sanitary conditions
- Germ-resistant environment
- All areas easy to clean and disinfect
- Hard, nonporous flooring
- Smooth, cleanable surfaces
- Disinfectable sick cots
- Nonpollutant, nonallergenic environment
- Proper ventilation, humidity, and temperature levels
- Water-impervious materials

Library/media center
- Quiet environment
- Nonglare, nonreflective surfaces for computer use

- Indirect lighting
- Comfortable for the age level of the students
- Controlled moisture and humidity levels

Classrooms
- Easily cleaned flooring
- Hard flooring, with a throw-rug option
- Environment conducive to concentration
- Glare from windows controlled
- Work surface/furnishing durability reflective of classroom function
- Durable storage areas (shelving)
- Water-resistant walls, cabinets, and floors around sink and toilet areas

Kitchen
- Adherence to sanitation regulations
- Hard, nonporous, nonslip flooring
- Ability to withstand heavy daily cleaning with chemicals and disinfectant
- Seamless surfaces for food preparation and cooking
- Splash-guard surfaces at sink area
- Floor and wall surfaces resistant to oil and cooking residues
- Heat-resistant finishes
- Smooth surfaces to resist the growth of bacteria

Cafeteria
- Hard, nonporous flooring
- Smooth surfaces to resist the growth of bacteria
- Finishes that can be cleaned with disinfectants
- Hard, smooth wall surfaces for cleaning (at least as a wainscot)

Gymnasium
- Resilient floor surface that allows true bounce and spring action

- Hard, durable wall surfaces for ball play
- Padded wall sections located strategically for game play
- Noise reduction via acoustical block, ceiling treatments, etc.
- Durability of all products used: lights, scoreboard, doors, clocks, etc.
- Vandal-resistant materials

Locker rooms
- Nonporous, nonslip flooring
- Ability to withstand heavy cleaning and student abuse
- Water- and humidity-resistant materials
- Mildew-resistant curtains
- Vandal-resistant materials
- Proper ventilation at clothing and equipment storage areas
- Durable lockers and furnishings
- Moisture-resistant wall surfaces

Auditorium
- Ease of cleaning beneath the seating area
- Soft floor finish on walking surfaces to reduce noise
- Hard and soft wall surfaces placed to achieve the best acoustical properties
- Vandal-resistant materials
- Hard surface or cushioned seating, as defined by client

- Flame-resistant finishes and curtains
- Resilient stage flooring
- Dark stage walls

Technology
- Ergonomic considerations
- Nonglare or antiglare surfaces
- Static-resistant materials
- Quiet environment
- Ability to control exterior light

Science
- Chemical- and acid-resistant materials
- Hard, cleanable floor finish
- Proper ventilation for chemical and gas use
- Water-resistant work surfaces, cabinetry, walls, and floors
- Chemical storage

Art
- Cleanable walls, floors, and ceilings (seamless preferred)
- Hard, smooth flooring
- Natural light
- Heavy-duty storage shelving
- Fire-resistant kiln area
- Water-resistant work surfaces, cabinetry, walls, and floors

CHAPTER 12
ACOUSTIC CONTROL

INTRODUCTION

The acoustical design of a space involves the attenuation of unwanted and disturbing sounds and the enhancement of desired sounds to the point at which they can be heard properly. Poor acoustical design in schools causes students to have trouble hearing and can thus hurt the learning process. The construction and mechanical systems of a building greatly affect its acoustics, which should therefore be a consideration as early as the schematic design phase. The best acoustic isolation occurs when isolation is not needed; in other words, when compatible adjacencies have been properly planned. With a clear understanding of acoustics, the architect can complete simple acoustic design alone, but in complex and critical cases should engage an acoustic consultant. It is almost impossible to fully attenuate noise, even with a double floor or double structure. With lack of proper acoustics in a classroom, reverberance can be so high that a teacher's speech can be distorted by the overlaying of reflected waves. This chapter outlines the areas of concern in the acoustics design of schools and suggests methods for creating effective acoustic spaces.

DEFINITIONS

We are concerned here with the clarification of those definitions directly applicable to the acoustic design of a school. We assume that the reader is acquainted with the fundamentals or basic nature of acoustics, and thus these are not considered.[1]

Sound is a wave, vibration, or change in pressure in an elastic medium, such as air, concrete, water, or glass. Note that sound can be defined as these disturbances themselves, or as the sensations they produce. We are concerned here with audible sound, or sound able to be heard by healthy ears within a detection range of 20–20,000 hertz (Hz). A sound radiates outward from its source until it strikes a room boundary or other surface, where it is partially absorbed, partially reflected, and partially transmitted to an adjoining space. Distance also attenuates sound intensity in large spaces.

Background Noise

Noise in a school can be generated inside or outside a space, by occupants, movement of furniture, HVAC systems, lighting systems, and ballasts, and can interfere with spoken messages; thus, louder speech is required. A range between two noise criteria (NC) curves has been developed to express typical background noise design criteria. The NC curves plot sound levels across eight standard frequencies at which sound levels in existing spaces can be tested.

1. Definitions are derived from the following: William J. McGuiness, Benjamin Stein, and John S. Reynolds, *Mechanical and Electrical Equipment for Buildings*, 6th ed. (New York: John Wiley & Sons, 1980). Charles M. Salter, *Acoustics: Architecture, Engineering, the Environment* (San Francisco: William Stout Publishers, 1998). *Federal Register* 36, *CFR*, chapter XI, "Architectural and Transportation Barriers Compliance Board: Petition for Rulemaking; Request for Information on Acoustics."

Maximum A-weighted steady background noise levels in unoccupied, furnished learning spaces (from ANSI S12.60):

Learning space Maximum one hour average A-weighted steady background noise level, in dB
Core learning <20,000 cu ft 35
Core learning >20,000 cu ft 40

ACOUSTICAL PERFORMANCE: MATERIALS AND SPATIAL PROPORTIONS

Three main criteria determine how effectively a student can hear and understand in a given space, and designers should consider these criteria from the preliminary design phase onward to ensure effective speech reception within a space:

Definitions

- *Sound absorption* is the process of removing sound energy, or the ability of materials, objects, and structures (e.g., a room) to absorb energy.
- *Reverberation* is an acoustical phenomenon that occurs in an enclosed space, such as a classroom, when sound persists in that space as a result of repeated reflection or scattering from surfaces enclosing the space or objects in the space, such as chairs or cabinets. A less reverberant environment allows sound events to be kept separate and is more suited to speech. A more reverberant environment should be designed for music.
- *A-weighted sound level* is sound pressure level measured with a conventional frequency weighting that roughly approximates how the human ear hears different frequency components of sounds at typical listening levels for speech. The A-weighting (see ANSI S1.4 or IEC 61672-1) attenuates the low-frequency (or low-pitch) content of a sound. A-weighted sound level is expressed in decibels (dB).
- *Noise criteria (NC) curves* are a set of spectral curves used to obtain a single-number rating describing the "noisiness" of environments for a variety of uses, and generally used to describe the maximum allowable continuous background noise. NC curves plot sound levels across the frequencies between 63 and 8,000 Hz, the speech-perception range. The NC curve of a room is the lowest curve that is not exceeded by sound levels measured at each frequency. NC criteria are often expressed as a range in specifying acceptable background noise levels. NC is typically used to rate the relative loudness of ventilation systems. Matching the NC curve will result in a rumbly or hissy sound and should not be used to design systems for masking speech and activity noise.
- *Noise reduction (NR)* is defined either as the reduction in sound-pressure level caused by making some alteration to a sound source, or as the difference in sound-pressure level between two adjacent rooms caused by the transmission loss of the intervening wall (in other words, the difference in background sound level between a source on one side of a wall and a receiver on the other).
- *Noise reduction coefficient (NRC)* is a single-number rating of the sound absorption of a material, equal to the arithmetic mean of the sound-absorption coefficients in the 250; 500; 1,000; and 2,000 Hz octave frequency bands, rounded to the nearest multiple of 0.05.
- *Sound transmission loss (STL)* is the decrease or attenuation in sound energy of airborne sound as it passes through a building construction. Generally, STL increases with frequency.
- *Sound transmission class (STC)* is a single-number rating of a wall or other assembly, describing the sound-insulating properties in the 100 to 4 kilohertz (kHz) range, primarily for assessing speech transmission through a structure.

Source: ASHRAE 1997 Fundamentals Handbook.

1. Distance of the student from the signal or source, and the effects of interference or loud background noise on the signal
2. The level of background noise from HVAC and lighting systems, or from sounds generated within or outside the room
3. The effects of reverberation

Designers can control background noise levels and reverberation, and thereby ensure good speech intelligibility. Typically, in terms of placement of acoustic control on the walls, floors, or ceilings, the surface of a room that is closest to all of the occupants all of the time is the surface that should be acoustically treated. In other words, where the length or width of a room is greater than the height of the ceiling, it is the ceiling that should be "softened," because it is the surface closest to most of the room's occupants.

It is equally acceptable to "soften" the floor by installing a carpet, but in terms of cost and maintenance, an acoustical tile ceiling with an NRC of at least 0.7 is often more practical in meeting the room's acoustical needs. With such a ceiling, there should be no need for additional control in a room during normal use. (Plaster ceilings should not be used in classrooms.)

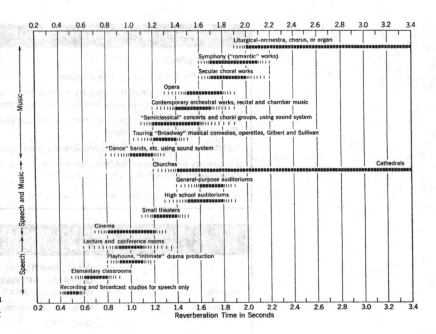

Walls in a classroom need not be treated unless the ceiling is unusually high and this height approaches the horizontal dimensions of the room.

Except in auditoriums, room dimensions are more important for audiovisual equipment than for acoustical applications. Most classrooms still work without audiovisual equipment other than basic video, television,

▲ Optimum reverberation (500–1,000 Hz) for auditoriums and similar facilities. Source: Stein and Reynolds 2000, p. 1537.

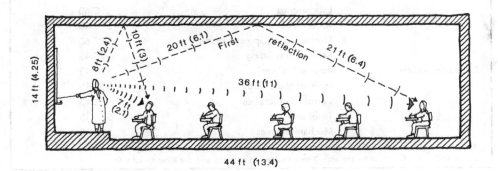

◀ Sound paths in a typical medium-size lecture room. The maximum path-length difference between direct and first reflection: 11 ft. Source: Stein and Reynolds 2000, p. 1536.

SUGGESTED NOISE-CRITERIA RANGES FOR STEADY BACKGROUND NOISE

TYPE OF SPACE	NC CURVE
Large auditoriums, large drama theaters	20–25
Small auditoriums, small theaters, music rehearsal rooms, large meeting and conference rooms (for good listening conditions)	
Libraries, private or semiprivate offices, small conference rooms (for good listening conditions)	30–35
Cafeterias, reception areas (for moderately good listening conditions)	35–40
Laboratory work spaces, lobbies, service areas, and engineering rooms (low speech intelligibility requirements)	40–45

Source: Adapted from McGuiness, Stein, and Reynolds, 1992.

RECOMMENDED SOUND TRANSMISSION CLASSES (STCS) FOR PARTITIONS IN NORMAL SCHOOL BUILDINGS

ROOM	WALL, PARTITION, OR PANEL BETWEEN ADJACENT AREAS	SOUND-ISOLATION REQUIREMENT
Classroom	Adjacent classrooms	STC 50
	Laboratories	STC 50
	Corridors or public areas	STC 45
	Kitchen and dining areas	STC 60
	Shops	STC 60
	Recreation areas	STC 60
	Music rooms*	STC 60
	Mechanical equipment rooms	STC 60
	Toilet areas	STC 53
Music or drama rooms	Adjacent music or drama rooms*	STC 60
	Corridors or public areas	STC 60
	Practice rooms*	STC 60
	Shops	STC 60
	Recreational areas	STC 60
	Laboratories	STC 60
	Toilet areas	STC 60
	Mechanical equipment rooms	STC 60
	Exterior of building	STC 45
Counseling offices	Adjacent offices	STC 45
	General office areas	STC 45
	Corridors or lobbies	STC 45
	Toilet areas	STC 45
	Mechanical areas	STC 60

*Requires decoupled construction such as double walls and floor, or a room within a room.
Source: ANSI S12.60 Acoustical Performance Criteria, Design Requirements, and Guidelines for Schools.

and overhead projector. Tele- and videoconferencing/distance has historically been available only in specially equipped classrooms, although this is changing as the use of computers and related technologies in classrooms becomes ever more widespread.

DESIGN GUIDES

Acoustic problems differ by room function.

Classrooms

Typically, classroom acoustic design is readily achieved through the location of sound-absorbing materials or treatments to reduce noise levels; by ensuring adequate privacy between adjacent spaces; and by controlling the noise of the mechanical systems. Classroom areas average 650–900 sq ft, with 10 ft high ceilings. Sound absorption is most easily provided by acoustic ceiling tiles with an NRC of 0.7. Alternatively, walls and floors may be treated. Full-height partitions should isolate and prevent disturbance from adjacent areas. The noise-reduction characteristics of any airtransfer ducts should be as good as those of the walls or doors they are penetrating.

Speech must be clearly heard, and the proper acoustic design for a classroom is a balance or compromise between the need for some reflection to achieve correct levels, and the need for absorption to maintain clarity and intelligibility. The optimum reverberation time for speech in a classroom with a volume less than 10,000 cu ft is 0.6 seconds, and for larger rooms and lecture halls, the reverberation time should be 0.7 seconds. A classroom should have a background noise of NC-30 or 35 dBA.

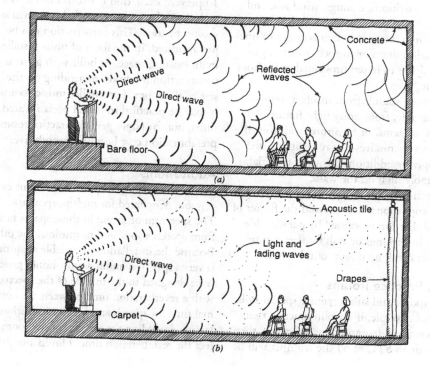

◀ Untreated space. In much of room (a), reverberant sound is the greatest part of received sound. Wall and ceiling absorption in room (b) eliminates most of these reflections. Source: Stein and Reynolds 2000, p. 1524.

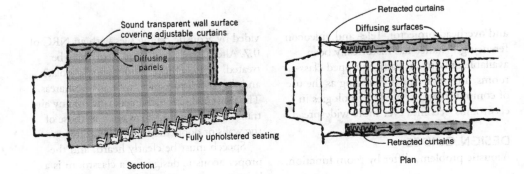

Section and plan of an auditorium with surface treatments. These control reflections and reverberation. Source: Stein and Reynolds 2000, p. 1544.

The following are guidelines for acoustic designs of classrooms:

- Minimize external noise.
- Where possible, locate classrooms away from noisy spaces such as gymnasiums and mechanical rooms.
- Design and specify adequate acoustic isolation in partitions, ceilings, windows, and doors.
- In certain cases it may be necessary to line ventilation ducts or to specify heavy, gasketed doors to lessen unwanted noise from outside.
- Unwanted sounds from inside a room— for example, from noisy light fixtures, HVAC systems, or furniture, and from the students themselves—may be attenuated by applying additional acoustic material, preferably high on the walls.
- There are no strict rules for room shapes and proportions, but to avoid the flutter of sound that can be caused by parallel side walls, furnishings or wall finishes can be used to break up direct sound waves.

Music Practice Rooms

Music rooms and suites require special isolation. For example, if a violin practice room is adjacent to a trumpet practice room, then even with an STC of 55 the trumpet will be heard in the adjacent room. A much higher STC is required, implying special construction. Generally, music rooms require decoupled construction: double walls and floor, or a room within a room.

Sound waves produced by music have a dynamic range and a tendency to excite the room construction into vibrating motion. To prevent excitation between both similar and dissimilar uses, decoupled construction should be used. This construction can be prefabricated, in the form of units installed in an existing space, or built with general construction methods, depending on the size of the room. For smaller music rooms, it may be practical to install prefabricated units, but for larger general practice rooms, prefabrication cost becomes prohibitive.

Auditoriums

School auditoriums are, almost without exception, designated for multipurpose use. The spectrum of sound in these spaces ranges from speech at one end to music at the other. Because the installation of variable acoustics is very expensive, auditoriums should generally be designed to the middle of the spectrum with a reverberation time between the optimal time for speech and for music. Various factors, including the volume of the room, affect the reverberation time. Elimination of extraneous noise and careful planning of the mechanical systems serving the space are important to the acoustic design.

When the reverberation time of a room has been established, acoustic materials should be placed in such a way that as the proper reverberation time is achieved, there are reflecting surfaces to help project sound and absorbing surfaces to prevent sound reflections. In an auditorium it is best to avoid placing absorptive surfaces on the ceiling or walls close to the stage; these surfaces should, rather, occur on the rear wall facing the stage. Open volumes to the roof deck can be used beneficially to maximize volume in the room and minimize the exterior height of the structure. In this case suspended open ceilings (i.e., "clouds") finished with a hard or smooth material may be used as reflectors. If needed, depending on the volume of the auditorium, soft absorptive surfaces can be placed on the side walls toward the rear of the room. Ceiling and side walls provide diffusion, and at the front of the auditorium they distribute sound to the audience. The reflective surfaces of ceilings and walls should be close enough to the performers to minimize delays between natural and reflected sound. Upholstered chairs are common, as they offer similar absorption characteristics for the audience that will occupy the space. Curtains can be used, where affordable, to achieve varying reverberation times, depending on the desired activity or function of the room. The use of circular spaces and curved side walls should be avoided, because such walls focus the sound waves rather than provide even reflection.

Air-handling systems serving auditoriums require special design, with low-pressure fans, slower-than-average air velocities (less

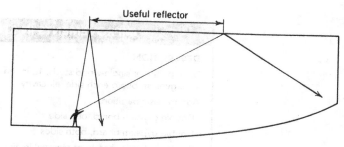

(a) Flat ceiling

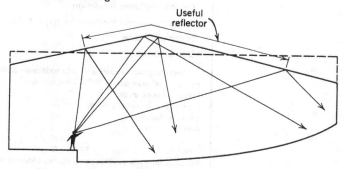

(b) Two panel ceiling increases useful reflecting area

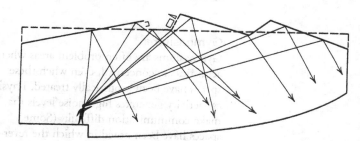

(c) Multifaceted ceiling incorporates lights and loudspeakers

than 1,000 ft per minute), and grilles and diffusers sized at maximum NC20, based on design air quantities.

Sound systems, incorporating microphones, loudspeakers, and control locations, are required in almost all auditoriums and should be part of the design of the space from the start.

▲ *Use of ray diagrams shown in section through a typical lecture room. Source: Stein and Reynolds 2000, p. 1542.*

IMPROVEMENTS IN STC RATING OF STUD[A] PARTITIONS

DESCRIPTION	STC
Basic partition: single-wood studs, 16 in. on centers. ½-in. gypsum board each side, air cavity	35
Add to basic partition:	
Double gypsum board, one side	+ 2
Double gypsum board, both sides	+ 4
Single-thickness absorbent material in air cavity	+3
Double-thickness insulation	+ 6
Resilient channel supports for gypsum board	+ 5
Staggered studs	+ 9
Double studs	+ 13

A. When using two improvements, add additional +2. When using three improvements, add additional +3.

Example: Improvements to 35 STC basic partition:

Staggered wood studs	+9
Double gypsum board, one side	+2
Single insulation	+3
Adder	+3
Total	+17
Total STC	35+17 = 52

For application to metal-stud partitions, use adders as above, except begin with STC = 40 for 3⅝ in. basic partition.

Source: Adapted from Stein and Reynolds 2000.

Gymnasiums

Gymnasiums are often problem areas where acoustics are concerned, even when these spaces have been acoustically treated. Physical activity generates high noise levels that make communication difficult. (Some spaces have been noted in which the reverberation times were so long that the instructor had to teach a physical education class in the hallway before sending the students back into the gym for the "physical" aspect of the class.) Although the acoustical design of gymnasiums is not nearly as critical as that of auditoriums, these spaces nevertheless require reasonable reverberation control. For practical reasons related to its use, the floor and walls of a gym must be hard, so the only surface that remains available for acoustical treatment is the ceiling. In most cases a gymnasium has a long-span roof structure, often with exposed trusses or beams, and acoustical material can be applied to the underside of the slab above. To afford adequate absorption to a lower frequency range, this material should be a minimum of 2 in. thick with an NRC of 0.7.

However, where a sound-amplification system is used, sound-absorbing wall treatment or devices may be required. Gymnasiums are sometimes used as auditoriums. In such cases, loudspeaker placement requires careful consideration, and it may be advisable to have flexibility in loudspeaker switching.

A gymnasium should never be located above any sensitive spaces, including classrooms. It is feasible, however, to place sensitive spaces above a gymnasium, inasmuch as the separating slab has a high STC and acoustic control is thus manageable. In addition, sensitive spaces should not be placed next to a gymnasium; instead, use mechanical space or a circulation zone as a buffer.

Laboratories

Fume hoods in chemistry and biology laboratories generate noise, because extraction is usually done by remote high-pressure fans. A hood has a pressure valve controlling the extracted air. This valve has to dissipate pressure, thereby generating noise. Thus, in selecting fume hood exhausts, the design team should review the acoustical performance and NC level of the equipment based on the pressure and air quantities to be controlled, and make sure that the NC level is no greater than 45–50 (a 10 decibel (dB) excedence over the ambient noise level).

Dining Areas

Cafeteria and lunchroom activities produce fairly high noise levels, so these should be separated from kitchens and serving areas. Sound-absorbing material, such as acoustic tile, should be applied to walls and ceilings. While ideally, the space should be carpeted for noise reduction, this may be impractical for maintenance and hygiene. The minimum NRC should be 0.8.

Shops

Tools and equipment in the metal, woodworking, and stage-scenery shops of schools generate very high levels of airborne and structure-borne noise. These areas should thus be carefully located in the initial planning of the building, preferably with an adjacency or combination of noisy areas, and should have ceiling and wall treatments with a minimum NRC of 0.75.

Swimming Pools

High humidity usually causes deterioration of the absorptive materials in the often unruly acoustic environments of school swimming pools. Special sound-absorbing and moisture-resistant materials, or combinations of materials, may have to be used to limit noise levels.

Mechanical Systems and Mechanical Rooms

Mechanical rooms with classrooms or other acoustically sensitive rooms located above or below need a minimum structural density in the floor slab so that the slab may act as a barrier to airborne sound and be sufficiently rigid to act as a stable platform for rotating equipment. Typically, the design team should look for 75–100 psf concrete to obtain a good shell in which to specify resilient mountings for the equipment. If the foundation is not sound, it has a tendency to resonate, and the decoupling provided by the mountings will be less efficient than theoretical predictions. Lightweight, flexible structures degrade isolation efficiencies of resilient mountings.

With proper planning, almost anything can be programmed over a mechanical space without designing an expensive, acoustically isolated structure. However, whenever practicable, direct adjacencies should be avoided. Mechanical rooms generate low-frequency sound; therefore, masonry is the better partitioning material inasmuch as it provides basic mass to absorb low-frequency waves. For speech privacy, on the other hand, masonry construction is not desirable, because the human voice lies midrange in the spectrum; drywall construction attenuates this sound effectively.

HEARING IMPAIRMENT AND ADA REQUIREMENTS

The Americans with Disabilities Act Accessibility Guidelines (ADAAG) state that in certain assembly areas where audible communications are integral to the use of the space (for example, in lecture and concert halls, playhouses, movie theaters, and meeting rooms), there must be a permanently installed assistive listening system in the following situations:

- If they accommodate at least 50 persons, or if they have audio-amplification systems
- If they have fixed seating[2]

A permanently installed assistive listening system, or an adequate number of electrical outlets or other supplementary wiring necessary to support a portable assistive listening system, must be provided for other assembly areas. The number of receivers that must be provided should be equal to a minimum of 4 percent of the total number of seats, but in no case should there be fewer than two receivers.

These regulations apply to new construction of classrooms seating at least 50 students or classrooms with fixed seating and audio-amplification systems. Sounds are

usually broadcast by the assistive listening system through infrared or FM signals transmitted from the speaker's microphone to listeners with special receivers and headsets. Such systems aid communication between teacher and student, but not between the students themselves.

A drawback of assistive listening systems is that they may be severely compromised by a reverberant noisy environment, where unwanted sounds are picked up by the microphone and transmitted to the listener, often impeding hearing ability. Design teams should thus take special care to prevent highly reverberant environments.

Published in the *Federal Register*, June 1, 1998, 36, *CFR*, chapter XI, the Architectural and Transportation Barriers Compliance Board's "Petition for Rulemaking: Request for Information on Acoustics" is highly recommended reading material as it sought to address the issue of poor classroom acoustics constituting an architectural barrier to education.[4] In 2000 the American National Standards Institute produced *Acoustical Performance Criteria, Design Requirements, and Guidelines for Schools* (ANSI S12.60-2002) which set voluntary standards for good classroom acoustics that have been widely adopted.

2. *Federal Register* 36, *CFR*, part 1191 4.1.3. 19(b).

4. The website may be accessed at http://www.access-board.gov/rules/acoustics.htm.

CHAPTER 13
LIGHTING DESIGN

INTRODUCTION

The lighting system is a critical factor in the design of a school, both in terms of its impact on energy costs and its effect on the health, performance, and stress levels of students. The Kats study *Greening America's Schools* cites the extensive research that supports the consensus finding that good lighting "improves test scores, reduces off-task behavior and plays a significant role in achievements of students" (2006, p. 10). It is vital that lighting and daylighting systems be carefully considered and that any value-engineering decisions take into account both first costs and long-term and maintenance costs, as well as the impact of any decision on the user. Inadequate lighting, glare, or conflicting lighting levels will cause eyestrain and make it hard for students to concentrate.

Classroom lighting requirements involve the illumination of the room, not just the desk, where light seems to be needed most. Classroom lighting is a diverse issue, inasmuch as classrooms are often used for different kinds of teaching and various types of classes, which may mean different lighting needs from day to day or from year to year. Thus the approach must be one whereby all problems are solved and all levels provided for without resulting in an over- or underlit space. This approach is especially important in elementary schools and kindergartens, where many activities can occur in a space at once, as compared with high schools and colleges, where the tasks tend to be more specific. There is no single solution or sim-

ple guideline for classroom lighting. A lighting method that perfectly illuminates a classroom with a 10 ft ceiling may not work in a room with a 9 ft ceiling.

Note that there is a vast difference between quantity and quality of light. The illumination of a classroom to 50 footcandles (fc), the generally accepted level, is often considered adequate, but no attention may be given to the way in which this illumination is achieved. The result can be a poorly lit space, even though the lighting level seems to be correct.

LIGHT LEVELS, LIGHT REFLECTANCE VALUES, AND GLARE

Research and experience point to the desirability of uniform brightness ratios in the field of vision and an average light reflectance value (LRV) of 50–60 percent in school environments. LRVs of surfaces and materials are shown in the table on the next page. The maximum brightness difference should not exceed 3 to 1.

Younger students require lower light levels—about 30–35 fc older students, for whom more detailed reading, requiring about 50 fc, must be accommodated. The table on page 221 shows recommended minimum illumination levels in schools.

A chemistry lab may need as much as 100 fc illumination on the benches, but not throughout the space, and the higher level on the benches may be achieved through task-lighting.

> Lighting can make a classroom come alive...Lighting must also contribute to the mood for learning...It must be a stimulant. Bland, coldly uniform, "scientifically planned" lighting usually has the opposite effect: it bores and depresses...The classroom can have lighting that changes, that is a shifting interplay of opposites—warm and cool, light and shadow, soft and hard, level light and accent light.
> (Perkins 1957, p. 37)

LIGHT REFLECTANCE VALUES (LRVS) OF SURFACES AND MATERIALS

SURFACE OR MATERIAL	LRV (%)
Furniture	40–50
Equipment	40–50
Doors and door frames	40–50
Floors	20–30
Walls	50–55
Teaching walls	45–50
Accent walls	45–50
Ceilings	90–100
Average for typical classroom	40–60

Source: Adapted from William C. Brubaker, *Planning and Designing Schools* (New York: McGraw-Hill, 1998).

RECOMMENDED LUMINANCE RATIOS

1 to 1/3	Between task and adjacent surroundings
1 to 1/10	Between task and more remote darker surfaces
1 to 10	Between task and more remote lighter surfaces
20 to 1	Between luminaires (or fenestration) and adjacent surfaces
40 to 1	Anywhere within the normal field of view

Source: Adapted from McGuinness, Stein, and Reynolds 1980.

Definitions

- *Candlepower (cp):* The unit of luminous intensity is the candlepower. A wax candle has a luminous intensity in the horizontal direction of about 1 candlepower.
- *Lumen (lm):* The unit of luminous flux, a measure of the perceived power of light, which is adjusted to reflect the varying sensitivity of the human eye to different light wavelengths. A candle radiates light equally in all directions. One lumen is the amount of luminous energy (flux) emanating from 1 sq ft of the surface of a transparent sphere with a radius of 1 ft surrounding a candle.
- *Footcandle (fc):* An illumination of one footcandle is produced when 1 lumen of luminous energy falls on 1 sq ft of area.
- *Illumination:* This can be expressed as the density of luminous energy, expressed in lumens per unit area, or footcandles. Measurements of illumination levels can be made with footcandle meters.
- *Luminance/brightness:* The luminous flux, or light, emitted, transmitted, or reflected from a surface. Luminance affects the acuity with which we see

objects, and, generally, visual performance increases with object brightness. The object's background, it should be noted, is important, and introduces the notion of contrast.
- *Contrast:* The contrast or luminance ratio between an object and its surroundings is important in creating and maintaining visual comfort. Depending on the task being performed, luminance ratios should decrease as luminance levels increase.
- *Light reflectance value* (LRV): The measurement of a material's ability to reflect light. The LRV of a material is used to establish the brightness ratio or luminance ratio of a room. Thus, it is important that the reflectances of the major surfaces in a room be considered and controlled.
- *Brightness ratios:* Although visual performance increases with contrast, the difference between the average luminance and that of the visual field or task should, conversely, be low. In other words, although contrast may be recommended in the *object* of view, it is detrimental to the *field* of view.

RECOMMENDED MINIMUM ILLUMINATION LEVELS IN SCHOOLS

TASK OR SETTING	FOOTCANDLES
Reading printed material	30
Reading pencil writing	70
Reading photocopied material:	
Good copy	30
Bad copy	100
Classrooms	
General	20–50
Chalkboards (supplementary illumination)	150
Drafting rooms	100
Laboratories	50–100
Lecture rooms	
General	70
Special exhibits and demonstrations	100–200
Auditoriums	10–20
Lip-reading classes	150
Shops	100
Sewing rooms	150
Sight-saving classes	150
Study halls	70
Social activity	5–10
Toilets and washrooms	20–50
Corridors and stairs	20–50

Figures are taken from Table 18.4 in McGuinness, Stein, and Reynolds 1980, and are based on IES standards and recommendations for maximum performance; and Gary J. Gordon and James L. Nuckolls, *Interior Lighting for Designers, 3d ed.* (New York: John Wiley & Sons, 1995).

In a teaching/lecturing type of class, it is important to reduce contrast for students looking up at the teacher and down at their books; a light balance is needed so that the students' eyes are not strained through constant adjusting. All surfaces should be lit.

The architect should ensure that desks, walls, blackboards, and screens are adequately lit. A brightness ratio of 5 to 1 ensures visual comfort and minimizes strain. From normal viewpoints, brightness ratios be-tween areas of appreciable size should be restricted to the approximate values shown in the table above so that a comfortable brightness balance is reached.

Glare, an effect of extreme contrast or luminance, can be disturbing and frustrating to students. If light is coming from the wrong direction because of too much luminance, there will be glare. To limit glare, the designer can either limit the amount of light emitted toward the eye of the observer or

▶ *The diagram shows direct and reflected glare light paths, with direct glare strongest in a head-up position, and reflected glare at a reading position. Glare can be controlled when lighting design takes into consideration room size, surface finishes, size and placement of light sources (including windows), and luminance ratios. Source: Stein and Reynolds 2000, p. 1084.*

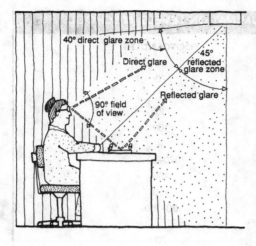

increase the area from which light is emitted (i.e., increase the number of fixtures). The careful location of light fixtures is also vital in the prevention of glare. In terms of the overall design of a space, one should remember that too many light fixtures that are poorly located can create "clutter" in the field of vision, which can be equated to static or noise in acoustic design. Reflected glare, which is as distracting as direct glare, results when there is too much uncontrolled luminance reflected by surfaces or objects. The designer should beware of reflected

glare from desk surfaces and, especially, computer screens. Direct and indirect glare are most easily avoided by indirect lighting systems.

There is no formula governing light fixture choice: this should be a function of what the architectural design, the LRV, and the brightness ratio of the spaces must be. Direct/indirect lighting is more comfortable with adequate ceiling heights (9–9½ ft).

The color of the walls is part of the lighting design. A colored accent wall in a classroom can help to relieve eyestrain and glare and to focus attention. Colors in the cool range, such as soft greens and blues, are usually best, although it must be noted that choice of color depends on the type of school environment. For example, in elementary schools, bright, warm colors are often used to inspire students.

Sophisticated audiovisual presentations have become more prevalent with advances in technology, especially in more affluent schools. Here the architect may have to introduce multilevel switching and dimming, whereby, for example, three or four rows of lights may be operated individually to set the required light levels. In all likelihood, the cost of school construction is such that

▶ *Size, luminance, and location in the field of view determine the glare afforded by a fixture. The diagram shows how, due to the apprehended solid angles of source, the glare from a small source, through luminance, is less objectionable than a source on a dark background. For this reason ceilings and upper walls should be light-colored to reduce glare. Source: Stein and Reynolds 2000, p. 1085.*

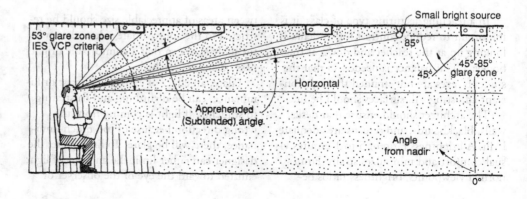

(a) (b) (c)

The diagrams show how reflected glare is reduced as the number of light fixtures is increased and luminance decreased, with an all-luminous ceiling producing the least glare. Source: Stein and Reynolds 2000, p. 1096.

this level of sophistication will never be sufficiently affordable to become the norm, but will be achieved primarily in specialized rooms. Nevertheless, audiovisual teaching methods and the use of computers are increasingly becoming the norm for learning.

ELECTRIC LIGHTING SYSTEMS

The most common electric lighting system is a two-by-four fluorescent lamp lay-in troffer. This is appropriate where students read books at their desks, but does not take into account multipurpose use or the increasing presence of computers in the classroom. Computers have introduced new lighting needs for which traditional prismatic lenses, although cost-effective, are not adequate.

Parabolic louvers can create a shielding zone to reduce glare and provide pleasant lighting levels. The disadvantages are that louvers add to the cost of a troffer and may cast shadows on walls, creating a dark ceiling zone even though the work surfaces are adequately illuminated.

Increasingly often, indirect lighting systems are being used in computer labs and classrooms, where it is important that glare and reflection on the computer screen be avoided. Indirect lighting systems use ceilings, and sometimes walls, to reflect light and illuminate a space softly and evenly.

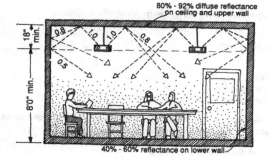

80% - 92% diffuse reflectance on ceiling and upper wall

18" min.

8'0" min.

40% - 60% reflectance on lower wall

Indirect fixtures directly illuminate ceilings and upper walls, which become secondary sources to illuminate the spaces below. A largely uniform brightness can be produced with good indirect lighting design. Source: Stein and Reynolds 2000, p. 1215.

Users of such a space tend to have fewer headaches and less eyestrain and visual fatigue than users of the aforementioned systems. Effective indirect lighting provides little contrast and no bright spots; thus, the fixtures typically must be suspended at least 18 in. from the ceiling and spaced in rows approximately 10 ft apart.[2] The ceiling height may need to be raised to maintain 8 ft between the bottom of the fixture and the floor. Indirect lighting is usually more expensive, in terms of first cost, than the other systems described earlier. However, spaces that are indirectly lit appear brighter owing to the elimination of shadows, and thus less

2. This spacing depends on the suspension length. For example, a row spacing of 12 ft is acceptable with a 24 in. suspension length. Some features are effective when mounted less than 12 in. from the ceiling.

LIGHTING SYSTEMS COMPARISON					
	PRISMATIC LENSES	PARABOLIC LOUVERS	INDIRECT LIGHTING	WINDOWS	SKYLIGHTS
Lens	A12, A19	3 in. deep, RP-24	None	Glass	Acrylic
ADVANTAGES	A12: Low cost A19: Slightly less glare and more comfort than with A12 lenses	3 in. deep: Reduces glare RP-24: Eliminates glare	Excellent visual comfort, especially in computer spaces	View, daylight	Daylight, color quality, savings, high light levels
DISADVANTAGES	A12: High glare, low comfort A19: Slightly higher cost Both: Not recommended for computer rooms	3 in. deep: Cost RP-24: High cost	Cost	Vandalism	First cost, potential leaks resulting from penetration of roof membrane, limitations on control of light levels
APPLICATION	A12: Low budget, no computers A19: Small budget, no computers	Computer spaces, low-ceiling aesthetics	Computer spaces, high ceilings	Classrooms and offices	Classrooms, media centers, gymnasiums, and offices

Source: Adapted from table in Paul N. Grocoff, 1995, "Electric Lighting and Daylighting in Schools," IssueTrak: A CEFPI Brief on Educational Facility Issues, http://www.eric.ed.gov/ERICWebPortal/custom/portlets/recordDetails/detailmini.jsp?_nfpb=true&_&ERICExtSearch_SearchValue_0=ED426580&ERICExtSearch_SearchType_0=no&accno=ED426580 (accessed 6/09).

lighting is needed. In fact, directly lit classrooms require illumination of 50–100 fc, as compared with 35 fc for indirectly lit spaces. The resultant energy savings usually compensates over time for the higher initial fixture cost.

The advantages and disadvantages of different lighting systems are described in the table above.

WINDOWS AND DAYLIGHTING

Windows bring air and light into a room and connect the room with the world outside. They introduce different ventilation and lighting requirements for a school, and the choice of a window system has an impact on both the owner and the user. The issue of windows in classrooms has been much debated, ranging from the introduction of windowless classrooms at one time in the State of Florida, to laws in New York State that require 50 percent of a window wall to be glazed. In some schools, windows are targets for vandalism and crime, and it has been argued that views to the outdoors are distracting to students. However, a report in the *Archives of Internal Medicine* advocates the compulsory use of windows as a necessary relief. The report states that the type of distraction caused by windows is "soft," and that without windows students become even more focused on doodling in their books and can less easily refocus their attention on the teacher.

Windows and daylight in a space can have the following effects:

- Daylighting introduces high contrasts, and north- and south-facing rooms have different lighting requirements. Northern Hemisphere south-facing windows can be designed with *brise-soleils*—"eyebrows" or shades against the summer sun—and winter sun can be used to advantage (e.g., for solar warming). West-facing windows should be avoided where feasible.
- In a classroom supplied with 60 fc of electric light, sunlight may introduce 8,000–10,000 fc and, hence, a large contrast.
- Daylighting can be used to control lighting costs through the careful design of the electric lighting system.
- Daylighting usually introduces the need for shading devices, inasmuch as too much sunlight can cause glare and heat up a room.
- Energy loss or heat gain through windows can be minimized by the orientation of classrooms in the plan, by the efficient design of the windows themselves, and by the use of shading devices.
- Vandalism can be countered by the organization of the plan around a courtyard or easily monitored areas, and by the use of skylights, which also provide good light levels.
- Interior windows are an excellent means of invigorating the design of a school, making visual links to different activities and displaying the educational process and its programs while, at the same time, trans-

mitting light. At times, the use of glass block is an appropriate device for lighting an interior space while maintaining its privacy, as is the use of skylights.

DESIGN GUIDES

Schools buildings and commercial, office, and institutional buildings in many ways have similar lighting requirements. However, school construction, renovation, and operating/maintenance budgets and allowances are nearly always small, and, thus, equipment, including lighting, must be:

- Maintenance-free, as much as possible
- Energy-efficient
- Long-lasting
- Tough and relatively damage-proof

In choosing light fixtures, the following guidelines should be noted.

In general

- Daylight is the most efficient light source.
- Fixtures and/or their ballasts may generate noise.
- To reduce maintenance, long-life lamps and fixtures are important. In corridors and less accessible or high-ceilinged spaces, extended-life fluorescent lamps are longer-lasting and require less frequent changing.
- Light fixtures are cleaned infrequently, which affects light levels. Generally, the design and selection of fixtures should be based on the assumption that maintenance will be infrequent.

Classrooms

- Surface reflectance is important.
- Compare life-cycle costs of different lighting systems.

▲ *This student union area makes effective use of natural light. Berkeley High School, Berkeley, California. ELS Architecture and Urban Design. Photograph by David Wakely.*

- Compare life-cycle costs with first costs.
- Maximize daylighting.
- Multiple lighting levels may be required for varying teaching applications, and this is achieved economically by multiple switching and multilevel ballasts.
- For direct-indirect and direct fixtures, use standard fluorescent cool and warm white lamps.
- Incandescent lamps are not advisable.

Auditoriums and multipurpose spaces
- Flexible, dimmable lighting is recommended.
- Incandescent lamps are often preferred, but new lamps and fixtures are changing preferences.
- Additional fluorescent or high-intensity discharge (HID) fixtures may be required to supplement light levels for writing and study tasks.
- Long-life lamps are advisable because of the relatively inaccessible higher ceilings.
- Install lights on steps or tiers for safety.
- Locate noisy ballasts carefully.

Gymnasiums
- Use tough, well-protected fixtures that can be relamped from the floor with a pole.
- Provide multilevel switching to allow multipurpose use of the space.
- Take into account the accumulation of dirt.

Lecture halls
- Lighting is similar to that of classrooms.
- Use switching and multilevel ballasts to achieve three-level fluorescent lighting.
- Locate clearly labeled light switches at the entrance and at the front of the room. Label switch cover plates so that users know which lights the switches control.
- Locate a row of adjustable fixtures to light the front of the room.
- Chalkboards and marker boards may be lit with fluorescent fixtures.
- Control the entry of light from outside the room, and use narrow vision panels in doors.
- In large lecture halls, spotlights are recommended to light the speaker/teacher during a film or slide presentation.
- In applications where a chalkboard and a screen are used concurrently, separate lights may be needed.

- If possible, locate doors so that light from outside the room does not fall on and wash out the screen when a door is opened during a class or lecture.

Art rooms

- Skylights or north-facing windows are recommended.
- Design for constant-color daylight.
- For artificial lighting, use deluxe fluorescent tubes.
- Provide task-lighting, adjustable by students.
- Use spotlights for certain focused, detailed applications.
- Provide track-mounted incandescent lights, adjustable wall-washing fixtures,

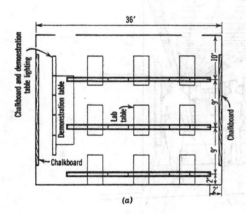

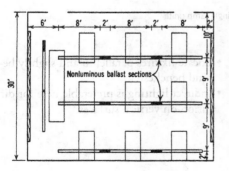

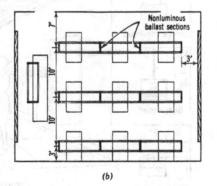

◀ *Laboratory lighting schemes. Running lights across tables or in aisles is preferable to the transverse direction from the aspect of reflected glare. (a) Pendant direct-indirect units. (b) and (c) variations of the single, semidirect design. The relatively high noise level of ballasts is generally not objectionable in labs, although quiet electronic ballasts are recommended for their acoustic and energy characteristics. Source: Stein and Reynolds 2000, p. 1304.*

▲ *This photograph of an exhibition room demonstrates good and bad lighting techniques. High windows give excellent daylight penetration. The art display is perfectly highlighted by track lighting, but the tracks should be carefully positioned to prevent glare and shadows, especially when the ceiling is lower than 10 ft high. Also, here the incandescent downlights for general lighting are used excessively and unattractively. Source: Stein and Reynolds 2000, p. 1302.*

LIGHTING DESIGN

▶ Library stack lighting is best accomplished by fixtures with lenses specifically designed for the purpose. Fixtures with baffles and plastic diffusers generally do not give adequate vertical surface illumination. Source: Stein and Reynolds 2000, p. 1305.

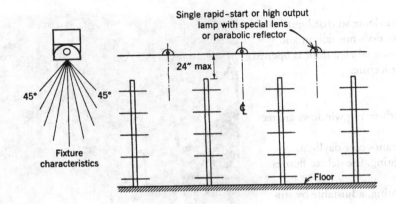

▶ Lighting of school corridors. High-reflectance walls, floor, and ceiling improve utilization of light and increase the feeling of cheerfulness. The lighting technique illustrated is appropriate for school corridors. The rows of luminaires at each side wall illuminate bulletin boards, special displays, and the faces of interiors of lockers more efficiently than do units centered in the ceiling. Source: Stein and Reynolds 2000, p. 1306.

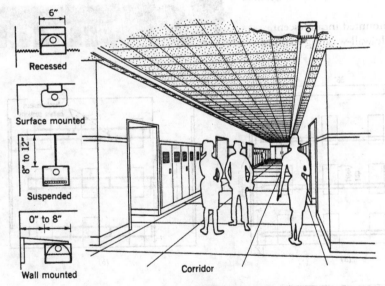

Wall lighting with single lamp units

or color-corrected fluorescent fixtures for display of artwork.

Laboratories

• Lighting approaches should take into account fixed, dark-colored benches and shiny surfaces.

• Locate fixtures parallel to and slightly behind benches.

• Indirect lighting is preferable here for diffusion on vertical surfaces.

Libraries

- Lighting should accommodate the various activities and areas that typically make up a library, primarily the reading room(s) and stacks.
- Reading rooms may be lit with the use of general lighting, such as fluorescent or HID sources, or lower-level general lighting reinforced by fluorescent task-lighting at the carrels or tables. Beware of noisy ballasts. Ceiling heights should be a minimum of 10 ft when HID fixtures, such as metal halide or deluxe mercury, are used.
- For the stacks, specially designed fluorescent fixtures, mounted between and 2 ft above the shelving, are available to light the vertical surfaces.
- Work and checkout areas require lighting similar to that of the reading room, with higher lighting levels.
- Direct-indirect lighting is recommended for computer areas.

▲ In this cafeteria, soft, even, glare-free light from cove lighting in a pyramidal coffer is of sufficient intensity to permit the cafeteria to double as a work/study and meeting space. Source: Stein and Reynolds 2000, p. 1303.

CHAPTER 14
INTERIOR ISSUES

While exterior architecture responds to the context of its community, interior architecture should accept the transition from the public to the more personalized student realm. With increased community use of school facilities being more common, it is important to create identifiable public, staff, and student zones that are unique in character and scale and are also securable for after-hours use. While the community should feel welcomed into public facilities, each student should feel that he or she has "a home within the school." To create this feeling, the scale of the building and the interior detailing should be based on the ages of the student population. Appropriately sized corridors, ceiling heights, furnishings, and toilet facilities are just some of the important ergonomic and design considerations.

CLASSROOMS

Classrooms should respond to the needs of the students they serve. This is particularly important in developing elementary school classrooms where children spend most of their day. Classrooms often define the success of a particular school design from the perspective of "user satisfaction." Major characteristics of good school design include appropriately sized furniture, adequate day lighting, and well designed mechanical, data, and electrical infrastructure systems.

Elementary School Classrooms

Square-footage requirements are driven by the need of the students to move around and participate in a variety of learning activities

◀ School interiors—in particular common spaces—can have surprising and whimsical details. The Bay School of San Francisco, San Francisco, California. Leddy Maytum Stacy Architects. Photograph by Tim Griffith.

as discussed in chapter 1. Elementary school children should feel a sense of ownership and be able to easily distinguish their space from other classrooms. Within the room, each student should have an area for personal space. Cubicles or cubbyholes for personal storage have traditionally served the smaller student, and individual desks or lockers have been used as the child grows older. A variety of areas should be offered within the classrooms so that the child can engage in group activity or move away for individual quiet study.

The classroom must reflect the teaching methods of the school; it must be an efficient tool and a suitable atmosphere for education, regardless of the educational approaches used (Perkins 1957, p. 22).

▲ Pairs of elementary classrooms open to each other to facilitate team teaching. Concordia International School, Shanghai, China. Perkins Eastman. Photograph by Tim Griffith.

◤ Cubicles for personal storage are an important fixture in most elementary schools. Courtesy of VS America, Inc.

For small children, it is important that spaces not be physically or emotionally overwhelming, but approachable and friendly. Areas regularly occupied by each child should be grouped into smaller subunits. For example, a young child should not have to travel far from the home-base classroom to special classes like art and music. In a large school, this may mean the creation of mini-schools to serve a number of home-base classrooms. This type of educational program is seen in the house concept discussed in chapter 1, in the section on middle schools.

The support areas of the classroom should also be sized to be accessible to the age group of the students served. Among the components to be considered are the following:

- Toilet facilities—sink height, fixture size and height, height of dispensers, etc.

- Appropriate opportunities for children with physical disabilities to participate as part of the group
- Depth of counter and sinks within the classroom
- Water fountains
- Cubicles
- Door handles
- Light switches

The ergonomic diagram on page 243 can aid in determining the appropriate height for placement of equipment and provisions for handicapped access and wheelchair clearances to meet the Americans with Disabilities Act (ADA) requirements. Height regulations, which tend to be higher than necessary for general students, must be balanced with the lower heights required for younger student populations.

Middle School and High School Classrooms

As students grow, the scale of the support areas gradually begins to conform to adult dimensions, and the spaces are adjusted to encourage the movement of students from classroom to classroom. In middle school, the corridors widen, with students' personal space becoming part of the public corridor areas, introducing informal gathering areas and breakout spaces.

General classrooms become more standardized in their layout, supporting specific academic subjects. General classrooms can also support cross-disciplinary learning where a variety of topics are all covered within one learning period. The shift toward cross-disciplinary learning can also be supported by enhanced technology such as tablet computers, smartboards, or even podcasting. Project breakout rooms can also be provided to allow students to work individually in response to their need to learn at different rates with different learning styles.

At the high school level, students are typically more mobile within their building. Travel from class to class occurs over a large area of the school. Students' contacts increase, and the building should provide opportunities for impromptu meetings along the travel paths. The interiors can have a dual focus with both public space and the academic classrooms.

Planning for Teams

The middle school students' home-base area is often the "house" to which they are assigned. The house is composed of a cluster of classrooms containing the core curriculum requirements—science, math, English, social studies—utilized by a student at any given period of the day. This area supports the students' main class subjects and also serves as a home base. Lockers are often also included in close proximity to the classrooms as part of the home-base area so as to promote positive social interaction. These areas should also be adjacent to administrative spaces that can serve as the "eyes and ears" on the corridor. Each house should have its own identity within the overall school. Color-coding and the use of particular materials can further support the identity of each house. Provided with the medium scale of the houses as learning environments, middle school students can grow and transition from the more intimate learning environment of the elementary school and be prepared for the more self-directed learning that occurs in high school.

Although the house or school-within-a-school concept has been used on large high school campuses, the buildings were traditionally designed with a departmental model focus like science, social studies, and math, surrounding the shared areas at the build-

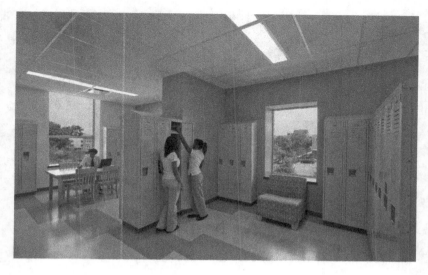

▲ The interior design should provide spaces for impromptu meetings. Ralph Ellison High School, Chicago, Illinois. OWP/P. Photograph by James Steinkmap.

A good school building is like a good house—or a hotel for kids and teachers—in that it has a variety of spaces that provide a variety of opportunities for interaction. (Strickland 1994)

▲ A project breakout room. Timberline Middle School, Alpine, Utah. VCBO Architecture. Photograph by Dana Sohm, Sohm Photografx.

ing's core. There are number of other organizational strategies that decentralize these departments into interdisciplinary teams; these are discussed in chapter 2. In addition to core classrooms, small "multipurpose" rooms are often provided as breakout space for student or faculty meetings, project work or tutoring. Disciplines with special requirements, such as the sciences or the graphic arts, which are increasingly technically complex, are shared between the various houses or teams.

In high schools, increased emphasis is placed on public areas like theaters, gymnasium, art studios, music facilities, commons areas and media centers. These spaces should be accessible, functional, include wireless network access, and be comfortable for visitors as well as students and staff.

GENERAL USE SPACE

Public and primarily adult-use areas, such as administrative and staff offices, conference rooms, nurse's room or "sick bay," and guid-

ance offices, along with other public gathering areas, should support adult users. Adjustments should be made to certain elements of these spaces, such as the reception desk, furnishings, and signage, as these areas will support both student and adult use. For example, a section of the reception desk may be at lower height to allow young children or students in wheel chairs visual contact with the receptionist. Areas of larger square footage, like the cafeteria, media center, and gymnasium, and those spaces students encounter directly, such as computer stations or food-service counters, should be sized for student use.

The use of materials, color, and furnishings can support different places within the building by emphasizing a variety of scales and uses available to all of the students. The textures, both physical and visual, of the interior should be age-appropriate. For younger students, a simple graphic or material pattern that is easily understood and relates to their travel through the building is preferred. As the student population ages, many more mature schemes can be pursued that lend a level of complexity and texture to the space. The weaving of natural light into the design texture of the building can support the students' daily enjoyment of the spaces. Natural light should be used creatively in all areas of the school building. Although mandated by many codes for instruction rooms, the use of daylighting as an aid in defining space should not be limited to classrooms. It can allow occupants to understand their relationship to the exterior at any given point within the building and can aid in their orientation. A number of studies, including one by Alberta Education's Light Study have shown similar positive effects of natural light in classrooms. Along with a reduction in electrical costs, natural light, studies have shown, can have beneficial health and educational effects:

- Children receiving trace amounts of ultraviolet (UV) radiation in their classrooms had 1.75 fewer cavities per child per year than children in non-UV schools.
- Children exposed to high pressure sodium vapor lighting were absent 3.2 days per year more than students under full spectrum and full-spectrum with UV enhancement.

Scholastic achievement was significantly linked to light. Students exposed to high-pressure sodium vapor lighting demonstrated the poorest rate of achievement.

FLEXIBILITY

The growing diversity in teaching and learning styles has influenced the design of classrooms and breakout spaces to become multifunctional learning environments. The specification of products and furniture for these spaces must be easily adaptable to different spatial configurations. Finishes, furnishings, and equipment need to be carefully considered, and audiovisual and acoustical criteria need to be appropriately defined for every space.

Movable and demountable walls can also be used to create additional flexibility within classroom areas. Two traditional classrooms can be opened up to each other to provide large-group instruction and team teaching. Furnishings for these areas should be considered part of the individual classrooms and should coordinate with the overall space whenever the spaces are combined.

In elementary schools, spaces such as the auditorium and the gymnasium or multipurpose room can join to form a "gymatori-

um," or combine the auditorium with a cafeteria to create a "cafetorium." Where space is a premium, other combinations can include

- Merging the seating areas of the media center and the cafeteria for shared use
- Using a movable partition to turn an auditorium balcony into a separate lecture room
- Aligning a black box theater with a gymnasium and providing an operable wall between them, allowing the black box to function as a stage and the gymnasium as the seating area or "house"
- Populating what was traditionally the "hallway" with breakout space, computer commons, and informal seating areas, within allowable tolerances and in conformance with fire and egress codes

▲ *Views to the exterior can aid student orientation when traveling through the school. Burr Street Elementary School, Fairfield, Connecticut. Skidmore, Owings & Merrill LLP. Photograph by SOM/Robert Polidori.*

▶ *The alignment of a green box theater with the gymnasium creates improved flexibility for a wide variety of uses. Courtesy of Perkins Eastman.*

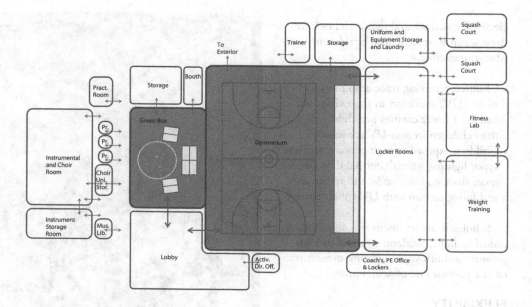

It should be remembered that successfully integrating audiovisual and acoustic criteria can be challenging when combining uses into a single flexible space.

Multiple-use space must be supported with the selection of appropriate materials, lighting, and furniture to better define alternative uses. For instance, theatrical lighting and a good sound system in a cafeteria can transform it into a presentation and meeting center. While there will be a cost premium for the interior construction and equipment, the savings can often be offset by the reduction in built space.

The following materials and furnishings should be considered in multipurpose rooms:

- Renewable resource flooring, such as linoleum rubber flooring made from recycled content
- Accent walls that can shift the focus of the room and provide some visual relief

- Multiple lighting levels
- Separate table and chair combinations
- An integrated sound and video projection system

If projection equipment or sound systems are built in, care should be taken to provide adequate protection from balls and activities that could strike and damage the equipment. Storage for furnishings and teaching materials is also very important to maintain the flexibility of the space.

FURNISHINGS

Furniture selection is an aspect of contemporary school design that is often underappreciated but can have tremendous impact on the success of the facility.

In selecting furniture for schools, several factors are considered: the age of the students, the appropriate height and size of furnishings, ergonomic features (dynamic back, adjustable height, etc.), the durability of construction and materials (recycled content or easily recycled furniture), and the proposed activity. For example, an art class in an elementary school will require child-sized chairs made of materials that allow for easy cleanup, whereas a computer class in a high school may have an "adult" upholstered computer chair.

Small children require small-scale desks, chairs, counters, and other furnishings. Chairs should be made of spill-resistant materials and should be light enough for children to maneuver. The base of the chair should be selected based on the flooring used in the room. Work surfaces should be of durable, wipe-off materials that hide scarring and resist scratches. With small children's susceptibility to germs, the ability to disinfect all pieces is important. Many products are resistive to the growth of bacteria and germs.

Furniture color and materials should also be selected to balance the facility's architectural palette. Selections should be relatively neutral and easily matched to other materials in the room, providing a visually quiet background to student work or subject material.

Furnishings provided within individual program areas should support the learning objectives of the space. Nowhere is this more apparent than in the classroom. Classroom furniture is changing. Tables and chairs are becoming the norm, in lieu of the tablet-arm chairs once the norm in middle and high schools This change facilitates the multiple teaching and learning opportunities, including small-group and project-based work, lecture, presentation, research and conference configurations.

Specialty programs have their own unique requirements. Art rooms and science

▲ Informal breakout spaces built into the circulation. The Urban School, San Francisco, California. SMWM. Photograph by Tim Griffith.

laboratories may need stand-up work areas at counters that support large projects, while a music room may need only a chair and a music stand for each student. Furnishings should allow some flexibility in space arrangement, except in areas of extremely specific functions, such as a graphics lab or distance learning center in a high school, where the incorporation of technology will dictate the selection of furniture.

Many school settings have ambiguous functions and are used for a variety of purposes. With the increase of multiple-use areas and multipurpose rooms, the flexible use of the space is increased but the exact function for which furnishing must be provided is less obvious to the designer. When faced with this circumstance, the client may have to compromise among the various uses. A cafetorium may be furnished with stacking chairs and foldable roll-away tables. When the space is in cafeteria mode, the chairs are

▲ More ergonomic, flexible, and durable furniture is an increasingly important design consideration. Ralph Ellison High School, Chicago, Illinois. OWP/P. Photograph courtesy of VS America Inc.

set up around the tables; when it is an auditorium, the same chairs are placed in rows for audience members and the tables are rolled away to storage.

Young people are becoming increasingly sophisticated in their tastes, and the furnishings in a high school must do likewise, creating a "workplace for learning." Although adult-dimensioned furnishings may be appropriate, the strength and life cycle of the pieces become critical. Schools should purchase furnishings that are durable, provide good ergonomic support for the children, are appropriate to the tasks assigned, are easily cleanable, and can be recycled when their life cycle has expired. The furnishings provided in the more private areas of the schools (e.g., classrooms) should be functional, durable, cleanable, and comfortable. The more public realms of a school should be comfortable for visitors and parents. For example, the furnishings in an administra-

tion reception area may be upholstered, cushioned, sofa-type furnishings, whereas classroom chairs may be high-density plastic on chrome structures.

In all the practical, functional, and flexible uses of furnishings, the designer should not underestimate the value of furniture in making an aesthetic statement. Furniture that fits the user group, the intended use, and the aesthetic scheme of the building is an essential part of a successful design.

There are a number of questions to consider in selecting furnishings:

Curriculum perspective
• Will the subject be taught to an entire class at once, to student teams, or both?
• Will students work in teams on their own?
• What books, electronic readers, and learning materials will the students require as they work at their desks, tables, or computers?
• How frequently and to what extent will the class work require reconfiguration of the furniture plan?
• Is the classroom subject-specific or interdisciplinary?
• Is there a laptop or electronic reader program in place, or anticipated in the near future?

Building interface perspective
• How are electrical power and computer cabling distributed in the classroom, and what will be required in the future? What kind of built-in flexibility has been incorporated?
• How is wire management addressed? Are there wireless capabilities? Should it be part of the building design or the furniture design?
• Is the lighting adjustable to allow for projection or large video display?

General perspective
- Are materials durable, safe, recyclable, and relatively maintenance-free?
- What is the best way to accommodate a broad range of student sizes? Should adjustments in table height require the efforts of maintenance personnel?
- Should a percentage of the total chair purchase include adjustable height capability?
- Are tables/counters handicapped accessible?
- How will storage of students' books and materials be accommodated?
- What kind of accommodation is provided for backpacks?

TECHNOLOGY

Certain basic issues should be considered where computers are being used regardless of the scale of the space, whether it is an individual classroom with a few stations or a computer learning laboratory for an entire class. Contemporary school design recognizes that it is difficult to predict where computers will be used in the future. It's safe to assume that it will be anywhere and everywhere and not confined to a "computer lab"; therefore, all spaces in the school should be designed for various technologies including electronic readers, smart boards, video display, and computers. Considerations for this provision include

- Appropriate lighting and control systems
- Proper relationship between table height (keyboard height) and the chair for a given user
- Power, data, and wireless accessibility

The following are some design considerations for the reduction of glare in computer environments:

- Even illumination, without hot spots or glare
- Automatic light-level sensors that balance daylight with artificial lighting to maintain constant levels of illumination and reduce energy costs
- Diffusion of natural light with blinds, louvers, or roof overhangs and sun shelves
- Arrangement of rooms and their furnishings to reduce the effects of glare
- Specification of absorptive rather than reflective finishes within classroom spaces

In an area dedicated to computer use, the floor treatment and construction are important. Although a hard-surface tile floor is not recommended because it may produce a glare, some types of carpeting can cause the buildup of static electricity in a dry atmosphere, which can harm sensitive electronics of a computer. Several manufacturers have developed carpeting systems that reduce or eliminate static buildup. Another flooring system often used in computer areas that require the option for frequent rearrangement of workstations is an elevated sectional computer floor. This system provides several inches of height between the permanent subfloor of a room and the finished walking surface, where computer wiring can run unrestricted by furnishings. Wireless technology and the cost of this option usually restrict use of raised computer floors.

Work surfaces available to schools for use with computers vary in design. In selecting tables or desks for computers, the proposed use is critical. A workstation setup for data entry and retrieval will vary compared to one for reading, music exploration, or computer drafting. It is mainly the use of technology tools, combined with the instruction method that will inform the selection of furnishings.

Any special needs should be documented with the client, solutions should be developed, and appropriate furnishings and equipment specified. Several issues are critical in the selection of furniture for use with computers:

• Keyboard height
• Monitor positioning in relation to the keyboard and the viewers eye level
• Depth of the workstation to accommodate the monitor, keyboard, and spare work surface
• Size of the user group
• Specific tasks for which the technology will be used
• Selection of comfortable, adjustable, rolling chairs with sturdy backs
• Flexibility of table and chair arrangement
• Instructional style of the teachers

While wireless technology is more and more common, areas with concentrated, fixed technology still exist. The wiring layout for areas with intensive computer technology is critical to locating the hub and head in rooms that service the entire facility. The type of system to be installed defines the location of these rooms. In general, hub locations should be centrally located in areas that allow for easy access by technicians. Wiring should be run in accessible locations for easy rerouting and servicing. Many schools have utilized a wiring trough or raceway hung from the structure above finished ceilings to condense computer cabling.

The options for dedicated stations within a classroom versus laptop technology on carts or distributed to every student will affect the overall requirements for wireless transmitters, data drops, and electrical outlets. One of the major decisions to be made by a district is their strategy for integrating computer technology into their schools. The types of systems, the location and number of computers within a school, and their relationship to the curriculum will affect the overall network and system designs. The technology policy adopted by the school system—as discussed in chapter 10—can have a profound impact on the interior design and furnishings.

COLOR AND LIGHT

Color psychology and selection is beyond the scope of this book, but it is an important component to successful school design. Appropriate color can have a number of effects: it can increase a child's sense of security, it can offer eye relief from the strain caused by heavy use of computers, and it can be part of a design strategy to make the school environment fun and stimulating. Designers should become familiar with color's influences in the learning environment.

There are excellent resources available for further research on this topic. Faber Birren was the leading authority on the effects of color on humans; in addition to his 25 books and numerous articles relevant to this topic, his collection of texts on color, with additional resources, is searchable via the Faber Birren Collection of Books on Color at Yale University Libraries.[1] The National Clearinghouse for Educational Facilities, a program managed by the National Institute of Building Sciences, presents a *Resource List on Color Theory for Classrooms and Schools*, with abstracts on references that explore the effects of color on perception, physiology, and learning.[2]

1. Available at http://www.library.yale.edu/art/ faberbirren/index.htm (accessed 6/2009).
2. Available at http://www.edfacilities.org/rl/ color.cfm (accessed 6/2009).

Color Basics

Faber Birren, in his book *The Power of Color* (1997), stated that "The term Functional Color is generally applied to uses and applications of hue in which beauty or appearance are secondary to more practical purposes." He goes on to say, "Functional color is concerned with measurable facts. It is founded on research, on known visual reactions, on data which may be statistically analyzed." Both beauty and function are not mutually exclusive and certainly all designers should strive to achieve both. With that in mind, the following points should be observed when selecting color for the learning environment:

- Color is a powerful tool in the learning environment.
- Color approach should avoid overstimulation and under stimulation.
- Color use varies according to both region and culture.
- Avoid a color palette made up completely of neutral colors (blacks, whites, off-whites, and grays)
- Lack of light wavelengths has been shown to cause an increase in nervousness, anxiety, and insecurity.
- It is believed that soft, subtle colors with cooler hues enhance the ability to concentrate.
- A front wall in a medium tone can help relax students' eyes when they look up from tasks.
- Some variation in wall color can be desirable. For example, side and back walls may be beige, sandstone, or light taupe, while the front wall may be a medium tone of blue-green or blue.
- Pale or light green tones are believed to encourage enhance quietness and concentration.

Lighting

Poor lighting in a classroom can cause the following negative effects:

- Increased blinking in an attempt to irrigate the eye, caused by repeated attempts to focus
- Muscular tension leading to neck, shoulder, wrist, and back strain
- Dilation of the pupil attempting to let in more light, which can lead to both increased blinking and muscular tension
- Glare
- Poor visibility
- The need to constantly adjust to conflicting brightness

To help prevent eye strain:

- Overhead ambient lighting levels should be kept low to avoid excessive glare and shadows.
- It can be helpful to supplement work areas with adjustable articulated-arm task-lighting to provide additional light.
- Window coverings should be used to eliminate VDT glare; position the screen away from uncovered windows.
- Position seating approximately one arm's length from the screen.
- Choose background and character colors with a high level of contrast (this applies to the room as well).

Reflectance values

All materials reflect light at different rates. The following general guidelines for light reflectance values (LRV) should be followed for the selection of classroom materials and finishes:

Floors

- LRV = 20–30 percent
- Appropriate floor materials can help in glare reduction and acoustic control, and can improve indoor air quality by being easy to clean and reducing maintenance.

Furniture and equipment

- LRV = 40–50 percent
- Furniture and equipment should have uniform LRVs with a maximum brightness difference between the furniture and the brightest part of the room of 2.5–1 (40 percent for furniture and 100 percent for ceilings).

Walls

- LRV = 50–55 percent
- Appropriate wall materials can help in glare reduction. Locate exterior windows to the side of the room's primary viewing wall.

Accent wall

- An accent wall in a classroom can help to relieve eyestrain, focus attention on the teacher, reduce overall glare from adjacent whiteboards, and provide visual relief by avoiding color monotony.

Ceiling

- LRV = 90–100 percent
- Bright ceilings reflect the natural world, and provide for uniform light levels and a consistent appearance.

1. The text in this section is derived from the VS International website; although marketing oriented, VS has historically been a leader in furniture and ergonomic research. The VS website address is http://www.vs-furniture.com/56.0.html?&L= 1&FL=9; a wide variety of research and guidance is available under the Schools tab and throughout the website.

ERGONOMICS

- Furniture manufacturers and others have conducted a great deal of useful research on ergonomics.[1] If one filters out the marketing messages, there are often useful guidelines for furniture planning, design, and procurement. For example, some of the recommendations in the literature of one leading manufacturer of school furniture make the following points related to proper ergonomic design: "The modern school…calls for great flexibility…to support the most varied activities.
- "Our muscles only have a limited ability to complete one-sided work. For this reason…dynamic sitting is called for in school.
- "Experts in industrial medicine are calling for more movement…in school—in other words, a natural balance of movements between sitting and standing.
- "Crucial to an ergonomic pupil's workstation are chairs and desks/tables that are adapted to height.
- "Even the best school furniture is only as good as its adjustment.
  - "First adjust the chair…when the seat depth is fully utilized, the front edge must not press against the lower leg. The backrest should support the back below the shoulder blade.
  - "[Then] adjust the desk/table height. In a sideways sitting posture to the table, bend the arms through 90°. The tips of the elbows [should be] situated two to three centimeters below the tabletop front edge of the table.
- "If the school furniture is not height adjustable, …at least…assign the available chair sizes to the children in such a way that they correspond as far as possible to the above mentioned points.

- "Adjustment should be carried out at least twice a year." [2]

SECURITY

The safety of children within the traditional haven of the schoolyard has come into question in recent years, so administration, faculty, and parents have become more focused on security. Choices between passive versus active security measures are often widely discussed. A balance of both can provide a safe and secure environment for all except in the most extreme circumstances.

Security measures installed on the interior of a school must be a planned part of every building, but security truly begins at the perimeter of the school site, as discussed in chapter 4. The site should be laid out to ensure lines of sight across main parking and play areas. Bright lighting and video camera recordings allow observation of the site, and directional signage and short direct access roads and sidewalks point the visitor to the main entry. A single point of entry for visitors allows visual control by limiting unobserved access to any other areas of the building. Some schools have installed metal detection systems and professional security staff at the entries. Part-time or full-time security personnel have become standard for many campuses, and office space should be provided for them. This area can be located within the administration suite, or perhaps in a more remote area of the campus in a larger facility to increase coverage of the areas more distant from the main entrance. Likewise, within the school itself, sightlines throughout the school should be maximized, "nooks and crannies" should be minimized,

2. Quoted material excerpted from VS International website, http://www.vs-furniture.com (accessed 3/2009).

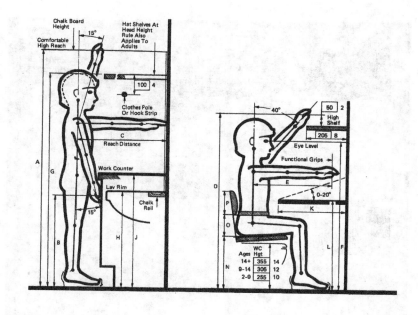

▲ Ergonomics has become an important issue in the design of new school furniture.

and administrative spaces should be distributed throughout the facility.

In addition to the possible threat from strangers, security concerns often arise within a building because of the actions of students. While efforts to create a more personalized learning environment where unusual activities by a student are more apparent can provide early intervention, student access to and potential use of weapons cannot be ignored.

Measures used to control such threats can include the following:

- Video surveillance
- Lockdown capabilities
- Metal detectors
- Search of person
- Search of property

Enacting these measures may limit the freedom or personal privacy of students.

▲ Security features can be built in without being intrusive, as is the case when the grilles recessed in the ceilings of this school are open. Middle school prototype, Broward County, Florida. STH Architectural Group.

A program that combines the various approaches specific to the individual school system should be clearly defined. The client should be comfortable with the level of security for the educational programs, as well as the protection of persons and property.

CODES

The regulatory agencies and the codes they enforce are intended to "protect human health, safety, and welfare" and help provide safe environments for all. The most consistent standard nationally is the Americans with Disabilities Act (ADA), as discussed in chapter 5. Since the passing of this legislation, there has been a movement toward universal design. Universal design provides equal access to all spaces regardless of an individual's abilities. Schools must integrate disabled students into the mainstream student population. Several school systems still function under particular requirements for dedicated special education classrooms or suites that segregate various groups, even though research has shown that many disabled students learn best when they are among age-appropriate nondisabled peers (Rydeen 1999).

Integration is a question of educational program; however, several items should be considered in providing access without barriers. The regulations set forth by the ADA must be met as part of the design.

Following is a brief list of measures that may be incorporated:

Many school systems choose a balance between such drastic, visible measures and more passive controls. The following is a list of passive measures to consider in the early phases of the design process:

- Ensure clear sightlines throughout the campus.
- Position administration adjacent to the front entrance.
- Position areas frequented by staff throughout the building.
- Provide reasons for staff to be seen in the corridors.
- Eliminate secluded areas.
- Provide ample corridors and circulation space for proper student flow.
- Provide a system of communication between administration and all other areas.

- Accessible parking areas adjacent to the entry
- Automatic entry doors with accessible vestibule areas
- Centralized vertical circulation

- Graphics with information given in large print and braille
- Wider classroom wing corridors to accommodate various user groups
- Adjustable furnishings and work surfaces to accommodate wheelchairs

Design decisions influence accessibility. Furnishings that adjust for wheelchair and regular use are recommended. The traditional classroom of 750–900 sq ft may not be adequate to provide accessible space for the instruction of disabled students. All marker boards and bulletin boards should be located within the reach of all students.

Code requirements have other significant impacts on the interior design. They mandate highly fire-resistant construction and allow only materials that support minimal flame spread. Although the codes in effect from state to state may vary slightly, the safety levels required in all school construction are strict. A thorough code review should be undertaken, beginning in the schematic design phase, with reviews at every interval of the design that follows. In design development and through creation of the construction documents, the interior finishes, materials, and furnishings should be reviewed periodically as the design progresses. Code requirements affecting interiors address the following:

▲ Barrier-free design often involves incorporating ramps into a school's circulation. Carrie Ricker Middle School, Litchfield, Maine. Harriman Associates.

◀ Although designing to accommodate people with various physical disabilities is important, the dimensions for chair-bound students and staff are often the most determinant factors in ADA compliance.

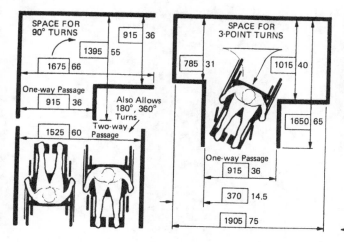

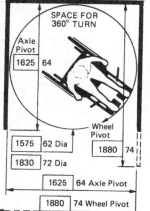

- Means of egress, path of travel, and size requirements
- Natural lighting
- Areas of refuge
- Area allowances within a single fire zone
- Area increases to existing buildings
- Fire-wall separations and their construction
- Fire-rated construction
- Flame-spread regulations
- Active versus passive life safety systems, including voice annunciation

The design will have to include fire extinguishers at regular intervals and may have to incorporate a sprinkler system. The construction of fire walls, separations, and enclosures for vertical circulation will affect material selections as the design develops. Some materials that have particularly high fire-resistant traits—for example, concrete and masonry—complicate the designer's task to make the school environment warm and supportive for children and young adults.

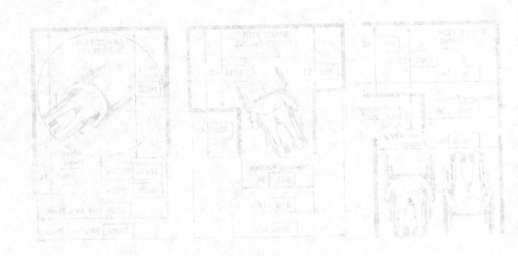

CHAPTER 15
WAYFINDING

Wayfinding refers to the way people orient themselves in a given environment and eventually find their destination. The ability to orient oneself is based on many pieces of information—visual clues, memories, knowledge of a place—and the ability to reason. Environmental psychology terms the ability to acquire, code, store, recall, and decode information about the physical environment "cognitive mapping." Cognitive maps are psychological impressions or representations of individuals' ability to understand space and the organizing elements by which they orient themselves.

The work of Kevin Lynch, presented in *The Image of the City* (1960), was based on studies that found three analytic components of environmental imaging:

• *Identity*, or objects in background
• *Structure*, or objects in relationship to each other
• *Meaning*, or personal, societal, or figurative belief

Lynch focused on the identity and structure of spaces to discern what makes cities imaginable or known. He notes:

Everything that has to do with movement, the architect should express strongly so that people can read it. An environment that is not well articulated is going to get someone lost. (Passini 1992)

▲ *Landmark elements such as chimneys, cupolas, and towers are often used to establish a school's image. Troy High School, Troy, Michigan. Perkins+Will.*

▲ Clear paths—often using natural light—should form the major circulation system. Left: Perry Community Education Village, Perry, Ohio. Perkins+ Will. Photograph by Hedrich/ Blessing. Right: Trent Elementary School, Spokane, Washington. ASLC Architects.

[Imageability is]…that quality of a physical object which gives it a high probability of evoking a strong image in any given observer. It is that shape, color or arrangement which facilitates the making of a vividly identified, powerfully structured, highly useful mental image of the environment. It might also be called legibility. (p. 9)

A highly imaginable space has components that relate in a well-structured manner. The way a space is mapped for an individual varies. There are certain images and visual clues that are perceived similarly by groups of people who share similar backgrounds, activities, routines, or recurrent features in the environment. For example, a group of schoolchildren may be of a similar age, share the learning and play activities of a school, and be aware of the physical features of the school building. The image and understanding of any environment is enriched by continual use. Lynch's research resulted in the identification of five categories of elements that people use to map an environment:

- *Paths:* channels of movement
- *Edges:* boundaries that break or contain or run parallel to the forms
- *Districts:* areas of recognizable identity or specific curricular focus
- *Nodes:* places of intense activity and can include breakout spaces or small group areas

• *Landmarks:* points of reference that are visually distinguishable

Cognitive maps usually combine several of the elements listed. These elements are not just formed by the floor or site plan. Instead, the three-dimensional characteristics of a space, the material choices, the colors, and the lighting can all impact the formation of edges, districts, or nodes.

The five categories can relate directly to the layout of a school campus. The *paths,* or circulation corridors, should be planned to provide clear, direct access to all major areas or districts within the school. Architecturally, this is analogous to a main street and takes you from one major area, or *district,* to another. In a school, this is the first level of intuitive wayfinding within the facility. Performing-arts wings, athletic facilities, media centers, and central administration suites are examples of districts. Where the boundaries of the districts meet, an *edge* may be formed, giving a student a clear sense of having exited one area and entered another. This is also an opportunity to zone the building not only to limit access during nontraditional hours of operation, but also to facilitate security should it be required that the building be "locked down."

A *node* works in conjunction with paths, edges, and districts, providing breakout areas of informal interaction at an intersection of activities or along paths where activity is concentrated. Nodes in contemporary schools provide seating areas for small group work or can be used to expand the learning environment beyond the classroom. As with the edges of districts, nodes can provide a convenient opportunity to zone the building and, used in conjunction with an expanded path, can greatly enhance the overall learning quality of the school.

Landmarks may be used by the designer to mark entrances or points of interest. For example, the traditional clock tower over a school's main entry serves as a major reference point and object of visual orientation for the students and the community.

In the 1960s, Donald Appleyard (1970) explored the differences in individuals' cognitive map forms and, in particular, the distinction between path-oriented and spatial styles of mapping. Almost 70 percent of the research subjects drew maps that were sequential images or series of events. This result indicates that the path is the dominating organizational element for the majority of people. Within a school building, the paths or corridors to and from different activities should be clearly planned and understandable. It may be helpful to link functionally related or sequentially visited spaces with color-coded corridors from the origin points to the destinations.

The process of learning involves an increase in perception of detail as a person

▲ *At key intersections and centers of activity, the design should clearly define a node as a visual reference point. Agassiz Elementary School, Cambridge, Massachusetts. HMFH Architects. Photograph by Wayne Soverns Jr.*

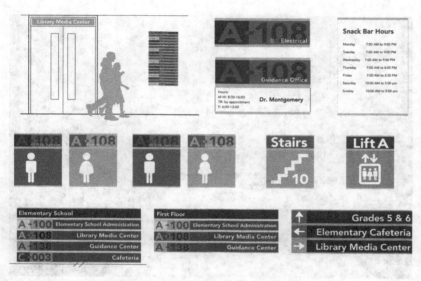

▲ *Songdo International School signage and wayfinding program, Songdo International School, Songdo, South Korea. Courtesy of Russell Design/Perkins Eastman.*

As adults, people tend to rely on maps, diagrams, and more highly abstract information for orientation and finding their way within a new area. As indicated in item 3 of the preceding list, an adult who is visiting an unfamiliar city will use a city map to reach a destination. Adults navigate wide-reaching, complex environments on a daily basis, whereas children's environments are more limited in overall range and tend to be perceived on the basis of reference points. The adolescent child's orientation system (above) may be based on a local hangout, the path of travel between home and school, local landmarks within the community, and similar points of reference.

The designer of learning environments for small children should be aware that children are naturally oriented in relation to their own positions, as seen above. Children see the world always in relation to themselves. For example, an especially enjoyable piece of equipment at the playground and its relationship to the toilet facility a child uses while at the playground may be the elements by which he or she organizes and understands that environment. A child's cognitive map will likely include detailed aspects of a space with which he or she is directly involved. Details of the play area within the classroom, shown on a child's drawn map, may include the floor material, number of toys, type of light, type of furniture, number of children playing in the space, and so forth. The social and natural elements of an environment are far more important in a child's world than built structures. Therefore, the school design should incorporate detailed elements at the child's level, in areas where children are active, and with which they can identify.

develops. The following reference system, proposed by Gary Moore (1976), relates the phases of development to the progress of perception from early childhood to the adult years:

1. An egocentric reference system; that is, one organized around the child's own position and actions in space
2. Several different possibilities of fixed reference systems organized around various fixed, concrete elements or places in the environment
3. An abstract or coordinated reference system organized in terms of abstract geometric patterns, including in special cases the cardinal directions (north, south, east, and west).

Signage is a wayfinding tool and an important part of directing people through a space. Building signage can include building identification, building layout illustration, directional signs, and place signs. A clearly designed signage package should be part of every school building design. The following are important considerations in developing signs for schools:

- Signs should be placed strategically at decision-making areas.
- Color-coding can be used to identify district areas or paths of travel.
- Signs for small children should incorporate graphics as well as text identification.
- The text and graphics should be appropriately scaled to the age of the user groups.
- A clear, sequential numbering system should be developed.
- Signs should be legible, direct to the point, and visible at reasonable distances.
- Signs should be designed and placed consistently throughout the facility.
- The overuse of signage and cluttered signage, which becomes ineffective, should be avoided.

A well-considered architectural wayfinding plan will be clear and uncluttered. Signage should also be considered a building enhancement, with care taken to use compatible materials and appropriate scale. Signs also create an identity and can strongly reinforce a sense of a school's community.

▶ *Design team should remember that for smaller children, landmarks are often near the floor. Lego Child Care Center, Enfield, Connecticut. Jeter, Cook, and Jepson Architects. Photograph by Wheeler Photographics.*

▲ *Clear main circulation paths, such as the one at Hamilton Southeastern High School, can be dynamic streets where students can interact between classes. Southeastern High School, Fishers, Indiana. Fanning/Howey Associates. Photograph by Emery Photography.*

▲ At the detail level, signage is an essential part of wayfinding. The Dalton School, New York, New York. Helpern Architects. Photograph by Durston Sailor.

should be coordinated with the requirements of the local police, fire department, and EMS if necessary. In certain parts of the country and in most international schools, signage will be required to be bilingual.

Increasingly, signage is becoming digital and integrated with a system of display monitors located throughout the building. In some cases, these digital signs may take the place of what would have traditionally been fixed signs and should be coordinated as part of an overall signage and information conveyance design.

In addition to signage, visual clues can be utilized to help orient the user. Architectural elements like lobbies, stairs, elevators, and areas of special use, such as a gymnasium, can create a framework within which users can place themselves. The following interior treatments, typically used for aesthetic effect, can also assist the designer in creating a highly understandable environment:

• Change of wall color, type, or texture
• Change in flooring
• Use of lighting to highlight or minimize areas
• Change of ceiling treatments
• Furniture arrangement or type

John Muhlhausen, in his article "Wayfinding Is Not Signage" (2006), also suggests that designers consider audible clues (PA system, elevator chimes, water fountains, etc.) and tactile clues ("trails" with different materials, "rumble strips" at stair landings, knurled door knobs on non-public doors etc.) as further methods to aid in the process.

The extent of wayfinding clues incorporated in the environment should vary from public to private spaces. Public areas require

Consideration should be given to messages used and the graphic/verbal "conversation" between governance and user. In addition to wayfinding and identification of specific space, schools have an "informational" level of signage that should be integral to the design. Signs such as "This is a smoke-free facility" or "Visitors must report to the office" can introduce visual clutter if not considered during the signage design phase. Signage

more information to be presented to aid visitors in locating their destinations. As the spaces become more private, fewer cues will be needed because of the occupants' knowledge of the environment. This is mainly true of older student populations and staff; however, the youngest students at the elementary level will benefit from the inclusion of color-coding or graphic representations along travel routes to and from the classrooms and most private instructional areas. The functional areas within a school building are listed here in order of most public to most private:

1. Site areas:
   a. Parking
   b. Drop-off drives
   c. Bus loading areas
   d. Sidewalks
2. Main entry
3. Administration area
4. Main public spaces:
   a. Gymnasium, accessed from the exterior and the interior
   b. Auditorium, accessed from the exterior and the interior
   c. Cafeteria, accessed from the interior
   d. Media center or library, accessed from the interior
5. Specialty education areas:
   a. Art
   b. Music
   c. Science
6. Dedicated instructional areas:
   a. Classrooms
   b. Houses (clustered classrooms around a home base)

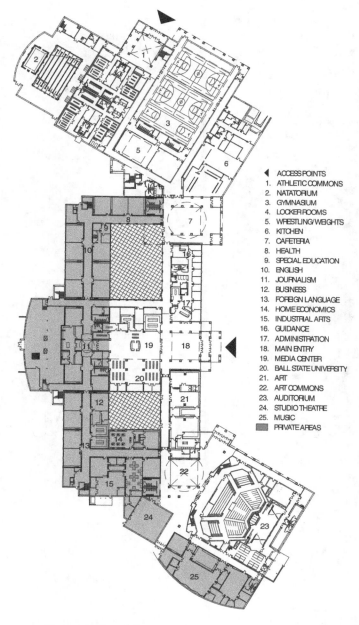

ACCESS POINTS
1. ATHLETIC COMMONS
2. NATATORIUM
3. GYMNASIUM
4. LOCKER ROOMS
5. WRESTLING/WEIGHTS
6. KITCHEN
7. CAFETERIA
8. HEALTH
9. SPECIAL EDUCATION
10. ENGLISH
11. JOURNALISM
12. BUSINESS
13. FOREIGN LANGUAGE
14. HOME ECONOMICS
15. INDUSTRIAL ARTS
16. GUIDANCE
17. ADMINISTRATION
18. MAIN ENTRY
19. MEDIA CENTER
20. BALL STATE UNIVERSITY
21. ART
22. ART COMMONS
23. AUDITORIUM
24. STUDIO THEATRE
25. MUSIC
PRIVATE AREAS

▲ *Clear plans are often organized with a hierarchy of public and private areas. As one moves toward the more private areas, fewer wayfinding cues are needed, because of occupants' knowledge of the space. Westfield High School, Westfield, Washington. Schenkel Shultz Architects.*

CHAPTER 16
RENOVATION

As Lawrence Perkins liked to note, "Buildings do not fall down; they are torn down" (Perkins 1957, p. 62). But because it is neither necessary nor realistic to replace the existing stock of tens of thousands of school buildings, most school building programs will involve renovations, restorations, additions, or adaptive reuse of existing buildings.

INTRODUCTION
A 1995 U.S. General Accounting Office (GAO) report presented to the United States Congress estimated that it would require $112 billion to repair or upgrade the nation's school facilities simply to establish good overall conditions. This report found that about two-thirds of America's schools reported being in overall adequate condition; however, the remaining one-third housed more than 14 million children. By 1999 the U.S. Department of Education estimated that it would require $127 billion to bring school facilities into overall good condition, and a year later, in a study released by the National Education Association, the price tag for fixing and modernizing the nation's schools and outfitting them with new technology was estimated at $322 billion (Richard 2000). The threefold increase over the GAO's number is partially attributed to NEA's comprehensive, state-by-state analysis, and partially to the inclusion of nearly $54 billion for technology improvements, such as wiring for access to the Internet, but it is also a reflection of the reality that deferring these costs only leads to increases over time.

The renovation needs of most school districts have grown steadily in recent decades for a number of reasons:

- Growth in enrollment
- Changes in class sizes and curricula
- Implementation of technology, including additional electrical capacity
- Energy conservation measures
- Adjusting to new legal requirements and mandates—the Americans with Disabilities Act (ADA), English as a Second Language (ESL) classes, mandatory preschool, women's athletic programs, etc.
- Removal of hazardous materials—asbestos, lead paint, etc.
- Improved security
- Correction of deferred maintenance
- Expiration of the useful life of a school building or its systems
- Conversion of underutilized areas to effective program use
- Reduction of inequalities between schools in the same district
- Implementation of air-conditioning to permit more community and year-round use

Of the $19.3 billion of school construction that was estimated to have been completed in 2008, approximately $4 billion was spent on additions and $3 billion on renovations.

The poor conditions described by Jonathan Kozol in *Savage Inequalities* (1991) and by many others are not limited to poor inner-city neighborhoods of the nation, nor are they limited to urban schools. These conditions also exist in middle-class and wealthy suburbs. It was estimated that almost 60 percent of school districts reported at least one school building in need of major repair or replacement of major building features.

Estimates show that school construction and renovation projects steadily increased over the last decade. According to the *School Planning & Management* magazine, in 2007 approximately 63 percent of all construction dollars were spent for new school construction, and the remaining dollars were split equally between additions and renovations to existing schools.[1]

TO BUILD NEW OR TO RENOVATE?

Many school buildings have already had numerous additions, and there comes a point at which a site will not allow for any more building. The age of the original building and its additions is one of the deciding factors as to which direction the school district should take. In many cases, when additions were designed, the electrical and mechanical systems, fire alarm systems, plumbing, and structural systems of the new construction were not made compatible with the original existing systems, either because of the age of existing systems or because it was less expensive to provide different systems for the addition. Adding onto existing systems can be quite expensive; moreover, many manufacturers no longer make parts and pieces for replacement in older systems, and it is thus impossible to upgrade them.

Is it better to renovate an existing building or to build a new one? Note the figures given in the accompanying tables. However, this question is not simply answered by

1. Paul Abramson, 2008, "The 2008 Annual School Construction Report," *School Planning & Management Magazine,* http://www.peterli.com/spm/pdfs/constr_report_2008.pdf (accessed 6/2009).

computing the cost of renovations, the expected building life, and the expected future renovation needs versus the cost of a new building. Many factors must be considered. The initial approach should include a thorough inspection of existing building systems and components to compile lists of strengths and weaknesses in regard to adaptability for immediate use and for anticipated future use:

- *General building appearance.* Is the building attractive and appealing, or is a lot of work needed to make it acceptable?
- *Building site location.* Is the building located in an area where the school district must accommodate increased enrollments, or will added capacity distort neighborhood school boundaries?
- *Building age and construction characteristics of the era when it was built.* Is the building in disrepair because of design and construction flaws, expiration of the normal life of existing systems, or lack of maintenance?
- *Building structural systems and adaptability to new functions and building requirements.* Does the structure permit adaptation, or will it seriously complicate or compromise renovation?
- *Accessibility to disabled persons.* Is the building easily adapted to accommodate ramps, elevators, accessible bathrooms, etc., or will it be hard to adapt?
- *Life safety code deficiencies.* Are the existing deficiencies easily remedied, or will large amounts of money have to be spent to bring the building up to today's codes (e.g., egress stairs, corridors, fire alarm systems, etc.)?
- *Energy usage.* What is the general energy-performance condition of building compo-

PROJECTED SCHOOL DISTRICT CONSTRUCTION, 2009–2011	
TYPE	COST ($000)
New	43,750,822
Additions/modernizations	19,605,268
Total	63,356,090

Source: Agron, 2009.

COST BREAKDOWN FOR NEW SCHOOLS	
	K–12 (% OF TOTAL COSTS)
Site purchase	3
Site development	8
Construction	69
Furnishings/equipment	12
Fees (& other)	8

Source: Agron, 2009.

▲ *Scarsdale High School created a safe student drop-off and pickup area as part of a general upgrade of the school site. Scarsdale High School, Scarsdale, New York. Peter Gisolfi Associates. Photograph by Norman McGrath.*

nents (e.g., does the building have single-pane windows, uninsulated walls, uninsulated roof construction, etc.)?

- *Capacity of existing electrical systems.* Can the electrical systems be upgraded to accommodate increased demand resulting from computer usage, increased classroom needs for electricity, more air-conditioning, new codes and regulations, and the like?
- *Capacity of existing HVAC equipment.* What is the expected life of the existing equipment, and can it be upgraded to accommodate demand resulting from computer usage, new codes and regulations, increased use of school facilities not limited to the academic year, and so forth?
- *Adaptability of existing conditions to accommodate security measures required today.* Is the existing facility configured, or can it be reconfigured, in such a way as to facilitate security measures to protect students, faculty, staff, and the building itself?
- *Hazardous materials required to be removed from facility.* Does the facility contain unencapsulated asbestos or other hazardous materials that would have to be removed in a renovation project?

The accumulated weight of the answers to these questions can—at times—make new construction more attractive than renovation.

There are, of course, those building assets that must be taken into consideration that do not necessarily appear in a monetary assessment: unusual spaces with high ceilings, unique plaster work and woodworking, tall windows, durable terrazzo flooring, hardwood flooring, brick and stone detailing, and the like. These features would most likely not be affordable in new construction considered by school districts today.

▲ Some districts have made efforts to upgrade a utilitarian exterior with a modest set of exterior changes, as at the Trent Elementary School, Spokane, Washington. ALSC Architects.

The age of a building is not the only consideration for replacement. School buildings constructed in the early 1900s were built to have a life span of 50 to 100 years. They generally have high ceilings, wide corridors, and large gymnasiums and auditoriums. These features may enable new computer cabling and HVAC ductwork to be more easily accommodated in older buildings than in schools designed at the middle of the century. Many schools built during the 1950s and 1960s were constructed with "modern" materials: single-story steel structures, metal-framed single-pane windows, flat built-up roofs, and brick veneers with concrete masonry unit interior walls. During this time energy conservation was not a priority; therefore, many buildings were not well insulated and contained a great amount of uninsulated glass.

Schools built during the 1970s typically incorporated systems with limited life spans of only 20 to 30 years. Many of these schools, built quickly and cheaply, continue to cause maintenance problems for school districts. During the oil embargo of the 1970s, energy consumption and alternative energy sources became a focus of the nation.

Cost of Renovation versus New Construction

Many school districts began replacing windows with less glazing and more insulated panels. A more radical approach by some school districts was to eliminate windows and skylights throughout each school building. At that time, this seemed like a logical response to the energy crisis. But, as we look back, we realize the full impact: decreased light transmission into interior spaces, as well as exteriors, making schools appear to be grim "jails." As noted in chapters 6 and 13, research indicates that students' concentration, performance, and attendance all increase when they have access to sunlight.

Significant advances in window and skylight design have prompted many schools in recent years to include window replacement in their major construction projects to return their school buildings to the original aesthetics while gaining better insulating values. Many of the windows being removed today were installed in the past 25 years.

During the 1950s and 1960s student enrollment peaked. The 1970s marked the beginning of a 13-year decline in public school enrollment from a high of 46 million in 1971 to 39.2 million in 1984. A steady increase began at about 1985 as the baby-boomers of the 1950s and 1960s sent their children off to school. The U.S. Department of Education estimated that 46.8 million students walked through the doors of public schools in the fall of 1998. Public school enrollment for the fall of 2009 was projected to be about 50 million (56 million with the inclusion of private school enrollment).[2]

School districts are looking for unused or underutilized spaces in existing facilities to alleviate present overcrowding. One school system found space for special education classrooms by completely gutting and renovating unused elementary school boys' and girls' locker rooms and shower facilities. This saved the district the time and money that would have been spent in building an addition to the school. Another school district was considering the necessity of building a larger gymnasium and locker room facilities at its high school to accommodate increased enrollments. The design team proposed to renovate the existing gymnasium and locker rooms to create a much-needed auditorium and music classroom/practice room suite.

High-ceilinged gymnasiums or auditoriums of older buildings, too small to accommodate the school population, have the potential to be converted to other uses

2. U.S. Department of Education, Institute of Education Sciences website, http://nces.ed.gov/fastfacts/display.asp?id=65 (accessed 6/2009).

through the insertion of a second level within the existing building volume. The school district may thus save the cost of building exterior walls and a new roofing system. However, this approach must be analyzed carefully. Inserting a new structure and new mechanical and electrical systems into an existing space may be far more costly than building new.

Often, additions are the only solution, but in some cases—particularly in older school buildings—there are underutilized or unused spaces that can be converted to academic use. One school system that was studied found spaces for several programs in the existing elementary schools by reclaiming basement areas that could—with some regrading—be opened to the outdoors.

One of the goals of any renovation or adaptive reuse should be to minimize the serious results of deferred maintenance and to

▲ *The Scarsdale, New York, school system initially used unattractive brown replacement windows in the older Georgian and Collegiate Gothic style schools and, because of community reaction, replaced them several years later with more architecturally appropriate units with superior energy conservation and operating characteristics. Peter Gisolfi Associates. Photograph by Norman McGrath.*

mitigate any physical inequalities between the older and the newer buildings in a school system. Unfortunately, this goal is unachieved in too many school systems.

The example given in the accompanying sidebar is not an isolated or unusual situation in many school systems, nor does it describe a problem found only in older, urban areas. Poor school facilities are a major problem across the country, and it presents one of the greatest design and construction challenges.

If maintained properly, many of the systems in a school building can be made to last for decades. If not maintained, many of the systems will deteriorate quickly to a point that the building is no longer a safe or appropriate environment for children. Jonathan Kozol writes in *Savage Inequalities* that even though the deterioration is well known and widely documented, many districts continue to defer the necessary funding because there are demands of higher priority on limited resources. "A year later, when I visit Morris High, most of these conditions are unchanged. Water still cascades down the stairs [when it rains]. Plaster is still falling from the walls. Female students tell me that they shower after school to wash the plaster from their hair. ... A plaque in the principal's office tells a visitor that this is the oldest high school in the Bronx" (Kozol 1991, pp. 99–100).

Removal of Hazardous Materials

The design team must know how to deal with the presence of hazardous materials. Not long ago the primary issue was asbestos, and a large part of many renovation budgets was devoted to removing all asbestos—even asbestos floor tile—when lower-cost options might have been appropriate. Asbestos can be found in many materials, including floor tile and mastics (typically found in 9 in. × 9 in. floor tile, but it is possible to find it in 12 in. × 12 in. floor tile produced during the same era), transite building panels (used for fire separations in some cases, as well as for exterior building cladding), piping insulation (typically found, but not limited to, plumbing piping and boiler breeching), plaster walls and ceilings, and roof shingles.

More recently, analyses of sites for the possibility of contamination by leaking underground oil tanks, lead paint, polychlorinated biphenyls (PCBs), and other hazards have become routine parts of the renovation process. If existing fuel storage tanks are not up to code, they should have been removed or closed in place by December 23, 1998, as mandated by the Environmental Protection Agency (EPA).

The presence of hazardous materials can greatly increase the cost of a reconstruction project and must be included in the designer's analysis and findings. However, if an existing building containing hazardous

In order to find Public School 261 in District 10, a visitor is told to look for a mortician's office.... The school is next door, in a former roller-skating rink. No sign identifies the building as a school.... The school's "capacity" is 900 but there are 1,300 children here.... Two first grade classes share a single room without a window, divided only by a blackboard. Four kindergartens and a sixth grade class of Spanish-speaking children have been packed into a single room in which, again, there is no window. A second grade bilingual class of 37 children has its own room, but again there is no window...I ask..."Do the children ever comment on the building?" "They don't say," [the teacher], answers, "but they know... All these children see TV...they know what suburban schools are like. Then they look around them at their school... They understand." (Kozol 1991, pp. 83–88)

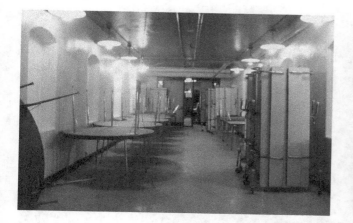

▲ At the Hastings Middle/High School, a number of spaces were recaptured, including this cafeteria space. Hastings Middle/High School, Hastings-on-Hudson, New York. Peter Gisolfi Associates. Photographs by Norman McGrath.

◄ At the Scarsdale High School, all of the older schools were renovated to remove unattractive renovations and restore the original design character. Scarsdale High School, Scarsdale, New York. Peter Gisolfi Associates. Photographs by Norman McGrath.

materials is demolished to make way for a new building, the hazardous materials will have to be removed under the guidelines applicable to any other hazardous materials removal project.

Technology Upgrades

Rapid changes in technology and how schools use this technology have also put a heavy burden on school districts to provide their children with the best the world has to

▲ At the Hastings Middle/High School, a sensitive renovation recreated an attractive lobby. Hastings Middle/High School, Hastings-on-Hudson, New York. Peter Gisolfi Associates. Photographs by Norman McGrath.

offer. Many schools in the United States were built before the current technological boom and are not easily adaptable to support the necessary equipment required for today's computers (computer wiring, computer cabinets, Internet exchangers), electrical loads, heating and ventilation requirements, and so on. (See chapter 10 for a more extensive discussion.)

ADA

See chapter 5 for a discussion of the requirements of the Americans with Disabilities Act (ADA).

Other Issues in Renovation

The design team working on an existing facility faces special challenges. Diagnostic skills are needed to identify hidden conditions in determining whether repair or replacement is required. Analyses of the remaining useful life of such basic systems as the roof, piping for water and heating, boilers, and windows are a common design

team task. Special techniques have been developed for many of these analyses, but others rely on such basic approaches as the cutting of sample pipe sections to measure the extent of corrosion. Window-by-window surveys are often required to identify rot, broken counterweights, and cracked panes.

The design team must also have knowledge of the building systems, materials, and techniques commonly found in older schools—plaster and clay tile walls, slate roofing, terrazzo floors, typical asbestos-containing materials, old electrical and HVAC systems, and large wood windows. Many of these are no longer commonly used in new designs, but they often raise important issues in additions and renovations. Thanks to the preservation movement, there are now reference materials available on most historic building materials and systems.

Knowledge of historic preservation has become a major consideration for the designer. Maintaining the unique character of their building or buildings, which are often the architectural centerpieces of their neighborhoods, is important to many communities and schools.

Design teams have also had to learn how to help sell unattractive bond issues. A difficult obstacle for a school district to overcome is how to explain to the public the millions to be spent to repair or replace roof systems or HVAC systems, remediate hazardous materials such as asbestos, upgrade old and deteriorating piping, or upgrade electrical systems to support increased demands. These are the areas of the school system that the public rarely observes and of which it has little knowledge. Renovations to existing classrooms, libraries, and toilet facilities; building additions; and new schools are things that the public can see, and such visible improvements help them to understand where their money is being spent.

Design and construction teams have had to learn how to schedule renovations around breaks in the school year. The careful management of key milestones (drawing completion, bidding, approvals, construction start, etc.) is a critical skill. Most projects—or at least, their disruptive phases—must be completed before school begins again.

CHAPTER 17

INTERNATIONAL DESIGN ISSUES AND OPPORTUNITIES

INTRODUCTION

In the elementary school in the mountain community of Pachali, Guatemala, where I was helping teach in 1965, the major issue for the school building was whether the community could afford to bring an electric line to the school to power a light bulb. A light bulb would make it possible to have evening classes for the children and adults whose work schedules made daytime classes infeasible. In many parts of the world, the problems of education facilities are just this basic.

Today, organizations like Schools for Children of the World (SCW) are facing similar issues in other areas of South America, such as Honduras. In 2004 the Honduras Ministry of Education adopted the *Honduras School Facility Master Plan.* To assist in the planning and construction of facilities to support the Master Plan, the Ministry, in conjunction with SCW developed a national *School Facility Design Guidelines* for use in developing and modernizing the country's educational facilities.

In many places around the world, however, school design requires experienced design teams. Over the past few years there have been design opportunities for North American architects that are among the most interesting projects available. In both developed and developing countries, there is an interest in sophisticated educational environments. Some are willing to hire international design expertise to create them. In some Asian countries where education is a high priority, for example, school clients have reached out to U.S. architects. And from time to time,

U.S. architects have been brought in to design schools for countries that do not have adequate architectural resources to plan and design a large school building program.

INTERNATIONAL SCHOOLS

One segment of this work is in American-curriculum-based international schools located abroad. These schools are operated for the most part by nonprofit entities to serve the needs of an expatriate population working in a particular country. These have predominantly English-based American or British curriculums and have designed their facilities accordingly. ISC Research Limited reported in its January 2008 newsletter that there were more than 4,600 international

▼ *The Boys Campus of GEMS World Academy, a K–12 International School. KAEC International School, King Abdullah Economic City, Saudi Arabia. Perkins Eastman. Courtesy of Perkins Eastman.*

schools, with a total student population of over 1,700,000. By the end of 2009 that number had already increased to more than 5,400 schools with over 2,350,000 students.

A small percentage of these schools receive some funding from the U.S. State Department. The Office of Overseas Schools reports that during the 2008–2009 school year, the OOS assisted 196 schools in 136 countries. Enrollment in the schools at the beginning of the 2008–2009 school year totaled 121,970, of whom 33,361 were U.S. citizens. Of 14,939 teachers and administrators employed in the schools, 6,429 were U.S. citizens.[1]

The State Department–assisted schools are truly international, as are most schools called "international." They are usually open to nationals of all countries, and their teaching staffs are multinational. These schools represent a key component of American foreign policy, with the objective of strengthening mutual understanding between the United States and the people of other countries.[2]

The facilities of international schools are usually intended to reflect the current standards one might find in a progressive public or private school in the United States. Nevertheless, there are often differences influenced by the host country's culture or expectations. Moreover, a school might also be influenced by its largest student population, regardless of host country. For example, a school in China at which the largest number of students are from Korea might function more like a Korean school than an American school, even though the curriculum would be American.

PLANNING AND DESIGN ISSUES

Many international schools are predominantly populated with students from their geographic region. For example, in Asian countries, schools often have significant percentages of Asian-country nationals. In such a case, most of the countries have factory-model economies existing in information-age societies. As a result, the "factory model" educational paradigm will be expected by many of the students' parents (see chapter 2).

At the same time, such a school's program is usually built around a more contemporary idea of western education that includes team- and project-based learning. It's the difference between a lecture-style setting and small-group and individualized settings. A new International School facility in this region must support the needs of this broad range of parent and student expectations.

Other factors influencing international school design worldwide include the following:

- The cultural context of the country in which the international school is constructed
- The special needs of a multicultural expatriate population
- The relationship formed with the local governmental bodies
- Significant accessibility, security, and safety concerns
- Very high parental expectations for student performance

As architectural practice becomes global, these international school design opportunities are likely to grow. Many of the issues related to international practice are beyond

1. Worldwide Fact Sheet: 2008–2009 American-Sponsored Elementary and Secondary Schools Overseas, http://www.state.gov/m/a/os/1253.htm (accessed 6/2009).
2. Ibid.

the scope of this book. Many are covered in another recent AIA book, *International Practice for Architects* (Perkins 2007). There are, however, some issues that are specific to designing schools overseas. Among the most common are the following:

1. The design is less likely to be governed by code and precedent. While this can open up the potential for design creativity, it places a greater burden on the design team to bring best practices to the project's program and design.
2. The client group is often led by a local administrative team and faculty subject to frequent turnover. It is not uncommon for changes in client leadership—combined with the issue above—to lead to late changes in program and design direction.
3. Unlike most U.S. schools, international schools are often campuses that contain preschool and/or kindergarten through high school. While this does increase opportunities for sharing of central resources, it also entails the complication of separating the several age groups.
4. In most countries, the American design team is expected (or required) to work with a local design team for contract documents and construction administration. Since many of these local associates are relatively inexperienced in school design, it is often necessary for the American team to provide very complete design documentation and some supplemental contract documents and construction oversight to achieve the intended design. Without these additional services, strange things often happen during the implementation phases. Be prepared to "design" a services package

▲ *Concordia International School: High School, Shanghai, China. Perkins Eastman. Photograph by Shutte.*

that might be called "concept design" but which will look a lot like a 50 percent design development set.
5. Although many international projects are less constrained by the types of codes and precedents that guide so much U.S. school design, they are often influenced by local codes and traditions. In some countries the local codes may ignore key life-safety issues, such as the need for two means of egress. Thus, in most countries, following international best practices for life safety—such as the International Building Code (IBC) published by the International Building Code Council—is advisable. The local associate team is typically the source for other areas of code interpretation and research.
6. Most countries have preferred construction materials and systems. In developing countries, most of these choices are heavily influenced by local material availability, the availability of

inexpensive and relatively unskilled labor, and the desire to minimize expensive and hard-to-maintain imported materials and systems. In many cases, this means the schools have a concrete or masonry structure, a stucco or tile wall and ceiling finish, a tile or stone floor, and simple mechanical and electrical systems—all systems that are common in many developing countries.

7. Building systems complexity is continually being discussed in the market. Many international schools do not have the ability to pay for or maintain sophisticated building systems. Sustainability and long-term operational costs versus the initial cost of construction are emerging issues. Many regions between 20° south latitude and 20° north latitude do not require a heating system but do have very heavy cooling loads. There is increasing availability of low-energy systems globally, and solar orientation, sun screening, and alternative energy sources should be investigated.

8. The American design team must also be sensitive to the local design traditions that have evolved in response to local climatic conditions. The climate extremes of regions such as the Middle East, for example, require an understanding of the traditional ways that these issues can be minimized by the building design.

9. The local availability of contemporary school technology design services may be limited depending on location. This is another area where services might be bundled under the international design team. Other specialty consultants that may be hard to access locally include theater and acoustic design, food service design, audiovisual design, and security design.

10. The construction cost can vary widely from one location to another; therefore, it is rarely wise to tie a professional services fee to the cost of construction. A school that costs $275/sq ft in Boston might cost $100/sq ft in Shanghai, China, for a similar building.

11. Because of the multinational population of international schools and the English-based curriculum, there is a greater commitment to English as a second language (ESL) classrooms and a greater emphasis on bilingual education in general.

12. When programs such as advanced placement (AP) and international baccalaureate (IB) form the basis of a school's curriculum, the programs for these facilities often call for more self-directed and team-based learning environments.

13. Cultural precedent can have a significant influence on design. In Saudi Arabia, for example, some international schools are designed to accommodate a gender-integrated population through the third grade, and segregated into boys' and girls' schools from grades 4–12.

14. As noted earlier, security is a major concern in most countries. International schools typically have a secure perimeter and large protected areas for safe pickup and drop-off. This issue is likely to grow in importance in the future.

15. The process is often similar to the planning and design stages for a U.S. project. Most projects begin with a master plan or facility evaluation phase to determine the scope of the project. Many projects involve the reconstruction of or major improvements to existing campuses.

Some involve entirely new campuses. Older international schools find themselves with property that has become extremely valuable since the time when the school was originally built. They may be moving to an area where there is very little development; in this case, access to utilities should be carefully evaluated. For example, the American School in the Pudong District was built in the 1990s, when the entire area surrounding the campus was agricultural land. Today, this thriving campus is in the center of a very large housing and commercial development.

It is preferable to have the owner engage the local architect/engineer at the same time as the international design consultant team. This allows for the international team to receive advice on codes, building materials, and construction means and methods during the early stages of the design phase.

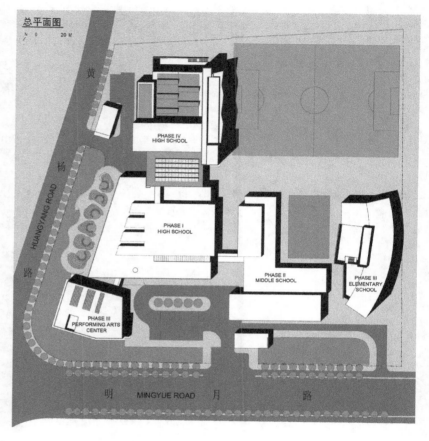

▲ This K–12 campus is just one of many international schools built in China in the last 20 years. Concordia International School campus, Shanghai, China. Perkins Eastman. Courtesy of Perkins Eastman.

CHAPTER 18

OPERATION AND MAINTENANCE

INTRODUCTION

A well-designed school will withstand the impacts and abuse to be expected from its students. The building should be easy to operate and maintain by its caretakers, and it should ultimately preserve the financial investment made by the community that authorized its construction. Operations and maintenance issues are different for new construction and existing buildings. This chapter considers both.

NEW SCHOOL CONSTRUCTION

A new school assignment is an ideal opportunity for an owner and a design team to develop a building that is operations- and maintenance-friendly. The design of the building should be tailored to the requirements of its educational program, consider the ability of its caretaker, and be easy to operate and maintain. Common sense is usually the best tool for making design decisions that create a school that is easy to operate and maintain. Locating primary mechanical equipment and controls for ease of access, positioning janitor's closets and equipment near the locations where they will be used, and sensitivity to the ability of the caretaker of the building—all contribute to the ease of operation and maintenance of the school. The architect should consider the following factors related to operations and maintenance:

- The design team's responsibility to advise the community on the best life-cycle strategy for any school construction program
- Utilities available to the site
- Sophistication of the building's caretakers

- Durability of building products and equipment
- Special considerations for specific program areas

One of the challenges of new school design for the design team is to balance the client's desire to keep first (construction) costs low against the desired longevity and durability of the resultant building. The architect's responsibility is to offer the community a building that will stand up to the punishment unique to school buildings. Throughout the twentieth century, a large percentage of schools used masonry materials for the exterior, as well as masonry, glazed tile, hardwood trim, plaster, and other durable materials for major interior corridors and common areas. The use of robust materials continues to offer the soundest approach for school design today.

The availability of and access to utilities at the site is an important factor in new school design. Early in the design process the architect must verify the potential infrastructure for heating fuel, electrical service, and water source that will serve the facility. The nature of the utilities that will enter the building and their access paths have a direct impact on the location and sizes of primary and secondary mechanical rooms in the building. By identifying potential fuel sources one can begin to narrow the choices of possible mechanical systems.

It is critical for the architect to understand the client's ability to maintain the building and operate the proposed systems.

The skills of a school's staff vary greatly from district to district. The size of the caretaking staff can range from a single custodian to a team of custodial and facility management people. The size of the staff is, of course, no indicator of its sophistication. For example, the most technically advanced mechanical building management system (BMS) is worthless if the school's personnel are not qualified to operate and maintain the system.

Likewise, extravagant and/or delicate landscaping is not appropriate if the caretakers are not accustomed or willing to meet the higher level of maintenance required.

The durability of building products and equipment is directly related to the expenditure of maintenance staff hours and the subsequent life-cycle costs of the building's systems. The architect must specify building products that anticipate vandalism, graffiti, and heavy use. The building design should make supervision as easy as possible for the adults who will work in the building. Such a plan includes simple sight lines and provides adult use areas throughout the building— staff meeting rooms and educational resource areas. Sound location of staff use areas (i.e., closer to the classrooms) can reduce adults' travel time to these spaces and ensure that an adult is always present in every area of the school. This arrangement can increase adult supervision and reduce vandalism and abuse of the school.

It is common for corridor and classroom partition walls to be built of painted concrete block or glazed masonry units. Because gypsum surfaces are easily scarred, these more durable walls have proven to be easier to maintain. Similarly, terrazzo flooring products have historically provided an attractive and durable floor surface in areas of heavy traffic. Owing to their cost, however, these products have been disappearing from new school construction in recent decades. Alternate products such as vinyl composition tile, epoxy tile, more durable sheet rock products, and carpet fibers much more durable than those of the past, where appropriate, are typically used today.

As indicated earlier, a new school will be operations- and maintenance-friendly if the design team carefully considers its plan and selection of building systems and finishes. The accompanying table highlights special considerations for specific program areas.

EXISTING SCHOOL BUILDINGS

Renovation of an existing school typically involves the correction of existing maintenance and operations problems. For obvious reasons, school districts generally tend to invest most of their financial resources in teaching staff and educational materials (books, technology, athletic equipment, etc.) The physical condition of the school is typically ignored until a problem occurs. Student overcrowding, a leak in the roof, and continuous shorting-out of the electrical power system are examples of such problems. Operations and maintenance considerations for new buildings, as discussed earlier, should be applied in renovations of existing buildings whenever possible. Specifically consider:

- The condition of the mechanical, electrical, and plumbing systems
- Energy conservation through replacement and upgrade of systems
- Sophistication of the building's caretakers
- Typical points of failure
- Identification and mitigation of hazardous materials

DESIGN CONSIDERATIONS FOR PROGRAM AREAS

SPACE	FLOOR FINISH	ELECTRICAL POWER/ COMMUNICATIONS REQUIREMENTS	SPECIAL MECHANICAL REQUIREMENTS*	COMMENTS
General classroom	VCT/carpet	Con. + Comp. + group Comm.		Plan for a minimum of a five-computer cluster in each classroom; special storage required.
Computer center	VCT/carpet (special type for computer room)	Con. + Comp. + Comm.	Cooling for special equipment load	Floor power/communications boxes and linear wall distribution systems maximize computer location options; floor outlets in VCT can obstruct polishing/waxing equipment.
Cafeteria	VCT	Con.	Ventilation	Ease of floor cleaning/disinfecting critical; adjacency to loading dock desirable.
Kitchen	Quarry tile	Con.+ special equipment	FP/ventilation/Ref.	Direct access to loading dock important; ease of cleaning/disinfecting required; kitchen use has high impact on floor/walls/ceiling.
Auditorium/ performance space	VCT/carpet	Con.+ special equipment + Comm.	Ventilation/air-conditioning "quiet" system	Special acoustical requirements; flat floor increases flexible use; adjacency to main entrance and proximity to loading dock are suggested.
Science laboratories	VCT	Con.+ special equipment + Comm.+ Comp.	FP/special ventilation/ natural gas	Instructional lab vs. combination instructional space and lab area; special storage required.
Art classroom	VCT	Con.+ special equipment + Comm.+ Comp.	Ventilation	Special FP and mech. requirements for kiln room; special storage requirements; proximity to loading dock is suggested.
Music classroom	Wood/VCT	Con.+ special equipment + Comm. + Comp.	"Quiet" system	Special acoustical requirements; furniture systems risers (for choral/orchestral practice) increase space flexibility; special storage requirements; close proximity to auditorium is suggested.
Gymnasium	Wood (special systems)	Con. + special equipment + Comm. + Comp.	Ventilation	Special storage requirements.
Locker room	Ceramic tile (floor and walls)	Con.	Ventilation	Ease of cleaning/disinfecting critical; simple sight lines—avoid plan layouts with hidden corners; special storage requirements.
Multipurpose meeting room	Carpet/VCT	Con. + special equipment + Comm. + Comp.	"Quiet" system	Consider furniture type and impact on floor finish; acoustical equipment; furniture storage adjacency to main entrance; proximity to loading dock is suggested.

Legend: Con. Convenience outlets / Comm. Communications (network tie-in) / Comp. Computer station(s) /
    FP Fire-protection system / Mech. Mechanical system / Ref. Refrigeration/freezer / VCT Vinyl composition tile
Source: Perkins Eastman.

EXPECTED LIFE OF MAJOR SYSTEMS

SYSTEM	EXPECTED LIFE IF PROPERLY MAINTAINED	RECOMMENDED INSPECTION/ MAINTENANCE CYCLE
Exterior envelope		
FOUNDATION		
Block	Indefinite	3 years
Concrete	Indefinite	5 years
STRUCTURE		
Steel	Indefinite	7 years
Concrete	Indefinite	5 years
Masonry bearing wall	Indefinite	5 years
Wood	Indefinite	3 years
EXTERIOR WALL		
Masonry	Indefinite	3 years
Stucco	40 years	2 years
Painted wood	30 years	Annually
EIFS	20 years	Annually
Brick joints	10 years	3 years
WINDOWS		
Aluminum/steel windows— long-life finish	40 years 5-year warranty	Annually, including weather stops, glass, and hardware lubricator
Aluminum/steel windows— (field) painted finish	40 years 2- to 5-year warranty	Annually, including weather stops, glass, and hardware lubricator
Wood windows	40 years	Annually, including weather stops, glass, and hardware lubricator
Brick/window joints	10 years	Annually
ROOF		
Slate shingles	Indefinite	Annually
Copper roofing	50 years	Annually
Fiberglass shingle	25–40 years	Annually
Aluminum or steel roofing	40 years	Annually
Asphalt or wood shingle	20–25 years	Annually
Built-up	20+ years*	Twice yearly—spring and fall; always after a major storm
Single-ply	20+ years**	Twice yearly—spring and fall; always after a major storm
BUILDING SYSTEMS		
Mechanical		
Boilers	25–40 years	Annually
Piping	20–50 years	Annually (depends on material)
Duct work	20–50 years	Annually
Electrical	15–20 years	Annually (limited by technical upgrades)
Plumbing	20–50 years	Annually
Fire Protection	15–30 years	Annually

*10-, 15-, or 20-year warranty with 2-year installers' warranty.
**10- or 15-year warranty with 2-year installers' warranty.
Source: Perkins Eastman.

The architect's design team must survey the school's mechanical, electrical, plumbing, and fire-protection systems. Part of the conditions assessment phase must include estimates of the remaining life of existing equipment. This phase should also include detailed interviews of the caretaker(s), teaching staff (user group), and administration of the school. These interviews can identify problems that are unique to the particular school building and that recur throughout the school year.

A study of the existing mechanical and electrical systems and the building envelope (windows and typical wall/roof section) can suggest upgrades of the systems through more efficient energy use; see chapter 6 for a more detailed discussion of energy efficiency.

Typical points of failure in the exterior envelope include brick joints, brick/window joints, and roofing materials. These three areas are among the most neglected in school buildings throughout the country. The table at left touches on these and other issues and outlines good practice methods associated with each.

An addition or major renovation to an existing school offers the architect an opportunity to understand the caretakers' ability to maintain and operate the building, and to become acquainted with the strengths and weaknesses of both the caretakers' abilities and the existing building systems. Such a study often indicates that the best course of action is to extend the existing building systems to the new construction. Fuel availability, system performance, and level of maintenance are historic facts; an addition can be an opportunity to correct existing undesirable conditions. There are no rules of thumb in this area; careful consideration of each facility and its caretaker group is the key.

Identification and mitigation of toxic substances and hazardous materials is critical to both the project budget and the schedule. It is essential to have a qualified environmental engineer complete thorough tests of an existing school as early as possible in the design process. Only the written report of a qualified inspector should be relied upon for determinations in this area. If left undetected until late in the design or construction process, the presence of asbestos, lead paint, or other hazardous substances can undermine the construction budget and cause serious delays in the schedule. It can also undermine the architect's credibility with the school board and the community.

CHAPTER 19
COST ISSUES

INTRODUCTION

Cost management is one of the most complex tasks facing a school's owner and design team. No single chapter can provide a comprehensive review of this topic, but there are several guidelines that are relevant to the effective cost management of a school building program. Specifically, this chapter includes an outline of the basic steps in a cost-management program, an introduction to the relative costs of typical school building choices, a review of some of the nonquantitative factors that can affect the cost of a project, a discussion of value engineering and life-cycle costing, and a review of the general sources of cost information.

MANAGEMENT

An effective cost-management approach includes setting a realistic budget; developing regular, careful cost estimates; and making adjustments to fit the design to the budget.

As school building programs have become more complex and expensive, there has been increased emphasis on a comprehensive, professional effort to manage costs. In summary, the key components of a cost-management program are the following:

1. Retain a design team, professional cost estimator, or a construction manager with proven cost-estimating and cost-management capabilities. Some schools retain all three, but at the very least the project team must have one member who can objectively and accurately analyze the cost impact of the thousands of program and design choices that will be made.

2. Start the budgeting process during the initial program phase. As stated in chapter 3, one of the most common errors is to start a project with an unrealistic budget. An experienced team should be able to translate a space program and evaluation of building conditions into a realistic budget.

3. Prepare detailed cost estimates for at least four points in the design process:
   - The end of schematic design
   - The end of design development
   - The midpoint of the construction document phase
   - The end of the construction document phase

These estimates should be more specific than one-page calculations based on past experience and square-foot cost data. Most experienced teams try to quantify the building components in increasing detail as the design progresses, apply accurate unit prices to each component, and add in appropriate contingencies for what is not yet designed and the inevitable extras that occur in most construction programs.

The earlier estimates tend to be more useful, as they can be used to adjust the design to bring the building program back within budget. The greater detail of the later estimates, however, also helps to identify potential budget problems, facilitates final design choices, and provides information useful in making decisions to keep the project within budget. The detailed estimates also help in the analysis of construction bids or contractor proposals to identify possible problems such as inadequate builder interest or a misunderstanding of the contract documents.

4. Make cost a factor in evaluating major design decisions. Most sophisticated owners and teams evaluate both the first cost and, as discussed later in this chapter, the life-cycle cost inherent in a design decision.

5. Use value engineering techniques to achieve the proper balance between cost and quality. Value engineering is often misused as a synonym for cost cutting. Instead, it should be used to describe efforts to achieve the same program, quality, and design goals for the originally determined budget or even less cost.

RELATIVE COSTS

Costs are always a function of local factors (local labor and material costs, contractor availability and interest, building systems required by local climate or site conditions, etc.), as well as regional and national factors. As a result, although *School Planning and Management*'s "2008 Annual School Construction Report" supplement estimated that a median elementary school costs $157.05 per sq ft to build, schools in New York City and other high-cost areas exceeded $400 per sq ft.

In communities of all types, however, the choice of building systems and materials, as well as issues inherent to the site, can have a significant impact on the cost. The accompanying table provides a partial comparison, illustrating the relative costs of a number of common choices. This information should

be used with great caution, because costs vary significantly over time and between locations. Moreover, the choices listed are far from comprehensive.

OTHER FACTORS THAT CAN AFFECT COSTS

Exact quantity takeoffs and careful unit pricing do not always ensure an accurate construction cost estimate. Care in both areas is essential, but there are many other factors that have significant effects on the final cost of a construction project.

Some of these factors—for example, the accuracy of the contractors' own estimators—defy prediction. Others, however, can be analyzed and, to some extent, quantified. Therefore, qualitative and quantitative analyses of local construction markets are important elements of cost-management programs. Adjustment factors can be found in published services that provide a general guide, but they are inadequate by themselves. Analyses of these factors do not adhere to a standard format, because each project differs from all others. However, the following are among the general areas that should be covered:

1. Local geographical, sociological, and economic factors
2. Contractors' interest in and capabilities for the job
3. Labor availability and cost
4. Availability of materials
5. Other factors relating to the owner and the designer

Local Construction Industry Issues

The first set of factors, including population density, proximity to urban centers, and accessibility via major traffic routes, can readily

COST COMPARISON FOR MAJOR BUILDING SYSTEMS

	STRUCTURAL SYSTEM	ARCHITECTURAL SYSTEM	PLUMBING SYSTEM	HVAC SYSTEM	ELECTRICAL SYSTEM
SIMPLE COST	• Unclassified earth excavation, minimal elevation deviations • Stockpiling of excavated material on-site • Balanced cut and fill • Uniform spread footings • Continuous wall footings, nonstepped • Concrete-block or poured-concrete foundation walls • Wood frame or roof truss (if permitted by code) • Block wall and simple joint roof framing	• Simple shaped building with minimal architectural features • Exterior brick or block with stock window shapes, some stonework or precast trim, low ratio of windows • Unplastered block or drywall partitions in most areas • Resilient tile floors, VCT predominantly used • Painted exposed ceilings in most areas • Suspended ceilings with 2 × 4 acoust. tile in corridors and offices • Flat roofs with parapets • Simple waterproofing requirements • Vitreous spray or epoxy enamel in lieu of ceramic tile, minimal use of vitreous materials except for floors in wet areas • Simple program requirements • Low ratio of interior work • Hollow metal doors and bucks at normal heights • Simple stair exiting and fire-protection requirements • Minimum provision for future flexibility • Minimum circulation space, double-loaded corridors	• Gravity-type sanitary and storm systems using extra-heavy cast-iron pipe and fittings • Domestic hot and return water systems utilizing submerged tankless coils in boiler • Gas distribution for gas unit heaters, rooftop cooling and heating units, and boilers • Austere fixtures • Economical toilet layouts (i.e., typical in-line facilities) • Fire standpipe system, if required • Insulation for mains, risers, water lines, and horizontal storm drains in finished areas • Fire sprinkler system	• Low-pressure, one-pipe system • Two-pipe circulating hot-water system • Ventilation of interior areas (toilets) • Self-contained, low-pressure heating and air-conditioning systems, all air • Forced-air heat only • Self-contained boiler rooms • Limited insulation of piping and supply duct work	• One main distribution panel (wall mounted) serving simple 120/208V • Feeders: runs feeding one or more panels at a time • Lighting fixtures: fluorescent fixtures mainly in continuous rows; few incandescent fixtures • Branch circuit work: use of one light switch per average room, minimal outlets • Motor work: individually mounted starters furnished by others • Fire-alarm system: master control board with stations and gongs at stairs and exits; noncoded, nonzoned • Sound system: master amplifiers with microphone and page common to all speakers • Inexpensive clocks, not connected to central system • Emergency lighting: wall-mounted battery units with headlamps

continues

	STRUCTURAL SYSTEM	ARCHITECTURAL SYSTEM	PLUMBING SYSTEM	HVAC SYSTEM	ELECTRICAL SYSTEM
AVERAGE COST	• Unclassified earth excavation, some variance of grade elevations • Stockpiling of excavated materials on-site • Balanced cut and fill • Spread footings of generally uniform dimensions with some oddities • Continuous wall footings, with stepped requirement • Poured-concrete foundation walls • Concrete slab on grade • Some interior foundation wall requirements • Usually uniform bay size layouts for structural system, including variances for special conditions • Reinforced-concrete frame and arches • Structural steel frame, masonry or spray-on fire protection • Simple-use precast concrete or architectural cast concrete members for structural purposes • Generally more complicated building shape with breaks, corners, and cantilevers requiring an experienced contractor	• More complex building shape expressing architectural features • Exterior glass brick, architectural concrete, larger ratio of windows, special size windows, moderate use of stonework, cast stone and other special exterior materials • Unplastered block partitions utilizing expressive bonds; use of more expensive interior finishes, especially in public areas • Resilient tile floors, VCT or similar products, predominantly used; some use of carpeting or other more costly finishes • Greater requirement for hung ceilings; simple suspension system and economic use of acoustical tile • Flat roofs with some setbacks on different levels • More complex waterproofing requirements • Greater use of vitreous materials on walls and floors in wet areas • More complex program requirements, modular design	• Includes "simple" category plumbing; plus the following items • Sump and ejector pump systems • Hot-water generator • Domestic water-pressure system • Emergency generator---gas connections • Standard fixtures • Kitchen work • Tempered water for showers	• Includes "simple" category HVAC, plus the following items • Central station heating and air-conditioning (single zone) • Feeders: runs feeding one or more panels at a time • Multizone heating and air-conditioning systems with reheat coils • Fan coil perimeter system, two- or four-pipe • Unit ventilator system, two- or four-pipe • Kitchen and "simple" science room exhaust • Mechanical equipment rooms, including converters, chillers • Acoustic lining • Automatic sprinkler system (fire prevention) • Pneumatic controls, electric-electronic controls • Basic rooftop heating/cooling/ventilation equipment, limited ducted distribution	• Service and panels: one main distribution board (freestanding) serving light and power panels; simple 120/208V service • Feeders: runs feeding one or more panels at a time • Lighting fixtures: basic 2 × 4, 1 × 4, or 2 × 2 fluorescent fixtures, mainly in continuous rows; few incandescent fixtures; specialty lighting where necessary, plus some architectural lighting for aesthetic purposes • Branch circuit work, two or more light switches for each major room controlling different rows of fixtures, use of three-way switching; more generous employment of receptacles---both duplex and special • Motor work: motor control center furnished by electrical contractor • Fire-alarm system: master control board with stations and gongs at stairs and exits, plus zoning and coding of fire signal; use of some heat and smoke detectors • Sound system: master amplifiers with microphone and page common to all speakers • Clock and program system; master-control cabinet plus devices in major rooms and halls • Television system: cable or antenna amplifier and receiving outlets throughout building • Emergency lighting system: emergency generator and auto transfer switch feeding one emergency panel • Basic wiring for computer lab and some other technology

	STRUCTURAL SYSTEM	ARCHITECTURAL SYSTEM	PLUMBING SYSTEM	HVAC SYSTEM	ELECTRICAL SYSTEM
AVERAGE COST *(continued)*	• Masonry bearing wall and plank structure • Simple structural steel frame, metal deck/concrete or plank deck	• Greater density of interior work • Solid-wood doors and metal bucks; heights may vary according to need and location • Greater fire-protection and exiting requirements • Modest provisions for flexibility • More circulation space requirements • Greater need for mechanical equipment space • Modest use of varied materials for interior finishes • Limited use of movable partitions			
ABOVE NORMAL COST	• Classified earth excavation, such as hardpan, clay, boulders, rocks, etc. • Great variations in grade • Dewatering problems • Required bracing, shoring, etc • Unbalanced cut and fill resulting in need for borrowed or exported material • Foundation complications requiring spread footings of varying sizes and shapes; special foundations, such as piles	• Complex building shape requiring architectural treatments such as frequent overhangs, setbacks, multilevels, etc. • Exterior walls expressing and accentuating architectural aesthetics, utilizing stonework, complex precast or architectural concrete units, special window shapes and details, high ratio of glasswork, high-quality windows with long-life finishes and low-e glass, greater use of metal alloys for trim and decorative purposes	• Includes "simple" and "average" categories of plumbing, plus the following items • Galvanized steel or cast iron above grade for sanitary and storm systems • Foundation drainage if required • Preheater for domestic hot water • Water treatment, if required • Gas piping for laboratories • Acid-neutralizing system for labs • Gas systems for labs	• Can include "simple" and "average" categories of plumbing, plus the following items • Variable air volume system with mixing boxes or terminal reheats • Induction system • Fume hood exhaust • Dust-collection system • Thermal wheel heat exchange • Heat reclamation • High-pressure steam, with PRV stations • Radiant ceilings and floors • Heat pumps	• Service panels: 480/177V service into building, one or more freestanding main distribution board 480/120–208V transformers, subdistribution panels, light and power panels • Feeders: multiple sets of feeders between main distribution boards and from main distribution boards to subdistribution panels; single feeder runs from subdistribution panels to light and power panels; possible use of bus duct for main feeders • Lighting fixtures: low-glare and up/down fluorescent fixtures; some incandescent fixtures and specialty lighting where necessary, plus some architectural lighting for aesthetic purposes; high-intensity lighting for special areas

continues

	STRUCTURAL SYSTEM	ARCHITECTURAL SYSTEM	PLUMBING SYSTEM	HVAC SYSTEM	ELECTRICAL SYSTEM
ABOVE NORMAL COST *(continued)*	• Grade beam requirements more often than typical; continuous wall footings and foundation walls • Structural slab not on grade • Interior requirements for foundation walls and footings • Varying bay sizes • Complicated reinforcing concrete frame and slab; structural steel frame encased in concrete fireproofing • Detailed precast concrete, architectural concrete, or cast stone details • Generally complicated structure shape requiring unique structural design solution, or considerations requiring high-caliber contractor • Design for future expansion	• Plastered interior partitions, greater use of vinyl wall • Greater use of vinyl tile floors and architecturally expressive finishes • Greater use of hung ceilings with Sheetrock or high-quality 2 × 2 acoustical tile in most areas • Multilevel roofs, setbacks, penthouses, promenade decks, etc. • Complex damp- and waterproofing requirements • Ceramic tile or glazed block used on floors and walls in wet areas • Complex program requirements for multipurpose occupancy • High-density requirements for interior work; single-loaded enclosed corridors • Expensive fire-protection requirements, substantial exiting needs • Large circulation and public areas • Large mechanical equipment space • Expensive vertical and horizontal transportation equipment • Large degree of flexibility inherent in layout and design to accommodate	• Emergency showers and eye-washing facilities • Deionized and distilled water systems for labs • Heavy kitchen work • Fire pump and jockey pump • Insulation of all domestic water piping and all horizontal storm piping • Luxury fixtures • Design for a high degree of flexibility	• Steam humidification • Snow-removal systems • Water treatment systems • Boiler feed system • CO_2 fire prevention system • Remote power plant installation • Central station, computerized monitoring for automatic temperature controls • Sound attenuation systems • Design requirements for future expansion	• Branch circuit work: two or more light switches per major room, controlling different rows of fixtures; use of three-way switching; more generous employment of receptacles---both duplex and special • Motor work: motor control centers, plus intricate interlocking and control devices; fan shutdown coupled with fire-alarm system • Fire-alarm system coded and supervised fire-alarm system plus complete smoke detection, heat detection, and sprinkler alarm systems; fan shutdown facilities coupled to motor control centers • Sound system: master system plus subsystems in other facilities, interconnected for selective paging • Clock and program system: master control cabinet, plus devices in major rooms and halls • Television systems: cable and/or antennas, amplifiers and receiving outlets throughout building, plus program originating and sending facilities; possible television studio • Emergency lighting system: emergency generator, plus complete system of feeders and panels to all areas • Telephone system with features (voice mail, etc.): complete system of feeder, conduits, terminal cabinets, and outlets • Stage lighting: theatrical stage lighting with complete dimming facilities • Intercom telephone system: automatic exchange plus handsets

	STRUCTURAL SYSTEM	ARCHITECTURAL SYSTEM	PLUMBING SYSTEM	HVAC SYSTEM	ELECTRICAL SYSTEM
ABOVE NORMAL COST *(continued)*		future changes and requirements for mechanical and electrical trades • Use of large movable partitions			• Lightning protection • Laboratory work; special lab panels with contactors, wire-mold raceway with multivoltage receptacles, lab bench wiring, explosion-proof areas • Surveillance and security systems: all exterior and stair doors, plus door to special rooms, wired to central security console; possible closed-circuit television hookup included • LAN and WAN wiring as well as wiring all classrooms for computers and Internet • Design for future expansion • Design characteristics reflecting high degree of flexibility

Source: Bradford Perkins, Perkins Eastman, 1999.

indicate potential problems. The capabilities of the construction industry in a smaller town can be strained by the requirements of a large project, so the estimator should take note of the work experience and size of local contractors' firms and labor pools.

The character of a town can also have an effect on costs. In some towns outside urban areas, for example, the construction industry can depend heavily on one owner for work. Therefore, local work must be suited to this employer's construction program. In other areas, the presence of organized crime and other circumstances can, unfortunately, determine the number and interest of bidders in some trades.

General market information, such as that described, rarely provides the detail necessary for either design decisions or final cost estimates, but it does indicate where further research is necessary. It is the research on local contractors, labor, material, and owner/architect factors that can and should shape the final plans.

Lack of Bidder Interest Raises Costs

The interest and capabilities of a contractor are often major cost considerations. It is not uncommon for there to be substantial cost overruns, owing largely to lack of interest and competition. In one such case, only two firms were willing to bid on a New York City educational project that would last four years, and neither was willing to take it without premiums that approached 100 percent. In years when there is a great amount of private-sector work, it may take creative bid packaging and bidder solicitation to attract adequate interest.

During a recession, "negative escalation" can be experienced on projects in many regions. Bid prices actually stabilize or go down as contractors and labor just try to stay employed. When the economy recovers, however, both contractors and labor are often quick to reestablish their normal markups, overtime requirements, and other costs. It is not uncommon for costs to jump rapidly, to amounts far greater than can be accounted for by normal increases in labor and material costs, when a local construction market gets busy.

Interest is only one of the two important considerations in selecting a contractor; the other is capability. In small cities and rural areas, local contractors may not be able to build a complex project efficiently. An inexperienced contractor facing a complex project or unusual materials and details usually adds a significant premium to his bid—if he bids at all. What usually happens is that outside contractors have to be encouraged to bid, inasmuch as they have to expect problems working in a new area with a limited labor and subcontractor pool; and large outside contractors add premiums as well.

On a smaller scale, many contractors add a premium for handling new materials or unfamiliar details. For example, architectural concrete, complex brick patterns, the newer curtain walls, radiant heating systems, and many other materials, systems, or details may be beyond the capabilities of the local construction industry.

Checklist of Key Questions

Unfortunately, there is no central source for the information needed to select a contractor. However, by calling Associated General Contractors (AGC) chapters, local contractors, and other industry sources, it is usually possible to obtain partial answers to the following key questions on the subject of contractor interest and capabilities:

- How many contractors in the area work in a given category of construction?
- How many bids does a project of a given size normally receive?
- Is there so much directly competing work in the area that there is a reduction in the number of potential bidders?
- Is the seasonal factor in this area any more pronounced than normal for the construction industry as a whole?
- Are there ways of stimulating contractor interest?
- What is the prevailing contractor attitude toward unusual design or site location?
- Are local contractors familiar with unusual materials or details that may be employed on the project?
- Is there likely to be any reduction in the number of bids or bid premiums resulting from minority hiring or training requirements?
- Are local contractors finding construction loans unusually difficult to obtain?

Labor Shortage May Restrict Design Options

A major factor in contractor interest and capability is, of course, the local labor force. A cost estimator must know the local wage rates and be aware of any shortages in critical trades, the prevailing premiums necessary to obtain local labor or induce migration, the trade jurisdictions, and any other factors that can have cost ramifications.

Shortages can be an important factor. An architect recently designing a project in upstate New York was informed of a shortage of carpenters. This helped him during schematic design as he realized that several design options, such as a poured-in-place concrete structure, were foreclosed. In other areas, a shortage of masons has made pre-cast and other exterior materials more attractive.

Local work practices are also important. In many areas prefabricated components, such as prehung doors, are disassembled and then reassembled on-site because of local union rules. In other areas, union locals prevent the use of any materials manufactured by nonunion labor.

Strikes are a similar risk and another unknown cost for the contractor to estimate. Therefore, it is important to check on the expiration date of existing contracts, the likelihood of strikes, the size of the increases likely to be negotiated in the next contract, and related factors.

Information on these and other labor-related cost factors can be supplied by local contractors and construction trade associations, minority group representatives, and other related sources. The following questions should be asked:

- Are the jurisdictions of unusual size?
- Are there any jurisdictional disputes that may affect the project?
- Are there significant variations in labor supply owing to seasonal factors?
- Are there extreme shortages in any trades, and if so, will they result in premiums and/or delays in construction schedules?
- What inducements are required to encourage labor to come to the area?
- What is the impact of training programs, and what is the availability of minority workers if the contractors are expected to meet minority hiring targets?
- What are the basic and fringe rates for each trade?
- When do local contracts expire, what in-

creases are scheduled in existing contracts, and what percentages are predicted for the next contract?
- Is local labor cooperative or belligerent, and what is its level of interest in the project?

Materials are usually a lesser problem than either contractors or labor, but on some projects material supply and cost volatility can be critical. Too often designs include materials that are either unavailable locally or unfamiliar to local contractors. In some cases too many projects are competing for the same material. Where any of these situations occurs, it is worth devoting part of the market study effort to this subject. Among the basic questions to ask are the following:

- Are any of the critical materials unusual or difficult to obtain?
- How far is the project site from the nearest major source of the materials incorporated in the design?
- Are there other projects in the area that may compete directly for the same materials?
- Are there complications—shipping limitations, delays, etc.—in supply because of unusual materials, shortages, or lack of capacity?
- Which materials are on national rather than local price scales? Are any local materials unusually expensive or inexpensive?

The last area, and most difficult to research for a full market study, includes owner/designer factors. There are a few good clients who actually attract additional bidders or an unusually large number of bidders for their projects.

▶ The ability of the project team to reduce cost is highest during the early phases, when plans and programs are easier to modify. Courtesy of Perkins Eastman.

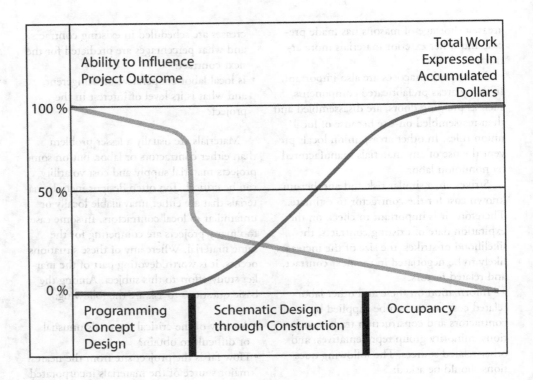

Most owner/architect cost factors are negative, however. Some subcontractor associations have told public clients that their members have added premiums to their bids on the clients' projects to account for slow payments, onerous contracts, and/or excessive paperwork.

Some architects, unfortunately, have also been known to cause contractors to add premiums. Their consistently incomplete construction documents, disruptive actions during the construction phase, and unnecessarily complex designs are among the most common reasons. Therefore, an increasing number of construction market studies are including such questions as the following:

• Do the owner's administrative, contract, payment, or inspection procedures cause significant problems for the contractor?
• Does the architect have a reputation for causing problems or providing inadequate construction documents?
• Are there problems that the owner or architect can help mitigate?

If a market study reveals serious problems in any of these areas, it is possible to save more money by concentrating on overcoming adverse market conditions than by refining costly segments of the design. The difference between an efficient and inefficient design may be less than 15 percent, whereas market conditions can add far more than that amount in premiums.

Adverse market conditions can usually be overcome. Split contracts, expedited payment procedures, careful selection of local materials, aggressive bidder solicitation, contractor orientation meetings, and careful timing of bids and other techniques are being used with increasing frequency to solve market problems. The first step, however, is to identify the problems.

VALUE ENGINEERING AND LIFE-CYCLE COST ANALYSIS

As noted earlier, value engineering is often confused with cost cutting. The term was originated, however, to describe a technique used to seek design options that achieve the original design objectives at a lower cost. Some school systems even use a formal process to develop and evaluate value engineering ideas. At the very least, most owners expect to see construction and operating cost comparisons of the major building system alternatives.

In a sophisticated value engineering effort, cost is defined not only as construction cost but also as life-cycle cost. Experienced owners and design professionals know that a building's design has a significant impact on its operating cost and its life-cycle cost. What has been less well understood is how and where to apply this concept in the design process. Unfortunately, the rhetoric of life-cycle cost analysis is more advanced than its application.

Some owners and design professionals have ignored this critical design parameter in favor of an overriding concern with construction cost control. Construction cost is certainly a critical factor, but life-cycle cost is an increasingly important design consideration.

The following examples are well known in school design:

- Should the school use low-maintenance finishes or lower first-cost finishes, such as paint, that require regular maintenance?
- Should the school install long-life light fixtures that have a higher first cost and bulb replacement cost in order to gain the benefits of the lower energy usage, reduced maintenance load, and lesser heat gain impact on the air-conditioning?
- Will a central mechanical system (versus a decentralized system of package units) justify a higher first cost with lower replacement, energy, and other costs?
- Should the school use more expensive aluminum windows with a baked-on long-life finish, or less expensive wood windows that require periodic painting?
- Should the school system build a new, more efficient building, or renovate an inefficient older building?
- Will proposed energy conservation measures, such as new windows or added insulation, be justified by their lower operating costs?

In response to these questions, a systematic life-cycle analysis can help identify the most appropriate design solution. Most such questions can be analyzed relatively simply, but others require an analysis of several or all of the following factors:

- *Capital investment costs:* often called "first costs"—the costs of construction, furnishings, equipment, design fees, and other related items

- *Financing costs:* the costs of construction or long-term financing
- *Staff costs:* costs associated with operating and maintaining the facility
- *Building operating costs:* the costs of energy and other related expenses
- *Maintaining costs:* the costs of custodial care and repair, annual maintenance contracts, and salaries of maintenance personnel
- *Alteration costs:* the costs related to interim changes required because flexibility or additional capacity was not built in
- *Replacement costs:* the costs of replacing systems or building components that

have a shorter life than other available choices

It is typical to create a spreadsheet that compares key choices, such as those listed previously, over time. Costs that occur after the first year are discounted by the cost of money to the school system to take into account the fact that costs incurred in future years have less financial impact than costs in the first year.

Cost management has become a central issue on every school project, and an increasingly complex. To be effective, a design team must be able to manage all aspects of this task.

CHAPTER 20
FINANCING

PUBLIC SCHOOL FINANCING

Most school building programs are financed with bond issues voted on by the residents of the school district. Private schools have to raise money from alumni and other private sources, special schools may be funded with state aid, and some others may draw upon still other sources; but the vast majority of programs that cannot be funded from the annual operating budget must go to public vote. Every year billions of dollars of school bond issues are on the ballot, and the majority pass. However, the failure of a bond issue, which is not uncommon, inevitably has serious negative consequences for the school district. This chapter outlines the basic issues involved in public financing of school construction, as well as the process used by many districts to gain the necessary public support for passage. A good source on the many steps and legal issues related to the public funding of school construction is *Planning and Financing School Improvement and Construction Projects*, published by the National Organization on Legal Problems of Education and the American Bar Association, Topeka (Bittle 1996), hereafter referred to as the NOLPE monograph. Some of the major points made in this monograph, as well as in other sources, are the following:

1. *Legal constraints.* There are a number of laws that govern the public financing of schools. Districts typically retain legal counsel to see that they stay within these laws. For example:

- Any irregularity in the notices and procedures—such as an incomplete environmental assessment or an inaccurate public notice describing the purpose of the bond issue—can void a referendum.
- A school district typically cannot do indirectly what cannot be done directly. As the NOLPE monograph (p. 7) notes, "A lease with an option to purchase was held [by the courts to be] beyond the authority granted by statute."
- There are strict rules governing any interest earned on bond proceeds prior to their use to fund construction and equipment.
- In some states, a school district cannot promote a "yes" vote; it can only provide information. In such cases it must rely on a citizens committee or other groups to be the advocates.
- Most districts must operate within debt limits established by law.

2. *Determination of need.* As discussed throughout this book, the financing process should begin with a careful analysis of the district's needs as well as a detailed estimate of the probable costs. This estimate should include adequate contingencies to cover the expansion of scope inherent in the implementation phases that follow the bond issue.

3. *Financial feasibility.* The school district typically retains bond counsel and a financial consultant. The financial consultant will help determine the financial feasibility of a bond issue and will compile the

financial data, projections, and related calculations needed to structure the bond issue. This consultant also develops the information that must be disclosed to potential purchasers of the bonds.

4. *Fees.* Part of the budgeting process should be a calculation of the various fees—for an architect, engineer, special consultant, bond counsel, financial consultant, investment banker, and so forth—that must be covered by the bond proceeds. Establishment of the design team fee has historically been guided by state or local fee schedules developed or negotiated directly by the school district. Many of the school district schedules are too rigid to recognize the inherent differences between projects (see also "Educational Specifications, Programming, and Predesign" in chapter 3). Therefore, most experienced design teams calculate the time (and thus the cost) it will take to provide both the prebond services and the services following passage.

As noted in the NOLPE monograph: "Bond counsel will ordinarily work for a fixed or hourly fee for work during the planning and election process... Financial consultants generally charge a fee at the time the bonds are issued. Bond counsel and financial consultant fees are generally based on the completion of the project, the complexity of the financing, and the amount of bonds to be issued" (p. 6).

5. *Managing a successful bond-issue referendum.* As typical bond-issue size and anti-tax sentiment have grown, most districts must carefully plan the campaign for a successful referendum. According to DLR Group Educational Facilities Con-

sultants, the basic precepts of a successful bond issue include the following:

- A unified school board
- A campaign that is citizen-led and staff supported
- Knowledge of what the community wants and expects from its facilities and curriculum
- A completed facilities study, clearly showing the need for improvements with all options studied and documented
- Informed district employees, who know the election issues and know how they can help
- A public relations plan that includes a free flow of information to the public about the need and costs associated with the improvements.
- A publicity plan that continually reminds the voters that the election is about educating students, who are the benefactors of the bond passage

DLR notes: "It's extremely rare to ignore these tools and still win." Therefore, most districts do the required initial planning and then involve one or more citizens committees that include respected leaders in the community to help achieve a positive vote. It is not uncommon to have several committees working in a coordinated fashion toward this end.

Among the most common committees formed to analyze and promote a potential bond issue are the following:

- A steering committee to coordinate the several committees. This committee may also be responsible for obtaining endorsements from organizations within the district and for identifying and getting out the vote by probable "yes" voters.

BUILDING COMMUNITY CONSENSUS FOR LONG RANGE MASTER PLANS

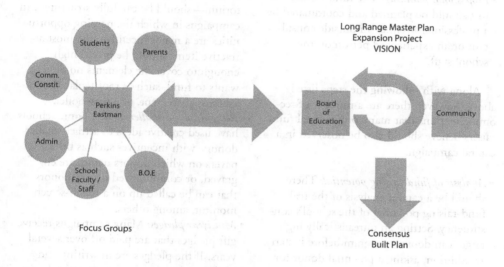

Focus Groups

Consensus Built Plan

◀ The creation of the consensus needed for a successful bond issue is typically created with significant input from many groups. Courtesy of Perkins Eastman.

- A facilities committee to help analyze and confirm the need and the options.
- A publicity committee to disperse accurate information about the need, the proposed solution, and the bond issue.
- Special subcommittees, such as a senior citizens committee, to deal with the special concerns of particular groups of potential voters. For example, senior citizens, who do not have children in the schools also tend to have a high voter turnout and are naturally concerned about the impact of the bond issue on their fixed incomes. They can often make or break a bond issue.
6. *Getting out the vote.* The final step is to get out the vote. The "no" voters are often more motivated, but it is usually apathy or confusion among the "yes" voters that dooms most unsuccessful bond is-

sues. Thus, it is important not only to establish a strong pre-referendum education and public relations effort but also to make sure an informed, supportive public goes to the polls and votes.

PRIVATE SCHOOL FINANCING
The financing of private schools must follow a process similar to that used in a well-planned public school bond referendum:

- *A clear definition of need:* The process should begin with a careful definition of the school's need.
- *Educating the school's constituency:* There must be a broad-based educational program for the school's consistency (primarily the alumni and families of the students).
- *The leaders must lead:* The school's leadership (the board, the head of the school,

and the individuals responsible for fund-raising) must take the lead in the fund-raising effort.

- *Professional planning:* The fund-raising effort should be planned and coordinated by a professional—either an outside consultant or an experienced person on the school staff.

Along with following the steps listed above, however, there are a number of recommendations that many professional fund-raisers believe should also be observed in a capital campaign:

- *Analysis of fund-raising potential:* There should be a careful analysis of the real fund-raising potential of the school's constituency. Setting an unrealistically high target can doom a program before it starts. In addition, asking a potential donor for an unrealistically large amount makes refusal likely.
- *Advance pledges:* Many campaigns try to obtain pledges for a third or more of the target from key donors before the campaign officially starts. These initial donations give the campaign credibility and momentum.
- *Board support:* Unified support—including financial support—from the school's board is essential. Donors expect to see that the school's leadership is committed to the campaign.
- *Donor recognition and naming opportunities:* Many campaigns provide a list of naming opportunities to potential donors as a reward, recognition, and/or incentive

for their gifts. The pricing of these opportunities—for example, a name on the building or a room or other element within the building, such as a seat in an auditorium—should be carefully structured. In campaigns in which the naming opportunities are a major incentive, the most attractive items should be priced high enough to cover the elements no one wants to fund, such as roof replacement, asbestos abatement, or a new boiler.

- *Recognition of smaller donors:* Some schools have used creative ideas to attract smaller donors, with incentives such as brick pavers on which donors names are engraved, or computerized lists of donors that can be called up on a touch-screen monitor, among others.
- *Multiyear pledges:* Many campaigns receive gift pledges that are paid off over several years. If the pledges are in writing and creditworthy, they become security for interim financing that allows the project to proceed. (Private schools can also borrow if tuition or endowment income is sufficient to cover the debt service.)
- *Follow-up:* Proper follow-up with, and treatment of, donors—no matter how small their contributions—is important to maintain goodwill and the potential for future donations.

Virtually all schools find the prospect of raising the money necessary for a building program a daunting task. With careful planning and implementation, however, thousands of public and private school building programs are successfully funded each year.

SAMPLE SPACE PROGRAM FOR AN ELEMENTARY SCHOOL, GRADES PK–5

750   planned students in grades PK–5

SPACE DESCRIPTION	SPACE COUNT	PROPOSED STUDENTS		NET SQUARE FEET		NOTES
		EACH	TOTAL	EACH	TOTAL	
1 CLASSROOM SPACE						
A. Pre-K, K–1 Cluster						provide exterior access
1. Classroom: pre-kindergarten	1	15	30	1,200	1,200	
2. Classroom: kindergarten	4	20	80	1,200	4,800	
3. Classroom: grade 1	5	24	120	1,000	5,000	
4. Classroom storage	10			50	500	
5. Classroom toilets	10			60	600	
6. Cluster lockers: 250 count	1			750	750	distribute in cluster
Subtotal:			230		12,850	
B. 2–3 Cluster						provide exterior access
1. Classroom: grades 2–3	12	24	288	1,000	12,000	
2. Cluster toilets	2			300	600	
3. Cluster lockers: 300 count	1			900	900	distribute in cluster
Subtotal:			288		13,500	
C. 4–5 Cluster						provide exterior access
1. Classroom	10	24	240	1,000	10,000	
2. Cluster toilets	2			300	600	
3. Cluster lockers: 250 count	1			750	750	distribute in cluster
Subtotal:			240		11,350	
D. Cluster Common Areas						
1. Cluster project space	3			1,200	3,600	one per cluster
2. Special education/breakout	3			300	900	one per cluster
3. Special education office	3			150	450	one per cluster
4. Speech/hearing	2			200	400	
5. Shared community room	1			200	200	
6. Tutoring space	1			650	650	
7. Project prep/storage	3			300	900	adjacent to project space
Subtotal:					7,100	
Total Student Learning Space:			758		44,800	

750 planned students in grades PK–5 SPACE DESCRIPTION	SPACE COUNT	PROPOSED STUDENTS EACH	TOTAL	NET SQUARE FEET EACH	TOTAL	NOTES
2 TEACHER AND ADMINISTRATIVE SUPPORT SPACE						
A. Administrative Suite						
1. Waiting and reception area	1			400	400	2 rec, 6–8 people, visual to nurse
2. Principal's office	1			225	225	visual to reception, visual to entry
3. Assistant principal's office	1			225	225	
4. General conference room	1			250	250	10–12 people
5. Workroom	1			200	200	needs sink
6. File storage	1			150	150	
7. Supply storage	1			150	150	
Subtotal:					1,600	
B. Special Services						
1. Office	1			100	100	
2. Psychologist's office	1			100	100	
3. Pupil services	1			150	150	optional
4. Shared conference room	1			150	150	
5. Time-out alcove	1			50	50	2 people, open to circulation
Subtotal:					550	
C. Clinic						
1. Nurse's office	1			120	120	
2. Exam/treatment rooms	1			200	200	2 cots, refrigerator, freezer, medicine cabinet
3. Storage/supplies	1			60	60	
4. Toilet	1			70	70	
Subtotal:					450	
Total Teacher and Administrative Space:					2,600	

750 planned students in grades PK–5

SPACE DESCRIPTION	SPACE COUNT	PROPOSED STUDENTS EACH	PROPOSED STUDENTS TOTAL	NET SQUARE FEET EACH	NET SQUARE FEET TOTAL	NOTES
3 MEDIA AND TECHNOLOGY SPACE						
A. Library/Media Center						
1. Stacks/reading	1			1,400	1,400	10,000 volumes, broadcast area
2. Circulation desk	1			120	120	
3. Workroom	1			200	200	
4. Library storage	1			150	150	includes periodical storage
5. School store	1			100	100	
6. Librarian's office	1			120	120	
7. Faculty professional space	1			800	800	
Subtotal:					2,890	
B. Media Technology						
1. AV storage/repair/production	1			500	500	laptop shop
2. Media distribution center	1			200	200	
3. Software/CD storage	1			200	200	
Subtotal:					900	
Total Media and Technology Space:					3,790	
4 CLASSROOM SUPPORT SPACE						
A. Public Spaces						
1. Lobby	1			400	400	
Subtotal:					400	
B. Cafeteria						
1. Commons/cafeteria	1			3,200	3,200	12 sq ft/student
2. Stage	1			1,200	1,200	
3. Storage	2			300	600	tables/chairs
4. Serving area	1			600	600	
Subtotal:					5,600	
C. Kitchen						3.2 sq ft per meal served x 800 = 2,560 (estimated)
1. Staff toilets/lockers	2			75	150	
2. Office	1			120	120	
3. Receiving/storage	1			150	150	
4. Janitor/cleaning	1			50	50	

750 planned students in grades PK–5 SPACE DESCRIPTION	SPACE COUNT	PROPOSED STUDENTS		NET SQUARE FEET		NOTES
		EACH	TOTAL	EACH	TOTAL	
5. Dry storage	1			150	150	
6. Prep/production	1			1,500	1,800	
7. Laundry alcove	1			120	120	
Subtotal:					2,540	
D. Interior Facilities						
1. Gymnasium	1			6,300	6,300	bleacher seating for 850
2. Gymnasium toilets (boys)	1			500	500	50 lockers, 100 sq ft shower
3. Gymnasium toilets (girls)	1			500	500	50 lockers, 100 sq ft shower
4. Athletic office/storage	1			1,000	1,000	
Subtotal:					8,300	
E. Exterior Facilities						
1. Play area: pre-K, K, & grade 1	1				0	
2. Play area: grades 2–3	1				0	
3. Play area: grades 4–5	1				0	
4. Play field	1				0	
Subtotal:					0	
Total Classroom Support Space:					16,840	

750 planned students in grades PK–5 SPACE DESCRIPTION	SPACE COUNT	PROPOSED STUDENTS		NET SQUARE FEET		NOTES
		EACH	TOTAL	EACH	TOTAL	
5 VISUAL AND PERFORMING ARTS SPACE						
A. Activity rooms						
1. Activity room: music	1			1,200	1,200	
2. Activity room: art	1			1,200	1,200	
3. Activity room: art & music	1			1,200	1,200	
4. Storage	4			150	600	
5. Kiln room	1			60	60	
Subtotal:					4,260	
Total Visual and Performing Arts Space:					4,260	

750 planned students in grades PK–5						
SPACE DESCRIPTION	**PROPOSED**			**NOTES**		
	SPACE	STUDENTS		NET SQUARE FEET		
	COUNT	EACH	TOTAL	EACH	TOTAL	
6 FACILITY MANAGEMENT AND SUPPORT SPACE						
A. Mechanical and custodial						
1. Central mechanical room	1			2,000	2,000	
2. Custodian's office	1			120	120	
3. Custodial closets	3			60	180	
4. Communication closets	3			60	180	
Subtotal:					2,480	
B. Property Control						
1. Shipping and receiving	1			500	500	
2. Recycle room	1			400	400	
3. Secured staging/storage	1			600	600	
4. Building maintenance supplies	1			400	400	
Subtotal:					1,900	
Total Facility Management and Support Space:					4,380	
TOTAL NSF			758		76,670	

750 planned students in grades PK–5		CAPACITY STUDENTS	NET SQUARE FEET TOTAL	GROSSING FACTOR	GROSS SQUARE FEET TOTAL
SPACE PROGRAM SUMMARY					
A.	**Area Summary**				
1.	Proposed new elementary school		76,670	1.37	105,038
B.	**Capacity Summary**				
1.	Teaching stations	758 students			
2.	Utilization factor	100%			
3.	Effective student capacity	758 students			
C.	**Area Analysis**				
1.	Square feet per student: planned	750 students			140
2.	Square feet per student: actual	758 students			139
D.	**Area Comparison**				
1.	Classrooms	58%			61,376
2.	Administration	3%			3,562
3.	Media and technology	5%			5,192
4.	Support space	22%			23,071
5.	Performing and visual arts	6%			5,836
6.	Facility support	6%			6,001
	Total GSF	100%			105,038

SAMPLE SPACE PROGRAM FOR A MIDDLE SCHOOL, GRADES 6–8

SPACE DESCRIPTION	Sample Middle School Program						NOTES
	SPACES		STUDENTS		NET SQUARE FEET		
1,200 planned students, grades 6–8							
1,200 core capacity	TEACHING	TOTAL	EACH	TOTAL	EACH	TOTAL	
1 ACADEMIC SPACE							
A. Grade Level Teaming Areas (one set per grade)							
1. Core classrooms	9	9	24	216	900	8,100	3 teams per grade level
2. ESL classroom	1	1	24	24	900	900	
3. Science classroom	2	2	24	48	1,250	2,500	water, gas, electric, movable furniture
4. Science prep room	1	–	–		150	150	shared between 2 labs
5. Bookroom	1	–	–		200	200	
6. Teacher planning workroom	1	–	–		300	300	
7. Student locker area							included in grossing factor
Subtotal:	12			288		12,150	
3 total grade levels	36			864		36,450	
B. Shared Academic Spaces (times 2 sets)							2 sets shared between 3 grade levels
1. Graphics and computer lab		1	–	–	1,000	1,000	
2. Storage		1	–	–	100	100	for lab above
3. World language classroom	1	1	24	24	900	900	
4. Teacher break room and restroom		1	–	–	300	300	
Subtotal:	1			24		2,300	
2 sets of shared spacess	2			48		4,600	
C. Distributed Administration Suites (1 per grade level)							
1. Assistant principal		1	–	–	150	150	
2. Assistant principal support space		1	–	–	100	100	
Subtotal:	–			–		250	
3 total suites	–			–		750	one per grade level
D. Special Education Suite (optional; may not be required)							near academic areas
1. Specialized needs classroom (orthopedic)		1	12	12	1,000	1,000	
2. Time-out room (optional)		1	–	–	100	100	
3. Storage, washer, dryer, kitchen		1	–	–	200	200	
4. Changing room and shower		1	–	–	150	150	

SPACE DESCRIPTION		Sample Middle School Program					NOTES
1,200 planned students, grades 6–8	SPACES		STUDENTS		NET SQUARE FEET		
1,200 core capacity	TEACHING	TOTAL	EACH	TOTAL	EACH	TOTAL	
5. Restroom		1	–	–	50	50	
Subtotal:	–			12		1,500	
E. Special Education Group Rooms							
1. Speech classroom	0.5	1	12	12	400	400	
2. Small group classroom	0.5	1	12	12	600	600	
3. Conference room		1	–	–	600	600	
Subtotal:	1			24		1,600	
F. Alternative Education (2 sets shared among 3 grade levels)							
1. Classroom	2	2	24	48	900	1,800	
2. Computer research lab	2	2	24	48	900	1,800	
3. Storage		2	–	–	150	300	
4. Mentoring conferencing room		1	–	–	350	350	
5. Break room and vending area		1	–	–	600	600	
6. Admin: counselor/facilitator		1	–	–	150	150	
7. Admin: administrative assistant		1	–	–	150	150	
8. Admin: teachers' office		1	–	–	150	150	
7. Student locker area							included in grossing factor
Subtotal:	4			96		5,300	
2 total suites	8			192		10,600	
G. Business Education (optional)							
1. Lab	1	1	24	24	1,000	1,000	
2. Office		1	–	–	100	100	
3. Storage		1	–	–	120	120	
Subtotal:	1			24		1,220	
H. Career Investigation (optional)							
1. Classroom	1	1	24	24	1,000	1,000	
2. Storage		1	–	–	100	100	
3. Office		1	–	–	100	100	
Subtotal:	1			24		1,200	
I. Family and Consumer Science (optional)							flexible; can adapt to future program requirements
1. Lab	1	1	24	24	1,800	1,800	
2. Storage	1	–	–	200	200		

SPACE DESCRIPTION	Sample Middle School Program						NOTES
	SPACES		STUDENTS		NET SQUARE FEET		
1,200 planned students, grades 6–8 1,200 core capacity	TEACHING	TOTAL	EACH	TOTAL	EACH	TOTAL	
3. Office	1	–	–	100	100		
Technology education							
4. Robotics lab	1	1	24	24	1,800	1,800	
5. R&D room		1	–	–	150	150	
6. Storage		1	–	–	150	150	
Subtotal:		2		48		4,200	
Total Academic Space:		51		1,236		62,120	

2 ADMINISTRATIVE AND STAFF SPACE							
A. Administration Area							near main entry
1. Reception area		1	–	–	250	250	
2. Secretarial reception		1	–	–	150	150	
3. Secretary		1	–	–	150	150	
4. Principal		1	–	–	180	180	
5. Conference room		1	–	–	215	215	
6. Workroom/copier/restroom		1	–	–	300	300	
7. Records file room		1	–	–	80	80	
Subtotal:		–	–	–		1,325	
B. Staff Support Space							adjacent to student entry
1. Staff offices		1	–	–	1,600	1,600	
2. Restrooms		2	–	–	120	240	
Subtotal:		–		–		1,840	
C. Clinic							adjacent to attendance office
1. Waiting area/info display		1	–	–	300	300	
2. "Nurse aide, exam, audio testing		1	–	–	120	120	
3. Nurse's office		1	–	–	150	150	
4. Cot room		2	–	–	120	240	
5. Restroom		2	–	–	50	100	
Subtotal:		–		–		910	
D. Guidance							
1. Counselor		3	–	–	150	450	
2. Reception/clerk		1	–	–	250	250	
3. Reception seating		1	–	–	150	150	
4. Workroom/copier/restroom		1	–	–	200	200	
5. Multipurpose counseling office		1	–	–	200	200	

SPACE DESCRIPTION	Sample Middle School Program					NOTES
1,200 planned students, grades 6–8	SPACES		STUDENTS		NET SQUARE FEET	
1,200 core capacity	TEACHING	TOTAL	EACH	TOTAL	EACH	TOTAL	

SPACE DESCRIPTION	TEACHING	TOTAL	EACH	TOTAL	EACH	TOTAL	NOTES
6. Conference office		1	–	–	150	150	
7. Vault/storage/secured test materials		1	–	–	150	150	
Subtotal:	–			–		1,550	
E. General Areas							
1. Parents' office		1	–	–	225	225	
2. Technology distribution room		1	–	–	200	200	
3. Entry lobby with reception/security counter		1	–	–	400	400	inviting, with display areas
Subtotal:	–			–		825	
Total Administrative and Staff Space:	–			–		6,450	

3 STUDENT DINING AND FOOD SERVICE SPACE

SPACE DESCRIPTION	TEACHING	TOTAL	EACH	TOTAL	EACH	TOTAL	NOTES
A. Student Dining	school population/number of planned lunch periods x 15 sq ft = (1,200/3) x 15 = 6,000						
1. Commons cafeteria		1	–	–	6,000	6,000	dining, performances, assemblies
2. School Store		1	–	–	400	400	
Subtotal:	–			–		6,400	
B. Kitchen	3.7 sq ft per meal served, including serving areas x 1,300 meals served = 4,810 (estimated)						
1. Receiving		1	–	–	230	230	
2. Custodial/laundry		1	–	–	120	120	
3. Chemical/paper		1	–	–	300	300	
4. Toilet/locker area		1	–	–	150	150	
5. Dry storage		1	–	–	500	500	
6. Freezer		1	–	–	300	300	
7. Cooler		1	–	–	170	170	
8. Office		1	–	–	150	150	
9. Office storage		1	–	–	65	65	
10. Custodial closet		1	–	–	65	65	
11. Food prep area		1	–	–	1,450	1,450	
12. Serving area		1	–	–	1,300	1,300	
Subtotal:	–			–		4,800	
Total Student Dining Space:	–			–		11,200	

SPACE DESCRIPTION	Sample Middle School Program						NOTES
1,200 planned students, grades 6–8	SPACES		STUDENTS		NET SQUARE FEET		
1,200 core capacity	TEACHING	TOTAL	EACH	TOTAL	EACH	TOTAL	
4 LIBRARY AND MEDIA CENTER SPACE							
A. Library/Media Center							
1. Library/media reading room		1	–	–	4,000	4,000	
2. Librarian's office		2	–	–	200	400	
3. Librarian's workroom		1	–	–	300	300	
4. Laptop repair and AV storage		1	–	–	600	600	
5. Media and periodical storage		1	–	–	500	500	
6. Multimedia production area		1	–	–	500	500	
7. Curriculum planning area		1	–	–	400	400	
Subtotal:		–		–		6,700	
Total Library and Media Center Space:		–		–		**6,700**	
5 FITNESS AND WELLNESS SPACE							
A. Physical Education							used after hours by the community (minimum; some districts may require a second gym)
1. Gymnasium	2	1	48	48	10,000	10,000	
2. Weight, aerobics room		1	–	–	1,500	1,500	
Subtotal:	2			48		11,500	
B. Storage Spaces							
1. PE equipment storage		2	–	–	200	400	1 PE and 1 team storage
2. Athletic equipment storage		2	–	–	550	1,100	
3. Outdoor equipment storage		1	–	–	300	300	doors directly to exterior
Subtotal:		–		–		1,800	
C. Locker Facilities							one shower/restroom per locker/team room
1. Team lockers: boys		1	–	–	1,500	1,500	
2. Team lockers: girls		1	–	–	900	900	
3. Shower/restroom: boys		2	–	–	550	1,100	
4. Shower/restroom: girls		2	–	–	700	1,400	
5. PE lockers: boys		1	–	–	750	750	
6. PE lockers: girls		1	–	–	750	750	
Subtotal:		–		–		6,400	

SPACE DESCRIPTION			Sample Middle School Program				NOTES
		SPACES	STUDENTS		NET SQUARE FEET		
1,200 planned students, grades 6–8							
1,200 core capacity							
		TEACHING	TOTAL	EACH	TOTAL	EACH	TOTAL
D.	**Coaches and Support Spaces**						
1.	Athletic director's office		1	–	–	180	180
2.	Physical education office		2	–	–	200	400
3.	Shower		2	–	–	300	600
	Subtotal:		–		–		1,180
E.	**Support Spaces**						
1.	Laundry room		1	–	–	120	120
	Subtotal:		–		–		120
F.	**Exterior Athletic Facilities**						
1.	Football/soccer field		1	–	–	–	–	55 x 100 yd + end zones
2.	Track		1					all surface, min. 6 lanes, inside lane 440 yd
3.	Bleacher seating		1	–	–	–	–	
4.	Softball field		1	–	–	–	–	55 x 100 yd
5.	Tennis		3	–	–	–	–	verify quantity 60 X 120 ft
6.	Hard surface play area		1	–	–	–	–	striped for basketball 60 X 100 ft
	Subtotal:		–		–		–	
G.	**Site Program**							general listing of possible requirements
	General items to include:							
1.	Monumental sign							
2.	Flagpole(s)							
3.	Perimeter fence (max. height 6 ft)							
4.	Possible future expansion zone							
5.	Site lighting							
6.	Parking/vehicular circulation							
7.	Bus queuing:							full size, dependent on transportation requirements and availability of public transit
8.	Bus queuing: mini bus							
9.	Automobiles: parent queuing							
10.	Automobiles: staff/visitor parking							dependent on local zoning and other code requirements

SPACE DESCRIPTION	SPACES TEACHING	SPACES TOTAL	STUDENTS EACH	STUDENTS TOTAL	NET SQUARE FEET EACH	NET SQUARE FEET TOTAL	NOTES
Sample Middle School Program							
1,200 planned students, grades 6–8							
1,200 core capacity							
11. Maintenance truck access							
12. Delivery truck access							
13. Custodial staff parking							
14. Pedestrian circulation							
15. Student plaza							
16. Loading/unloading (wide sidewalks)							
17. Service court							
18. Can wash area							
19. Dumpster area							
20. Loading dock							
Subtotal:	–			–		–	excluded from building area
Total Fitness and Wellness Space:		2		48		21,000	
6 VISUAL AND PERFORMING ARTS SPACE							
A. Visual Arts							arranged in suites; first-floor access to art patio
1. Art classroom	2	2	24	48	1,200	2,400	
2. Art storage		1	–	–	400	400	
3. Graphics and digital photography lab	1	1	24	24	1,200	1,200	
4. Kiln room		1	–	–	120	120	
5. Art office		1	–	–	120	120	
Subtotal:	3			72		4,240	
B. Performing Arts							
1. Choral classroom	1	1	24	24	1,400	1,400	double-volume ceiling height preferred
2. Band/orchestra room	1	1	24	24	2,000	2,000	double-volume ceiling height preferred
3. Choral library	1		–	–	100	100	
4. Choral director office	1		–	–	100	100	
5. Choral uniform storage	1		–	–	400	400	
6. Choral individual practice	4		–	–	60	240	
7. Choral ensemble practice	2		–	–	90	180	
8. Band/orchestra instrument storage	1		–	–	600	600	
9. Band/orchestra office and library	1		–	–	400	400	
10. Band/orchestra group practice	1		–	–	200	200	
11. Band/orchestra individual practice	4		–	–	60	240	
Subtotal:	2			–		5,860	

SPACE DESCRIPTION			Sample Middle School Program				NOTES
	SPACES		STUDENTS		NET SQUARE FEET		
1,200 planned students, grades 6–8							
1,200 core capacity	TEACHING	TOTAL	EACH	TOTAL	EACH	TOTAL	
C. Auditorium							
1. Auditorium		1	–	–	4,500	4,500	450 seats
2. Stage		1	–	–	2,000	2,000	dance, drama, instrumental
3. Control booth		1	–	–	120	120	
Subtotal:	–			–		6,620	
D. Drama							near auditorium and stage
1. Drama classroom		1	24	24	900	900	
2. Drama storage		1	–	–	750	750	
3. Drama teacher's office		1	–	–	100	100	
Subtotal:	4			72		1,750	
Total Visual and Performing Arts Space:	9			144		18,470	
7 FACILITY MANAGEMENT AND SUPPORT SPACE							
A. Mechanical and Custodial							
1. Lawn equipment storage		1	–	–	150	150	
2. Receiving and storage		1	–	–	400	400	
3. Office		1	–	–	150	150	
3. Locker/restroom		1	–	–	175	175	
Subtotal:	–			–		875	
Total Facility Management and Support Space:				–		875	
TOTAL NSF	62			1,428		126,815	

1,200 planned students, grades 6–8 1,200 core capacity	CAPACITY STUDENTS	NET SQUARE FEET TOTAL	GROSSING FACTOR	GROSS SQUARE FEET TOTAL
SPACE PROGRAM SUMMARY				
A. Area Summary				
1. Total area		126,815	1.42	180,077
2. Target area				
Difference		126,815		180,077
B. Capacity Summary				
1. Teaching stations	62	1,428 students		
2. Utilization factor	85%			
3. Effective student capacity		1,214 students		
Area Analysis				
1. Square feet per student: planned		1,200 students		150
2. Square feet per student: actual		1,428 students		126
D. Area Comparison				
1. Academic	49%	62,120		
2. Administration	5%	6,450		
3. Community	9%	11,200		
4. Library/media	5%	6,700		
5. Fitness	17%	21,000		
6. Performing arts	15%	18,470		
7. Facility support	1%	875		
Total NSF	100%	126,815		

SAMPLE SPACE PROGRAM FOR A HIGH SCHOOL, GRADES 9–12

SPACE DESCRIPTION	Sample High School Program						NOTES
	SPACES		STUDENTS		NET SQUARE FEET		
1,600 planned students, grades 9–12 1,600 core capacity	TEACHING	TOTAL	EACH	TOTAL	EACH	TOTAL	
1 ACADEMIC SPACE							
A. General Classrooms							
1. Core classrooms	40	40	24	960	775	31,000	3 teams per grade level
2. Small group rooms		8	12	96	350	2,800	
3. Science classroom/labs	10	10	24	240	1,200	12,000	water, gas, elec, movable furniture
4. Science prep room		5	–	–	150	750	1 shared between 2 labs
5. General storage		1	–	–	400	400	
6. Team storage		4	–	–	325	1,300	
7. Studio space		1	–	–	1,500	1,500	for self-directed project-based work included in grossing factor
8. Student locker area							
Subtotal:	50			1,296		49,750	
B. Shared Academic Spaces							
1. Graphics and computer/commons		2	–	–	1,200	2,400	can be enclosed or open space
2. Computer commons storage		1	–	–	100	100	
3. World language classrooms	4	4	24	96	775	3,100	
4. World language lab	2	2	24	48	1,200	2,400	
Subtotal:	6			144		8,000	
D. Special Education Group Rooms							
1. Tutorial space	0.5	2	12	24	400	800	
2. Conference room	1	–	–	600	600		
3. Time-out room (optional)		1	–	–	100	100	
4. Office space	1	–	–	200	200		
5. Storage, washer, dryer, kitchen		1	–	–	200	200	
6. Restroom		1	–	–	50	50	
Subtotal:	1			24		1,950	

SPACE DESCRIPTION			Sample High School Program				NOTES
		SPACES		STUDENTS		NET SQUARE FEET	
1,600 planned students, grades 9–12							
1,600 core capacity		TEACHING	TOTAL	EACH	TOTAL	EACH	TOTAL	

		TEACHING	TOTAL	EACH	TOTAL	EACH	TOTAL	NOTES
E.	**Business Education**							
1.	Lab	2	2	24	48	1,000	2,000	
2.	Business classroom	2	2	24	48	775	1,550	
3.	Office		1	–	–	100	100	
4.	Storage		1	–	–	120	120	
	Subtotal:		4		96		3,770	
	Total Academic Space:		61		1,560		63,970	
2	**ADMINISTRATIVE AND STAFF SPACE**							
A.	**Administration Area**							
1.	Reception area		1	–	–	150	150	
2.	Waiting		1	–	–	125	125	
3.	Secretary		1	–	–	150	150	
4.	Principal		1	–	–	220	220	
5.	Additional administrative offices		3	–	–	150	450	to be determined
6.	Academic advisor		1	–	–	180	180	
7.	General office space/file space		1	–	–	450	450	
8.	Conference room large		1	–	–	450	450	
9.	Conference room small		1	–	–	215	215	
10.	Kitchenette		1	–	–	80	80	
11.	Workroom/copier/restroom		1	–	–	300	300	
12.	Records file room		1	–	–	80	80	
	Subtotal:		–		–		2,850	
C.	**Distributed Administration Suites**							distributed near general classrooms
1.	Assistant principal		2	–	–	150	300	
2.	Assistant principal support space		2	–	–	100	200	
	Subtotal:		–		–		500	
B.	**Staff Support Space**							distributed near general classrooms
1.	Staff workrooms		2	–	–	1,200	2,400	
2.	Copy center		1	–	–	750	750	
	Subtotal:		–		–		3,150	
C.	**Clinic**							
1.	Waiting area/info display		1	–	–	300	300	
2.	Nurse aide, exam, audio testing		1	–	–	120	120	

SPACE DESCRIPTION		Sample High School Program				NOTES
	SPACES		STUDENTS		NET SQUARE FEET	
1,600 planned students, grades 9–12						
1,600 core capacity	TEACHING	TOTAL	EACH	TOTAL	EACH	TOTAL	

SPACE DESCRIPTION	TEACHING	TOTAL	EACH	TOTAL	EACH	TOTAL	NOTES
3. Nurse's office		1	–	–	150	150	
4. Exam room (optional)		1	–	–	120	120	
5. Cot room		2	–	–	120	240	
6. Restroom		2	–	–	50	100	
7. Kitchenette		1	–	–	80	80	
Subtotal:		–		–		1,110	
D. Guidance							
1. Counselor offices		4	–	–	150	600	
2. Reception/clerk		1	–	–	250	250	
3. Reception seating		1	–	–	150	150	
4. Workroom/copier/restroom		1	–	–	200	200	
5. Vault/storage/secured test materials		1	–	–	150	150	
Subtotal:		–		–		1,350	
E. General Areas							
1. Parents' office		1	–	–	250	250	
2. Entry lobby		1	–	–	1,500	1,500	inviting, with display areas
Subtotal:		–		–		1,750	
Total Administrative and Staff Space:		–	–			**10,710**	

3 STUDENT DINING AND FOOD SERVICE SPACE						
A. Student Dining						school population/ number of planned lunch periods x 15 sq ft = (1200/3) x 15 sq ft per student = 8,000
1. Cafeteria	1	–	–	8,000	8,000	Maximum as calculated by formula above. Can be reduced depending on lunch policy, which may allow off-campus dining or other options.
2. School store	1	–	–	400	400	
Subtotal:	–		–		8,400	

SPACE DESCRIPTION			Sample High School Program				NOTES
1,600 planned students, grades 9–12	SPACES		STUDENTS		NET SQUARE FEET		
1,600 core capacity	TEACHING	TOTAL	EACH	TOTAL	EACH	TOTAL	

								NOTES
B.	**Kitchen**							3.7 sq ft per meal served, including serving areas x 1300 meals served = 4,810 (estimated)
1.	Receiving		1	–	–	230	230	
2.	Custodial/laundry		1	–	–	120	120	
3.	Chemical/paper		1	–	–	300	300	
4.	Toilet/locker area		1	–	–	150	150	
5.	Dry storage		1	–	–	500	500	
6.	Freezer		1	–	–	300	300	
7.	Cooler		1	–	–	170	170	
8.	Office		1	–	–	150	150	
9.	Office storage		1	–	–	65	65	
10.	Custodial closet		1	–	–	65	65	
11.	Food prep area		1	–	–	1,450	1,450	
12.	Serving area		1	–	–	1,300	1,300	
	Subtotal:		–	–	–		4,800	

Total Student Dining and Food Service Space:	–		–			13,200	

4	**LIBRARY AND MEDIA CENTER SPACE**						
A.	**Library/Media Center**						
1.	Library/media reading room	1	–	–	4,000	4,000	
2.	Librarian's office	2	–	–	200	400	
3.	Librarian's workroom	1	–	–	300	300	
4.	Laptop repair and AV storage	1	–	–	600	600	
5.	Media and periodical storage	1	–	–	500	500	
6.	Multimedia production area	1	–	–	500	500	
7.	Curriculum planning area	1	–	–	400	400	
8.	Project Rooms	2	–	–	250	500	glass-enclosed
	Subtotal:	–		–		7,200	
B.	**Media Technology**						
1.	TV studio	1	1	24	24	1,000	1,000	
2.	TV studio ontrol booth	–	1	–	–	400	400	
3.	AV storage, repair, and production	–	1	–	–	400	400	
4.	File server room	–	1	–	–	250	250	

SPACE DESCRIPTION	Sample High School Program						NOTES
	SPACES		STUDENTS		NET SQUARE FEET		
1,600 planned students, grades 9–12 1,600 core capacity	TEACHING	TOTAL	EACH	TOTAL	EACH	TOTAL	
5. Technology support	–	1	–	–	200	200	
6. Technology office	–	1	–	–	125	125	
Subtotal:	1			24		2,375	
C. Student Services and Career Center							
1. Waiting and display	–	1	–	–	500	500	
2. Receptionist	–	1	–	–	125	125	
3. Counseling offices	–	5	–	–	125	625	
4. Display space	–	1	–	–	50	50	
5. Guidance storage	–	1	–	–	75	75	
6. Conference room	–	1	–	–	250	250	
Subtotal:	–			–		1,625	
D. Internet Café							near library or commons area
1. Service counter	–	1	–	–	225	225	
2. Seating	–	1	–	–	300	300	
3. Storage	–	1	–	–	125	125	
	–		–	–	–	–	
Subtotal:	–			–		650	
Total Library and Media Center Space:	1			24		11,850	
5 FITNESS AND WELLNESS SPACE							
A. Physical Education							used after hours by the community
1. Gymnasium	2	1	48	48	12,600	12,600	two practice courts, competition court
2. Auxiliary gymnasium	1	1	24	24	7,800	7,800	practice court
3. Health classroom	2	2	24	48	775	1,550	
4. Weight, aerobics room	1	1	24	24	1,500	1,500	
5. Dance	1	1	24	24	1,500	1,500	
6. Trainer		1	–	–	600	600	
Subtotal:	7			168		25,550	
B. Storage Spaces							
1. PE equipment storage		2	–	–	200	400	1 PE and 1 team storage
2. Athletic equipment storage		2	–	–	550	1,100	
3. Outdoor equipment storage		1	–	–	300	300	doors directly to exterior
Subtotal:	–		–			1,800	

SPACE DESCRIPTION	Sample High School Program						NOTES
	SPACES		STUDENTS		NET SQUARE FEET		
1,600 planned students, grades 9–12							
1,600 core capacity	TEACHING	TOTAL	EACH	TOTAL	EACH	TOTAL	
C. Locker Facilities							one shower/restroom per PE locker and team locker room
1. Team lockers: boys	1		–	–	1,500	1,500	
2. Team lockers: girls	1		–	–	900	900	
3. Shower/restroom : boys	2		–	–	550	1,100	
4. Shower/restroom: girls	2		–	–	700	1,400	
5. PE lockers: boys	1		–	–	750	750	
6. PE lockers: girls	1		–	–	750	750	
7. Community use/team lockers: boys	1		–	–	750	750	includes showers and toilets
8. Community use/team lockers: girls	1		–	–	750	750	includes showers and toilets
Subtotal:	–		–		7,900		
D. Coaches and Support Spaces							
1. Athletic director's office	1		–	–	180	180	
2. Physical education office	2		–	–	200	400	
3. Shower	2		–	–	300	600	
Subtotal:	–		–		1,180		
E. Support Spaces							
1. Laundry room	1		–	–	120	120	
2. Uniform storage	1		–	–	400	400	
Subtotal:	–		–		520		
F. Exterior Athletic Facilities							
1. Football/soccer field	1		–	–	–	–	55 x 100 yd + end zones
2. Track	1						all surface, min. 6 lanes, inside lane 440 yd
3. Bleacher seating	1		–	–	–	–	
4. Softball field	1		–	–	–	–	55 x 100 yd
5. Tennis	6		–	–	–	–	verify quantity 60 X 120 ft
6. Hard surface play area	1		–	–	–	–	striped for basketball 60 X 100 ft
Subtotal:	–		–		–		
Total Fitness and Wellness Space:	7			168		36,950	

SPACE DESCRIPTION		Sample High School Program					NOTES
		SPACES		STUDENTS		NET SQUARE FEET	
1,600 planned students, grades 9–12							
1,600 core capacity		TEACHING	TOTAL	EACH	TOTAL	EACH	TOTAL	
6	**VISUAL AND PERFORMING ARTS SPACE**						
A.	**Visual Arts**						arranged in suites; first-floor access to art patio
1.	Art classroom	2	2	24	48	1,200	2,400	
2.	Art storage		1	–	–	400	400	
3.	Graphics and digital photography lab	1	1	24	24	1,400	1,400	
4.	Kiln room		1	–	–	120	120	
	Subtotal:	3			72		4,320	
B.	**Performing Arts**						
1.	Choral classroom	1	1	24	24	1,400	1,400	double-volume ceiling height preferred
2.	Band/orchestra room	1	1	24	24	2,200	2,200	double-volume ceiling height preferred
3.	Music classroom	1	1	24	24	900	900	
4.	Choral library		1	–	–	100	100	
5.	Choral director's office		1	–	–	100	100	
6.	Choral uniform storage		1	–	–	400	400	
7.	Choral individual practice		4	–	–	60	240	
8.	Choral ensemble practice		2	–	–	90	180	
9.	Band/orchestra instrument storage		1	–	–	600	600	
10.	Band/orchestra office and library		1	–	–	400	400	
11.	Band/orchestra group practice		1	–	–	200	200	
12.	Band/orchestra individual practice		4	–	–	60	240	
	Subtotal:	3			72		6,960	
C.	**Theater**						
1.	House		1	–	–	6,500	6,500	650 seats
2.	Stage		1			2,400	2,400	
3.	Orchestra pit		1			950	950	
4.	Lobby area and public assembly		1			2,000	2,000	
5.	Box office		1			75	75	
6.	Projection, lighting, sound		1			175	175	
7.	Scene shop		1			1,000	1,000	
8.	Scene storage		1			500	500	
9.	Prop storage		1			800	800	
10.	Piano storage		1			125	125	
11.	Performance riser storage		1			150	150	
12.	Dressing rooms		4			400	1,600	

SPACE DESCRIPTION	Sample High School Program						NOTES
	SPACES		STUDENTS		NET SQUARE FEET		
1,600 planned students, grades 9–12 1,600 core capacity	TEACHING	TOTAL	EACH	TOTAL	EACH	TOTAL	
13. Black box theater	1	1	24	24	3,250	3,250	
14. Bleacher seating stack area		1			275	275	
15. Projection, lighting, sound		1			125	125	
16. Performance riser storage		1	–	–	150	150	
Subtotal:	1			24		20,075	
D. Drama							near theater and stage
1. Drama classroom	1	1	24	24	900	900	
2. Drama storage		1	–	–	775	775	
3. Drama teacher's office		1	–	–	100	100	
Subtotal:	1			24		1,775	
Total Visual and Performing Arts Space:	8			192		33,130	

7 FACILITY MANAGEMENT AND SUPPORT SPACE

A. Mechanical and Custodial							
1. Lawn equipment storage	1	–	–		150	150	
2. Receiving and supply storage	1	–	–		500	500	
3. Recycling room	1	–	–		400	400	
4. Book storage	1	–	–		400	400	
5. Shop	1	–	–		800	800	
6. Office	1	–	–		150	150	
7. Locker/restroom	1	–	–		175	175	
Subtotal:		–	–			2,575	
B. Site Program							general listing of possible requirements

General items to include:

1. Monumental sign
2. Flagpole(s)
3. Perimeter fence (max. height 6 ft)
4. Possible future expansion zone
5. Site lighting
6. Parking/vehicular circulation
7. Bus queuing: full size

dependent on transportation requirements and availability of public transit

SPACE DESCRIPTION	Sample High School Program						NOTES
1,600 planned students, grades 9–12	SPACES		STUDENTS		NET SQUARE FEET		
1,600 core capacity	TEACHING	TOTAL	EACH	TOTAL	EACH	TOTAL	
8. Bus queuing: mini bus							
9. Automobiles: parent queuing							
10. Automobiles: staff/visitor parking							dependent on local zoning and other code requirements
11. Maintenance truck access							
12. Delivery truck access							
13. Custodial staff parking							
14. Pedestrian circulation							
15. Student plaza							
16. Loading/unloading (wide sidewalks)							
17. Service court							
18. Can wash area							
19. Dumpster area							
20. Loading dock							
Subtotal:		–		–			excluded from building area
Total Facility Management and Support Space:				–		2,575	
TOTAL NSF		77		1,944		172,385	

1,600 planned students, grades 9–12			NET SQUARE		GROSS
1,600 core capacity	CAPACITY		FEET	GROSSING	SQUARE FEET
	STUDENTS		TOTAL	FACTOR	TOTAL
SPACE PROGRAM SUMMARY					
A. **Area Summary**					
1. Total area			172,385	1.53	263,749
2. Target area					
Difference			172,385		263,749
B. **Capacity Summary**					
1. Teaching Stations	77	1,944 students			
2. Utilization Factor	85%				
3. Effective Student Capacity		1,652 students			160
Area Analysis					
1. Square feet per student: Planned		1,600 students			165
2. Square feet per student: Actual		1,944 students			136
D. **Area Comparison**					
1. Academic	37%		63,970		
2. Administration	6%		10,710		
3. Community	8%		13,200		
4. Library/Media	7%		11,850		
5. Fitness	21%		36,950		
6. Performing Arts	19%		33,130		
7. Facility support	1%		2,575		
Total NSF	100%		172,385		

BIBLIOGRAPHY AND REFERENCES

GENERAL

Abramson, Paul. 2008. "The 2008 Annual School Construction Report." *School Planning & Management Magazine*. http://www.peterli.com/spm/pdfs/constr_report_2008.pdf (accessed 6/2009).

Agron, Joe. 2009. "35th Annual Construction Report." *American School and University*, May.

The American Architect. 1915. *Modern School Houses Part II: Illustrating and Describing Recent Examples of School House Design Executed in the United States*. New York: The American Architect.

American Architectural Foundation. 2006. *Design for Learning Forum: School Design and Student Learning in the 21st Century, A Report of Findings*. Washington, D.C. http://www.archfoundation.org/aaf/documents/report.designforlearning.pdf (accessed 6/2009).

American National Standards Institute. *Acoustical Performance Criteria, Design Requirements, and Guidelines for Schools*. ANSI S12.60-2002.

American Society of Heating, Refrigerating, and Air-Conditioning Engineers (ASHRAE). 2006. *ASHRAE GreenGuide: The Design, Construction, and Operation of Sustainable Buildings*, 2nd ed. Atlanta, Ga.: ASHRAE.

———. 2007. *2007 ASHRAE Handbook—HVAC Applications*.

———. 2008. *Advanced Energy Design Guide for K–12 School Buildings*.

Anderson, L. W., and D. R. Krathwohl, eds. 2001. *A Taxonomy for Learning, Teaching and Assessing: A Revision of Bloom's Taxonomy of Educational Objectives*. Complete edition. New York: Longman.

Appleyard, Donald. 1969. "Why Buildings Are Known." *Environment and Behavior* 1 (no. 3):131–156.

———. 1970. "Styles and Methods of Structuring a City." *Environment and Behavior* 2 (no. 3):100–107.

Biehle, James T. "Renovate or Replace: Deciding the Fate of Your School." *E Architect*. http://www.e-architect.com/pia.cae.renovate_cae.asp.

Birren, Faber. 1997. *The Power of Color: How It Can Reduce Fatigue, Relieve Monotony, Enhance Sexuality and More*. Secaucus, N.J.: Carol Publishing Group.

Bittle, Edgar H., ed. 1996. *Planning and Financing School Improvement and Construction Projects*. Topeka, Kan.: National Organization on Legal Problems of Education and American Bar Association.

Bliss, Lynne. 1996. "Six Keys to the Twenty-Second-Century High School." *School Planning and Management*, May. http://www.spmmag.com/articles/may_1996/article010.html.

Bloom, Benjamin S. 1956. *Taxonomy of Educational Objectives Ltd.* New York: Longmans, Green and Co.

Brubaker, William C. 1998. *Planning and Designing Schools.* New York: McGraw-Hill.

Chuang, Jeffrey. 1997. "Classroom Cacophony." *The Dallas Morning News*, June 30. http://www.dallasnews.com.

Conant, James B. 1959. *The American High School Today.* New York: McGraw-Hill.

Deasy, C. M. 1985. *Designing Places for People: A Handbook on Human Behavior for Architects, Designers and Facility Managers.* New York: Whitney Library of Design.

Dorn, Michael. 1998. "Make School Safety a Priority." *School Planning and Management*, October. http://www.spmmag.com/articles/1098_6.html.

Dryden, Ken. 1995. *In School.* Toronto: McClelland and Stewart.

Edwards, Carolyn P., George Forman, and Lella Gandini, eds. 1993. *The Hundred Languages of Children: The Reggio Emilia Approach to Early Education.* Norwood, N.J.: Ablex.

Erb, Tom. 1996. "'School' No Longer Means What You Thought." *Middle School Journal* 27 (March).

Federal Register 36 CFR Chapter XI. "Architectural and Transportation Barriers Compliance Board: Petition for Rulemaking; Request for Information on Acoustics." Washington, D.C.

Fickes, Michael. 1998. "The Security Factor in School Renovations." *School Planning and Management*, February. Available on the Internet: http://www.spmmag.com/articles/Feb_98/security.html.

Freedman, D. S., W. H. Dietz, S. R. Srinivasan, and G. S. Berenson. 1999. "The Relation of Overweight to Cardiovascular Risk Factors among Children and Adolescents: The Bogalusa Heart Study." *Journal of Pediatrics* 103 (no. 6): 1175–1182.

Gahala, Jan. 2009. "Critical Issue: Promoting Technology Use in Schools." North Central Regional Educational Laboratory website through Learning Point Associates. http://www.ncrel.org/sdrs/areas/issues/methods/technlgy/te200.htm (accessed 6/2009).

Gardner, Howard. 1983. *Frames of Mind.* New York: Basic Books.

Gordon, Gary J., and James L. Nuckolls. 1995. *Interior Lighting for Designers.* 3d ed. New York: John Wiley & Sons.

Graves, Ben E. and Clifford A. Pearson, eds. 1993. *Schools Ways: The Planning and Design of America's Schools.* New York: McGraw-Hill, Inc.

Grocoff, Paul N. 1995. "Electric Lighting and Daylighting in Schools. IssueTrak: A CEFPI Brief on Educational Facility Issues." http://www.eric.ed.gov/ERICWebPortal/custom/portlets/recordDetails/detailmini.jsp?_nfpb=true&_&ERICExtSearch_SearchValue_0=ED426580&ERICExtSearch_SearchType_0=no&accno=ED426580 (accessed 6/09).

Honawar, Vaishali. 2008. "Working Smarter By Working Together." *Education Week*, April 2. http://www.edweek.org/login.html?source=http://www.edweek.org/ew/articles/2008/04/02/31plc_ep.h27.html&destination=http://www.edweek.org/ew/articles/2008/04/02/31plc_ep.h27.html&levelId=2100 (accessed 6/2009).

Jackson, Lisa. 1997. "Learning from Your Mistakes." *School Planning and Management*, October. http://www.spmmag.com/articles/may_1996/article010.html.

————. 1998. "Right Sizing for Tikes." *School Planning and Management*, May. http://www.spmmag.com/articles/may_1998/tykes.html.

Jacobowitz, Robin, Meryle G. Weinstein, Cindy Maguire, et al. 2007. *The Effectiveness of Small High School, 1994–95 to 2003–04*. New York: Institute for Education and Social Policy, Steinhardt School of Education, New York University. http://steinhardt.nyu.edu/iesp.olde/publications/pubs/IESP_SmallHighSchoolEffectiveness_April2007.pdf (accessed 6/2009).

Kantrowitz, Barbara Kantrowitz and Pat Wingert. 1991. "10 Best Schools in the World." *Newsweek*, December 2.

Kats, Gregory. 2009. *Greening America's Schools: Costs and Benefits*. October 2006. A Capital E Report http://www.cap-e.com/ewebeditpro/items/O59F9819.pdf (accessed 6/2009).

Kerr, Stephen T. 1996. *Technology and the Future of Schooling*. Chicago: University of Chicago Press.

Kozol, Jonathan. 1991. *Savage Inequalities: Children in America's Schools*. New York: Crown.

Lackney, Jeffrey A. 1998. "Changing Patterns in Educational Facilities." *DesignShare Planning News*. http://www.designshare.com.

Lang, Jon. 1987. *Creating Architectural Theory: The Role of Behavioral Sciences in Design*. New York: Van Nostrand Reinhold.

Lawton, Millicent. 1999. "School Design Can Say a Lot About Teaching and Learning." *Harvard Education Letter*, January–February.

Lee, V. E., and J. B. Smith. 1997. "High School Size: Which Works Best, and for Whom?" *Educational Evaluation and Policy Analysis* 19 (no. 3): 205–227. http://www.eric.ed.gov/ERICWebPortal/custom/portlets/recordDetails/detailmini.jsp?_nfpb=true&_&ERICExtSearch_SearchValue_0=ED396888&ERICExtSearch_SearchType_0=no&accno=ED396888 (accessed 6/2009).

The Little Institute for School Facilities Research. 1997. *The School Technology Primer: A Non-Technical Guide to Understanding School Technology*. Wilkesboro, N.C.: The Little Institute for School Facilities Research.

Livingston, Pamela. 2008. "E-Learning Gets Real" *Technology & Learning*, May 22. http://www.techlearning.com/article/8856.

Lynch, Kevin. 1960. *The Image of the City*. Cambridge: MIT Press.

McGuinness, William J., Benjamin Stein, and John S. Reynolds. 1980. *Mechanical and Electrical Equipment for Buildings*. 6th ed. New York: John Wiley & Sons.

McQuade, Walter, ed. *Schoolhouse*. 1958. New York: Simon Schuster.

Moore, Gary T. 1976. "The Development of Environmental Knowing: An Overview of an Interactional-Constructivist Theory and Some Data on Within-Individual Development Variations." In *Psychology and the Built Environment*, ed. Davi Canter and Terrence Lee. London: Architectural Press.

Muhlhausen, John. 2006. "Wayfinding Is Not Signage: Signage Plays an Important Part of Wayfinding—But There's More." April 3. http://signweb.com/content/wayfinding-is-not-signage (accessed 6/2009).

National Middle School Association. Summary 3. "Number of Middle School Students."

———. Summary 8. "Grade 5 in Middle School."

Nixon, Charles W. 1998. "Today's Schools, Tomorrow's Classrooms." *School Planning and Management*, November.

Packard, Robert T., and Stephen A. Kliment, eds. 1989. *Ramsey/Sleeper Architectural Graphic Standards: Student Edition Abridged from the Seventh Edition*. New York: John Wiley & Sons.

Passini, Romedi. 1992. *Wayfinding in Architecture*. New York: John Wiley & Sons.

Perkins, Bradford. 2007. *International Practice for Architects*. New York: John Wiley & Sons.

Perkins, Lawrence B. 1957. *Workplace for Learning*. New York: Reinhold.

Perkins, Lawrence B., and Walter D. Cocking. 1949. *Schools*. New York: Reinhold.

Porter, Jessica. 1995. "State-of-the-Art School Seeks to Take a Bite Out of Crime." *Education Week*. Sept. 6.

Powderly, H. Evan. *A User's Guide for the H. C. Crittenden Middle School*. Armonk, N.Y.

Richard, Alan. 2000. "NEA Pegs School Building Needs at $332 Billion. *Education Week*. May 10. http://www.edweek.org/ew/articles/2000/05/10/35nea.h19.html?tkn=TSUFvH%2B41wr5X7TwU8%2BpUdlVNh7GP%2FJarHwR&print=1 (accessed 6/2009).

Salter, Charles M. 1998. *Acoustics: Architecture, Engineering, the Environment*. San Francisco: William Stout Publishers.

Seyffer, Charles. 1999. "Clearing the Air About IAQ." *School Planning and Management*, February. http://www.spmmag.com/articles/Feb99/articles0179.html.

Shen, Fred. 1999. Personal interview conducted with principal of Shen Milsom & Wilke, Inc., New York, N.Y.

Stein, Benjamin, and John S. Reynolds. 1992. *Mechanical and Electrical Equipment for Buildings*. 8th ed. New York: John Wiley & Sons.

———. 2000. *Mechanical and Electrical Equipment for Buildings*. 9th ed. New York: John Wiley & Sons.

Stiefel, Leanna, Amy Ellen Schwartz, Patrice Iatarola, and Colin C. Chellman. 2008. *Mission Matters: the Cost of Small High Schools Revisited*. Working Paper #08-03 (March). New York: Institute for Education and Social Policy, Steinhardt School of Education, New York University. http://steinhardt.nyu.edu/scmsAdmin/uploads/001/403/IESPWP0803.pdf (accessed 6/2009).

Strickland, R. 1994. "Designing the New American School: Schools for an Urban Neighborhood." *Teachers College Record* 96:32–57.

Thompson, Thomas, and Ellen Sears. 1999. Personal interview conducted with principals of Thomas Thompson Lighting Design, New York, New York.

"Tools for Schools." 1998. *American School and University*, May.

U.S. Green Building Council. 2009. *Green Building Design and Construction*, version3 (formerly known as the *USGBC LEED for Schools Reference Guide*.) Washington, D.C.: USGBC.

Wasley, Patricia A., et al. 2000. *Small Schools: Great Strides*. New York, Bank Street College of Education.

Whittle, Chris. 2005. *Crash Course: Imagining a Better Future for Public Education*. New York: Riverhead Books.

Winkel, Steven R., David S. Collins, and Steven P. Juroszek. 2007. *Building Codes Illustrated for Elementary and Secondary Schools: A Guide to Understanding the 2006 International Building Code*. Ed. Francis D. Ching. Hoboken, N.J.: John Wiley & Sons.

Wood, George H. 1992. Schools That Work. New York: Dutton.

STANDARDS AND CODES

Americans with Disabilities Act Accessibility Guidelines for Buildings and Facilities. 1994. 28 CFR Part 36. Available through the Department of Justice website at www.ada.gov, under ADA Design Standards.

American National Standards Institute. Published standards. www.ansi.org.

ANSI/IESNA RP-3-00 *Lighting for Educational Facilities*.

ANSI S1.40 *Specifications and Verification Procedures for Sound Calibrators*.

American Society of Heating, Refrigerating, and Air-Conditioning Engineers. Available through the ASHRAE website, http://www.ashrae.org/publications/

2009 ASHRAE Handbook: Fundamentals.

2008 Advanced Energy Design Guide for K–12 School Buildings.

2007 ASHRAE Standards & Guidelines.

2007 ASHRAE Handbook—HVAC Applications.

2006 ASHRAE GreenGuide: The Design, Construction, and Operation of Sustainable Buildings, 2nd ed.

Barrier-free Design: Selected Federal Laws and ADA Accessibility Guidelines. New York: Eastern Paralyzed Veterans Association, 1996.

Building Officials and Code Administrators International Code. Published standards. www.bocai.org.

Building Officials and Code Administrators International, Inc. *The BOCA National Building Code/1993*. Country Club Hills, Ill.: Building Officials and Code Administrators International, Inc, 1993.

Department of Justice. *Code of Federal Regulations: 28 CFR Part 36*. Department of Justice, July 1, 1994.

Electronics Industries Alliance / Telecommunications Industry Association (EIA/TIA).

EIA/TIA 568-B Commercial Building Wiring Standard.

EIA/TIA 569 Commercial Building Standard for Telecommunication Pathways and Spaces.

ANSI/J-STD—607-A-2002 (formerly EIA/TIA 607) – Grounding and Bonding

Federal Register 36 CFR Chapter XI. "Architectural and Transportation Barriers Compliance Board: Petition for Rulemarking; Request for Information on Acoustics." Also available at http://www.access-board.gov/rules/acoustic.htm.

"Indoor Air Quality Rules." 1998 *American School and University*, May.

International Electrotechnial Commission (IEC) 61672-1 – Electroacoustics – Sound level meters – Part 1: Specifications.

International Code Council. ICC/ANSI A117.1–2003.

National Association for the Education of Young Children. Published accreditation standards. Washington, D.C.: NAEYC.

National Conference of States on Building Codes and Standards, Inc. *Directory of Building and Codes Regulations*. www.ncsbcs.org.

National Fire Protection Agency (NFPA) 70–National Electrical Code.

National Fire Protection Agency (NFPA) 101–Life Safety Code.

New York State Education Department.

Building Code of New York State, http://publiccodes.citation.com/st/ny/st/index.htm.

Manual of Planning Standards for School Buildings. http://www.emsc.nysed.gov/facplan/publicat/mps1998.pdf.

U.S. Department of Education, Office of Civil Rights. 2006. *Compliance with the Americans with Disabilities Act: A Self-Evaluation Guide for Public Elementary and Secondary Schools.* Doc. ED401688. Available at www.eric.ed.gov. See also the state standards for, for example, California, Florida, and Virginia, which are available through the state departments of education at Sacramento, Tallahassee, and Richmond.

WEBSITES

American Architectural Foundation: www.archfoundation.org/aaf/aaf/index.htm

American Council on Education: www.acenet.edu

The American Montessori Society (AMS): www.amshq.org

American Society of Heating, Refrigerating, and Air-Conditioning Engineers (ASHRAE): www.ashrae.org

ASHRAE Advanced Energy Design Guide for K–12 Schools: Register for free download at www.ashrae.org/publications/page/1604

Americans with Disabilities Act (ADA): www.ada.gov

Association for Career and Technical Education (ACTE) (American Vocational Association): www.acteonline.org

Arc of the United States: www.thearc.org

Association for Childhood Education International: www.acei.org

Children's Technology Review (reviews of software for children): www.childrenssoftware.com

Council for American Private Education: www.capenet.org

Council on Education Facility Planners International: www.cefpi.com

Architectural Lighting magazine: www.archlighting.com

Educational Resources Information Center (ERIC): www.accesseric.org

Education Week links: www.edweek.org

Florida Solar Energy Center, Energy Efficient Schools: www.fsec.ucf.edu/en/research/buildings/schools/index.htm

The Green Building Information Center: http://greenbuilding.ca

The Green Building Program Sustainable Building Sourcebook: http://sustainablesources.com

IBM K–12 education: http://www-03.ibm.com/industries/education/us/index.html

IBM K–12 news releases: http://www-03.ibm.com/industries/education/us/list/solution/all/index.html

"I Have a Dream" Foundation: www.ihaveadreamfoundation.org

International Code Council (ICC): www.iccsafe.org

Learning Disabilities Association of America: www.ldanatl.org

Library of Congress Periodicals Reading Room: www.loc.gov or http://memory.loc.gov/ammem/awhhtml/awser2/periodicals.html

Merit Network K–12 Education Resources: www.merit.edu/members/k12

National Association for the Education of Young Children: http://www.naeyc.org

National Association of Independent Schools: www.nais.org

National Catholic Educational Association: www.ncea.org

National Center for Research in Vocational Education: http://vocserve.berkeley.edu

National Clearinghouse for Educational Facilities: www.edfacilities.org

National Crime Prevention Council (NCPC): www.ncpc.org

National Education Association: www.nea.org

National Middle School Association: www.nmsa.org

National School Boards Association: www.nsba.org

National Renewable Energy Laboratory: www.nrel.gov

New York State Energy Research and Development Authority's New York State High Performance School Design online training: www.nyserda.org/hps/default.asp

North Central Regional Education Laboratory: www.ncrel.org/tech

Northwest Educational Technology Consortium: www.netc.org

Northwest Regional Educational Laboratory: www.nwrel.org

Renewable Energy Policy Project: www.repp.org

Sustainable Architecture, Building and Culture: www.sustainableabc.com

Tech&Learning: www.techlearning.com

U.S. Department of Energy, Energy Efficiency and Renewable Energy Network: www.eere.energy.gov

U.S. Environmental Protection Agency (EPA): www.epa.gov

Energy Star program: www.energystar.gov/index.cfm?c=k12_schools.bus_schoolsk12

Indoor Air Quality Tools for Schools: www.epa.gov/iaq/schools

U.S. Green Building Council: http://www.usgbc.org

10 Best Websites for Educational Technology: www.fromnowon.org

INDEX

BUILDING TYPE BASICS FOR
ELEMENTARY AND SECONDARY SCHOOLS:

1. Program (predesign)
What are the principal programming requirements (space types and areas)?
Any special regulatory or jurisdictional concerns?
11–89, 144–45, 183, 191–92

2. Circulation
What are the desirable primary and secondary spatial relationships?
91–102, 140–41

3. Unique design concerns
What distinctive design determinants must be met?
103–133

4. Site planning/parking/access
What considerations determine external access and parking? Landscaping?
135–47, 159–63

5. Codes/ADA
Which building codes and regulations apply, and what are the main applicable provisions?
(Examples: egress; electrical; plumbing; ADA; seismic; asbestos; terrorism and other hazards)
149–55, 175–76, 181–82, 189–91, 204, 218, 244–46

6. Energy/environmental challenges/sustainability
What techniques in service of energy conservation and environmental sustainability can be employed?
146–47, 157–74, 204–6

7. Structure system
What classes of structural systems are appropriate?
175–79

8. Mechanical systems
What are appropriate systems for heating, ventilating, and air-conditioning (HVAC) and plumbing?
Vertical transportation? Fire and smoke protection? What factors affect preliminary selection?
163–74, 181–87

9. Electrical/communications
What are appropriate systems for electrical service and voice and data communications?
What factors affect preliminary selection?
164–65, 169–70, 189–92

10. Special equipment
What special equipment is required, and what are its space requirements? Is security a factor?
191, 193–99, 239–40